Syrian Civil War

Syrian Civil War

THE ESSENTIAL REFERENCE GUIDE

Robert M. Kerr, Editor

ABC-CLIO®

An Imprint of ABC-CLIO, LLC
Santa Barbara, California • Denver, Colorado

Copyright © 2020 by ABC-CLIO, LLC

Library of Congress Cataloging-in-Publication Data

Names: Kerr, Robert M., 1972– editor.
Title: Syrian Civil War : The Essential Reference Guide / Robert M. Kerr, editor.
Description: Santa Barbara, Calif. : ABC-CLIO, An Imprint of ABC-CLIO, LLC [2020] |
    Includes bibliographical references and index.
Identifiers: LCCN 2019035109 (print) | LCCN 2019035110 (ebook) | ISBN 9781440859212
    (hardback) | ISBN 9781440859229 (ebook)
Subjects: LCSH: Syria—History—Civil War, 2011–
Classification: LCC DS98.6 .S974 2020 (print) | LCC DS98.6 (ebook) |
    DDC 956.9104/23—dc23
LC record available at https://lccn.loc.gov/2019035109
LC ebook record available at https://lccn.loc.gov/2019035110

ISBN: 978-1-4408-5921-2 (print)
      978-1-4408-5922-9 (ebook)

24   23   22   21   20   1   2   3   4   5

This book is also available as an eBook.

ABC-CLIO
An Imprint of ABC-CLIO, LLC

ABC-CLIO, LLC
147 Castilian Drive
Santa Barbara, California 93117
www.abc-clio.com

This book is printed on acid-free paper ∞

Manufactured in the United States of America

Contents

List of Entries

List of Primary Documents

1. Executive Order 13582—Blocking Property of the Government of Syria and Prohibiting Certain Transactions with Respect to Syria (August 18, 2011)
2. United Nations Security Council Resolution 2042 (April 14, 2012)
3. President Barack H. Obama: Remarks by the President in Address to the Nation on Syria (September 10, 2013)
4. United Nations Security Council Resolution 2118 (September 27, 2013)
5. Vladimir Putin's Address Following Adoption of a Joint Statement by Russia and the United States on Syria (February 22, 2016)
6. Presidential Memorandum on the Plan to Defeat the Islamic State of Iraq and Syria (January 28, 2017)
7. President Donald J. Trump, Statement on the Anniversary of the 2013 Syrian Chemical Weapons Attack (August 21, 2017)
8. Statement by President Trump on Syria (April 13, 2018)
9. United Nations General Assembly Summary Report on the High-Level Panel Discussion on Violations of the Human Rights of Children in the Syrian Arab Republic (May 15, 2018)
10. Statement by H. E. Walid al-Moualem, Deputy Prime Minister of the Syrian Arab Republic, Made to the 73rd Session of the United Nations General Assembly (September 29, 2018)
11. Letter from the Representatives of the Islamic Republic of Iran, the Russian Federation, and Turkey to the United Nations (February 18, 2019)
12. Statement by UNHCR Special Envoy Angelina Jolie as Syria Crisis Enters Its Ninth Year (March 14, 2019)
13. Statement of the Secretary-General on Syria (March 15, 2019)

Overview of the Syrian Civil War

The Syrian Civil War is a popular and ongoing rebellion against Syrian president Bashar al-Assad's government and his Ba'ath Party that began in March 2011. Since then, events within Syria have sharply escalated as Syrian armed forces have attempted to quell the rebellion using violent means. Antigovernment protesters, meanwhile, have become better organized and equipped, leading to an escalatory spiral of attacks and counterattacks that have frequently claimed the lives of innocent civilians. One complicating factor, however, is that there is no single opposition group. Rather, there are multiple groups representing a variety of ethnic, political, and religious agendas, and at times they have fought each other as intensely as they have Syrian government forces. The Syrian government has been roundly condemned in the international community, but outside attempts to mediate a peaceful resolution to the conflict have proven elusive. By 2015, the conflict had grown in complexity and scale with the deployment of Russian troops to Syria in late 2015 to counter growing American involvement as they intensified their fight against the Islamic State (IS). In addition to American and Russian involvement, the conflict has also drawn fighters from Turkey, Iran, Lebanon, Great Britain, and Syria's Arab neighbors as the scope of the civil war has grown to a level that the

conflict has become larger, with truly far-reaching geopolitical consequences.

Although the immediate catalyst of the Syrian Civil War seemed to have emerged from the wider Arab Spring, which saw protests sweep other Arab nations, including Tunisia, Yemen, Libya, and Egypt, the violence in Syria is actually rooted in its immediate past. Since al-Assad's father, Hafez, began ruling the nation with an iron hand in the early 1970s, Syrians have been routinely subjected to severe political repression, human rights abuses, and periodic crackdowns against alleged government dissidents that resulted in thousands of deaths over the past few decades. The government also routinely employs torture and incarceration of suspected political opponents and dissidents without due process. Some Syrians had hoped that Bashar al-Assad would liberalize their country when he took power in 2000. However, despite some early rhetoric, al-Assad apparently had no intention of instituting meaningful political reform. To make matters worse, al-Assad and much of the leadership in his government are Alawite, a subgroup of Shiite Islam that represents only 12 percent of the Syrian population; Sunni Muslims comprise nearly 75 percent of the population.

In addition to the obvious problems caused by minority rule, Syrians began to chafe under their government's restrictive laws that limited or eliminated freedom of expression, assembly, or association. The al-Assad regime strictly censors the press, and until 2011 many popular websites were blocked. Women and ethnic minorities—especially the Kurds—have also been subjected to discrimination and even violence, especially in the wake of increasing Kurdish demands for an independent state in the wake of their military successes against the Islamic State in Iraq. At the same time, the economic situation in Syria began to badly deteriorate, particularly after the global financial crisis and recession that began in 2007. Unemployment rates soared, government aid to the poor declined, and government subsidies for basic food crops resulted in climbing prices. This all happened against a backdrop of millions of Iraqi refugees flowing into Syrian cities in the wake of the U.S. invasion of Iraq in 2003.

By 2011, Syria seemed ripe for popular unrest, and by then many Syrians had taken notice of rebellions occurring in other Arab nations. Protests in Syria commenced on January 26, 2011, when anti-government activist Hasan Ali Akleh immolated himself in a public square in the town of Hassakeh. Sporadic protests occurred throughout Syria thereafter, but not until mid-March did the protests begin to escalate. The al-Assad government moved swiftly, and with an iron fist, to quash the rebellions. Thousands were arrested and detained for indefinite periods of time. Many of those arrested were tortured or treated abhorrently. By April, the government had sent troops and tanks into towns and cities across Syria; troops frequently opened fire, killing or wounding scores of civilians. Although al-Assad imposed an absolute blackout of all media and news coverage, the outside world nevertheless learned of the atrocities and was deeply disturbed by them. Foreign journalists caught in Syria were subject to arrest, and several were killed.

By the summer of 2011, a sizable number of Syrian soldiers and officers began to defect, claiming that they could not support a government that wages war on its own people. By the end of July, many of these defectors formed the Free Syrian Army (FSA), which would soon become the chief adversary of the regular Syrian Army. Throughout the autumn of 2011, government troops continued to quash protests by force, but on November 3, al-Assad's government agreed in principle to a plan put forth by the Arab League to end the violence. That overture, however, was virtually stillborn, as government forces continued to fire on civilians. In February 2012, the United Nations (UN) appointed Kofi Annan, former UN general-secretary, as UN-Arab League envoy to Syria. A cease-fire was agreed to on April 12, but Syrian armed forces, including the pro-government Shabiha (militia), and rebel forces routinely violated it. By June, the UN-Arab League effort had collapsed, and Annan resigned and left Syria in August 2012.

Meanwhile, reports of atrocities in Syria proliferated. On May 25, 2012, at least 108 civilians (49 children and 34 women) were killed in the Houla Massacre after Syrian forces shelled the village of Taldou. On June 6, some 78 civilians died in the al-Qubair Massacre, when government forces shelled a civilian area. The al-Assad government has indiscriminately shelled many other areas, including large towns and cities, and even unleashed Syrian military jets on areas that were inhabited by innocent civilians. In 2013, al-Assad's forces apparently deployed chemical weapons, provoking international outrage. In September of that year, Russia and the United States co-brokered a deal that witnessed the destruction or removal of Syria's chemical weapons stockpiles. The agreement helped the al-Assad regime avoid punitive airstrikes by the United States and other allied nations. The last of Syria's chemical weapons left the country in the summer of 2014.

The UN has issued several statements condemning the civilian killings in Syria, but China and Russia have been unwilling to take stronger action against Syria for both political and economic reasons. Unless their intransigence changes, the UN is unlikely to take any more substantive steps to quell the uprising. Syria has a strong backer in Iran, which has been a longtime strategic ally and has sent supplies and troops to Syria, but the Arab League has sharply condemned al-Assad's actions.

A major consequence of the Syrian Civil War has been the rise of the Islamic State of Iraq and Syria (ISIS), which in 2013 began seizing large swaths of territory in Syria and neighboring Iraq. ISIS has benefitted enormously from the power vacuums created by the long-running civil war. The ISIS insurgency also made the complex dynamics of the conflict even more convoluted, as many anti-government rebel groups began fighting ISIS as well as al-Assad's forces, essentially creating a civil war within a civil war.

In 2013, Hezbollah, headquartered in Lebanon, entered the conflict to aid al-Assad's forces. During 2014 and much of 2015, ISIS seized and occupied more and more Syrian territory as it terrorized local populations and forced millions to flee their homes. Because of the ISIS insurgency, the percentage of Syrian territory controlled by al-Assad dropped from roughly 35 percent in July 2013 to just 16 percent in August 2015. At the same time, an American-led coalition put together in the fall of 2014 began waging an air war against ISIS targets in Syria, but the situation in that nation continued to

deteriorate. In the late summer of 2015, Russia, at the invitation of al-Assad, began to construct air bases in the country, and in late September, Russia began its own intervention in the civil war, employing withering airstrikes against ISIS and anti-government rebels. The West, however, claimed that the Russian air campaign was chiefly targeting anti-government forces rather than strictly ISIS insurgents, a claim Moscow repeatedly denied.

By early 2016, peace talks aimed at ending the bloody civil war were again underway, sponsored by Russia, the United States, several European powers, China, and a number of Arab countries. The results of those negotiations remain highly uncertain, however, as Russia in particular seems reluctant to drop its support for al-Assad or demand his immediate removal. The Russian intervention in the Syrian Civil War undoubtedly made the conflict more complicated. Turkey's downing of a Russian warplane in November 2015 was a stark reminder of how the conflict could result in a direct confrontation between Russia and the Western powers. In late 2015, the Obama administration sent a small contingent of special operations troops to Syria in recognition that an air war alone might not be enough to destroy ISIS.

Al-Assad and most rebel groups agreed to a truce in February 2016 as preparations were made for peace negotiations. The following month, the Russians began withdrawing most of their air assets from Syria in a bid to boost peace talks. Moscow was careful to point out, however, that it was not dismantling its Syrian bases and that it could resume airstrikes at any time, and on relatively short notice. In the meantime, Russian artillery continued to support al-Assad's forces. While it remains to be seen if a permanent peace will be achieved, Russia's intervention in the civil war certainly strengthened al-Assad's hand as well as Moscow's position in Syria and the larger Middle East.

It was the rise of ISIS that prompted the largest response by the United States in Syria, and as part of the U.S.-designed military operation carried out by the predominantly Kurdish Syrian Democratic Forces known as Operation Wrath of Euphrates, the Islamic State was dealt a decisive blow and effectively defeated at Raqqa in 2017. Assad, while obviously not happy with the U.S. military involvement, no matter how small, in his country, was able to seize the opportunity presented by the U.S. and Kurdish fight against ISIS by focusing his attention against other rebel groups—primarily the Free Syrian Army (FSA). The FSA had been one of Assad's biggest threats, and through a series of military operations throughout 2017 and 2018, and aided by Russian and Iranian troops, the Syrian government was able to isolate the last significant bastions of anti-government militia activity to the country's northwestern Idlib Governorate. It is feared by many in the international community that Assad deliberately created a safe haven in Idlib in order to gather his last remaining opposition into one area where he can launch a massive military campaign to kill all of them at one time. This has not happened, but he has not given any indication that he intends to do otherwise.

The Syrian conflict endured far longer than most would have ever guessed when the first major anti-government protests erupted in Daraa and then spread throughout the rest of the country. What started as peaceful calls for government reform in response to decades of harsh rule by a government dominated by a privileged minority quickly grew into chaos, with various interests, both Syrian and international, competing to topple the Assad regime with the goal of gaining power and creating a government that would suit their individual group's needs. Average citizens wanting more democracy, religious zealots wanting to create various incarnations of an Islamic Utopia, international neighbors with designs on Syria's natural resources or geostrategic position, and even people just simply looking for a fight; all of these groups could be found throughout the civil war trying to take down a government, and sometimes each other. Amid this complexity, however, the regime of Bashar al-Assad endures, and it shows few signs of ending anytime soon.

Paul G. Pierpaoli Jr. and Robert M. Kerr

Further Reading

BBC News. "Syria's War." September 6, 2012. http://www.bbc.co.uk/news/world-middle-east-17258397. Accessed September 13, 2018.

Dam, Nikolaos van. *The Struggle for Power in Syria: Politics and Society under Asad and the Ba'th Party.* I. B. Tauris, 1996.

Hinnebusch, Raymond. "Syria: From 'Authoritarian Upgrading' to Revolution?" *International Affairs* 88(1) (2012): 95–113.

Causes of the Syrian Civil War

It could, and indeed has been argued that the Syrian Civil War is the result of a complicated web of sectarian competition, political infighting, authoritarian governance, and even centuries' old ethnic hatreds. To make this argument, however, is to essentially throw one's hands in the air and assume the roots of the conflict are too complex to fully comprehend, and therefore, there is really no conclusion to reach other than that people there, and throughout the Middle East, are doomed to live an everlasting cycle of violence. This is indeed the prevailing "wisdom" of even people who claim to be experts on the peoples and places of the Middle East, and it is not uncommon to hear them claim in international media outlets that without outside, primarily Western intervention or even strong, authoritarian governments, people in the region will fight one another. The reality is that while the history of the Middle East is indeed complex, it is no more so than anywhere else in the world, and to assume that people in the Middle East are somehow predisposed to kill one another is to ignore the chain of events set in motion by empire building, colonialism, and great power politics that have made violence the predictable, though not inevitable, outcome. To understand the Syrian Civil War, one must look at its three main catalysts: the social policies of the Ottoman Empire, French attempts to construct a society that was advantageous to its goals during its Mandate Period after the First World War, and the regional instability caused by the 2003 invasion of Iraq. It was these three conditions that paved the way for the Syrian Civil War in the wake of the Arab Spring in 2011.

Syria in the Ottoman Empire

It is not that the Ottomans did anything in particular to cause the Syrian Civil War, but it is important to understand that during the period of Ottoman rule from 1516 through 1918, foundational conditions were set that the French would later exploit that did, indeed, have a direct impact on the Syrian Conflict in the wake of the 2011 Arab Spring. In order to understand the Ottoman roots of the conflict, however, it is essential to understand that nationalism—the strong emotional bond one has with people they've never met who live on land far beyond that which they can see on the horizon—did not exist at this time or in this place. Historians agree that nationalism, as we know it today, emerged in France and fueled that country's eighteenth-century revolution (an important fact to remember in the next section when France's role in Syria is discussed). In the Ottoman Empire, Islam was a unifying factor to some degree; but as long as people paid their taxes and did not work against the Ottoman political and economic machine, their lives revolved around people in their local vicinity speaking their own languages, living according to their own customs, and focusing on their immediate concerns.

For the early Ottomans in the sixteenth and seventeenth centuries, Greater Syria was simply an administrative unit of the empire, broken down into two main regions called eyalets, Aleppo and Damascus. Both of these eyalets were broken down further into sanjaks, with Aleppo having 10 separate sanjaks within it while Damascus had nine. These administrative divisions were set up primarily for taxation purposes, and few, if any people living within them developed any sort of emotional attachment with being from a particular sanjak or even eyalet. Instead, people identified with their close kin, and maybe their neighborhoods, villages, or segments of their ethnic groups.

The Ottomans did go through periods of readjustment in terms of how they divided Syria during their 400 years running the region, but even during times of official crackdowns on local populations the problems tended to be with taxation and not loyalty to any sort of Ottoman identity. Thus, the people who lived in Syria, like virtually anywhere else in the Ottoman Empire, never really developed a common, widely held sense of identity beyond that which they shared with the people and places they interacted with every day. Another important aspect of the Ottoman Empire was an approach to dealing with religious minorities called the millet system.

Under the millet system, the Ottomans, who were Sunni Muslims, allowed monotheistic minority groups, such as the Zoroastrians, Jews, and Christians, living within

the empire to practice their religions, with some restrictions. Islam mandates that these monotheists, especially Jews and Christians (referred to as the "People of the Book" based on the three religions' common Abrahamic roots), are under no obligation to convert to Islam, and that Muslims actually have an obligation to protect them. The People of the Book, under Ottoman law, fell into the category of *dhimmi*, which literally translates to "protected person," and could practice their religion with a few stipulations. The first stipulation was that the religious minorities could not proselytize or make any attempts to gain converts to their religion. They also had legal disadvantages if they ever came to a dispute with a Muslim; and most famously, they had to pay a tax called the *jizya*. Islam requires all Muslims to pay a tax called *zakat*, which is typically about two to two and a half percent of one's income. This tax forms the basis of Islam's welfare system and is designed to guarantee that the poor are provided with the basic necessities of food, shelter, and water. Because the vast majority of people in the Muslim world pay the *zakat*, it does not have to represent a large amount of an individual's income because so many people are paying it; it is an economy of scale issue in that the more people pay into the system, the less money each person has to pay. *Dhimmi*, however, are not entitled to *zakat* funds (unless, of course they convert to Islam, which many *dhimmi*, such as the Circassians and other peoples of the Caucasus region, for example, did), so they were required to pay a higher percentage of their income: 18 to 19 percent. While this practice might look inherently discriminatory on the surface (and perhaps even in practice, especially toward the end of the Ottoman Empire), it was actually designed to make sure the *dhimmi* had a fund of money that only they would have access to in order to maintain their temples, synagogues, and churches, and to provide welfare for their own people. Because these communities were far smaller than those of their Muslim neighbors, they had to pay more as individuals in order to meet the economic needs of their communities. It was, again, an economy of scale issue in which fewer people paying into the system means each person pays more.

In the end, the legacy of the Ottoman Empire in Syria was that the people who lived there had strong, very locally focused senses of identity that would later be exploited by the French, who would use this reality to pit the peoples of Syria against one another in an attempt to prevent widespread resistance to French governance. This is not to say, however, that there was not a Syrian nationalist movement. Among the many groups within Syria at the fall of the Ottoman Empire was a small, but very ardent group of Syrian nationalists who would actually have a profound impact on laying the foundations of the Syrian Civil War.

Syria under the French Mandate

During World War I, the imminent fall of the Ottoman Empire grabbed the attention and imaginations of France and Great Britain. Both countries saw unimaginable wealth in the acquisition of the Ottoman lands of the Levant and northern Arabia, and in 1916 they made a secret deal known as the Sykes-Picot Agreement to divide these lands among themselves upon Ottoman defeat. In 1918, the two powers made good on that agreement, and France took administrative control of Syria and Lebanon. One factor both the British and the French overlooked, however, was that throughout the war the British

were stirring up Arab nationalism in order to rally their support against the Ottomans. Given promises by the likes of T. E. Lawrence (aka Lawrence of Arabia) that their dedication to the fight against the Turks would be rewarded after the war, the Arabs felt, and indeed still feel, that the agreement made between the British and the French was the ultimate betrayal of trust. Unlike the Brits, who established an immediate presence in their agreed-upon territory immediately after the war in 1918, the French were largely absent from Lebanon and Syria between 1918 and 1920; and the Arab troops who had fought alongside Lawrence seized the opportunity to gather their supporters and in 1919 declare an independent Arab state from Damascus and under the leadership of Prince Faisal (who had fought alongside T. E. Lawrence in their final push to seize Damascus from the Turks the previous year). The French were not amenable to this idea.

In 1920, the French seized Damascus in the Franco-Syrian War and sent Faisal into exile (he would later become the king of Iraq). The experience of almost losing their foothold in the former Ottoman lands had a profound impact on how the French governed Syria until the end of the mandate in 1943. Fearful of the Arab nationalists who lived primarily in Damascus, the French did two things that would have direct implications for the later instability in Syria. First, they severely limited the role Sunni Muslim Arabs could play in their militia, the Troupes Speciales du Levant, choosing instead to recruit heavily from Syria's minority groups (particularly from the Alawites). Second, they gave two minority groups, the Druze and the Alawites, their own autonomous states, thereby giving them disproportionate influence in Damascus.

The Troupes Speciales du Levant was a militia formed by the French in their newly created territories of Syria and Lebanon. The French deliberately recruited heavily from the region's ethnic and religious minorities. Sunni Muslims were recruited as well, but the relatively large presence of the minority groups gave them representation and status in the military disproportionate to their overall population. The French had long employed techniques to divide and rule over their colonial subjects, and the ethnic diversity that was the legacy of the multiethnic Ottoman Empire created fertile ground on which to do so. The French tended to recruit into their proxy military forces around the world according to what they perceived to be the greatest threat to their rule. In the case of Syria, the greatest threat was clearly the Arab nationalists who were mainly Sunni Muslims, so the French made sure to promote interests contrary to the Arab nationalists', which had the desired effect of sowing discontent among the various groups in the region. The French were also very adept at identifying, and then exploiting, potential rifts within respective groups, and it did not take them long to discover the political, ideological, and tribal rivalries within the Sunni Muslim community itself. Their divide-and-rule policies within the military force that would eventually become the Syrian and Lebanese armies had a tremendous impact on paving the way for the Alawite Hafez al-Assad and his allies to rise to power in the 1960s.

First, because of perceived favoritism toward minorities within the military, the Sunni Muslims in Syria never developed a widespread dedication to military service. This meant that in Syria's independence era, minorities were far more eager to serve in the military than their Sunni countrymen. Second, the factions within the Sunni community the French so effectively exploited spilled into the military, where high-ranking Sunni officers organized themselves into rival factions within the military early in the independence era. Each faction felt it had the correct vision of how the young country should be run, and after a series of failed coup attempts led by the respective factions between 1949 and 1954, the government turned toward its mid-level officers who had proven to be loyal to them; these officers tended to be Alawites and other religious minorities, and they quickly found themselves being elevated in rank and status as a reward for their loyalty. This reality extended beyond the military as well, as the Alawites found themselves being promoted to higher positions throughout the government. This paved the way for the secularist Ba'ath Party, to which a large number of Alawites and other minorities belonged, to take over the government in 1963, with the Alawite Assad taking power in 1970.

The second major legacy of the French Mandate that has a direct impact on the cause of the Syrian Civil War is related to the issue of the Alawites' rise to power outlined above; it was the fact that the French gave them their own autonomous state centered around Syria's most important port city, Latakia. In July 1922, only two years after the Franco-Syrian War in which the predominantly Sunni Arab Nationalists were defeated, France created the Alawite state of Latakia. The main result of this move was to give Alawites disproportionate influence in the affairs of Syria, and it gave them the privilege of being able to work directly with the French in what was the country's most important port city. This period led to great resentment on the part of the Sunni Arabs toward the Alawites, as well as a general mistrust that has only been exacerbated since Assad came into power in 1970. Of course, the Alawites lost their state after Syrian independence, and suffered many consequences in the newly created state, which was led by Sunni Arab nationalists. This brief period in which the Alawites fell from grace convinced them they had to do whatever it took to gain control of the state, and unlike in the case of the Arab nationalist movement, which had distinct religious overtones, they promoted a secularist Syrian nationalism. It is not surprising that this secularist nationalism was very popular among not just the Alawites, but almost all of Syria's minority groups, and under the secularist, minority-dominated Syrian Ba'ath Party. This key division, between most of Syria's minority groups and the country's various Sunni political and religious factions, is still clearly visible in the civil war.

The U.S. Invasion of Iraq

Volumes have been written on the United States' invasion of Iraq to topple Saddam Hussein in 2003, and the most obvious destabilizing effects for the rest of the region need only be mentioned here. Perhaps the most important, from an American perspective, is the emergence of the Islamic State; a group that clearly emerged from a series of events, including many bad decisions on the part of the U.S. government, set in motion in the period immediately following President George W. Bush's famous "Mission Accomplished" speech from the deck of the USS *Abraham Lincoln*. From the Syrian perspective this was also extremely important, but the Islamic State did not cause the Syrian Civil War; it simply took advantage of the conditions set by it. From the perspective of Bashar al-Assad, the most significant impacts of

the U.S. invasion of Iraq were the presence of the U.S. military itself, and even more importantly, the hundreds of thousands of refugees, asylum seekers, disaffected Ba'athists, soldiers, and others who flooded into his country from Iraq.

The UNHCR reports that between 2003 and 2005 as many as 700,000 Iraqis fled into Syria, and that by 2007 the number of Iraqis in the country was well over 1 million. Bashar al-Assad's government before 2003 was functional; certainly Syria was not the wealthiest country in the region, but the people in the region were largely content, and even his detractors were comfortable enough to not organize against him. Syria maintained an open-door policy for Iraqis fleeing the U.S. occupation of their country from 2003 until 2007. Four years of providing refuge placed a huge strain on Syrian society, and while the country was able to absorb much of this burden early on, it became harder and harder as time went on. The refugees, especially in Damascus where they put a huge strain on resources, overburdened the outdated electrical grid and sewage system, stressed the real estate market at all levels of income, flooded the employment market with cheap labor, and overwhelmed the health-care system. One of the largest costs to the government was water—shortages were common after 2007. The Iraqi refugee crisis in Syria leading up to the civil war is rarely mentioned in the international media as one of its main causes, but it is widely discussed in media and intellectual circles throughout the Middle East. It created a situation in which the Assad regime was overstretched in providing essential services, especially in its own capital, which arguably led to a situation in which the government became extremely sensitive to maintaining its grip on power as it watched the Arab Spring sweep across North Africa and heading it its direction.

Conclusion: The Arab Spring as the Straw That Broke the Camel's Back

Syria is a country where ethnic and local identities and loyalties have always existed at the expense of a larger collective consciousness; and with a postcolonial legacy in which these identities and loyalties were used to divide people even further, the strains of a massive geopolitical powerhouse asserting its dominance in the country lit the fuse of a powder keg filled with explosive material. The Arab Spring accelerated the burning fuse; and a people and a government intimately tied together yet bitterly divided lost all inhibitions, and the powder keg exploded.

Robert M. Kerr

Further Reading

Bou-Nacklie, N. E. "Les Troupes Speciales: Religious and Ethnic Recruitment 1916–1946." *International Journal of Middle East Studies* 25(4) (1993): 645–660.

Fromkin, David. *A Peace to End All Peace: The Fall of the Ottoman Empire and the Creation of the Modern Middle East.* Henry Holt, 2009.

Khoury, Philip. *Syria and the French Mandate: The Politics of Arab Nationalism 1920–1945.* Princeton University Press, 1987.

Reilly, James A. *Fragile Nation, Shattered Land: The Modern History of Syria.* Lynne Rienner Publishers, 2019.

Consequences of the Syrian Civil War

It is difficult to determine the consequences of the Syrian Civil War because it is still ongoing. Bashar al-Assad has, no doubt in large part because of support from Russia's Vladimir Putin, retained his hold on power; the Islamic State exists only in small isolated pockets throughout his country; and his military forces have not suffered a significant defeat in a long time. On the other hand, millions of Syrian refugees will likely never return to his country, he has few friends or allies in the international community, and the Idlib Governorate in northwestern Syria remains a stronghold of a host of militia groups fighting against him. In short, the future of Syria is completely up in the air and not likely to be resolved anytime soon. That being said, there are some things that can be called consequences of the war no matter what happens next, and those are the unresolved issues surrounding Syria's domestic political and social future as it tries to rebuild; the country's tenuous geopolitical status in relation to the United States, Russia, and its Middle Eastern neighbors; and the crisis surrounding the millions of people who have fled to countries around the region, as well as the rest of the world.

Syria's Domestic Future

The unresolved issues for Syria in terms of its domestic future center around the questions of politics and rebuilding. Politically, Bashar al-Assad's government is still on a war footing, which means that his priority is putting down the last of his opposition, which is largely isolated to the Idlib Governorate along the country's northwest border with Turkey. He has given no indication that he intends to introduce any significant government reforms, and no viable opposition group seems to have the means to depose him. As fighting has decreased in intensity and frequency since 2018, however, many Syrians have turned their attention toward rebuilding, and it is likely people will start demanding routine government services be returned to their pre-conflict state. Will Assad face a new round of protests if he is not able to provide the basic functions of government? Will his primary allies, Russia and Iran, be willing to foot the bill in order to prop him up until Syria can rebuild some semblance of an economy? These are questions that currently have no clear answers.

Syria's Geopolitical Future

The consequences of Syria's Civil War are not just local or even regional, they are global. While the anti-Assad protests that sprang up in the southern city of Daraa in 2011 may have seemed very local in focus, especially for the protestors, the reality is that they were part of something much bigger, the Arab Spring. A movement fueled by an overall sense of dissatisfaction with the entrenched status quo in countries all the way from Morocco to Iran, the Arab Spring was not something that just happened spontaneously. It was the result of a melding of local discontent with encouragement from the United States and its Western allies to demand accountability and democracy from authoritarian, oppressive governments throughout the Middle East. This is not to take away from the very real hope, dreams, and optimism of the people who took part in demonstrations and who committed the ultimate act of self-sacrifice for their cause, but it is important to see that the Arab Spring was also a key focus of American foreign policy in the wake of Operation Iraqi Freedom. At the very least, Russia painted the Arab Spring as the United States' attempt to overthrow Middle Eastern regimes in order to replace them with overtly pro-Western governments, and Russian foreign and military policy explicitly states that. Russia's chief of the General Staff, General Valery Gerasimov, has spoken repeatedly about the Arab Spring as an act of "soft war" against the regimes of the Middle East, and part of Russia's decision to intervene in Syria on the side of the government was to stand up against what it sees as an aggressive American strategy to reestablish its base of power in the region. Thus, the Syrian Civil War's greatest consequences are for the Syrian people themselves, but the geopolitical consequences have pitted two old enemies, the United States and Russia, against each other in a way that could have far-reaching and potentially devastating consequences for the entire world.

The other major players besides the United States and Russia that will determine the geopolitical consequences of the Syrian Conflict are Turkey and Iran. One of the most significant questions to be determined in the wake of not only the Syrian Civil War but of Operation Iraqi Freedom as well is that of the Kurds. A stateless nation for all of its existence, the Kurdish people have all the ingredients needed to have their own country: a common language, a common culture, a common economy, and they occupy a contiguous ancestral homeland with bountiful resources. The problem is this homeland crosses the current borders of four countries that have no interest in allowing a Kurdish state to exist: Iraq, Syria, Iran, and Turkey. The Turks, in particular, have made it very clear since the birth of their modern nation that the Kurds who live within their boundaries will never have their own state. The Kurds, however, have been longtime, very reliable allies of the United States in their fight in Iraq against Saddam Hussein as well as al-Qaeda and other insurgent groups, and in Syria they were instrumental in leading the U.S.-designed plan to defeat the Islamic State in Raqqa—Operation Wrath of Euphrates. Regardless of what happens next in Syria, the Kurdish issue is one with the potential to pit the United States, Turkey, Russia, and no doubt Iran against one another; possibly sooner rather than later. Iran is the other, and for Syria maybe the most important, player in the region. The Assad regime has long counted on Iran as its most trusted (and generous) ally, and Bashar al-Assad still values that relationship, as seen in the deal he made with Tehran to lease the port at Latakia outright to them starting in 2019. This deal not only has the potential to provide Iran with direct access to the Mediterranean and all the economic benefits that go with it, but it remains to be seen whether they will try to establish a naval presence in the eastern Mediterranean as well. That would have profound geopolitical implications for the United States and Israel.

The Refugee Crisis

Along with the destruction of life and property, including many ancient and irreplaceable artifacts resulting from the Syrian Civil War, the issue with the most significant consequences for the Syrian people themselves is the refugee crisis. It is estimated there are at least 5 million refugees who fled Syria, and another 6 million homeless Syrians still living in the country. These people will either need to be returned to their homes (most of which need to be rebuilt by somebody) or settled elsewhere. Millions have been resettled and have started to build lives in their new home countries, but all face the profound challenges of fitting into new places and cultures, many of which do not want the Syrians there in the first place. It is too soon to estimate the impact that these diaspora communities will have on their new host countries, or to guess how many will try to return to Syria. But on a personal level, the sheer number—at least 11 million people—displaced from their homes will have second- and third-order consequences for them and their descendants for generations to come.

Conclusion: The Consequences of the Syrian Civil War Are Yet to Be Determined

Outlined here are just some of the consequences of the Syrian Civil War. It is too soon to know what will become of the Bashar al-Assad regime, the security and stability of the region, or the Syrian people, both in and out of Syria. It is certain, however, that the effects of the civil war will be felt far into the future, and that conflicts such as this one, in which historical, social, and geopolitical complexities make it difficult to identify who is on what side and for what desired end state, will likely become the norm in our increasingly interconnected world.

Robert M. Kerr

Further Reading

Agha, Husayn. *Syria and Iran: Rivalry and Cooperation.* Pinter Lab, 1995.

Barkey, Henri J., Scott B. Lasensky, and Phebe Marr, eds. *Iraq, Its Neighbors, and the United States: Competition, Crisis, and the Reordering of Power.* United States Institute of Peace, 2011.

Betts, Alexander. *Refuge: Rethinking Refugee Policy in a Changing World.* Oxford University Press, 2017.

Smith, Lee. *The Consequences of Syria.* Stanford, CA: Hoover Institution Press, 2014.

van Dam, Nikolaos. *Destroying a Nation: The Civil War in Syria.* I. B. Tauris, 2017.

A

Al-Abbas Brigade

The al-Abbas Brigade consists of Shiite foreign fighters who traveled to Syria from Iraq and Lebanon in 2012 to defend the Shiite population and holy sites from Sunni rebel groups. The group's full name is Abu al Fadl al-Abbas Brigade.

The al-Abbas Brigade is considered a front organization for armed Shiite groups based in Iraq. Media reports suggest its fighters were members of Iraqi cleric Muqtada al-Sadr's Mahdi Army, Lebanese Hezbollah, or Iranian-funded groups Asa'ib Ahl al-Haq (a splinter of the Mahdi Army) and Kata'ib Hezbollah, known to operate in Iraq and Syria. The name of the group refers to al-Abbas ibn Ali, the martyr son of Imam 'Ali, and was used by fighters connected to Kata'ib Hezbollah (KH) and Asa'ib Ahl al-Haq (AAH) during the Iraq War.

The arrival of al-Abbas Brigade in 2012–2013 highlighted the sectarian aspect of the war. Social media posts stressed the importance of defending the shrine of Sayyida Zeinab on the southern edge of Damascus, and videos shared by the group highlighted other religious holy sites destroyed by Sunni rebels in Syria. Its members were typically concentrated in southern Damascus near the shrine, but al-Abbas Brigade was involved in fighting alongside Syrian regime forces and Hezbollah in northern areas of the country.

Little is known about the group's activities in Syria since 2013. Some analysts speculate al-Abbas Brigade fighters returned to Iraq to fight ISIS alongside other armed Shiite groups. A Shia Popular Mobilization Unit (PMU) known as the al-Abbas Combat Division is active in Iraq and worked alongside Iraqi Security Forces and Kata'ib Hezbollah in Tal Afar to defeat the Islamic State. The al-Abbas Combat Division claims it was formed in June 2014 following a religious fatwa from Iraq's senior Shia cleric, Grand Ayatollah Ali al-Sistani, and works under Iraqi Ministry of Defense authority.

Melia Pfannenstiel

Further Reading

Fulton, Will, Joseph Holliday, and Sam Wyer. "Iranian Strategy in Syria." AEI and Institute for the Study of War, May 2013. http://www.understandingwar.org/report/iranian-strategy-syria.

Karouny, Mariam. "Shiite Fighters Rally to Defend Damascus Shrine." *Reuters*, March 3, 2013. https://www.reuters.com/article/us-syria-crisis-shiites/shiite-fighters-rally-to-defend-damascus-shrine-idUSBRE92202X20130303.

Knights, Michael, and Hamdi Malik. "The al-Abbas Combat Division Model: Reducing Iranian Influence in Iraq's Security Forces." The Washington Institute for Near East Policy, Policywatch 2250, August 22, 2017. https://www.washingtoninstitute.org/policy-analysis/view/the-al-abbas-combat-division-model.

Salhy, Suadad al. "Iraqi Shiites Flock to Assad's Side as Sectarian Split Widens." *Reuters*, June 19, 2013. https://www.reuters.com/article/us-iraq-syria-militants/iraqi-shiites-flock-to-assads-side-as-sectarian-split-widens-idUSBRE95I0ZA20130619.

Alawites/Alawis

The Alawites, also known as the Alawis, are a minority group within Syria. Making up about 15 percent of the total population of modern-day Syria, the Alawites have enjoyed power at the national scale disproportionate to their relatively small numbers since the assent of Hafez al-Assad to the top of the Ba'ath Party in the early 1970s.

The Alawite identity is based primarily on religious affiliation rather than race or ethnicity. Alawite religion, Alawism, is a subsect of Shia Islam, but is unique because it retains many beliefs and practices from religions that predate Islam; Zoroastrianism and Christianity, in particular. Alawites do not traditionally worship in mosques, but conduct religious rites around shrines near revered tombs and groves. Alawites consider themselves to be fully Muslim, however, and reject any claims that their religious traditions are in any way contrary to Islamic tradition. Based on the teachings of tenth-century Shia religious scholar Muhammad Ibn Nusayr al-Namri, Alawism emphasizes the importance of Ali, the Prophet Muhamad's son-in-law and the first convert to Islam. Venerating him as having almost deity-like status, Alawites treat the Five Pillars of Islam as symbolic gestures rather than religious obligations. This puts them at odds with their Muslim brothers and sisters, Sunnis in particular, and they have been the target of much persecution as a result. It is important to note that the Alawites themselves are very secretive about many of their religious beliefs and practices, and this has led to many suspicions and a sense of distrust among their neighbors about them, their beliefs, and their motives.

The Alawites were strong supporters of the French Mandate in Syria after World War I. The French were the first to recognize them as a legitimate ethnic group within Syria, and the first to give them legal standing and the opportunity to hold official positions within the government. Alawite support for the French was driven primarily by the fear that the Syrian nationalist movement, led largely by Sunni Muslims, would have marginalized Syria's minorities. By casting their lot with the French, the Alawites took a gamble that eventually paid off when the secularist Ba'ath regime took power in 1963. Their moderate religious views fit nicely with the secularism of the Ba'ath Party; and in a political movement that overlooked religious piety as a prerequisite for membership, Alawites, along with other minority groups, found a voice that was eventually amplified when Hafez al-Assad, himself an Alawite, came to power in 1971.

In the wake of the Syrian Civil War, the relationship between the Assad regime and his Alawite community has become complicated. The larger Alawite community began to quietly distance itself from the regime as the conflict dragged on because they started to see they were in an untenable situation. On one hand, they could not support their Alawite brother too emphatically because he could not guarantee their protection as the conflict wore on and tensions and hatred toward the regime (and them, by association) put them at great risk for retaliation. On the other hand, they could not distance themselves from the government overtly because that would be disloyal and they would suffer the consequences. With an uncertain future for the country of Syria, it may well be that the Alawites have the most uncertain future of all as a result of the conflict, and why they, even reluctantly, have a vested interest in the long-term victory of the Assad regime.

Robert M. Kerr

Further Reading

CIA World Factbook. https://www.cia.gov/library/publications/the-world-factbook/geos/sy.html.

Foreign Policy Research Institute. "Primer on the Alawites in Syria," 2016. https://www.fpri.org/article/2016/12/primer-alawites-syria/.

Held, Colbert C. *Middle East Patterns: Places, Peoples, and Politics*. Routledge, 2015.

Aleppo

Aleppo is an ancient city in northwest Syria, located about 60 miles south of the Turkish border. With a population of just under 2 million people, Aleppo is Syria's largest and one of its most important cities; it has been the scene of some of the Syrian Civil War's most intense fighting. In fact, the bloodshed has been so extreme in Aleppo that current population estimates are significantly lower than they were before the conflict, with the city's 2004 population being roughly 2.1 million. While many of these people undoubtedly fled the violence, the United Nations (UN) estimates that the death toll in Aleppo between 2012 and 2016 was over 400,000 people. Aleppo's strategic location, historical significance, and large population made it almost inevitable that it was going to be the scene of immense bloodshed as the conflict unfolded from its earliest days.

Aleppo, along with Damascus (Syria's capital), is one of the world's oldest continuously inhabited cities. Archaeological records indicate that people have been living on the site since at least the third millennium BCE, and perhaps even before that. What made the site so appealing to its earliest inhabitants was its geographic site and situation. The original settlers are thought to have lived on a hill located at the center of the modern city.

Providing a defensive advantage, the early inhabitants were able to take advantage of the area's fertile soil, as well as a source of fresh water in the form of the Quwayq River—though today the river struggles to maintain its flow due to damming upstream in Turkey and is fed only by diverting some of the flow of the Euphrates into its banks.

With an advantageous defensive position, good farmland, and a source of fresh water, Aleppo soon grew into an important center of trade and commerce. By the eighteenth century BCE it had grown into the capital of an Amorite kingdom that came to dominate most of the territory of modern-day Syria. The kingdom eventually fell, and Aleppo was controlled by the Hittites, Egyptians, Mitannians, and then Hittites again from the seventeenth through fourteenth centuries BCE. The Assyrians took it by force in the eighth century BCE, and then the Persians ruled it for 200 years from the sixth through fourth centuries BCE. Aleppo's modern history is really tied to its rise as an important center of commerce under the Greeks and then the Romans in the first century BCE.

It was in the first century BCE that Aleppo became what we would recognize as an international city. Substantial numbers of Jews settled in and around Aleppo at this time, and it became one of the most important Jewish cities in the region. Not long after, the Romans came, and the city became a crucial node of the Great Silk Road, linking the Roman Empire to China and all points in between. Aleppo became known as a diverse city, with traders from the east mingling with the city's many ethnic groups. When the Romans adopted Christianity as the state religion in the third century CE, they placed many restrictions on the city's Jewish population, and many of the city's inhabitants adopted Christianity for personal and political reasons. Roman/Christian rule lasted for almost 300 years until the Arab Muslim conquest of the city in 636.

Modern-day Syria was one of the first places to which Islam spread outside the Arabian Peninsula, and the cities of Aleppo and Damascus became important centers within the young but expanding Muslim world. Aleppo in particular was crucial in providing finance to the young empire, and its traders from around the world and of various religious traditions enjoyed more freedoms in many ways than they had under the Romans; this was particularly true for the city's Jewish population. Under the new Islamic law, Christians and Jews, officially known in the new system as *al-Ahl al-Kitaab*, or "the People of the Book," were not forced to accept Islam as their religion and were allowed to freely practice their religious traditions. However, they were considered a "protected class" (*dhimi*), and as such were not allowed to proselytize, and they did have to pay an extra tax to make up for the fact they did not belong to a mosque, and therefore could not pay the *zakat*, an obligatory tax for all Muslims. While they did not enjoy total freedom, life for the region's Jews under this system in the early Islamic Empire was far less restrictive than it had been under Roman and Christian rule. As an important city in the new Empire, a Great Mosque was built in Aleppo to accommodate the city's rapidly expanding population and the large number of increasingly Muslim traders traveling to and from the city.

Aleppo was not to rest peacefully under Arab Muslim rule; its strategic value would not allow for that. In 1260, the city was sacked by the Mongols, who saw it as a key point in their plans for westward expansion. Their rule did not last long as the Egyptian Mamluk armies soon retook the city, only to fall victim to both plague and continued Mongol

aggression, most notably by Tamerlane in 1400. Finally, in 1516, Aleppo was brought into the fold of the Ottoman Empire, to which it belonged until after the First World War. It is important to note, however, that Aleppo remained a city with an antiestablishment, rebellious streak as illustrated in its many trade guilds challenging Ottoman rule resulting in riots in the nineteenth century; so it is perhaps no surprise that Aleppo became the focus of so much conflict during the Syrian Civil War.

The establishment of the French Mandate in Syria after World War I had a negative impact on Aleppo in that it was effectively cut off from some of its historically most important trade partners in Iraq, which fell under the British Mandate, and Turkey, which was struggling to establish itself as an independent country. What it lost in trade revenue, however, it made up in industrial investment, and Aleppo saw incredible growth in the twentieth century as people moved from the countryside into the city in order to claim the growing number of factory jobs. Most of the people that moved into Aleppo were Sunni Muslims, and the city became an important center of Sunni commerce and intellectualism, and served as an effective counterbalance to the rise of Syria's new political elite, which came to be dominated by the Alawites, a Shia minority sect.

At the beginning of the Syrian conflict in 2011, Aleppo remained quiet and did not see any significant government protests; early protests were centered primarily in the country's Kurdish areas. As the conflict grew into a full-blown civil war, however, Aleppo became the base of many Sunni armed resistance groups and drew the attention and ire of Syria's president, Bashar al-Assad. Knowing the strategic and symbolic importance of Aleppo, he spared no effort in putting down any and all resistance within the city, a fact that can be seen in the total devastation of much of its buildings and streets. Not even the city's Great Mosque, built in the earliest days of Muslim expansion, was spared, as it suffered serious damage by both government and rebel forces in 2012 and 2013. It is interesting to note that Aleppo has been fought over by most of the major opposition groups, including the al-Nusra Front as well as the Kurdish Peoples Protection Units (the YPG). In fact, the YPG was one of the last groups fighting there before Syrian troops retook the city in February 2018. Fighting in the civil war has been devastating to the city in terms of the loss of life, destruction of the economy, and the destruction of buildings and historical artifacts. In fact, as much as 30 percent of the city recognized as World Heritage Sites by UNESCO has been destroyed. Given Aleppo's inherent strategic location, proven economic importance, and historical significance, it is likely that it will emerge from the ashes.

Robert M. Kerr

Further Reading

Burns, Ross. *Aleppo: A History*. Routledge, 2016.

Held, Colbert C. *Middle East Patterns: Places, Peoples, and Politics*. Routledge, 2015.

Mansel, Philip. *Aleppo: The Rise and Fall of Syria's Great Merchant City*. I. B. Taurus, 2016.

Al-Nusra Front (*Jabhat al-Nusra*)

The al-Nusra Front (known officially as Jabhat al-Fateh al-Sham [JFS] as of 2016) is a Sunni Islamic insurgent group in Syria. Formerly affiliated with al-Qaeda (AQ), JFS is a direct competitor with the Islamic State (IS) in Syria, and it is the second largest and second most influential anti-government group in the country; surpassed only by IS. This is, at least in part, due to its official ties to al-Qaeda from 2013 through 2016, allowing it to tap into AQ's vast global supply network. This gave al-Nusra access to money, guns, and equipment that was surpassed only by IS in the pantheon of players in the Syrian Conflict. In fact, al-Nusra and IS have both, at various times throughout the conflict, been better sourced and supplied than even the Syrian Armed Forces (especially before the involvement of the Russians in the conflict).

Al-Nusra was formed in 2012 with the blessing of al-Qaeda with the intention of helping to bring down the Assad regime and replacing it with an AQ-backed religious government. The Arab Spring, and more specifically the unpopularity of Assad within Syria, presented AQ with an opportunity to assist in the toppling of a secularist regime, and to fill what it saw as the impending power vacuum with its first real opportunity for an openly pro-AQ government in the Middle East. Appointing Syrian-born Abu Muhammad al-Golani as its leader, al-Nusra had the advantage of being able to present itself as an internationally supported organization with a Syrian face. Unlike IS, which is dependent on a large number of foreign fighters recruited from around the world, al-Nusra was comprised primarily of Syrians, and claimed legitimacy in the fight for power in Damascus based on this fact. Al-Nusra also enjoyed greater appeal for many within Syria because it was seen as more moderate (or at least less violent) relative to IS.

Al-Nusra's religious teachings, while still militant in nature, stress the importance of providing social services to people within the community, avoiding being seen as extremists, avoiding armed conflict with other militant groups fighting against the Syrian Armed Forces, and keeping the focus on what it considers the real enemy: the corrupt, anti-Islamic Assad regime. While al-Nusra, like al-Qaeda, wished to eventually impose sharia law throughout all of Syria, that goal was second to deposing the government, and the leaders of the group refrained from imposing it over localities that resisted giving up civil law entirely in exchange for that city or town's support in their fight against the government. Al-Nusra was openly critical of IS's more brutal approach and presented itself as the more moderate and level-headed, and distinctly Syrian alternative to a movement most Syrians saw as needlessly brutal, violent, uncompromising, and foreign in nature. It must be noted, however, that in spite of these comparisons with IS, al-Nusra was a violent organization; and in areas considered to be their strongholds, sharia law was strictly and violently enforced on many occasions, and opposition to their supremacy was dealt with swiftly. Their record with non-Sunni minorities in Syria was also one of violence and discrimination, though it must be noted that some of this violence toward minorities such as the Alawites, Druze, and Yezidis was the result of their varying degrees of support of the Assad government.

Robert M. Kerr

Further Reading

Gerges, Fawaz A. *ISIS: A History*. Princeton University Press, 2016.

Hubbard, Ben. "Al-Qaeda Tries a New Tactic to Keep Power: Sharing It." *New York Times*, June 9, 2015. https://www.nytimes.com/2015/06/10/world/middleeast/qaeda-yemen-syria-houthis.html.

Tomass, Mark. *The Religious Roots of the Syrian Conflict: The Remaking of the Fertile Crescent*. Palgrave MacMillan, 2016.

Al-Qaeda

Al-Qaeda is an international terrorist organization, whose hallmark is the perpetration of terrorist attacks against various Western and Western-allied interests. In the late 1980s, al-Qaeda (meaning the "base" or "foundation" in Arabic) fought against the Soviet occupation of Afghanistan. The organization is, however, best known for the September 11, 2001, terrorist attacks in the United States, the worst such attacks in the history of that nation. The founding of al-Qaeda, which is comprised chiefly of Sunni Muslims, is shrouded in controversy. Research from a number of Arabic scholars indicates that al-Qaeda was created sometime between 1987 and 1988 by Sheikh Abdullah Azzam, a mentor to Osama bin Laden. Azzam was a professor at Jeddah University in Saudi Arabia. Bin Laden attended Jeddah University, where he met and was strongly influenced by Azzam.

Genesis and Early Years

Al-Qaeda grew out of the Afghan Service Bureau, also known as the Maktab al Khidmat lil-mujahidin al-Arab (MaK). Azzam was the founder of the MaK, and bin Laden funded the organization and was considered the deputy director. This organization recruited, trained, and transported Muslim soldiers from any Muslim nation into Afghanistan to fight the jihad (holy war) against the Soviet armies in the 1980s. Sayyid Qutb, a philosopher of the Muslim Brotherhood, developed the credo for al-Qaeda, which is to arm all Muslims in the world and to overthrow any government that does not support traditional Muslim practice and Islamic law.

Following the mysterious death of Sheikh Azzam in November 1989, bin Laden took over the leadership of al-Qaeda. He continued to work toward Azzam's goal of creating an international organization comprised of mujahideen (soldiers) who would fight the oppression of Muslims throughout the world. Al-Qaeda actually has had several goals: to destroy Israel; to rid the Islamic world of the influence of Western civilization; to reestablish a caliphate form of government throughout the world; to fight against any government viewed as contrary to the ideals of Islamic law and religion; and to aid any Islamic groups trying to establish an Islamic form of government in their countries.

The organization of al-Qaeda follows the Shur majlis, or consultative council form of leadership. The emir general's post has been held by Osama bin Laden, who was succeeded by Ayman al-Zawahiri upon bin Laden's death in May 2011. Several other generals are under the emir general, and then there are additional leaders of related groups. There are 24 related groups as part of the consultative council. The council consists of four committees: military, religious-legal, finance, and media. The emir general personally selects the leader of these committees, and each committee head reports directly to the emir general. All levels of al-Qaeda are highly compartmentalized, and secrecy is the key to all operations.

Ideology and Activities

Al-Qaeda's ideology has appealed to both Middle Eastern and non-Middle Eastern groups that adhere to Islam. There are also a number of Islamist extremist groups associated with al-Qaeda that have established a history of violence and terrorism in numerous countries in the world today. Most notably, these associated groups have included al-Qaeda in Iraq, which merged with the Islamic State of Iraq and Syria (ISIS), and the al-Nusra Front in Syria. ISIS has been waging a bloody insurgency in both Iraq and Syria since 2011 and became a key player in the Syrian Civil War. The al-Nusra organization has also been involved in the civil war in Syria and, like ISIS, is waging war against President Bashar al-Assad's government. Nigerian-based Boko Haram, another organization of jihadist extremists, also has alleged ties to al-Qaeda.

Bin Laden was able to put most of the Islamist extremist groups under the umbrella of al-Qaeda. Indeed, its leadership spread throughout the world, and its influence penetrates many religious, social, and economical structures in most Muslim communities. The membership of al-Qaeda remains difficult to determine because of its decentralized organizational structure. By early 2005, U.S. officials claimed to have killed or taken prisoner two-thirds of the al-Qaeda leaders behind the September 11 attacks. However, some of these prisoners have been shown to have had no direct connection with the attacks. Al-Qaeda has continued to periodically release audio recordings and videotapes, some featuring bin Laden and Zawahiri, to comment on current issues, exhort followers to keep up the fight, and prove to Western governments that it is still a force with which to be reckoned.

Al Qaeda After 9/11

Despite the decimation of al-Qaeda's core leadership in Afghanistan and Pakistan after 9/11, it continues to be a major threat. According to experts, the organization moved from a centralized organization to a series of local-actor organizations forming a broad, loosely organized terrorist network. Al-Qaeda in Iraq was substantially weakened by the end of the Iraq War in 2011, but it subsequently regained control of many of its former staging areas and the ability to launch weekly waves of multiple car bomb attacks. It also joined forces with ISIS, and in so doing has greatly amplified its ability to sow chaos and terror within Iraq. On May 1, 2011, bin Laden was killed in an attack mounted by U.S. Special Forces on his compound in Pakistan. President Barack Obama called it the "most significant achievement to date" in the effort to defeat al-Qaeda.

In July 2013, however, more than 1,000 people were killed in Iraq, the highest monthly death toll in five years. Most of the attacks were led by al-Qaeda and its affiliates, including ISIS. That same year, in Syria, al-Qaeda's affiliate, the al-Nusra Front, rose to prominence. Until recently, Al-Nusra reported directly to al-Qaeda's leadership hierarchy. Between 2009 and 2018, in Libya, al-Qaeda-affiliated terror groups have been blamed for scores of attacks, many of them including civilians. Indeed, al-Qaeda has been blamed for the Sept. 11, 2012, attack on the U.S. consulate in Benghazi, Libya, that left the U.S. ambassador and three other Americans dead. In Yemen, al-Qaeda leaders in strongholds in the country's south have not been vanquished by a Yemeni military backed by U.S. and Saudi forces and drone strikes. al-Qaeda affiliates in Iraq, Syria, Yemen, and West Africa have expanded their operating areas and capabilities and appear poised to continue their expansion.

By January 2014, a resurgent al-Qaeda, along with ISIS, had secured much of Iraq's Anbar Province, including Fallujah, and was making significant headway in Afghanistan, often colluding with a resurgent Taliban. Al-Qaeda has also successfully established itself in parts of Lebanon, Egypt, Algeria, and Mali. By early 2014, the Obama administration had begun shipping Hellfire missiles and other weaponry to the Iraqi government in order to suppress the growing

insurgency there, which is now dominated by ISIS. In a telling sign of ISIS's recent excesses, al-Qaeda formally disassociated itself from the group in February 2014, citing the organization's brutality and inability to submit to authority.

In June 2015, al-Qaeda's second-in-command, Nasir al-Wuhayshi, died in a U.S. airstrike in Yemen. The Obama administration trumpeted this as a major blow to the al-Qaeda leadership, but the organization appears not to have suffered unduly because of it. In Afghanistan, meanwhile, President Obama reluctantly agreed to keep a force of more than 10,000 troops there through 2016, in part because of increased activity by al-Qaeda and its affiliates throughout 2015. Saudi Arabia mounted a major military intervention in the Yemeni Civil War in 2015, which was designed in large measure to defeat al-Qaeda in the Arabian Peninsula. Perhaps al-Qaeda's greatest influence in recent years has been its ability to form spin-off organizations—like ISIS—and to encourage allied groups such as Boko Haram.

In 2017, the Donald Trump administration sent additional troops to Afghanistan, where the Taliban, ISIS, and al-Qaeda insurgency has continued. In 2018, al-Qaeda remained a viable terrorist group with the potential to carry out attacks in many corners of the world. While it lacks the extreme potency of the late 1990s and early 2000s, it still poses a serious threat to Western interests. In 2016, al-Qaeda and al-Nusra split, with the al-Nusra leadership claiming that its alliance with al-Qaeda was inviting Western military operations within Syria.

Harry R. Hueston II

Further Reading

Bergen, Peter L. *The Holy War, Inc.: Inside the Secret World of Osama bin Laden*. Free Press, 2002.

Gunaratna, Rohan. *Inside Al Qaeda: Global Network of Terror.* Berkley Publishing Group, 2003.

Hueston, Harry R., and B. Vizzin. *Terrorism 101.* 2nd ed. XanEdu Press, 2004.

Zuhur, Sherifa. *A Hundred Osamas: Islamist Threats and the Future of Counterinsurgency.* Strategic Studies Institute, U.S. Army War College, 2006.

Al-Qubeir Massacre

Sometimes referred to as the Hama Massacre, this event occurred at al-Qubeir, a farming settlement near Hama, on June 6, 2012. Al-Qubeir was a Sunni settlement in the northwest Syrian province of Hama, and is surrounded by Alawite villages. It is believed the villagers of al-Qubeir were supportive of the Free Syrian Army, a rebel group comprised of dissident military officers who had left the Syrian Armed Forces to fight against the Assad regime. The Syrian Armed Forces began shelling the village with artillery early in the afternoon, and then a pro-government militia, the Shabiha, entered the village and began an hours-long massacre. Seventy-eight people, almost the village's entire population, were murdered; there were only five survivors.

The few eyewitness accounts that exist come from people who were talking to victims on cell phones before they were killed. These witnesses claim that militiamen were moving house to house while singing pro-Assad songs and indiscriminately killing men, women, and children with no explanation. Western media, specifically the British Broadcasting Corporation (BBC), were the first on the scene and reported a grisly scene of death.

The al-Qubeir Massacre occurred two weeks after a massacre in the village of Houla where 108 people were killed by government forces and their supporting militias. These massacres, which occurred relatively early in the Syrian Civil War, served as a wake-up call to the international community that the Assad regime was not only digging in its heels in Damascus, but actively striking against any opposition to its legitimacy. It was after these massacres that the United Nations Security Council, with the notable opposition of Russia and China, began to discuss the possibility of forming a group to help end the violence under the urging of former UN secretary general Kofi Annan, then working as the UN-Arab League envoy. Annan called for a special UN contact group to work on the Syrian problem, but his proposal failed in the wake of a Russian and Chinese veto. The result was the creation of The Friends of Syria Group, a diplomatic collective of countries dedicated to discussing the Syrian Civil War. In 2017, a contact group was initiated by French president Emmanuel Macron.

Robert M. Kerr

Further Reading
Yassin-Kassab, Robin, and Leila al-Shami. *Burning Country: Syrians in Revolution and War.* Pluto Press, 2018.

Al-Qusayr Offensive

The al-Qusayr Offensive was a two-month-long military operation led by the Syrian Arab Army (SAA) forces lasting from April 4 through June 8, 2013. Along with the Iranian-backed Lebanese militia group Hezbollah and the National Defense Forces, a pro-government Syrian group of militants, the offensive against rebel forces in the city of al-Qusayr in Homs Province resulted in a decisive victory for the Assad regime in its fight to cut off rebel supply lines. The victory not only secured al-Qusayr and all of its surrounding villages, but also allowed the Syrian government to regain control of an important stretch of the Syrian border with Lebanon; a border that had previously been controlled by rebel groups that used it to smuggle arms, fighters, and equipment into Syria.

In the long list of battles between the SAA and the wide range of anti-government militia groups involved in the Syrian Civil War, the Battle of al-Qusayr stands out for a number of reasons. First, al-Qusayr's strategic location on the Syrian border with Lebanon meant that control of this city was a high priority for both the government and insurgents. Second, the battle marked a significant shift in Hezbollah's operations in that it showed that the militia group could operate outside the borders of Lebanon on an expeditionary basis. Finally, the victory of the SAA and its allied militias during the al-Qusayr Offensive shifted the strategic advantage of the conflict decidedly toward the Syrian government at a time when their supremacy was not a given.

At the time of the military operation, al-Qusayr had been a rebel stronghold for over a year. Located roughly five miles from the Lebanese border, the town, with a population of around 30,000, is made up of a majority of Sunni Muslims, but also has a significant Christian population as well. Sunni anti-government militias had established control of al-Qusayr in early 2012, and began waging a campaign to drive Shia Muslims in the region, primarily on the Lebanese side of the border (hence Lebanese Hezbollah's interest in allying with the SAA against the dissident Sunni groups), out of their homes and away from the region. The strategic intent of this initiative was to create a friendly belt of Sunni Muslims on both sides of the border in order to facilitate the free movement of weapons, supplies, and fighters into Syria to be used in the fight against the Assad regime. This was to be the hub of a corridor stretching eventually from Damascus all the way to the Mediterranean and serve as a backdoor for anti-government forces to bypass the Syrian coastal areas, which tended to be more loyal to the government. The combination of rebel strategy and control over roads and trade routes made al-Qusayr a strategic keystone; whichever side in the conflict controlled the city and the route to and from Lebanon was going to gain a significant advantage in the fight. This is why the Syrian government had the SAA align with Hezbollah, an extremely powerful (and Iranian-backed) Shia militia based in Lebanon.

Hezbollah is an organization that goes beyond the level of militia and functions as a quasi-government in Lebanon. Hugely influential, militarily powerful, and politically and financially tied to the Iranian government, Hezbollah had not typically run military operations outside of Lebanon, but they had a vested interest in both helping Assad, their ally in Damascus, and establishing credibility as a fighting force hardened to take on the region's toughest armies— namely the Israeli Defense Forces. The al-Qusayr Offensive gave Hezbollah the opportunity to war-game its command and control functions, as well as its operations and tactics. During the conflict, Hezbollah performed well, and would occasionally get involved in the Syrian Civil War at the behest of the Syrian government in the following years—though not as frequently as Assad may have liked; it seems as though Hezbollah's real interest was in testing its developing military capabilities more than anything else. The al-Qusayr Offensive was strategically important for the Syrian Arab Army in gaining a distinct advantage in the Civil War, but for Hezbollah it was a strategic victory in establishing itself as a major military player in the region.

As of the beginning of 2019, Bashar al-Assad is still firmly in control of the Syrian government in Damascus. In part, this is due to the success of the SAA and Hezbollah at al-Qusayr in 2013. Without this strategic victory—had Sunni rebel forces been able to maintain control of the city and its strategic importance on the Lebanese border and as a base of operations—the Syrian Civil War may have gone in a very different direction. The victory of Syrian forces and their allies had more than practical value in securing a vital strategic location, however; it had a powerful psychological impact on the anti-government movement as well. While there have been many different players in the Syrian Civil War with varying degrees of power (with the Islamic State and the al-Nusra Front/JSF remaining powerful after al-Qusayr), the momentum of the rebellion against the government in Damascus reverberated throughout the country.

Robert M. Kerr

Further Reading

Yassin-Kassab, Robin, and Leila al-Shami. *Burning Country: Syrians in Revolution and War*. Pluto Press, 2018.

Al-Sham

Al-Sham is the name of the notional and aspirational region envisioned by the Islamic State (IS) as the core area of the Islamic caliphate they envision. The toponym al-Sham refers to a region that, in reality, exists today more in the geographic imaginations of people than on any map, and constitutes what geographers refer to as a vernacular region. Historically, however, the great geographers of the Islamic world referred to the area of southern Syria and Northern Iraq as "Greater Syria," or Bilad al-Sham.

Vernacular regions exist in the geographic imaginations of groups of people, and are extremely difficult to demarcate on a map. The United States has many such regions, such as the West, the Midwest, and the South. All Americans use these terms and have a general understanding of where each of these regions is located, but there is no authoritative source that can tell you exactly where their boundaries lie. Where, specifically is the Midwest on a map? If you try to get a group of people to agree on the Midwest's exact location, you will have accomplished a great feat! While it is virtually impossible to find on a map, very few Americans would argue that the Midwest is not a real place. Al-Sham is the same way in the modern-day states of Iraq, Syria, and the surrounding areas.

The area of the vernacular region of Bilad Al-Sham corresponds roughly with the area that people in the West refer to as the Levant (which is itself a vernacular region); that is, parts of modern-day Syria, Lebanon, Israel, Jordan, and Iraq. Like the example of the Midwest in the United States, however, it is difficult to discern its boundaries. In the Iraqi geographic imagination, al-Sham begins just north of Baghdad, and is even marked by the existence of a small industrial town called Bab al-Sham (the Gate to al-Sham) just northeast of Baghdad along the highway to Baqubah. For most Syrians, however, al-Sham does not extend as far south as Baghdad, and it includes the economically vital Mediterranean coast stretching all the way from Turkey in the north to the Gaza Strip in the south. For this reason, IS's claim of al-Sham as its aspirational homeland should be understood metaphorically rather than literally, though IS leadership certainly believes that all the land of the eastern Mediterranean will one day be included in the caliphate.

There are many theories about the origins of the term *al-Sham*. Many predate Islam and refer to the ancient speakers of Aramaic who worshipped a sky god called Baalshamin, or Lord of the Heavens. Known by most as Baal, or Lord, the second half of his name has been largely forgotten. The use of some derivative of the word *Sham,* or sky (*shamin* being plural, thus *heavens*), spread from Aramaic into other Semitic languages, all of which have words derived from Sham to refer to the sky. It is no coincidence, perhaps, that the vernacular region of Al-Sham corresponds roughly with the areas in which Baal was worshipped in ancient times. Despite the prevalence of Islam in the area since the eighth century CE—it was an important power base under the early Islamic Umayyad caliphate centered in Damascus—the linguistic reference to the ancient sky god persists.

In reality, there is evidence that al-Sham was more than just a vernacular region; it was also what cultural geographers refer to as a functional region. That is a region that is defined by intense and continuous interactions over a given space. These interactions are often economic in nature, and in ancient and even through Islamic times—that is, Syria's entire history before the French and British Mandates and the Ba'ath Party's rise to power in the twentieth century—there was no boundary between what are today's countries of Syria and Iraq. Intense trade relationships between Aleppo and Mosul, for example, were far more important than either city's relationships with other cities, and the people who lived in the area between Mosul and Aleppo had far more in common with one another than they did with any of their future countrymen.

It is on the region's historical tie to the Umayyad caliphate that IS rests its argument that the vernacular region al-Sham be seen as the heartland of its own dreams to reestablish the Islamic caliphate in modern times. By referring to al-Sham, IS is attempting to gain credibility among the world's Muslims, especially among the learned class of legal and religious scholars, from whom it craves recognition and legitimacy. This is a craving that continues to go unquenched, however, as hardly any mainstream, respected Islamic leaders have validated their claims, while some have rejected the legitimacy of claims that any region known as al-Sham even exists in any meaningful way in the twenty-first century.

Robert M. Kerr

Further Reading

Sluglett, Peter and Stefan Weber, eds. *Syria and Bilad al-Sham under Ottoman Rule: Essays in Honour of Abdul Karim Rafeq.* Brill Academic Publications, 2010.

Teixidor, Javier. *The Pagan God: Popular Religion in the Greco-Roman Near East.* Princeton University Press, 2015.

van Dam, Nikolaos. *Destroying a Nation: The Civil War in Syria.* I. B. Tauris, 2017.

Arab League

The Arab League, also called the League of Arab States, is a voluntary organization of Arabic-speaking nations. It was founded at the end of World War II with the stated purposes of improving conditions in Arab countries, liberating Arab states still under foreign domination, and preventing the formation of a Jewish state in Palestine.

In 1943, the Egyptian government proposed an organization of Arab states that would facilitate closer relations between the nations without forcing any of them to lose self-rule. Each member would remain a sovereign state, and the organization would not be a union, a federation, or any other sovereign structure. The British government supported this idea in the hopes of making Arabic nations allies in the war against Germany. In 1944, representatives from Egypt, Iraq, Lebanon, Yemen, and Saudi Arabia met in Alexandria, Egypt, and agreed to form a federation. The Arab League was officially founded March 22, 1945, in Cairo. The founding states were Egypt, Iraq, Lebanon, Saudi Arabia, Transjordan (Jordan and Lebanon), and Syria. Subsequent members include Libya (1953), Sudan (1956), Tunisia (1958), Morocco (1958), Kuwait (1961), Algeria (1962), South Yemen (1967, now Yemen), Bahrain (1971), Oman (1971), Qatar (1971), United Arab Emirates (1971), Mauritania (1973), Somalia (1974), Djibouti (1977), and Comoros (1993).

The original goals of the Arab League were to liberate all Arab nations still ruled by foreign countries and to prevent the creation of a Jewish state in Palestine, as well as to serve the common good, improve living conditions, and guarantee the hopes of member states. In 1946, the League members added to their pact a cultural treaty, under which they agreed to exchange professors, teachers, students, and scholars in order to encourage cultural exchange among member nations and to disseminate Arab culture to their citizens.

The league's pact also stated that all members would represent the Palestinians together so long as Palestine was not an independent state. With no Palestinian leader in 1945, the Arab states feared that the British would dominate the area and that Jews would colonize part of Palestine. In response to these fears, the Arab League created the Arab Higher Committee to govern Palestinian Arabs in 1945. This committee was replaced by the Arab Higher Executive in 1946, which again became the Arab Higher Committee in 1947.

The State of Israel was declared on May 14, 1948. On May 15, Egypt, Iraq, Lebanon, Saudi Arabia, Syria, and Transjordan declared war on Israel in response. Yemen also supported the declaration. Secretary General Abdul Razek Azzam Pasha declared that the league's goal was to conduct a large-scale massacre and extermination. Though Jordan claimed to be the legitimate ruler of Palestine, the league did not want to see Jordan in control of the area, and thus established its own government on behalf of the Palestinians, creating the All Palestine State on October 1, 1948. The mufti of Jerusalem, Haj Amin Husseini, was its leader and Jerusalem its capital. Though ostensibly the new government ruled Gaza, Egypt was the true ruler. In response, Jordan formed a rival temporary government, the First Palestinian Congress, which condemned the government in Gaza. After thousands of Arabs from league states died, the Arab-Israeli war ended in 1949, with Jordan occupying the West Bank and East Jerusalem and Egypt controlling Gaza. Israel had become a sovereign state.

In 1950, the Arab League formed the Joint Defense and Economic Cooperation Treaty, which declared that the members of the league considered an attack on one member country to be an attack on all. The treaty created a permanent military commission and a joint defense council.

During the 1950s, Egypt effectively led the Arab League. In 1952, General Muhammad Naguib overthrew Egypt's King Farouk. In 1954, Gamal Abdel Nasser assumed rule of the nation as a strong proponent of Arab unity, calling for a union of all Arab nations, including Palestine. Nasser ended the All Palestine Government in Palestine, formed a union called the United Arab Republic with Syria, and called for the defeat of Israel. In 1956, he closed the Suez Canal to Israeli shipping and announced that Egypt would henceforth control the canal completely, despite the fact that British businesses held a large ownership stake in it. Israel invaded Gaza in October with French and British aid, in what would come to be known as the Suez War. Egypt and the United States drove them back, and by 1957 all Israeli troops had withdrawn from Sinai, leaving it in Egyptian control, increasing Nasser's stature in the Arab world, and raising the visibility of Pan-Arabism and of the Arab League.

During the 1950s, the Arab League did not ardently pursue the liberation of Palestine from Israel, but it returned to this effort in the early 1960s. In 1964, the Arab League provided support for the creation of the Palestine Liberation Organization (PLO), whose express purpose was to attack Israel. Yasser Arafat became leader of the PLO and the face of the Palestinian resistance in 1969, a position he would hold until his death on November 11, 2004. After the Six-Day War of 1967, the Arab League issued the Khartoum Resolution, in which they vowed not to recognize Israel, negotiate with Israel, or enter into peace with Israel.

Egypt was suspended from the Arab League in 1979 in the wake of President Anwar Sadat's visit to Jerusalem and agreement to the 1978 Camp David Peace Accords. The league headquarters moved from Cairo to Tunis as a result. When the PLO declared an independent State of Palestine on November 15, 1988, the Arab League immediately recognized it. Egypt was readmitted in 1989, and the league's headquarters returned once again to Cairo. In the 1990s, the league continued its efforts to resolve the Israel-Palestine dispute in Palestine's favor.

In 2003, the Arab League voted 21–1 to demand the unconditional removal of U.S. and British troops from Iraq. The lone dissenting voice was the tiny nation of Kuwait, which had been liberated by a U.S.-led coalition of 34 nations in the 1991 Persian Gulf War. After the outbreak of the Syrian Civil War in 2011, the league suspended Syria's membership because its government was waging war against its own people. This left the organization with 21 active members. That same year, the group considered suspending Yemen because of violence against civilians and government resistance groups, but that move was not approved by the requisite majority.

Amy Hackney Blackwell

Further Reading

Hourani, Albert. *A History of the Arab Peoples.* Warner, 1992.

League of Arab States. http://www.arableague online.org/. Accessed August 8, 2019.

Smith, Charles D. *Palestine and the Arab-Israeli Conflict: A History with Documents.* 6th ed. Bedford/St. Martin's, 2006.

Arab Spring

The term "Arab Spring" refers to a wave of popular protests and demonstrations, beginning in Tunisia in December 2010, that swept rapidly throughout North Africa and the Middle East in 2011 and 2012. Although responding in part to economic difficulties, including rising fuel and food costs and high unemployment, protesters generally also rebelled against repressive, authoritarian, and corrupt governments, demanding more open political systems. Most expressed frustration with regimes that were often effectively one-party systems or family dictatorships.

The precise form and course of protests varied across different countries, as did the responses of different governments. Jordan, Algeria, Iraq, Kuwait, and Morocco all experienced significant protests and unrest, which resulted in the implementation of a range of political, economic, and social reforms and constitutional changes. In Tunisia and Egypt, expressions of popular discontent were so widespread and intense that within weeks they forced the president then in power from office and brought the overhaul of the political system. In Yemen, the process was slower, extending over the better part of a year, and further complicated by long-term sectarian violence from two rival groups of Muslim insurgents, one Shiite, the other the Sunni al-Qaeda in the Arab Peninsula.

While many Arab governments eventually made at least some concessions to protesters, others were determined to repress all dissent, using whatever force might be needed for the purpose. In both Libya and Syria, opposition to the entrenched one-party governments of Colonel Muammar Qaddafi and President Bashar al-Assad was met by government military crackdowns. In both cases, a brutal and violent civil war was the result. In Libya, estimates of the numbers killed between February and October 2011 ranged from several thousand to 50,000 or more. United Nations declaration of a "no-fly zone" and air strikes by Western NATO forces played a significant part in the relatively swift resolution of the war, which ended in Qaddafi's capture and execution.

In Syria, civil war began in March 2011. The Syrian conflict proved a magnet for Islamic militia forces of different complexions, while the international community was divided over whether to support the government or the rebels. Militia units from Hezbollah and the Muslim Brotherhood, longtime allies of the Syrian government and its president, Bashar al-Assad, rallied to its support, as did Russia and Iran. Al-Qaeda forces with backing from Saudi Arabia, by contrast, threw their lot in with the rebels. While calling on al-Assad to negotiate, the United States declined to intervene militarily. By September 2013, over 120,000 Syrians had reportedly been killed, while 6.5 million were refugees, 2 million of whom sought safety outside Syria. By late 2013, the balance appeared to be tilting in favor of the rebels, but the outcome was still far from certain.

Initially, many outside commentators, especially Westerners, hailed the Arab Spring with delight, believing that it would usher in the swift and near painless spread of democracy throughout the Middle East and the Arab world. Many also hoped that any new governments that emerged would be liberal in outlook, committed to supporting human and civil rights, including women's rights and religious freedom, political transparency, democracy, equality, and the cause of peace. Yet it soon became clear that the governments that emerged from the upheavals of 2011 might well be strictly limited in terms of democracy and liberal values, and that the reforms that were implemented, far from representing a wholesale remodeling of the entire political, social, and economic fabric, would often be rather limited in scope.

Moreover, not all the political forces unleashed by the Arab Spring were liberal or secular in nature. In Egypt, Jordan, and Algeria, for example, for decades governments had sought to discourage sectarian Islamic political parties, for fear that allowing religious extremists too much influence might prove politically destabilizing, both domestically and externally. In Egypt, in particular, the overthrow of President Hosni Mubarak in February 2011 opened the way for Mohamed Morsi, an official of the Muslim Brotherhood, to gain the presidency in July 2012. Within months, he sought to implement drastic increases in his own powers, which many feared marked the beginning of a new dictatorship. After several months of ever larger demonstrations in which millions of Egyptians ultimately participated, in July 2013 the Egyptian military finally ousted Morsi, installing a caretaker president until a new constitution could be drafted and new elections held. In Jordan and Algeria, constitutional reforms meant that Islamic political parties also made some gains. Given that sectarian extremism enjoyed significant political support among the general population on the "Arab street," greater democracy might even inflame such issues as the ongoing Israeli-Palestinian dispute.

In some cases, especially in Libya and Syria, and perhaps Yemen, the fighting and violence that characterized the Arab Spring were in themselves destabilizing, unleashing tribal and other antagonisms and rivalries that were liable to continue indefinitely. And, just as in Iraq and Afghanistan in the early twenty-first century, in those states, outside groups and elements that participated in the fighting might well stay on and become political forces to reckon with in their host countries. The initial optimism that the Arab Spring betokened an era in which democracy and liberalism would spread swiftly and benignly throughout the Middle East, transforming the region permanently for the better, soon came to seem premature and misplaced. While change might indeed be on the agenda, progress in the broad direction of civil society was, it seemed, likely to be slow and somewhat erratic in nature.

Priscilla Roberts

Further Reading

Achcar, Gilbert. *The People Want: A Radical Exploration of the Arab Uprising.* Translated by G. M. Goshgarian. University of California Press, 2013.

Amar, Paul, and Vijay Prashad, eds. *Dispatches from the Arab Spring: Understanding the New Middle East.* University of Minnesota Press, 2013.

Bradley, John R. *After the Arab Spring: How Islamists Hijacked the Middle East Revolts.* Palgrave Macmillan, 2012.

Dabashi, Hamid. *The Arab Spring: The End of Postcolonialism.* Zed Books, 2012.

Danahar, Paul. *The New Middle East: The World after the Arab Spring.* Bloomsbury, 2013.

Dawisha, Adeed. *The Second Arab Awakening: Revolution, Democracy, and the Islamist Challenge from Tunis to Damascus.* New York: Norton, 2013.

Noueihed, Lin, and Alex Warren. *The Battle for the Arab Spring: Revolution, Counter-Revolution and the Making of a New Era.* New Haven, CT: Yale University Press, 2012.

Ramadan, Tariq. *Islam and the Arab Awakening.* New York: Oxford University Press, 2012.

Wright, Robin. *Rock the Casbah: Rage and Rebellion across the Islamic World.* Updated ed. New York: Simon and Schuster, 2012.

Armenians

Armenians have a long history in Syria. There have been Armenian communities in the country since the Byzantine era, but not really in significant numbers until after the Armenian genocide perpetrated by the Ottomans between 1914 and 1923. It is estimated that before the Syrian Civil War there were approximately 100,000 Armenians living primarily in Aleppo, but most estimates put the population of Syrian Armenians at or around 15,000 to 20,000 in 2019. Like other diaspora communities such as the Circassians that have settled in Syria as a result of conflict or economic conditions, the Armenians held no strong nationalist sentiment toward Syria or loyalty toward the Ba'ath Party, which explains why as many as 70,000 of them fled the country during the course of the Syrian conflict after 2011.

Like the Circassians who made Syria home after the Russo-Circassian War of 1864, most of the Armenians living in Syria at the time the civil war broke out had moved there to flee a genocide. While the Circassians were fleeing the Russians, however, the Armenians were fleeing their country after a systematic attempt by the Ottoman Turks to wipe out their population in their homeland. Between 1914 and 1923, more than one and a half million Armenians were killed by the Ottomans in an attempt to eliminate a population that had grown increasingly dissatisfied with their treatment by the government and had started to push, with some success, for an improvement of their status as minorities within the empire.

The Ottoman Empire was famous for its treatment of minority groups under what was known as the *millet system*. Under the millet system, the Ottomans, who were Muslim, allowed monotheistic minority groups, such as the Zoroastrians, Jews, and Christians, living within the empire to practice their religions, with some restrictions. Islam mandates that these monotheists, especially Jews and Christians (referred to as the "People of the Book" based on the three religions' common Abrahamic roots) are under no obligation to convert to Islam, and that Muslims actually have an obligation to protect them. The People of the Book, under Ottoman law, fell into the category of *dhimmi*, which literally translates to "protected person," and could practice their religion with a few

stipulations. The first stipulation was that the religious minorities could not proselytize or make any attempts to gain converts to their religion. They also had legal disadvantages if they ever came to a dispute with a Muslim, and most famously, they had to pay a tax called the *jizyah*. Islam requires all Muslims to pay a tax called *zakat*, which is typically about two to two and a half percent of one's income. This tax forms the basis of Islam's welfare system and is designed to guarantee that the poor are provided with the basic necessities of food, shelter, and water. Because the vast majority of people in the Muslim world pay the *zakat*, it does not have to represent a large amount of an individual's income because so many people are paying it; it is an economy of scale issue in that the more people pay into the system, the less money each person has to pay. *Dhimmi*, however, are not entitled to *zakat* funds (unless, of course they convert to Islam, which many *dhimmi*, such as the Circassians and other peoples of the Caucasus region, for example, did), so they were required to pay a higher percentage of their income: 18 to 19 percent. While this practice might look inherently discriminatory on the surface (and perhaps even in practice, especially toward the end of the Ottoman Empire), it was actually designed to make sure the *dhimmi* had a fund of money that only they would have access to in order to maintain their temples, synagogues, and churches, and to provide welfare for their own people. Because these communities were far smaller than those of their Muslim neighbors, they had to pay more as individuals in order to meet the economic needs of their communities. It was, again, an economy of scale issue in which if there are few people paying into the system, each person needs to pay more money.

The millet system predates the Ottoman Empire, at least in practice if not in name.

Because this system is mandated by Islam, early Islamic empires practiced it, and many were renowned for their fair treatment of the monotheist minorities living within their communities. The most famous example of the "golden age" of Islam's treatment of Jews and Christians is found in the Moorish rule of Spain from the year 711 until 1492 when historians say that some of the best philosophers of Judaism (Maimonides, Abu Fadl ibn Hasdai, Solomon ibn Gabirol), Christianity (Abu Umar ibn Gundislavus, Revemund), and Islam (Abu Bakr Muhammad ibn al-Walid al-Turtushi, Ali ibn Hazm al-Andalusi, ibn Razin al-Tujibi) met, debated, and wrote their best works; some of them, such as Loubna al-Qortobiya and Maslama al-Majriti, were women. Things in al-Andalus, as Muslim Spain was known, were not always perfect as there were times when minority groups were, in fact, persecuted by the Muslim majority, but these incidents were infrequent and more related to local politics than wholesale discrimination. The example of Jews, Christians, and Muslims prospering in al-Andalus represents the best of the structure that would later become known as the millet system under the Ottomans, and it illustrates that such an arrangement can work. However, the case of the Armenians in the twentieth century illustrates how this system went horribly wrong.

Armenians are primarily Christians, and were officially classified as *dhimmi* under Ottoman law. It is estimated that there were roughly 3 million Armenians living in the Ottoman Empire in the late nineteenth century, and most were very poor and lived in rural towns and villages, away from cities. There were some wealthy Armenian merchants and traders who lived in cities, but most lived outside the reach of the government, and many were often subjected to overtaxation and forced conversions by unscrupulous local authorities trying to profit from the *jizya* tax. While the millet system was once an example of how to treat minority populations, as the Ottoman Empire matured into the late nineteenth and early twentieth centuries, discrimination within the empire became rampant. The problem became so bad that by the mid-1800s Christian nations such as France, Russia, and the United Kingdom pressured the Ottomans to improve the treatment of Christians within their empire, and the sultan gave into the pressure by introducing a series of reforms referred to as the *Tanzimat*. These reforms included a number of measures designed to bring non-Muslim minorities into the Ottoman mainstream by guaranteeing them full rights as Ottoman subjects, and even abolished slavery for the first time. However, despite the reforms modernizing some governmental functions, they actually did very little to improve the status of minorities—especially in rural areas. During this era of reform, however, a wave of revolutionary ideals began to emerge within Armenian society.

Fueled by ideas brought home by an increasing number of wealthy Armenians educated in some of Europe's most famous universities and by American missionary schools that had been established throughout Turkey in the 1800s, Armenians began to demand that the reforms being introduced be taken seriously, and they tried to elevate their status within Ottoman society. Much of the missionary work conducted by Americans in the late 1800s was focused on the Armenian population throughout northern Turkey, and as the Ottoman Empire's global influence declined in the years leading up to the First World War, the ideas of freedom, democracy, and most importantly, religious liberty had a profound effect on Armenian demands that the sultan grant them the rights they deserved. This situation was complicated by matters following the Russo-Turkish War (1877–1878) when the Armenian lands became a geopolitical football being tossed around such that the rule of law deteriorated and many abuses were committed against them. One of the problems the Armenians faced was that the Ottoman government refused to recognize that they made up the majority of the people in the areas where they lived and therefore did not merit any special recognition or rights under the empire's legal code. Sultan Abdul Hamid II was pressured by the international community to grant the Armenians rights guaranteed under the political reforms, but while he agreed to do so, no changes were implemented. This spurred a large group of Armenians to go to the capital to protest on October 1, 1895, but the sultan's police met them with force, and a wave of anti-Armenian violence spread throughout the country, with hundreds of thousands of Armenians killed in what would later become known as the Hamidian Massacres.

In 1908, a group of young military officers staged a coup against the sultan and forced him to step down to make way for a constitutionally based monarchy (similar to the United Kingdom today). The officers were part of what was known as the "Young Turk" movement, and they wanted to modernize the empire to be in line with European standards. There were two factions of the coalition that overthrew the sultan, however, and they had very different ideas about what a modern Turkey should look like. The first group, and the one that initially held power in the new government, was made up of constitutionalists who saw the *Tanzimat* as a good guide to bring minorities into the fold while recognizing their right to more or less retain their traditions. The other faction was the Turkish nationalists.

Nationalism was sweeping across the Western world in the late nineteenth century, and history shows that the wars of nationalism were some of the most fierce the world has ever seen. In the nationalist's view, modern Turkey should be built upon Turkish language, culture, traditions, and Islam; there was no room for minorities in this conceptualization, and this made the Armenians very nervous. A year after the coup, a countercoup took place that was led by some dissident members of the military as well as students who wanted Islam to play a bigger role in the government. This countercoup was not just aimed at the fledgling government, however, it was also aimed at its supporters; and the insurgents initiated mass violence against Armenians, especially in the town of Adana where tens of thousands were killed throughout the month of April 1909. Things got worse for the Armenians after Turkey's defeat in the First Balkan War in 1912. As a result of its defeat, Turkey lost almost all of its land on the continent in Europe, and Turkish society was scrambling for answers as to how one of the world's greatest empires could have suffered such a staggering defeat. The answer for many was found in the religious community who saw Turkey's defeat as evidence that God was displeased with their attempts to secularize and adopt modern European ways of governance; and the Turkish nationalists found great support in merging their platform with the religious community. The Armenians bore the brunt of the anger of many of these nationalists. Their situation did not improve as Turkey entered World War I, as the Armenians were seen as an internal security threat, assumed to be disloyal, and many were exterminated during this period that was a precursor to the genocide that was to come after the war. The years between 1914 and 1923 saw Armenians forced into concentration camps and murdered on a grand scale with more than one and a half million ultimately dying at the hands of the Turks.

Syria was the location of notorious concentration camps run by the Turks for the extermination of Armenians just outside the town of Deir ez-Zor. More than 100,000 Armenians were forced into death marches across the Syrian desert toward the camps. Early during the massacre, the camps were under the protection of the area's Arab governor, Ali Suad Bey. Known by his nickname "The Good Governor," Ali Suad Bey did what was in his power to make sure the Armenians were protected, and actually had medical facilities and housing built for the displaced Armenian families. However, dissatisfied with Ali Suad Bey's compassion toward the Armenians, the Turkish authorities had him replaced with someone more sympathetic to their view toward the Armenians, Zeki Bey, who was notoriously cruel— tens of thousands of Armenians starved to death in the camps under his direction.

Aleppo was the main Syrian city where Armenians who survived the death camps, along with others who came to Syria afterward, ended up settling. As minorities themselves under the Ottomans, the Arabs of the region welcomed the Armenian refugees and helped them integrate into their societies. There were other times of Armenian immigration into Syria after the genocide, and by 1944 it is thought that there were more than 60,000 Armenians living in Aleppo.

Early in the Syrian Civil War, the Armenians of Aleppo were largely sympathetic toward Bashar al-Assad. Like many minority groups in Syria who liked the fact that Assad himself is a minority (from the Alawite community), the Armenians feared the possibility of an overtly religious, Arab government. After July 2012, when the Christians of Aleppo became targets of various Arab militias, however, the Armenians decided that neutrality was the best position to take.

Between 2012 and 2018, ten of Aleppo's churches were destroyed, along with eleven Armenian schools. It has been reported that most Armenians that had been living in Syria have left the country, with tens of thousands actually seeking refuge in Armenia. It is important to note, however, that these people consider themselves refugees as Syria is the only homeland they have ever known; and while most speak Armenian, they are also fluent in Arabic and have adopted enough Arab cultural norms that they have had some difficulty fitting into Armenian society.

Not all Armenians left Syria, and as of 2018, those who remained are trying to reclaim their normal lives. For them, they will forever live under the specter of the war and constant reminders of the community that once was and neighbors who are likely to never return. For those who left, they will find themselves foreigners in strange lands, and even those who sought refuge in Armenia will struggle with fitting into a society that is both familiar and foreign. For all Armenians, as is the case for so many in Syria, the civil war will forever change them and their lives will never be the same.

Robert M. Kerr

Further Reading

Lewis, Bernard. *What Went Wrong: The Clash between Islam and Modernity*. Harper Perennial, 2003.

Umit, Devrim. "The American Protestant Missionary Network in Ottoman Turkey, 1876–1914." *International Journal of Humanities and Social Science* 4(6)(1) (April 2014).

Walker, Christopher J. *Armenia: The Survival of a Nation*. St. Martin's Press, 1980.

Army of Conquest/Jaish al-Fatah (JAF)

The Army of Conquest, or Jaish al-Fatah (JAF), was the name of a significant alliance of Sunni Muslim militia groups that operated primarily in western Syria, though for a time affiliated groups also operated in other parts of the country. Formed in Idlib Province, located along Syria's northwest border with Turkey, JAF originally included seven militant groups who had decided to pool their resources in order to better counter Assad's governmental forces north of Damascus. Three of those original seven groups, Jabhat al-Nusra, Ahrar al-Sham, and Jund al-Aqsa, had direct ties to al-Qaeda and were therefore well funded, with access to good training and weapons. A fourth militia group, Faylaq al-Sham, was linked to the Syrian arm of the Muslim Brotherhood, an organization that had long been persecuted by Middle Eastern regimes and was deeply involved in anti-government movements, both politically and militarily, throughout the Arab Spring. It too brought international support and funding to the JAF alliance. The remaining three original militias, Jaish al-Sunna, Liwah al-Haqq, and Ajnad al-Sham, were smaller, more localized Syrian movements with shared ideology with the larger coalition members.

One of the defining characteristics of JAF, and the one that perhaps makes it so noteworthy, was that while conducting combined military operations, each of the organizations abandoned their distinctive identities and symbols and functioned seamlessly as one fighting unit, with troops integrated and organized by function rather than faction. It is said that during operations militants were not even allowed to use each organization's distinctive name, and could only refer to themselves as the Jaish al-Fatah.

This unit cohesion could explain, in part, JAF's rapid military successes in northwestern Syria against the Syrian Arab Army and its allies. In 2015, JAF seized the city of Idlib and other strategic locations along transportation routes throughout Idlib Province. By the end of 2015, they had made significant inroads into Latakia Province, which is home to Assad's Alawite power base.

After their initial successes in the northwest, JAF expanded, setting up similar alliances in western and southern Syria. These groups found success against government forces in these regions, but as is the case with many coalitions made up of different groups promoting different interests, fractures developed and the coalition began to unravel. These fractures began, primarily, after military successes had left JAF and its component organizations in charge of governance over the territories they had seized. Disagreements over the application and interpretation of law, the influence of outside organizations such as al-Qaeda and the Muslim Brotherhood, and the day-to-day strains of providing essential services to the people proved insurmountable. By 2016, significant groups within the JAF alliance began to break away in order to pursue their own interests, and by 2017, the coalition was effectively dead. Even as the alliance broke apart, however, elements remained and still posed a threat on the international stage. In December, 2016, Jaish al-Fatah, or at least its remnants, claimed responsibility for the assassination of Russia's ambassador to Turkey in Ankara. This assassination was at the end of JAF's final military offensive against Aleppo, however, and with the aid of Russian air strikes they suffered their final defeat.

Jaish al-Fatah provides an important case study in the power of organizations with common military goals to set aside their differences in order to meet their objectives.

The coalition was so effective that some believe their successes spurred Bashar al-Assad to request Russian intervention specifically to combat JAF: in 2015, they presented the most viable opposition to the Syrian Arab Army among all the opposition groups in the Syrian Civil War, and the Russians did indeed engage JAF forces on numerous occasions throughout 2016. JAF also provides lessons on the dangers of groups working toward a common military goal without coordinating their political objectives. JAF seized territory through effective military means very quickly, but they were ultimately unable to agree on what should be done once they had taken that territory. Ultimately, this gave the Assad regime the advantage in the long run.

Robert M. Kerr

Further Reading

Hubbard, Ben. "A Look at the Army of Conquest, a Prominent Rebel Alliance in Syria." *New York Times*, October 1, 2015. https://www.nytimes.com/2015/10/02/world/middleeast/syria-russia-airstrikes-rebels-army-conquest-jaish-al-fatah.html.

Jenkins, Brian Michael. "The Dynamics of Syria's Civil War." RAND Corporation, 2014. https://www.rand.org/pubs/perspectives/PE115.html.

van Dam, Nikolaos. *Destroying a Nation: The Civil War in Syria*. I. B. Tauris, 2017.

Assad, Bashar al-

President of the Syrian Arab Republic (2000–present) and head of the Ba'ath Party. Bashar al-Assad was born in Damascus, Syria, on September 11, 1965. His father was Hafez al-Assad, strongman and president of Syria from 1971 to 2000. The Alawi sect to which al-Assad belongs encompasses approximately 12 percent of the Syrian population. Bashar was not as well known to the Syrian public as his popular elder brother, Basil, who died in an automobile accident in 1994.

Beginning in the mid-1980s, the younger al-Assad studied medicine at the University of Damascus, training in ophthalmology at the Tishrin Military Hospital and then the Western Eye Hospital in London. After Basil's death, Bashar enrolled in the military academy at Homs. He became a colonel in the Syrian Army in 1999.

Although Syria is technically a republic, President Hafez al-Assad first groomed his son Basil, then Bashar, as his successor although never openly declaring this intent. Bashar's acquisition of both military and Ba'ath Party credentials was imperative to his legitimacy, but most observers believed that the senior power brokers in the Syrian government assented to his succession as a matter of convenience. In 2000, he was elected secretary-general of the Ba'ath Party and stood as a presidential candidate. The People's Assembly amended the constitution to lower the minimum presidential age to 35, and al-Assad was duly elected president for a seven-year term. A general referendum soon ratified the decision.

A reform movement, dubbed the Damascus Spring, emerged during the first year of al-Assad's rule. Some Syrians hoped that their young president, who had announced governmental reforms, an end to corruption, and economic liberalization, would open Syria to a greater degree. Indeed, reformers hoped to end the State of Emergency Law, which allows for the abuse of legal and human rights, and issued public statements in 2000 and 2001. Political prisoners were released from the notorious Mezze Prison, and certain intellectual forums were permitted. However, by mid-2001, the president reined in the reformists, some of whom were imprisoned and accused of being Western agents.

Under al-Assad, at least prior to the civil war that commenced in January 2011, Syria opened somewhat in terms of allowing more media coverage than in the past, although censorship remained. Cell phones are now prevalent, and Syria finally allowed the Internet, whereas under Hafez al-Assad even facsimile machines were prohibited. Economic reform and modernization received top priority. Job creation, the lessening of Syria's dependence on oil revenue, the encouragement of private capital investments, and the mitigation of poverty are the key goals in the economic sphere. The government created foreign investment zones, and private universities as well as private banks were legally permitted. Employment centers were established after 2000, and al-Assad announced his support of an association with the European Union (EU). However, these changes were too gradual to instill much confidence in Syrian modernization.

Under al-Assad, Syria's relations with Iraq had improved prior to the change of regime in the latter country in April 2003, and for a time Syrian-Turkish relations were also less tense than in the past. However, the United States demonstrated great irritation with evidence that foreign fighters were crossing into Iraq from Syria and that former Iraqi Ba'athists were using Syria for funding purposes. The ensuing 2004 sanctions against Syria under the Syria Accountability Act, first enacted by the U.S. Congress in 2003, have discouraged investors and the modernization of Syrian banking systems.

Syria adamantly and consistently opposed the American presence in Iraq after the Anglo-American invasion there in March 2003, and the country's own Islamist movement reemerged. President al-Assad also had to deal with an influx to Syria of Iraqi refugees, who put an additional burden on the economy. Furthermore, al-Assad did not wish to encourage radical Islamists on Syrian territory and made efforts to contain them.

In terms of the Arab-Israeli situation, al-Assad inherited a hard-line position toward Tel Aviv along with sympathies toward the Palestinian cause during the Second (al-Aqsa) Intifada and its aftermath. Yet internally, the public saw the president as promoting an honorable peace for Syria, deemed necessary for further economic development. While Syria has continued to express hopes for a peace agreement, it insists on Israeli withdrawal from the Golan Heights. Syria demonstrated its lack of desire for war during the Israeli invasion of southern Lebanon in 2006, despite public statements that seemed bellicose.

Other important changes came with the shift in Syria's position in Lebanon. When former Lebanese prime minister Rafik Hariri was assassinated in a bombing in February 2005, suspicions fell on Syria. Anti-Syrian Lebanese demonstrated, as did pro-Syrian groups such as Hezbollah. The United Nations (UN) inquiry into Hariri's death as well as comments by former Syrian vice president Abd al-Halim Khaddam implicated Syrians at the highest level and pro-Syrian elements in Lebanon intelligence services in the assassination. A tribunal was scheduled, although the Syrian government sought to postpone its formation and caused a political crisis in Lebanon. Syrian troops withdrew from Lebanon in April 2005, however, thereby ending a long period of direct and indirect influence over the country. Lebanon has also been a good economic partner for Syria through trade and the absorption of large numbers of Syrian laborers. The U.S. government continued to charge al-Assad with aiding and bolstering Hezbollah in Lebanon, but the Syrian view was that the organization was a wholly Lebanese entity. It could, however, encourage its quiescence along the Israeli border. Assad has remained generally antagonistic toward Israel, though he is said to have discussed the possibility of a peace treaty with Israeli prime minister Ehud Olmert in 2008 via Turkish diplomats. (Turkey, unlike Syria, maintains diplomatic relations with Israel.)

In early 2011, the political unrest that had been brewing for some time in Syria began to boil over as popular uprisings in other Arab countries—most notably Tunisia and Egypt—successfully challenged long-standing dictatorial regimes. Relatively small protests began in January 2011 and seemed to diminish in February. But in mid-March, large protests erupted in cities around the country, triggering a mass movement against the Assad regime. Some believed that the Syrian government would fall, as the Egyptian and Tunisian ones did. However, unlike in Egypt and Tunisia, the loyalty of the military to the regime was carefully cultivated and maintained by the Assads over the past four decades. The army did not side with the protesters, and when Assad charged the military with breaking the demonstrations, it complied. Toward the end of March, the government began to crack down with great violence against the protesters, even as Assad offered concessions, including a proposal to lift the state of emergency. The protests and violence intensified during April and May, and the military even besieged and occupied cities where protests were particularly large, arresting hundreds of dissidents and killing or injuring many others.

By mid-2012, the violence had continued to escalate, as had Assad's willingness to use brute force to quell the unrest. In July, the International Committee of the Red Cross declared that Syria was in the midst of a full-scale civil war. In early 2013, rebel groups appeared to be gaining the upper hand against Assad's regime, and had seized a number of town and cities. Assad's difficulties were compounded by a number of defections by high-ranking government and military officials, although much of the Syrian army's rank and file remained loyal to the regime. At the same time, rebel groups like the Islamic State of Iraq and Syria (ISIS) were taking advantage of the chaos in Syria in an attempt to form an Islamist state within Syria and Iraq. Reports that Assad's forces had employed chemical weapons to stymie rebel gains precipitated international outrage, and in the fall of 2013, Assad agreed to destroy his chemical weapons arsenal under international supervision or face Western air strikes. By early 2014, Assad's forces had gained the upper hand in the conflict, but ISIS was threatening to change the calculus of the war.

The Syrian Civil War has decreased in intensity; by mid-2019, the last significant rebel stronghold was the Idlib Governorate along the border with Turkey, and there are indications Assad may be planning a final, large-scale military operation to wipe out this last bastion of resistance. The conflict has claimed the lives of more than 500,000 Syrians. At least 6 million have been internally displaced during the course of the conflict, and another 5 million fled to other countries as refugees. ISIS managed to seize control of wide swathes of Syrian territory by 2015, but a concerted Syrian military effort aided by a number of nations, including Russia, to defeat ISIS and reclaim lost territory was paying handsome dividends by 2016. The fight against ISIS also included heavy involvement by the United States and their Kurdish allies with the Kurdish fighters and their American military advisers dealing a fatal blow to the Islamic State in Raqqa in 2016. In late 2017, Assad's government declared victory over ISIS, although Syria remained riddled with violence and instability. Thanks to Russian intervention in Syria in 2015, Assad's grip on power has been greatly enhanced, despite his use of chemical weapons against his own people, which invited two U.S. retaliatory missile strikes in 2017 and 2018.

Sherifa Zuhur

Further Reading

Darraj, Susan Muaddi. *Bashar al-Assad*. Chelsea House, 2005.

George, Alan. *Syria: Neither Bread nor Freedom*. Zed, 2003.

Leverett, Flynt. *Inheriting Syria: Bashar's Trial by Fire*. Brookings Institution Press, 2005.

Assad, Hafez al-

Hafez al-Assad (1930–2000) rose from an impoverished background to become the president of Syria (1971–2000). He began his political career by joining the Ba'ath Party in Latakia, Syria, at age 16. He was an Alawite, a small sect of Shia Islam. However, as a secular party, the Ba'ath Party actively recruited members from all sects and branches of Islam as well as from Christian groups. Ba'athism also opposed imperialism and colonialism and espoused nonalignment except with Arab countries. As a youth, Assad participated in Ba'athist demonstrations against the French occupation of Syria and for Syrian independence.

He graduated from the Syrian (Hims) Military Academy as an air force lieutenant pilot in early 1955 and received advanced fighter training by the Soviet military that assisted in his advancement to squadron leader (1959). Assad was exiled to Egypt (1959–1961) after he opposed the union of Syria and Egypt that created the United Arab Republic. His joining with other military officers committed to the resurrection of the Syrian Ba'ath Party led to a coup popularly known as the "8th of March Revolution" (1963). The Ba'ath Party used this coup to seize governmental control of Syria and make the Ba'ath Party the only legal Syrian political party. Assad become the commander of the Syrian Air Force in 1964. A new ruling military junta removed the remaining party founders after another coup (1966) led by a group of Alawite military officers that included al-Assad. He was elevated to minister of defense (1966–1970), but the loss of the Golan Heights to Israel in the Six-Day War (June 1967) seriously weakened his political position. This led to a protracted political struggle with his mentor Salah al-Jadid, then chief of staff of the Syrian armed forces.

The party and the military government remained divided into nationalist and progressive wings until the nationalists led by General al-Assad seized control in November 1970 by arresting Prime Minister Nureddin Atassi al-Jadid, the effective leader of Syria, and other members of the government. Assad and the nationalists were more committed to Arab unity and the destruction of Israel than to socialism, while Atassi's progressive wing had been more committed to neo-Marxist economic reform. Assad became prime minister and was elected president for the first of five times in 1971. Under his rule, political dissenters were subject to arrest, torture, and execution.

A number of unresolved territorial disputes between Israel and Egypt and Syria remained after the Arab-Israeli War of 1967.

Egypt wanted the Sinai returned, and Syria wanted the Golan Heights returned, but Israel refused to withdraw to the pre-1967 armistice lines. After six years without resolution, Assad and Anwar el-Sadat felt the legitimacy of their leadership was threatened by the intractability of Israel. Egypt and Syria launched a two-pronged surprise attack against Israel on October 6, 1973, Yom Kippur. This was the fourth war between Israel and its neighboring Arab states and is known popularly as the Yom Kippur War or the Ramadan War. Israel was at first caught off guard, but the tide of battle turned on October 10; and as the Israeli Defense Force surrounded the Egyptian Third Army in Egyptian territory after crossing the Suez Canal, the United Nations called a cease-fire that took effect on October 22. El-Sadat's effective surrender was blamed by al-Assad for Syria's military defeat and resulted in lasting enmity between Assad and Sadat. Assad's continued insistence throughout his presidency on the return of the Golan Heights without reciprocity prevented any fruitful peace negotiations with Israel. He opposed all peace accords between the Palestinians and the Israelis as well Jordan's decision to end the state of war that existed with Israel (1994).

Assad sent troops into Lebanon in 1976 in an attempt to end the civil war raging there and assumed a permanent peacekeeping presence under the sponsorship of the Arab League. Israel's invasion and occupation of southern Lebanon (1982–1985) allowed Assad to impose changes in the constitution of Lebanon that granted Muslims equal representation with Christians in the Lebanese government while securing Assad's virtual control of Lebanon.

The only major internal threat that Assad faced was a 1982 rebellion in Hamah by the fundamentalist Muslim Brotherhood.

Assad's security forces suppressed the uprising by dispersing poison gas, killing 10,000 to 35,000 civilians, and by razing a good portion of the city. Ironically, Assad supported radical Palestinian and Muslim terrorist groups based in Lebanon and allowed them to establish bases and administrative centers in Syria. Syria was also accused of state-sponsored terrorism in the 1985 TWA hijacking. Assad and Iraq's Saddam Hussein did not develop close ties until 1998, when Israel began to develop a strategic partnership with Turkey. In fact, Assad had supported Iran in the Iran-Iraq War (1980–1990) and had participated in the coalition formed to remove Iraq from Kuwait in the first Persian Gulf War (1990–1991).

Hafez al-Assad died of a heart attack in 2000 and was succeeded by his son, Bashar al-Assad.

Richard M. Edwards

Further Reading

Patterson, Charles. *Hafiz Al-Asad of Syria*. Charles Patterson Digital, 2015.

Seale, Patrick. *Assad of Syria: The Struggle for the Middle East*. University of California Press, 1990.

Assyrians

The Assyrians are a people of three distinct civilizations, two ancient and one modern, all bearing the same name and general geographic origin. The second of these civilizations, the "Neo-Assyrian," of the ninth to the seventh centuries BCE, is the best known due to its reputation as a mighty military empire.

The original Assyrian civilization formed gradually from the remnants of the fallen Sumerian Kingdom and sundry generations of settlers and raiders in the treasured land of Mesopotamia, emerging as a distinct people around 1300 BCE. Like Athens, its capital shared the name of its god, Ashur.

During the following two centuries, the Assyrians grew in power, competing with, and sometimes dominating, their enduring archnemesis Babylon. By about 1200 BCE, the Assyrians controlled much of northern Mesopotamia, but after the death of Emperor Tiglath Pilesar I, the empire declined and nearly vanished for two centuries.

In the ninth century BCE, a new power, the Neo-Assyrian civilization, arose and continued the expansion of its predecessor. In the seventh century, the empire reached its high-water mark, stretching from the convergence of the Tigris and the Euphrates Rivers, east to the Zagros Mountains, north to Urartu (modern-day Armenia), west to modern-day Turkey, south along the Mediterranean coast and far into the Nile River Valley. Along with its original capital of Ashur, it also possessed the famous ancient cities of Ur, Babylon, Nineveh, Damascus, Tarsus, Tyre, Samaria, Memphis, and Egyptian Thebes.

The height of the Neo-Assyrian period commenced during the reign of Tiglath Pilesar III (r. 745–727 BCE) when he conquered Ururtu in the north, and inaugurated a tradition of deportation and resettling of occupied lands. Later conquests incorporated the territories of the northern Kingdom of Israel and its people were exiled, rendering them the legendary "lost tribes." The Neo-Assyrian lands also grew to include the Nile Valley, bringing the empire to its zenith.

Esarhaddon was succeeded by his son Assurbanipal III (r. 668–627 BCE), who reigned an impressive 42 years and was the last of the great emperors. He lost control of Egypt during his reign, but he brutally crushed revolts in Babylon and Elam. Assurbanipal was proud of his knowledge of mathematics and history, and established a library at Nineveh containing captured Babylonian scrolls as well as original Assyrian documents. In spite of his erudition, he was depicted as a decadent and sadistic oriental despot in Eugène Delacroix's controversial painting *The Death of Sardanapalus* (1828). Within a generation of Assurbanipal's death, an alliance of Babylonians and Medeans conquered and destroyed Nineveh, bringing the Assyrian Empire to a sudden, complete, and permanent end.

Assyria was comprehensively a military civilization, expanding and overwhelming its rivals through superior organization and technology. Its engineers were skilled in road construction, bridge building, and siege weapon design. Its forces were specialized and diverse, and included cavalry, light and heavy infantry, archers, and chariots with two or more horses each. Assyria's adoption of iron around 1000 BCE gave it an edge over those civilizations still dwelling in the Bronze Age.

The Assyrians were not driven by ideology. They fought for land and tribute, not for the expansion of their religion. However, those cities that resisted domination were met with bitter reprisals, including slaughter, torture, deportation, and enslavement. It is estimated that 4 million people were displaced by the Assyrians during their neo-imperial period.

The modern Assyrian community, though centered in the same geographic location as its ancient antecedents, has a very different culture compared to its militaristic predecessors. It is a Christian community of about 2 to 4 million people, most of whom live in their ancestral land, now divided among the modern states of Iraq, Syria, Turkey, and Iran. Since 2003, when an American-led coalition overthrew Saddam Hussein's Iraqi regime and unleashed several years of sectarian strife, most Assyrian Christians have fled Iraq due to violent persecution.

According to legend, the Assyrians adopted Christianity in the first century CE, when the apostle Thomas, en route to India, visited their land and converted the people to the new faith. The church he established became known as the Church of the East, or the Assyrian, or Nestorian, or Persian Church. Services are still conducted in Syriac, a dialect of the biblical-era language of Aramaic.

They were persecuted by the Persians beginning in the fourth century, and therefore supported the early Muslims who challenged Persian rule in the seventh century. The Assyrians developed a reputation as well-educated, diligent professionals, and thus served in high positions in government, science, and medicine under the early Abbasid caliphs. However, this relationship deteriorated under the later caliphs, and the Assyrians once again faced persecution at the hands of their rulers.

From the thirteenth to the fifteenth centuries, they were violently repressed by the Mongols, particularly the merciless Tamerlane. This led several Assyrians to take refuge in the Hakkari Mountains of modern Turkey, where they became skilled fighters in a hazardous wilderness. They had a long-standing feud with Kurdish chieftains, which intensified in the nineteenth and early twentieth centuries. During the First World War, many Assyrians, hoping for independence from the Ottoman Turks, sided with the Allied powers. When Russian forces pulled back from their attacks on Turkey, the Ottomans visited reprisals upon their rebellious subjects. An estimated quarter of a million Assyrians were killed during the war. The Assyrians hoped to form their own country following the collapse of the Ottoman Empire, but in 1925 the League of Nations officially recognized the continued Turkish control of the region.

In recent years, Assyrians have been subjected to further persecution and violence from the Islamic State of Iraq and Syria (ISIS), leading to appeals for asylum or the establishment of a new Assyrian state. In 2015, more than 200 Assyrians were kidnapped by the Islamic State—their fate is unknown—and the Assyrians of Raqqa were specifically targeted during the ISIS occupation of the city, and it is believed that only a handful of Assyrian families could be found in the city after it was liberated by Syrian Democratic Forces in 2017. These outrages include the destruction of artifacts and sites of the ancient Assyrians, such as the bulldozing of the ruins of Nimrud near Mosul. Though many Assyrians have fled the area, many others have no wish to leave a land that has been home to their ancestors for millennia.

Christopher G. Marquis

Further Reading

Burenhult, Goran. "Babylonians and Assyrians: Struggling Powers in Mesopotamia." In *Old World Civilizations: The Rise of Cities and States*, vol. 3 of *The Illustrated History of Humankind*, ed. by Goran Burenhult. HarperSanFrancisco, 1994.

Chaliand, Gérard. *A Global History of War: From Assyria to the Twenty-First Century.* Translated by Michèle Mangin-Woods and David Woods. University of California, 2014.

Costa-Roberts, Daniel. "8 Things You Didn't Know About Assyrian Christians." *PBS News Hour Weekend*, March 21, 2015. https://www.pbs.org. Accessed June 2, 2019.

Ghareeb, Edmund A. *Historical Dictionary of Iraq*, Historical Dictionaries of Asia, Oceania, and the Middle East, No. 44. Lanham, MD: Scarecrow Press, 2004.

Himel, Martin. "Former US Soldier Joins Militia to Defend Christian Faith in Iraq." *PBS News Hour*, March 20, 2015. https://www.youtube.com. Accessed June 18, 2019.

"Isis Extremists Bulldoze Ancient Assyrian Site Near Mosul." Reuters in Baghdad. *The Guardian*, March 6, 2015. https://www.theguardian.com/world/2015/mar/05/islamic-state-isis-extremists-bulldoze-ancient-nimrud-site-mosul-iraq. Accessed June 2, 2019.

Jones, Sam, and Owen Bowcott. "Religious Leaders Say Isis Persecution of Iraqi Christians Has Become Genocide." *The Guardian*, August 8, 2014. www.theguardian.com/world/2014/aug/08/isis-persecution-iraqi-christians-genocide-asylum/print. Accessed June 2, 2019.

McQuade, Romsin. "Iraq's Persecuted Assyrian Christians Are in Limbo." *Telegraph*, July 30, 2014. https://www.telegraph.co.uk/news/worldnews/middleeast/iraq/11000168/Iraqs-persecuted-Assyrian-Christians-are-in-limbo.html. Accessed June 2, 2019.

Mieroop, Marc Van de. "The Empires of Assyria and Babylonia." In *The Great Empires of the Ancient World*, ed. by Thomas Harrison. Thames & Hudson, 2009.

Simons, Geoff. *Iraq: From Sumer to Saddam*. St. Martin's Press, 1994.

B

Ba'athism

Ba'athism (also spelled Ba'thism) means "resurrection," "rebirth," or "renaissance," and is the core doctrine of the Ba'ath Party (also known as the Arab Socialist Ba'th Party, Arab Socialist Renaissance Party, or Al Baath Arab Socialist Party). The basic Ba'athist beliefs are revealed in their motto and economic dogma: Wahdah, Hurriyah, Ishtirrakiyah, meaning "Unity, Freedom, Socialism," with "Unity" referring to Pan-Arab unity; "Freedom" referring to freedom from non-Arab countries, in particular, Western interests; and "Socialism" referring to Arab socialism. Ba'athism is thus a combination of pan-Arabism, Arab socialism, nationalism, and militarism. The Ba'ath Party has as its goal the formation of a single, secular, Arab, socialist state.

The secular socialist emphasis of Ba'athism is attractive to marginalized and disadvantaged peoples in the Middle East. Hafez al-Assad rose to the presidency of Syria (1971–2000) after joining the party in Latakia, Syria, at age 16. Assad came from an impoverished background and was an Alawite, the member of a small sect of Shia Islam, but the party found many active adherents from other sects and branches of Islam as well as from Christian groups.

Ba'athism opposes imperialism and colonialism, embracing only alliances with Arab countries. As a youth, al-Assad, for example, participated in demonstrations against the French occupation of Syria and for Syrian independence (achieved April 17, 1946). Foreign domination, especially European and particularly French colonialism, was seen in the early development of Ba'athism as responsible for the cultural and moral deterioration that had weakened the Arab world and had dampened the positive values of Islam while giving rise to class divisions. This was seen as particularly true of the older generations of Syrian Arab nationalists. Ba'athism was founded on the conviction that Arabs needed a secular revival of the unity that had once transcended their differences through shared Islamic values and beliefs.

Ba'athism did not espouse an Arab nationalism rooted in the personal charisma of any one individual. Its earliest proponents were three-middle class educators, Zaki al-Arsuzi, Salah al-Din al-Bitar, and Arab Christian Michel Aflaq. The movement spread slowly throughout Syria in the 1930s. As the Ba'ath Party began to form in Damascus, Syria, in the early 1940s, Salah and Aflaq began to promote Ba'athism in Iraq by organizing demonstrations against the British presence in Iraq. The growth of Ba'athism stalled until World War II ended and the United Nations partitioned Palestine (1947), creating the state of Israel. The effective defeat of the Arab nations in the ensuing war solidified the existence of Israel (1948) and fanned the flames of Arab unity, the lack of which was widely seen as the reason for the defeat.

The Ba'ath Party traces its initial founding to 1943, but the official founding of the party is best dated from its first party congress in Damascus on April 7, 1947. It was at this congress that an executive committee was established and a constitution was approved. The Ba'ath Party then merged with the Syrian Socialist Party in 1953 to form the Arab Socialist Ba'ath Party. Branches of the party were soon founded in Iraq, Jordan, and Lebanon between 1954 and 1958.

The Ba'athists seized power in Syria in 1963 in a military coup, popularly known as the "8th of March Revolution," that made the Ba'ath Party the only legal Syrian political party; all official opposition groups were outlawed. The ruling military junta removed Aflaq and Bitar from the party in 1966, but the party remained divided into nationalist and progressive wings until the nationalists led by General Hafiz al-Assad seized control in November 1970 by arresting Prime Minister Nureddin Atassi; Salah al-Jadid, chief of staff of the Syrian armed forces and the effective leader of Syria; and other members of the government. Al-Assad and the nationalists were more committed to Arab unity and the destruction of Israel than to socialism, while Atassi's progressive wing had been more committed to neo-Marxist economic reform. Al-Assad died of a heart attack in 2000, and his son, Bashar al-Assad, succeeded him as president.

The Iraqi Ba'athists briefly seized control of the Iraqi government (February 1963), making Abdul Salam Arif president, but it was not until 1968 that the Iraqi Ba'ath Party took complete control. This control lasted until 2003 when, in the Iraq War (second Persian Gulf War), a coalition led by the United States removed Ba'athist Saddam Hussein from the presidency and banned the Iraqi Ba'ath Party (June 2003) from participation in the new government.

The Syrian Ba'ath Party is no longer guided by its founding ideology. Having abandoned its commitment to socialism and having failed to foster Arab unity, the party is more committed to the orderly management of the country under a military dictatorship. Though Ba'athism in Syria remained

somewhat splintered into smaller factions, the major internal threat to the party was from religious extremists such as the Muslim Brotherhood that continues to plague Egypt as well. The Ba'ath Party in Syria has suffered major setbacks since early 2011, when the Syrian government under Bashar al-Assad commenced a brutal crackdown against anti-government rebels and Islamist groups. The ensuing civil war went on to claim the lives of more than 500,000 Syrians and displaced at least another 11 million. The conflict involved open warfare between government forces, allied militias, and Shia groups on the one hand, and mainly Sunni rebels and militant groups on the other. Both sides were receiving aid from outside groups and other nations including Iran, Turkey, Russia, and the United States, among others. International extremist organizations such as al-Qaeda and the Islamic State were also involved. Throughout the fighting, however, the Ba'ath Party has survived, and all indications are that its hold on power in Syria will remain intact for the foreseeable future.

Richard M. Edwards

Further Reading

Alahmar, Abdullah. *The Baath and the Regenerating Revolution: A Search in the Aspects of the Baathist Arab Socialist Party and Its National Guiding Experience*. Dar Albaath, 1991.

Chand, Attar. *The Revolutionary Arabs: A Study of the Arab Baath Socialist Movement*. Homeland Publications, 1981.

Kienle, Eberhard. *Ba'th v Ba'th: The Syro-Iraqi Conflict, 1968–1989*. I. B. Tauris, 1990.

Baghdadi, Abu Bakr al-

Abu Bakr al-Baghdadi was the leader of the Islamic State of Iraq and Syria (ISIS). Born near Samarra, Iraq, in 1971 (his given name was Ibrahim Awwad Ibrahim Ali Muhammad al-Badri al Samarrai), he claimed to be a descendent of the Prophet Muhammad and thus should have been respected as a religious scholar and accorded the title of "caliph," or leader of the Muslim peoples. (The term "caliph" is a historical title held by the person who led the global community of Muslims, known as the *umma*. Tradition dictated this person must be able to claim familial ties to the Prophet Muhammad.) What is interesting about al-Baghdadi's claim, however, is that it ran through a line of Shia, rather than Sunni succession. As most Sunnis consider Shia tradition to be unorthodox, and even heretical, al-Baghdadi's claim to the title of "caliph" was rejected by the vast majority of Islamic scholars and leaders.

Al-Baghdadi, a Sunni Muslim, was not unique in terms of his Shia ancestry. It is very common in Iraq for families to intermarry between sects, and there are many prominent tribes that have both Sunni and Shia members. Culturally, Iraq is a mixture of Sunni, Shia, and even Christian traditions, and Iraqis are well known throughout the Middle East for blending the cultural aspects of all these traditions into one very unique culture. It is for this reason that ISIS, a Sunni Islamic movement born in Iraq and led by Iraqis, contains many elements that are traditionally thought of as distinctly Shia, such as its focus on prophecy about the end-times.

It is well known that al-Baghdadi was a poor student when it came to math and science and that he was rejected for military service due to poor eyesight. His family was pious, however, and he excelled at religious studies; eventually earning a bachelor's degree in Islamic studies from the University of Baghdad and then a doctorate in Quranic studies from Saddam University for Islamic Studies (now called Nahrain University), also

in Baghdad. It was during his time in graduate school that he joined the Muslim Brotherhood, and began to gravitate to some of that organization's more violent members. This was pivotal in solidifying his role in the anti-U.S. resistance after the invasion in 2003.

Shortly after that invasion, al-Baghdadi cofounded the militant group known as Al-Jaysh Ahl al-Sunnah wa al-Jammah (The Army of the People of the Ways of the Prophet and Communal Solidarity), which made a name for itself in the early days of Operation Iraqi Freedom (OIF)—such a name, in fact, that Coalition Forces arrested al-Baghdadi in Fallujah, Iraq, and held him in a detention facility for 10 months. It was in this detention facility, known as Camp Bucca, that al-Baghdadi widened his influence by becoming the inmates' spiritual leader. In this role, he developed a wide network of supporters, religious people and secularists alike, that would eventually form the foundation of ISIS. When al-Baghdadi was released from Camp Bucca in December 2004, and with the suggestion that he assume leadership of al-Qaeda in Iraq (AQI), with whom he had developed a relationship in detention, he traveled to Damascus, Syria, where he oversaw AQI's public relations campaign.

In 2006, AQI's leader, Abu Musab al-Zarqawi, was killed by U.S. forces. Its new leader, an Egyptian named Aby Ayyub al-Masri, disbanded AQI and called his new organization the Islamic State in Iraq (ISI). Al-Baghdadi slowly rose through the organization's ranks; used his connections to grow support for it beyond Iraq's boundaries (adding Syria, or al-Sham, to its title in 2013); and after al-Masri's death in 2010, became the leader of ISIS. In 2014, he declared himself "caliph" of the Islamic State and initiated a worldwide recruiting effort.

Abu Bakr al-Baghdadi was a reclusive leader. He made very few public appearances, and few video or audio recordings of his speeches and sermons exist. Western media outlets have reported his death numerous times, but in 2018, ISIS released an audio message of al-Baghdadi sending greetings for the Islamic holiday of Eid al-Adha; and in April 2019, he released a 20-minute video that analysts conclude was recorded shortly before it was posted. In this video, al-Baghdadi reassured his followers that despite the setbacks suffered in Iraq and Syria, the fight was far from over. Despite this rallying cry, al-Baghdadi was killed by U.S. forces in October 2019.

Robert M. Kerr

Further Reading

Gerges, Fawaz A. *ISIS: A History*. Princeton University Press, 2016.

McCants, William. "ISIS Leader Abu Bakr al-Baghdadi's Family Tree." The Brookings Institute, September 2015. https://www.brookings.edu/blog/markaz/2015/09/10/isis-leader-abu-bakr-al-baghdadis-family-tree.

Tomass, Mark. *The Religious Roots of the Syrian Conflict: The Remaking of the Fertile Crescent*. Palgrave MacMillan, 2016.

Wood, Graeme. "What ISIS Really Wants." *The Atlantic*, March 2015.

Battle of Haffah

Haffah is a town in northwest Syria, situated about 16 miles to the west of Syria's major port city, Latakia. The town itself is believed to have had a pre-conflict population of about 4,500 people, roughly half of whom were Sunni Muslims. About 40 percent of the townspeople were Alawites (the same ethnic group as Syrian president Bashar al-Assad), and the remaining 10 percent were Christian. The agricultural town's Sunnis, Alawites, and Christians lived together for centuries until almost the entire population left after fighting erupted in 2012.

Though small, Haffah has a very old history that dates back to the Phoenicians. Located in the hinterlands of Salah al-Din Castle, a UNESCO World Heritage Site, Haffah has always been known for its olives, figs, pomegranates, apples, and pears. The town is laid out in an elongated pattern along a road with a northeast/southwest orientation running along the top of a narrow mountain ridge with fairly steep sides. It provides whomever controls the town with a unique tactical advantage because any military force trying to take the town is always on the low ground.

Haffah was a quiet town at the outset of the Syrian uprisings in 2011. Its rural population was, no doubt, aware of all of the tragic events that ensued after the government crackdown against protestors in Daraa, but it did not see any mass protests against, or shows of support for, the government. However, on June 5, 2012, looking for bases from which to launch attacks against Latakia, Syria's port city that was once the capital of the autonomous Alawite state, Free Syrian Army forces launched attacks against Haffah's police stations. Latakia, as the heartland of Alawite culture in Syria, was a top priority for Bashar al-Assad since it became clear that the conflict would evolve into a much larger civil war; so his response to the Free Syrian Army's attack in a town so close to Latakia, and one with a large Alawite population, was swift. Within hours of the attack on Haffah's police station, Syrian Arab Army forces were in the city taking on the rebel forces. Free Syrian Army forces maintained the advantage throughout the first day of fighting, however, and held on to the police stations and managed to take out Syrian tanks and armored personnel carriers with rocket-propelled grenades (RPGs).

On the second day of fighting, the Syrian military was reinforced with more tanks and helicopters from the Syrian Air Force. It is unknown how many casualties there were, but estimates hover around 20 Syrian Army soldiers and 10 rebels over 24 hours of fighting. On June 7, two days after the rebels took the police stations, a number of rebels took the police officers hostage and bulldozed one of the police stations. The government was not able to retake the city, however, as Free Syrian Army fighters put up a fierce resistance. Unable to defeat them, the Syrian Arab Army brought in more reinforcements on June 10, and they proceeded to bombard the town indiscriminately (by this time almost all of the town's Alawite residents had fled, mostly to Latakia, under the protection of government forces). Finally, on June 12, a week after the initial assault on Haffah's police stations and after as many as 70 soldiers, 30 civilians, and 25 rebel fighters had been killed, the Syrian Arab Army retook the mountain town.

As mentioned above, Haffah's geography gives the town a unique advantage in terms of defense. It is on the high ground running along a narrow mountain ridge with steep, heavily forested sides. Any forces trying to take the town are forced into a bottleneck on the road at either the northeastern or southwestern entrances, which gives a defending force a distinct advantage. Unfortunately for the town, however, the geography gave the Syrian Army only one real option, and that was to park tanks and pieces of artillery on the parallel mountain ridges and, along with air support from helicopters, pummel the rebels into submission. The geography made a movement into the city by the army with the goal of occupation unrealistic, and as a result the city suffered greatly. Once the 200 rebels who had endured the barrage of artillery retreated (most likely into Turkey, where

they regrouped with other members of the Free Syrian Army from other parts of northern Syria), the Syrian Arab Army moved in to occupy the town, but almost the entire population of civilians had fled; the Syrian forces had liberated a ghost town.

Robert M. Kerr

Further Reading

Cooper, Tim. *Syrian Conflagration: The Civil War 2011—2013*. Helion and Company, 2016.

Ibrahim, Azeem. *The Resurgence of Al-Qaeda in Syria and Iraq*. Strategic Studies Institute Press, 2014.

Phillips, Christopher. *The Battle for Syria: International Rivalry in the New Middle East*. Yale University Press, 2016.

Battle of Maaloula

Maaloula is a very unique town in the mountains northeast of Damascus. Located almost 5,000 feet above sea level and built into the rugged mountain landscape, most of Maaloula's population is Christian (about 70 percent), and it is one of the last places on earth where the Western dialect of the Aramaic language is spoken. Interestingly, while Arabic is generally understood and used for religious purposes among the village's Muslim population, which makes up about 30 percent of the total population, even they resisted the "Arabization" of the region and primarily speak Aramaic as their first language. Aramaic is the language that Jesus of Nazareth would have spoken as his native tongue, and while the dialect spoken in Maaloula is not the same as that of Nazareth, many linguists see the Syrian mountain town as a vital link to an ancient language that has largely died off. The population of Maaloula fluctuates throughout the year; the permanent population of about 5,000 typically increases to around 10,000 during the summer months; it has traditionally been a popular destination for people from Damascus, about 35 miles away, to escape the summer heat in the mountains. The town also attracts a large number of linguists interested in studying ancient Semitic languages because of the inhabitants' fluency in Aramaic.

Because of its many ancient shrines and churches, Maaloula is being considered as a candidate as a UNESCO World Heritage Site. The United Nations established the World Heritage Site designation in order to recognize locations around the world that are considered to be so important to world history that great efforts should be taken to ensure their protection and maintenance. One of Maaloula's most famous structures is the Convent of Saint Thecla, a disciple of Saint Paul who fled to the mountain village to hide in the building from Roman persecution. Many of Maaloula's Christian structures contain pristine artwork such as frescoes dating to the twelfth century, and icons and mosaics that date back as far as the fourth century. This is why, in addition to the possibility of the massive loss of human life, the world community gasped in horror as the Free Syrian Army (FSA) and the al-Qaeda–affiliated Jabhat al-Nusra launched an offensive against Maaloula in September 2013.

In addition to its important Christian history and distinctiveness, Maaloula also has significant strategic value, especially for a militia that wants an easily defended stronghold from which to launch operations against government forces in Damascus. FSA and Jabhat al-Nusra forces had set up camps near Maaloula as early as March 2013, but did not make any significant moves against the town. This was, in part, because the Syrian government provided some security in the region to try to maintain life "as

normal" and allow for the annual movement of people from Damascus into the mountains as safely as possible during the summer months. Some Christian residents of the town suspected that their Muslim neighbors, with whom they had enjoyed good relations for more than a thousand years, had been working with the al-Qaeda–linked militants to help them overthrow the village. The security situation for Maaloula's Christians deteriorated in the fall of 2013 when it became necessary for farmers to have a Muslim escort to go to their farmlands on the outskirts of the town. The Christians' fears were realized when on September 4 a suicide bomber blew up a vehicle-borne improvised explosive device (VBIED) at a Syrian Army checkpoint on the road into Maaloula. What followed was an attack by the FSA and Jabhat al-Nusra that killed the remaining Syrian soldiers and disabled their tanks. The rebels then seized control of a popular mountainside hotel and began firing on the villagers below. By the end of the day, the al-Qaeda fighters occupied several sections of the town, which they held for two days. On September 6 and 7, the Syrian Army, with the help of air strikes from the Syrian Air Force, launched a successful counter offensive and retook those areas, as well as the checkpoint. On September 8, however, reinforcements helped the rebels drive out the Syrian military forces, and the FSA and Jabhat al-Nusra took control of Maaloula.

Militants killed Christians, burned a church, and after the Syrian Army briefly regained control of the city, took 12 nuns hostage from the Convent of Saint Thecla in November. World media outlets such as CNN, the BBC, and al-Jazeera quickly covered the invasion of Maaloula with a sense of dread; all were worried that Maaloula would be later known as a town where thousands were massacred and thousands of years of history and culture would be erased. The number killed, however, did not reach the thousands because it turned out that almost all of the town's Christian residents had fled the city during the initial assault. Most had reported that sacred sites had been desecrated but that the loss of life had remained low, with only a handful of inhabitants being killed in the initial attack. Later, international news agencies reported, correctly, that the amount of damage to the sacred sites had actually been relatively minimal. There was widespread concern over the condition of the nuns, however, and their status would remain unclear for months to come. Maaloula residents who remained during the attack mostly belonged to a pro-government militia known as the National Defense Force, and fought fiercely alongside government forces through the days of the battle. Under siege from November 2013 until April 2014, when Syrian forces, with the help of Iranian-backed Hezbollah, retook the city and began the assessment of the damage.

The nuns who had been kidnapped turned out to be alive, and were part of a prisoner exchange between the rebel militias and the Syrian government. Damage to the town's Christian buildings was significant, but not as bad as most had anticipated; and thanks to almost the entirety of Maaloula's Christians fleeing in the early days of the attack, massive loss of life was avoided. The town is far from recovered, however, and one year after the jihadists attacked, only around 150 families had returned from their exile to Damascus, Beirut, and elsewhere. In the subsequent years, more families returned, however, and the Russians had begun helping to rebuild and restore the Christian sites that had been damaged. In 2018, Russian television posted a video showing how one of the town's two monasteries had reopened and that Christmas religious services had attracted the largest number of worshippers since before the attack in 2013.

Like many of Syria's minorities, the Christians of Maaloula initially tried to stay neutral in the conflict. However, as more extremist elements within Islam came to dominate the motives of many of the anti-government forces, Christians largely supported the government for fear of being persecuted under a government influenced by al-Qaeda, the Muslim Brotherhood, or the Islamic State. Their position is that they would prefer a secularist government that, while oppressive, did not discriminate against them based on religion over an Islamist government that might not be so accommodating to their existence.

Robert M. Kerr

Further Reading

Cragg, Kenneth. *The Arab Christian: A History in the Middle East.* Westminster John Knox Press, 1991.

Karabell, Zachary. *Peace Be Upon You: The Story of Muslim, Christian, and Jewish Coexistence.* Knopf, 2007.

Sharkey, Heather J. *A History of Christians, Muslims, and Jews in the Middle East.* Cambridge University Press, 2017.

Battle of Saraqeb

In March 2012, just a week and a half after the Syrian Arab Army made significant strategic gains in retaking the city of Idlib from rebel control, government forces turned their attention to Saraqeb, Idlib Province's second-largest city. Saraqeb is strategically located at the junction of three roads: one leading to Aleppo; one to Hama, Homs, and then Damascus; and the third leading toward

Latakia. Rebels had seized the city because of its strategic location, and after having based many coordinated attacks against Syrian military targets there, the Syrian Army placed a high priority on retaking the city after its recent victory in Idlib city as quickly as possible. Rebel resistance was strong, however, and the government's inability to gain a permanent foothold in Saraqeb led to it utilizing a chemical weapon against its people almost a year after the initial battle began.

Located east of the city of Idlib, the largest city in the region, Saraqeb was first established as a center of commerce by itinerant traders during the Ottoman Empire. Known colloquially in the region as *Nawar*, these traders were not necessarily viewed favorably by the dominant society, and it is likely they settled this community as a way to escape harassment from their trade partners in Idlib and elsewhere. They likely met little resistance in setting up the town as it offers little in the way of natural resources. It does have strategic value, however, as it is situated at the junction of three vital trade routes connecting northwestern Syria with key centers of commerce throughout the region. There are roughly 250,000 Nawari throughout Syria practicing both Sunni and Shia Islam; the majority of Saraqeb's 35,000 residents are Sunni Nawari. There are three things Saraqeb is known for: its distinctive black, embroidered cloth, its skilled tradesmen who are particularly adept at fixing well-drilling equipment, and a fierce sense of independence and general distrust of outsiders.

In March, 2011, a small group of men in Saraqeb decided to hold a peaceful but poignant protest. During Friday prayers they stood up and argued that God is greater than the Assad regime and then held a quick march down the town's very small main road chanting "With our blood, with our souls, we

sacrifice for you, oh Daraa." This was in reference to the town in southern Syria where the anti-government protests began in earnest and escalated after the Syrian Arab Army led a series of brutal crackdowns on protestors. Over the ensuing weeks, Friday prayers attracted more and more protestors, and while they remained peaceful, they were forceful in their assertions that democratic reform in Syria was desperately needed.

The mood of the protests changed, however, when the government sent the protestors a message in the form of the body of a soldier from Saraqeb who had supposedly been killed by protestors in Daraa. Saraqeb's residents, however, were skeptical of the government's story and took their message as a warning. Rather than being scared into submission, however, the people were emboldened; and rather than calling for democratic reforms, they began calling for the overthrow of the Assad regime. In April, 2011, the army sent a small unit to control the city, but the protests only grew. In June, Syrian forces killed the first protester in Saraqeb, yet the protests did not stop. In August, the army sent in tanks, arrested protestors, destroyed shops, and burned houses. The main opposition leaders, however, escaped into the olive groves surrounding the city and devised a plan to resist the government forces. They did not stay hidden for long, however, and they were all arrested and held for months, during which they were interrogated, tortured, and endured horrific conditions. While the leadership was in captivity, however, the people of Saraqeb had organized themselves into a militia, allied with the Free Syrian Army resistance group, and began fighting back, eventually pushing the Syrian Army out of the town. This lasted until March 2012, when the army launched an offensive and took control of the streets once again. The army's offensive was well coordinated, and within a day they were able to retake the city. Key rebel leaders were arrested. This battle was well publicized, and news outlets such as al-Jazeera broadcast images of the battle in real time around the world.

The Syrian Army held the city until a counteroffensive led by the Free Syrian Army succeeded in retaking the city and placing it under rebel control. From November 2012 through March 2013, the rebels maintained control of the town without much interference from the Syrian forces. On March 23, 2013, however, observers noted a Syrian Arab Air Force helicopter circling the city. Suspecting a standard barrel bomb attack, rebels prepared to take cover but then noticed a trail of white spray coming out of the back of the helicopter and then three objects falling from it. Saraqeb was under a chemical weapon attack; there were barrel bombs being dropped, but instead of shrapnel the barrel bombs were full of chlorine gas. No deaths were reported, but dozens were treated for respiratory problems.

An interesting development that has happened in Saraqeb is worth noting. All throughout the battle for Saraqeb, locals allied with the Syrian Free Army but continuously resisted al-Qaeda, despite Idlib Province being a hotbed of al-Qaeda activity and support. As a town firmly against the Assad regime and attempts by foreign militias to take over the city, Saraqeb lived up to its reputation as an independent town that is beholden to no one. Fed up with waiting for outside help from any source, the people of Saraqeb decided to try to return to a state as close to normal as possible and hold town-level elections. In the fall of 2017, the people held a full election cycle, complete with debates, campaign posters, and ultimately an election for a new local governing council. While things are far from normal, the people

of Saraqeb have taken concrete steps to take matters into their own hands and to take care of themselves, the way they always have.

Robert M. Kerr

Further Reading

Cooper, Tim. *Syrian Conflagration: The Civil War 2011—2013*. Helion and Company, 2016.

Gopal, Anand. "Syria's Last Bastion of Freedom." *The New Yorker*, December 3, 2018. https://www.newyorker.com/magazine/2018/12/10/syrias-last-bastion-of-freedom.

Ibrahim, Azeem. *The Resurgence of al-Qaeda in Syria and Iraq*. Strategic Studies Institute Press, 2014.

Phillips, Christopher. *The Battle for Syria: International Rivalry in the New Middle East*. Yale University Press, 2016.

Binnish

Binnish is a town in northeast Syria's northeastern Idlib Province with a pre-conflict population of around 50,000 people, though it is believed that around 10,000 people fled the city in the year between the beginning of the conflict in the spring of 2011 and the first large-scale government military offensive against rebel groups inside the city in February 2012. Situated just northeast of the city of Idlib, Binnish is located on the road connecting Idlib and Aleppo, two of the Syrian conflict's most consequential cities. The city is the center of extensive, flat agricultural land, and its economy is based on the local agricultural products that are traded from there, primarily to Idlib.

Binnish established itself as an enclave of anti-Assad sentiment early in the conflict. In the summer of 2011, residents of Binnish began to hold rallies against the government in Damascus every Friday, and international media outlets regularly covered these peaceful gatherings of people of all ages calling for governmental reform. As was the case in other areas throughout Syria, the government did not look favorably on the peaceful protests. In February 2012, after months of growing crowds holding rallies every Friday afternoon, the Syrian Army launched an artillery attack against the people in the city. The Free Syrian Army and the Syrian Liberation Army had set up bases of operation within the town, so that along with peaceful protestors, the movement's more militant elements had emerged in Binnish early in the conflict. The February artillery attacks did not stop the protests, however, and the following month the American news outlet CNN reported that the peaceful anti-government protests had grown larger than ever. While the peaceful demonstrations continued, however, the Free Syrian Army and the Syrian Liberation Army continued to dig in as well.

Between 2012 and 2016, Idlib Province grew into one of the most significant strongholds of anti-Assad militias in the entire country. Bordering Turkey, the area benefitted from a political boundary that was difficult to control in places, and this allowed for the flow of militants and weapons into the northwestern province without too many hindrances. In 2016, the Associated Press reported that Idlib Province was the only region in Syria in which neither government forces nor the Islamic State had any real presence, which meant that it was seen by rebel groups as both a symbolic and strategic heartland of a movement that uniquely represented a future that was distinctly Syrian. While each of the groups agreed that Syria needed a new direction, they all represented very different ideas about what that future should look like, and one of the government's strategies in the area was to patiently wait and allow the groups to start

fighting amongst themselves. This did indeed happen to some degree, though it did not become as large an issue as the Syrian government had perhaps hoped. This strategy might explain, in part, why Idlib is one of the regions where the Syrian military largely took its time and set up strategic bases from which to launch large-scale assaults only after they believed the militias had the opportunity to fight each other. One of Assad's deliberate strategies even involved capturing militants from all over Syria and deporting them to Idlib Province in order to fracture the rebel unity in the region. The Associated Press reported that thousands of militants and their families had been moved from Homs and Damascus to areas throughout Idlib Province, and the region quickly filled up with anti-government forces with varying agendas ranging from secular socialism to religious extremism. By 2016, it was reported by the Institute for the Study of War that as many as 50,000 fighters had regrouped under the umbrella of the Jaish al-Fatah (Army of Conquest) and funded by al-Qaeda. Of course, aside from hoping to weaken the unity among his opposition, Bashar al-Assad's other motivation was to try to contain as many militants in one area as possible in order to justify a massive military offensive against them at a future time.

The United States has taken advantage of Assad's strategy, and while many of the American-supported anti-Assad militias are based in Idlib Province, so is its enemy, al-Qaeda. Once rebels established their stronghold in northwest Syria, U.S. air strikes targeting al-Qaeda targets began in July 2015. Primarily, the United States was interested in taking out the leadership of an al-Qaeda branch called the Khorasan Group, which U.S. intelligence had discovered was planning attacks against Western interests from what they thought was a new safe haven in Syria. From 2016 through 2017, Idlib Province, including Binnish, was targeted by air strikes from the aforementioned American Air Force against al-Qaeda targets, as well as Syrian and Russian air strikes against any target they deemed hostile.

Bashar al-Assad's hope to sow disunity among the dissident militias was not realized as fully as he might have hoped, and while there was certainly some fighting among the groups in Idlib Province, they tended to set aside their differences more effectively than many expected. This is perhaps because they were well supplied by their al-Qaeda sponsor, as well as the growing kinship they felt based on their shared fight against a regime they were determined to defeat. The Free Syrian Army was perhaps the biggest barrier to unity among the groups in Idlib, but even they set aside their differences with the other groups when the Russians and Turks brokered an agreement to institute a cease-fire in Idlib Province in September 2018. Suspicious that the deal was meant only to weaken the rebel position in the region as a precursor to a large-scale Syrian government assault, the rebel groups used the cease-fire as an opportunity to unify while they cautiously adhered to the agreement. In Binnish, thousands of people took to the streets waving the three-starred flag that had become the symbol of Syrian opposition; they had clearly not softened their anti-Assad feelings, and observers knew this peace was likely to be a short one.

As a sign that rebel groups were taking the opportunity afforded by the cease-fire to prepare for what they felt was the inevitable coming attack from Syrian and Russian forces, they started heavily taxing the commercial and aid traffic that had begun to flood into the region as a result of the improved security situation. In fact, the U.S. and British governments even cut off aid to Idlib Province due to what they called the "terror tax" being imposed by the rebel groups. The British *Telegraph* newspaper reported in October 2018 that rebel groups had possibly raised more than £2.5 million through these taxes.

As of the summer of 2019, the Russian-Turkish–brokered cease-fire remains in effect officially, but fighting has resumed in many places, including air strikes and artillery barrages in Binnish. In May 2019, fears of a massive Syrian offensive were rekindled as a new wave of heavy bombardment by Syrian forces took place throughout Idlib Province, with more than 200,000 people reportedly fleeing into surrounding areas. It is believed that Russian jets conducted some of the air strikes in the area their own government, along with Turkey, has designated as a safe zone. As Binnish is a key city in a region that is the last stronghold of anti-government forces in Syria, it is safe to say that as of 2019, Binnish's final story in the chapter of the Syrian Civil War remains to be written.

Robert M. Kerr

Further Reading

Abouzeid, Rania. *No Turning Back: Life, Loss, and Hope in Wartime Syria.* W. W. Norton, 2018.

Baresh, Manhal. "The Sochi Agreement and the Interests of Guarantor States: Examining the Aims and Challenges of Sustaining the Deal." European Universities Institute, Robert Schuman Center for Advanced Studies, 2019.

C

Carter, Ashton "Ash"

Ashton Baldwin Carter served as the 25th secretary of defense under Presidents Barack Obama and Donald Trump from February 2015 to January 2017. Educated at Yale University with a double major in physics and medieval history in 1976, he earned a doctorate in theoretical physics at Oxford University in 1979. He transitioned to working in the field of government policy after writing a report critical of President Ronald Reagan's "Star Wars" missile defense program, which he argued, based on physics, could not stop a Soviet nuclear attack against the United States. He joined the faculty at Harvard University's Kennedy School of Government, where he taught until joining the administration of President Bill Clinton as the assistant secretary of defense for international security policy in 1993. During his time in the Clinton administration, Secretary Carter was responsible for overseeing the Cooperative Threat Reduction Program (more commonly known as the Nunn-Lugar Program), which dealt with reducing and eliminating nuclear weapons from Russia and its former satellite states of Ukraine, Georgia, Azerbaijan, Belarus, Uzbekistan, and Kazakhstan in the wake of the fall of the Union of Soviet Socialist Republics (USSR). Secretary Carter also worked on the post–Cold War Strategic Defense Initiative as well as other programs dealing with science and technology issues in the realm of national security.

From 2009 through 2011, Carter served as undersecretary of defense for acquisition, overseeing logistics for one of the biggest and most resource-hungry organizations in the world. His most noteworthy accomplishment during this time was the rapid fielding of the much-needed Mine Resistant Ambush Protected (MRAP) vehicles to Iraq and Afghanistan to counter the threat to Coalition Forces from improvised explosive devices. From 2011 through 2013, he oversaw the Department of Defense's personnel system. All of these experiences, coupled with his education, were reasons President Obama appointed him to replace Chuck Hagel as the secretary of defense in 2015, a time when the Syrian Conflict had grown extremely complex for the United States after Russia came to the aid of Bashar al-Assad as he attempted to hold on to power.

As secretary of defense under President Obama, Carter led U.S. efforts in Syria to identify allies and bolster their efforts to remove Bashar al-Assad from power. At the same time, he is credited with leading the effort to counter Russian involvement in Syria while walking the fine line between relatively peaceful coexistence and all-out armed conflict. His main effort, however, was always the defeat of the Islamic State by taking out their strongholds in Mosul (Iraq) and Raqqa (Syria). At the time of Secretary Carter's nomination in December 2014, the Islamic State had made substantial gains, claiming territory in and around Tikrit, Mosul, and key oil and natural gas fields in northern Iraq. It had declared a caliphate (Islamist government) in Iraq and Syria, and its leaders announced their plans to expand throughout the Middle East. The rapidity and relative ease with which the Islamic State had spread in Iraq and parts of Syria made the international community take notice, and IS's claims for regional expansion were taken very seriously by all interested parties. It was during this time that two regional powers, Turkey and Jordan, initiated military offenses aimed specifically at taking out Islamic State targets before they had the chance to make good on their stated ambitions. Secretary Carter was also very concerned with a few actions taken by the Islamic State aimed directly at the West, including the very public and brutal execution of American journalist James Foley and British aid worker David Haines. He was also reconciling with the international outcry at the Islamic State's treatment of ethnic minorities in both Iraq and Syria, including the enslavement and mass murder of groups such as the Yezidis, whom the Islamic State painted as heretical unbelievers. It should be noted that Bashar al-Assad shared the fear and outrage over the Islamic State's treatment of minorities since, as a member of the minority Alawite community, his people, who practice a religious tradition that is an offshoot of Shia Islam, are themselves considered heretical in the eyes of IS leadership.

Over the first few months of Secretary Carter's tenure, Islamic State forces continued to expand their territory, taking the important cities of Ramadi in Iraq and the ancient city of Palmyra in Syria where they destroyed countless precious architectural sites, including part of the city's famous Roman amphitheater. Finding that the Department of Defense did not have a comprehensive plan for defeating the Islamic State when he entered office, Carter set about leading efforts to develop one. It was a long process, taking almost two years of full-time work, but in the process of building a new strategy while continuing to prosecute the fight against IS, Secretary Carter changed the way the U.S. government approached the complex problem by becoming more careful about which groups it would support in the overall Syrian Civil War, how it managed its delicate relationship with Russia, and focusing its efforts on operations that would hit the core of Islamic State's ability to wage war—thereby resulting in its lasting defeat. While the Syrian Civil War occupied much of President Obama's time, he tried to keep the military's role as focused on the Islamic State fight as possible.

Secretary Carter oversaw the creation of a task force headed by a single commander, U.S. Army lieutenant general Sean MacFarland, with a single mission—destroy the Islamic State. For U.S forces, this meant assisting their main allies in the fight against IS in Syria, the primarily Kurdish Syrian Democratic Forces (SDF). The key battle for the United States and the SDF centered on Manbij northeast of Aleppo, where SDF captured key ground and killed key leaders of the Islamic State. This fight, known as the 2016 Manbij Offensive, also uncovered a lot of intelligence that would later be used to deal a series of decisive blows to the Islamic State in both Syria and Iraq, and was made possible largely by Secretary Carter's organization of U.S.-led efforts in its fight against Abu Bakr al-Baghdadi's dreams of establishing an Islamic caliphate in the Middle East.

Robert M. Kerr

Further Reading

Carter, Ashton B. "Ash Carter: Behind the Plan to Defeat ISIS." *The Atlantic*, October 31, 2017. https://www.theatlantic.com/international/archive/2017/10/isis-plan-defeat/544418.

Frantzman, Seth, J. *After ISIS: How Defeating the Caliphate Changed the Middle East Forever*. Gefen Publishing House, 2019.

United States Department of Defense. "Ashton B. Carter: Former Secretary of Defense." https://dod.defense.gov/About/Biographies/Biography-View/Article/602689/ashton-b-carter.

Chemical Weapons and Warfare

Chemical weapons use the toxic effects from man-made substances to kill or incapacitate enemy forces. Chemical weapons range from riot control agents such as tear gas and pepper spray, which cause short-term incapacitation, to lethal nerve agents such as tabun and sarin, which can kill humans with only a minuscule exposure. The use of living organisms, such as bacteria, viruses, or spores, is not classified as chemical warfare but rather is considered biological warfare. However, certain chemical weapons such as ricin and botulinum toxins use products created by living organisms.

Chemical weapons are typically described by the effects they have on victims. The major classes of chemical weapons are nerve agents, blood agents, vesicants, pulmonary agents, cytotoxic proteins, lachrymatory agents, and incapacitating agents. Nerve agents quickly break down neuron-transmitting synapses, resulting in the paralysis of major organs and quick death. Blood agents cause massive internal bleeding or prevent cells from using oxygen, leading to anaerobic respiration, seizures, and death. Vesicants, also known as blistering agents, burn skin and respiratory systems, either of which can be fatal. Pulmonary agents suffocate victims by flooding the respiratory system. Cytotoxic agents prevent protein synthesis, leading to the failure of one or more organs. Lachrymatory agents cause immediate eye irritation or blindness, although the effects are deliberately temporary. Incapacitating agents, also temporary, cause effects similar to drug intoxication.

Primitive chemical weapons were used as early as the Stone Age, when hunter-gatherer societies used poison-tipped weapons for hunting. Sources of poisons included animal venoms and vegetable toxins. Undoubtedly, poison-tipped weapons were also used in intertribal warfare. Ancient writings describe efforts to poison water systems to halt invading armies. Chinese texts from approximately 1000 BCE describe methods to create and disperse poisonous smoke in war. Ancient Spartan and Athenian armies both used chemical weapons by the fifth century BCE. The Roman Army, however, considered the use of poisons abhorrent, and Roman jurists condemned enemies for poisoning water supplies. With the dawn of the gunpowder era, besieging armies launched incendiary devices and poisonous projectiles into enemy fortifications. By the nineteenth century, inventors in Britain and the United States proposed the development of artillery shells containing toxic gases.

During World War I (1914–1918), more chemical weapons were used than during any other war in history. At the Second Battle of Ypres (April 22, 1915), German troops opened canisters of chlorine gas and waited for the wind to push the gas into Allied trenches. Soon both sides were using artillery shells to deliver chemical attacks, incorporating a wide variety of chemical agents.

During World War II (1939–1945), chemical weapons were used in a few isolated instances, although both the Axis and the Allies had developed large arsenals of extremely toxic agents. Both sides feared retaliation by the enemy, and neither chose to use its massive stockpiles of chemical weapons.

In the Middle East, the first modern large-scale use of lethal chemical agents occurred during the Iran-Iraq War (1980–1988). Early in the war, Iraq dropped bombs containing mustard agent and tabun on Iranian troops, causing 100,000 casualties including 20,000 deaths. Iraq accused Iran of having used chemical weapons first, but the allegations were never confirmed by United Nations (UN) investigators. Near the end of the war, the Iraqi government used chemical weapons against rebellious Kurdish Iraqi citizens.

During the Persian Gulf War (1991), Iraq was accused of launching Scud missiles with chemical warheads against Israel, although no traces of chemical weapons were found. Iraq did not strike the attacking coalition forces with chemical weapons. One possibility is that the Iraqis feared that the coalition would retaliate with its own chemical weapons or perhaps even tactical nuclear weapons. A more likely possibility, however, is that the Iraqis never had the planning and coordination time necessary to employ chemical weapons. Virtually every successful use of chemical weapons in the twentieth century was in an offensive operation, where the attacker had the initiative and necessary time to plan and tightly control the use of such weapons and their effects. Being on the defensive from the start, the Iraqis never had that flexibility.

There have been many attempts to prohibit the development and use of chemical weapons. In 1874, the Brussels Declaration outlawed the use of poison in warfare. The 1900 Hague Conference banned projectiles carrying poisonous gases, as did the Washington Arms Conference Treaty of 1922 and the Geneva Protocol of 1929. None of the prohibitions proved sufficient to eradicate chemical warfare, however. The most recent effort to eliminate chemical weapons was the multilateral Chemical Weapons Convention (CWC) of 1993. The CWC came into

effect in 1997 and prohibited the production and use of chemical weapons. Numerous nations known to maintain or suspected of maintaining chemical weapons stockpiles refused to sign or abide by the treaty, including several in the Middle East. Egypt, Libya, and Syria, all known to possess chemical weapons, refused to sign the CWC, although Libya acceded to the treaty in early 2004 and vowed to dismantle its chemical weapons program. Bashar al-Assad of Syria agreed to the treaty in 2013, but he has taken no substantive actions to eliminate is stockpile of chemical weapons.

In the spring of 2013, it is suspected, President Assad launched chemical weapons attacks against rebel positions near Aleppo (March) and in the town of Saraqeb (April), but the most famous attack was on the Damascus suburb of Ghouta in August. The sarin nerve agent attack on Ghouta sparked international outrage, but this did not deter Assad from using chemical weapons repeatedly throughout the conflict. Some of the more notable attacks occurred in Jobar and Ashrafiyat Sahnaya (August 2013), Talmenes (April 2014), Sarmin and Qmenas (March 2015), Uqairabat (December 2016), Khan Shaykhun (April 2017), and Douma (April 2018). The 2017 attack on Khan Shaykhun resulted in a direct response from U.S. president Donald Trump, who authorized air and missile strikes against the airbase from which the attack was launched, but even this use of military force did not deter Assad from using his chemical weapon stockpile again.

Paul J. Springer

Further Reading
Butler, Richard. *The Greatest Threat: Iraq, Weapons of Mass Destruction, and the Crisis of Global Security.* Perseus Books, 2001.

Morel, Benoit, and Kyle Olson. *Shadows and Substance: The Chemical Weapons Convention*. Westview, 1993.

Solomon, Brian. *Chemical and Biological Warfare*. H. W. Wilson, 1999.

Torr, James D. *Weapons of Mass Destruction: Opposing Viewpoints*. Greenhaven, 2005.

Christian Militias in Syria

While the Syrian Conflict involved mostly various Muslim groups, Syria is a multiethnic country; so it was perhaps inevitable that its various Christian groups were brought into the fight. Syria's various Syriac/Assyrian, Arab, and Armenian Christian communities each formed militia groups for various purposes, but most often for self-preservation. Some of these groups include Assyrians from neighboring countries (primarily Iraq), as well as Christians from Western countries interested in helping to protect Syria's Christian minorities.

Christianity in Syria is almost as old as Christianity itself. In fact, St. Paul, the writer of so many books and letters of the Christian Bible, himself famously became a follower of Jesus, quite literally, on the road to Damascus. Some Christians in Syria, the Chaldeans, even still speak Aramaic, which was the native language of Jesus. While Christians today make up only a small number of Syrians, their presence predates Islam by almost 600 years; and at one point, Christians were the majority of people in this part of the world.

Today only about 10 percent of Syrians are Christian, the smallest percentage of the area's population since the first century. Under the Ottomans, all monotheists, Zoroastrians, Jews, and Christians were allowed to freely practice their religions as long as they did not try to proselytize in order to convert new followers, and they paid the *jizyah* tax. Every Muslim had to pay the welfare tax mandated by Islamic law and practice, the *zakat*, which was typically about two and a half percent of one's income. Other tolerated religious groups were freely permitted to practice their religions, but they did have to pay the *jizyah*, which was typically 18 to 19 percent of one's income. The reason for this disparity was not necessarily discrimination, but practicality. The welfare tax was meant to be a welfare system that people could draw from during hard times; it was a way to provide for the poor. There was a mandate that Muslim money should be used primarily, though not exclusively, to help other Muslims, and since the majority of people were Muslim, it allowed the tax to be much lower (a basic principle of an economy of scale). The people who weren't Muslim were in the minority, and the Ottomans believed that each group within its empire should be self-sustaining, meaning that Zoroastrians, Jews, and Christians should have their own pots of money to provide for their own communities. The Ottoman government, especially in the empire's early years, believed that this money could not be used by the Muslim community, but since there were far fewer religious minorities, they had to pay more in order to cover their expenses (again, a basic economy of scale issue). Christians in Syria lived under this system until the end of the Ottoman Empire, and while they continued to practice their religion under the French Mandate and then in an independent Syria, life did get more and more restrictive for minorities who did not practice Islam. Many Syrian Christians left the country in the period following World War II, with many settling in the American city of Detroit, Michigan where they found manufacturing jobs with the "Big Three" auto companies, Ford, Chrysler, and General Motors.

Damascus was at one time the largest Christian city in the world, with St. Peter himself ministering to the city on numerous occasions. Most of Syria's Christians belong to branches of the Eastern Orthodox Church, and most live in cities; Damascus in particular still has a sizable Christian population, though Aleppo is another city historically important to Syrian Christians. Most of Syria's Christians live in cities and tend to congregate in neighborhoods populated by other Christians. Even after the civil war, many Christians remain in Syria.

The largest Christian militia in Syria is the Syriac Military Council. Known by its Syriac name Mawtbo Fulhoyo Suryoyo, or MFS, the Syriac Military Council is made up of Syriac/Assyrian Christians aligned with the Kurdish Peoples Protection Units (Kurdish YPG). By and large, Christian militias in Syria are aligned with either the Syrian government or, as is the case with the Syriac Military Council, Kurdish interests because they fear a Syrian state governed by groups loyal to al-Qaeda or the Islamic State. This means that Christians in Syria do not represent a single interest group as some support the Assad regime, while others actively rebel against it with their Kurdish allies.

MFS is the largest and most significant of the Christian militias in Syria. Aligned with the Kurds in Syria's northeastern province of Rojava, MFS has fought against both Syrian and Muslim insurgent groups with its most significant battles being against the al-Nusra Front. With just over 2,000 members, MFS is not extremely large, but does provide a significant boost to their Kurdish allies in a conflict where every fighter counts. Like their Kurdish allies, the Syriac Military Council encourages women to join the fight and even sponsors an all-female unit knows as the Bethnahrain Women's Protection Forces.

In addition to the Syriac Military Council, other Christian militias in the conflict include, or have included, an Armenian group called the Martyr Nubar Ozanyan Brigade, an Armenian nationalist movement aligned with the Kurds; a Syriac/Assyrian pro-government organization called the Gozarto Protection Force (not even all Syriac/Assyrian Christians are on the same side of the fight as this group's goals are contradictory to the MFS, but again centered on self-preservation and protection of the Christian community, in this case centered in the northeastern city of Saded, which has been repeatedly attacked by the Islamic State); the Guardians of Dawn, a pro-government coalition of Christians throughout southern Syria; and a group called Sotooro, another pro-government Syriac/Assyrian group in Rojava province that has clashed with MFS's Kurdish allies, among others.

The situation of Christian militias in Syria illustrates the complexity of the Syrian Conflict. It is impossible and unwise to try to understand the conflict in terms of ethnicity or religion it is clear that even the Christian communities in Syria are divided between those who support the Assad regime and those who work against it. The one commonality among all of these Christians, however, is the desire to protect their communities and ensure self-preservation; each group is willing to do that even if it means disagreeing with other Christians about what needs to be done. At the end of the day for all of these groups, surviving the conflict intact, and not desiring to spread any particular religious or political ideology, is what motivates them to pick up arms and form allegiances among the various parties.

Robert M. Kerr

Further Reading

Sharkey, Heather. *A History of Muslims, Christians, and Jews in the Middle East.* Cambridge University Press, 2017.

Tejirian, Eleanor, and Reeva Spector Simon. *Conflict, Conquest, and Conversion: Two Thousand Years of Christian Missions in the Middle East.* Columbia University Press, 2014.

Circassians

The Circassians are an ethnic group originating from the northern Caucasus region along the northeast shore of the Black Sea. They lived in their native homeland, Circassia, from ancient times until the Russian conquest of the Caucasus region in the nineteenth century. After the Russo-Circassian War of 1864, the majority of Circassians who survived were displaced, and the Circassian diaspora spread into modern-day Turkey, Jordan, Syria, Israel, Egypt, and even as far afield as Germany, the Netherlands, and the United States. The families of those who were forced to flee have never been allowed to return to their homeland, which has been Russified and completely integrated into the Russian nation; there are very few existing signs of Circassian culture or identity anywhere in the region. Today, nearly half of all Circassians live in Turkey in communities throughout the country. Sochi, the former Circassian capital, was the site of the 2014 Winter Olympic Games, and much controversy surrounded them. The Circassian diaspora community criticized the Russian government for holding the games in facilities built on the sites where large numbers of Circassians had been systematically murdered; this, coupled with the fact that the games were held during the 150th anniversary of the Circassian genocide, added insult to injury for the global community.

The native language of Circassia is Cherkess, related to other Caucasian languages. The Caucasus region is very mountainous, and therefore many distinct dialects of Cherkess emerged that are particular to a valley, town, or village. In reality, Cherkess is best understood as a group of dialects that are more or less similar in terms of syntax and grammar, but are largely distinct from one another. It is not uncommon to find two people who speak Cherkess have difficulty understanding one another. Since Circassia is located in a strategically advantageous area on the Black Sea, it saw wave after wave of invaders since at least the first century CE when the Bulgars from Central Asia conquered them. Later, Greek and Byzantine influence brought Christianity to the region, and while some Circassians retained their native religious practices, especially those who lived in the mountains away from the coast, the majority adopted Christianity and treated it as their national religion. Christian influence continued to grow in the early medieval period as Georgia became the dominant power along the east coast of the Black Sea, and Christianity remained dominant in Circassia until the seventeenth century when the Crimean Tatars, an ethnically Turkish group, and the Ottoman Empire expanded its influence in the Black Sea region; the Turks brought Islam with them into the area, and the Circassians adopted the new religion for a variety of reasons.

Today, the vast majority of Circassians are Sunni Muslims, and Islam has become a defining characteristic of Circassian culture. This is, in large part, due to the spread of Ottoman influence in the sixteenth century. The Circassian elites who, because they were traders, lived along the coast were seemingly more interested in trade and smooth relations with this large Islamic empire from the south than they were with maintaining their Christian religious practices. While the Ottoman Empire tolerated other monotheistic religions such as Zoroastrianism, Judaism, and Christianity, there were social and economic benefits to being Muslim. For example, every Muslim had to pay the welfare tax mandated by the religion, the *zakat*, which was typically about two and a half percent of one's income. Other tolerated religious groups were freely permitted to practice their religions (though they were not allowed to try to spread their religions by seeking converts), but they did have to pay an additional tax called the *jizyah*, which was typically 18 to 19 percent of one's income. The reason for this disparity was not necessarily discrimination but practicality. The welfare tax was meant to be a welfare system that people could draw from during hard times; it was a way to provide for the poor. There was a mandate that Muslim money should be used primarily, though not exclusively, to help other Muslims, and since the majority of people were Muslim it allowed the tax to be much lower (a basic principle of an economy of scale). The people who weren't Muslim were in the minority, and the Ottomans believed that each group within its empire should be self-sustaining, meaning that Zoroastrians, Jews, and Christians should have their own pots of money to provide for their own communities. The Ottoman government, especially in the empire's early years, believed that this money could not be used by the Muslim community, but since there were far fewer religious minorities, they had to pay more in order to cover their expenses (again, a basic economy of scale issue). In the case of the Circassian elites, they decided it was better to be part of the ingroup rather than the minority for both economic and

political concerns, and they adopted Islam as the new government religion.

Due to the mountainous geography of Circassia, Islam was accepted to varying degrees according to how much contact the people of any given valley had with their neighbors. Generally, Islam was initially an official state religion, but by the eighteenth century, more and more people came to follow the religion in a very real way. In part, people also saw Islam as a way to differentiate themselves from the Christian Russians who continually tried to assert their influence in the region. Circassia's historical relationship with Russians has always been strained. Because of the North Caucasus region's strategic importance and mineral wealth, Russians have always seen it as a vital part of Russian national prosperity. Even well before the Russo-Circassian War of 1864, Russians had made multiple attempts to assert their dominance by Russifying the region in order to quell resistance among the different ethnic groups there. This resistance lives on today in the form of the independence movement in Chechnya. In fact, the Chechen resistance is Vladimir Putin's top security concern within his own country; the drive of the Caucasian peoples to resist Russian influence runs deep throughout the region. In fact, it was a Chechen who was responsible for the spread of Islam throughout the northern Caucasus region, including Circassia.

Ushurma, a Chechen man from the area near Grozny, became the spiritual father of Caucasian resistance to Russian influence. He was a man who, in the minds of the people of the Caucasus, represented not only spiritual enlightenment, but also the rough and rugged independence of the region's mountain people. He not only was able to inspire the imaginations of the people as their spiritual leader; he also put together an army and declared war against the Russians, defeating them in 1785 along the Sunja River and pushing north to retake other Caucasian towns from the Russian army. He amassed an army of more than 20,000 Chechens, Circassians, and other mountain peoples and forever set the tone for all subsequent interactions between the Russians and the people of the mountainous peninsula along the Black Sea. It was this series of military setbacks that set the stage for the Russian army's push to claim dominance in the Caucasus, culminating, at least for the Circassians, in the Russo-Circassian War of 1864 that would have dire consequences for all subsequent generations of Circassians.

Diaspora communities are large groups of people who have been displaced, or have either moved due to some sort of push factor away from their homeland or have been drawn by some sort of pull factor to another location. The most obvious push factor driving people from their homes is war, such as in the case of large numbers of Vietnamese people leaving their homeland during the decades-long conflict in that country and settling in France, the United States, and elsewhere around the world—the Vietnamese diaspora is global, and its members commonly intermarry, maintain their language and religious traditions, and increasingly strengthen ties back to Vietnam now that the Vietnamese government and economy have become more favorable toward them, despite their families' resistance to the Communists in the 1950s, 1960s, and 1970s. Another famous diaspora community displaced by the push factor of war is the Palestinians who live in concentrated communities in Jordan and Lebanon, and dispersed throughout the rest of the world as a result of the

Arab-Israeli War in 1948. The other, less violent push factor driving diasporas actually functions as a pull factor as well, and that is economics. The early twenty-first century has seen a dramatic increase in the number of people leaving their homes in Central America and Mexico due, in large part, to the lack of jobs in their own counties. Drawn by the significant pull factor of the United States' economy, diaspora communities of Mexicans, Guatemalans, Salvadoreans, and others have settled in the United States; and like other diasporas throughout history, they each maintain their own customs, traditions, and ties with one another that form a strong sense of community for people within those groups. It is this tie to tradition, however, that makes diaspora communities unwelcome in many societies that are afraid of losing their own sense of identity in the wake of large numbers of foreigners moving to their countries.

The Circassian diaspora created by the Russo-Circassian War is more than 150 years old. However, the Russians were not the only ones who caused the mass movement of Circassians out of the region. Outside of the coastal areas, Circassia was a very poor place, and there was intense social stratification between the area's social classes. Many of the poorest and most disenfranchised lived in the mountains, and through a series of complex events, many of them were enslaved by the Ottomans and spread throughout the empire. This is, in part, why the majority of Circassians now live in Turkey. That said, the Russians not only drove out the majority of Circassians who remained in their homeland, they also effectively erased Circassia from the map itself. In some cases, such as in Egypt, the Circassians have been fully assimilated and have completely integrated into the culture of the country. In other cases, such as in Syria and Israel, they retained much of their culture.

It is estimated that the Circassian population of Syria before the civil war was about 100,000. It is believed that the Ottomans settled Circassians in Syria after the Russo-Circassian War because they needed a group of loyal subjects in Syria to balance out some of the anti-Ottoman sentiments spreading among the various ethnic groups throughout the Levant. Most of the Circassians settled in the area of the Golan Heights and near the Sea of Galilee. Other important settlements could be found in areas north of Homs and in Damascus. While most Circassians learned Arabic over time, they retained their own culture and customs and still speak their native dialects as their first language.

Part of the reason the Ottomans encouraged the Circassians to settle in the Golan Heights, an area renowned at the time for its lawlessness and conflict among Druze and Bedouin tribes, was the fact that as warriors hardened by battle with the Russians, the government in Istanbul felt they could exert some official power among notoriously disloyal subjects. One of the tribal customs the Ottoman sultan found most troublesome was the Bedouin tradition of extracting "protection money" from people throughout the region; much like an organized crime organization, the Bedouin demanded people pay them for "protection" or suffer the consequences. The Ottomans felt cheated by money lost to this system, and the Circassians were, in fact, able to stem the tide of money being diverted from Istanbul to the Bedouin and Druze tribesmen. After this initial period of conflict, however, the Circassians and the Arabs of Syria got along very well. Some Circassians who lived along the Jordan Valley fought for Israel in the Arab-Israeli War, and in 1967, many of the Circassians who lived in the Golan Heights either fled from the area or stayed in the area now occupied by Israel. Those who stayed have integrated fairly well into Israeli society; and while they retain their own culture and religion, they are the only Muslims in Israel whose children complete mandatory service in the Israeli Defense Force.

Circassians are on all sides of the Syrian Civil War that broke out in the wake of the 2011 Arab Spring. Some who have integrated more fully into Syrian society actually serve in Assad's government and in the military. Others have joined rebel groups in attempts to protect their towns and villages from either Syrian forces or various militia groups. Some have undoubtedly joined the ranks of Jabhat al-Nusra or the Islamic State—as is the case with many long-term diasporic groups, the Circassians have lived in Syria too long to represent a single, monolithic set of interests or values. Perhaps not surprising, however, are the large number of Circassians who have decided to leave Syria in the face of the country's implosion. Feeling no particular allegiance to Syria or Assad's Ba'ath Party, these Circassians have sought asylum in Turkey, where they feel they can easily integrate into that country's old Circassian communities. Others have fled to Jordan for similar reasons, where they can live with distant cousins. Interestingly, more than 1,000 Circassians have sought asylum in Russia.

The Circassian experience is one worth exploring because it indicates the complexity of the roots of the Syrian Conflict. As a country that was never dominated by a single ethnic group, Syria is a pastiche of hundreds of different peoples coming together over thousands of years to create a place that defies easy categorization. As a people driven from a now extinct homeland, the Circassians help us understand the multicultural and multilayered fabric of Syrian society, and the historical reasons why Russia,

Turkey, and other countries throughout the region are all interwoven geopolitically.

Robert M. Kerr

Further Reading

Chatty, Dawn. *Syria: The Making and Unmaking of a Refuge State*. Oxford University Press, 2018.

Henze, Paul B. "The North Caucasus: Russia's Long Struggle to Subdue the Circassians." RAND Corporation, 1990.

Jaimoukha, Amjad. *The Circassians*. Routledge, 2015.

Richmond, Walter. *The Circassian Genocide*. Rutgers University Press, 2013.

D

Dabiq (Magazine)

Dabiq was an online magazine written and disseminated by the Islamic State (IS) from 2014 through 2016. Published on the "dark web," the journal spread rapidly through Internet sources and reached a huge number of readers throughout not only the Middle East but the entire world. It served as an effective means for IS to not only disseminate its particular teachings, but to recruit others to its cause as well.

Named for a small town in northern Syria where IS members believe it was prophesied by Muhammad that the forces of Islam would defeat, once and for all, the armies of the Christian West, Dabiq was published 15 times and received praise in the West not for its content, but for its high production values. It was clear that IS had communication experts in its ranks, and this worried the West and IS's other enemies because it appealed to many young and vulnerable recruits from around the world. Part of what made *Dabiq* unique in the realm of militant jihadist literature was the fact it was published in multiple languages; again proving that IS took public relations and information operations very seriously.

While it is impossible to know how many people were recruited to the IS cause because of *Dabiq*, it is clear its publication was part of a very effective web-based recruiting strategy that brought thousands of recruits from all parts of the globe, including the West. Rather than calling people to violence, *Dabiq* attempted to legitimize the Islamic State as the new caliphate and published articles explaining IS's particular interpretation of Islam, which focuses heavily on the end-times. While *Dabiq* ceased production after Syrian militias defeated IS in the actual town of Dabiq in 2016, IS's online efforts did not stop. A new online publication, *Rumiyah* (*Rome*), began to be disseminated over the Internet in late 2016 and lasted until late 2017. The new e-publication's name was a reference to IS's interpretation of a *hadith* that is said to prophesy the defeat of Rome by a great Muslim army. Unlike *Dabiq*, the focus of *Rumiyah* was on encouraging readers to carry out specific attacks throughout the world. In October 2016, for example, *Rumiyah* encouraged readers to carry out knife attacks on targets of opportunity, and it is believed to have been the inspiration for stabbings in the United States, the United Kingdom, and Australia.

Robert M. Kerr

Further Reading

Welch, Tyler. "Theology, Heroism, Justice, and Fear: An Analysis of ISIS Propaganda Magazines Dabiq and Rumiyah." *Dynamics of Asymmetric Conflict: Pathways toward Terrorism and Genocide* 11(3) (2018): 186–98.

Dabiq (Place)

Dabiq is a small town in northern Syria with big implications for the territorial aspirations of the Islamic State (IS). Situated 30 miles or so northeast of Aleppo, Dabiq is a town of just over 3,000 people. It has no significant resources and no real strategic value, yet it is absolutely vital to the Islamic State's existence because of its significant symbolic value to the IS worldview.

According to the Islamic State's apocalyptic worldview, the Prophet Muhammad spoke of Dabiq as one of two places in which the forces of Islam would, once and for all, defeat the Christian West in an epic battle that would herald the end-times. Islam's authoritative text, the Quran is looked at by Muslims as God's indisputable word, and can therefore not be questioned theologically. However, Islam also looks to another collection of writings for guidance in certain matters: the *hadith*, or the sayings of the Prophet.

Because Muhammad's status as a prophet was well known and accepted by his contemporaries, they took it upon themselves to record as many of his sayings and actions as possible to capture the essence of what a man favored by God should say and how he should act. Through time, however, there has been much debate as to which sayings constitute a legitimate *hadith* and which ones do not. The problem is that outside of those that historians and theologians know were written at the time of Muhammad, it is difficult to know if some were added by people trying to pass off their own ideas as something the Prophet himself said or did. It is within those debated *hadith* that one finds references to the dusty town in northern Syria that now lies just south of the Turkish border—most Muslim religious leaders, while not necessarily rejecting the *hadith*, are generally open to the idea that it is not considered one of the essential sayings of the Prophet either. In part, this is because most Muslim religious scholars are generally uncomfortable with discussion of prophecies about the end-times and usually shy away from discussing the matter at all—at least those

Muslim scholars in the Sunni tradition. Shi'a Islam is much more comfortable with eschatological discussions, but the Islamic State is unique in that it is virtually obsessed with the idea of the end-times, but it is a Sunni movement.

According to the Islamic State's interpretation of the Prophet's *hadith* about Dabiq, a great war between the forces of Islam and those of the "Romans" (interpreted by them to mean the Christian West) will culminate on the plains of Syria at the town of Dabiq. It is important to note that a great battle had taken place at Dabiq, but it is not the one envisioned by IS. In that battle, which took place in 1516 CE, it was two Muslim armies that met, with the forces of the Ottoman Empire defeating those of the Mamluk Sultanate. The Islamic State is noticeably quiet on this historical fact and chooses instead to focus on the coming apocalypse that it believes it can play a key role in bringing about.

Dabiq is so important to the IS ideology and worldview that it named its online magazine after the town as a way to keep it at the forefront of its followers' minds. In 2016, however, IS lost Dabiq to Syrian militias backed by Turkey in a fight that was relatively quick and easy. Despite the town's symbolic importance, IS had decided its military assets could best be utilized elsewhere. No doubt Dabiq still represents the ultimate goal of IS's plans, but the group's main focus seems to have shifted away from Syria as it seeks to overcome its significant military setbacks.

Robert M. Kerr

Further Reading

BBC. "Dabiq: Why Is Syrian Town So Important for IS?" https://www.bbc.com/news/world-middle-east-30083303.

Samaan, Jean-Loup. "An End of Time Utopia: Understanding the Narrative of the Islamic

State." NATO Defense College Research Division, 2015.

Weiss, Michael, and Hassan Hassan. *ISIS: Inside the Army of Terror.* Regan Arts, 2015.

Wood, Graeme. "What ISIS Really Wants." *The Atlantic*, March 2015. https://www.theatlantic.com/magazine/archive/2015/03/what-isis-really-wants/384980.

Damascus

Located in southwestern Syria, Damascus is the capital of the modern state of Syria. It is the second-largest city after Aleppo, though it is believed that Damascus's population actually surpassed that of Aleppo during the bloodiest days of the civil war. Though titled the *Damashq* in Arabic, the city is known colloquially in Syria as al-Shām. Damascus is considered to be the oldest continuously inhabited city in the world, with evidence of settlement as far back as the second half of the seventh millennium BCE; pottery and stone tablets mentioning "Damaski" date back to the third millennium.

The first recorded reference to the existence of Damascus comes from the hieroglyphic tablets of Tell el-Amarna, where it is recorded as a conquest of Pharaoh Thutmose III in 1490 BCE. The Damascus region, along with most of Syria, became a battleground between the Hittites from the North and the Egyptians from the South circa 1260 BCE. The end of this conflict came in 1259 BCE with a signed treaty between Hattusili and Ramesses II that handed control of the Damascus area to Ramesses II. However, Damascus was only a peripheral part of the Egyptian lands.

While the existence of Damascus had been previously recorded in history, it was fairly obscure in terms of importance until the arrival of the Arameans (Semites from Mesopotamia) in the eleventh century BCE. Many of the incoming Aramean tribes gave up their nomadic lifestyle and instead formed sedentary Aramaic kingdoms. One such kingdom, Aram-Damascus, centered their capital in the city of Damascus, and those who settled in the city began calling the city *Dimashqu*. These new Aramaean kingdoms then formed a loose federation known as Aram-Zobah and made Damascus an outpost of their federation. While initially just a member city of Aram-Zobah, Damascus would soon rise to power under the leadership of Rezon the Syrian.

Rezon the Syrian was a claimant to the throne of Aram-Zobah, whose claim was denied, and he was forced to flee Aram-Zobah. However, he returned to Damascus in 965 BCE and conquered it. Upon conquering Damascus, he overthrew the city's tribal government, reestablished Aram-Damascus as an independent state, and named himself the ruler. Aram-Damascus then began pushing its borders further and further south. This brought it into conflict with the Kingdom of Israel, which was trying to expand its northern borders. The conflict between these two kingdoms persisted until Ben-Hadad II was captured by Israel after unsuccessfully besieging Samaria. In order to secure his release, he was forced to grant Israel trading rights in Damascus. This relationship later proved invaluable when the Neo-Assyrian Empire attempted to invade Syria as it laid the groundwork for the Levantine Coalition between Aram-Damascus and the Kingdom of Israel. While the coalition was successful in stopping the first Assyrian invasion, it collapsed before the second Assyrian invasion, thereby allowing the Assyrians to move into Syria and claim it as their own.

As of the eighth century BCE, Damascus was practically engulfed by the Assyrians and entered a dark age. Nonetheless, it remained the economic and cultural center of the Near East as well as the Aramean resistance. After a revolt in 727 BCE was put down, the Assyrians began a large-scale campaign of crushing all Aramean resistance to their rule. This led to Damascus becoming totally subjugated to Assyrian rule. It also led to stability for the city as well as greater benefits from the spice trade with Arabia. The Assyrians remained in control of Syria until 572 BCE, when it was completely conquered by the Neo-Babylonians; however, there was a marked decline in Assyrian authority as of 605 BCE. After the complete takeover of Syria by the Babylonians in 572 BCE, relatively little is known about Damascus until it was reconquered by Alexander the Great in 333 CE.

The conquest of Damascus by Alexander the Great brought it into the Hellenistic world for almost a thousand years. This led to the city being rebuilt in different architectural styles multiple times. It was first rebuilt in the Greek Hippodamian style by Demetrius III Philopator, and then later rebuilt into a Roman style after it was annexed by the Roman General Pompey in 64 BCE. The ownership of Damascus then began to rapidly shift between various groups until it became a key military outpost of the Byzantine Empire 369 CE. During that phase, the cultural differences between Constantinople and Damascus led to Damascus willingly opening its gates to the invading Muslim Army in 635 CE.

Damascus's first interaction with Islam came in 628 CE when Muhammad sent a letter to Haris bin Ghasanni, the king of Damascus. This letter essentially said that it was foolish to stand against Islam, and anyone who did would be crushed under the Muslims' heel; but if they willingly joined Islam, then Damascus would still be theirs to rule. In 635, the city of Damascus accepted this offer by letting the invading Muslim army in its gates. Fearing the loss of Damascus, their most prestigious city in the Near East, the Byzantines decided to wrest back control of it. Fielding a superior army in terms of size, the Byzantines advanced into southern Syria during the spring of 636 CE, causing the Muslim forces, under the command of Khalid ibn al-Walid, to withdraw from Damascus in order to prepare for renewed confrontation. The two armies met and fought a major battle in August along the Yarmouk River. This battle ended in a decisive victory for the Muslim forces, which solidified Muslim rule in Syria and Palestine.

While Muslims now controlled Damascus, the majority of the population was still mostly Christian. In order to prevent non-Muslims from gaining power in the city's government, Arabic—a language the Christian Armenians did not know—was declared the official language of the state. As such, the first Islamic governor of Damascus was Mu'awiya ibn Sufyan, founder of the Umayyad Dynasty and the father of the man who would be responsible for setting in motion the deep division between Sunni and Shi'a Muslims. Under the Umayyads, Damascus became the political capital of a burgeoning empire, and this change in status greatly benefited the city. As the capital of an empire, Damascus was the home of the Imperial Treasury, which brought great wealth to the city. In recognition of the city's importance, construction began on the Great Mosque of Damascus in 706 CE. Soon after the mosque was completed, however, its sponsor, Caliph Al-Walid died, and in 715 his successor moved the capital, and the importance of Damascus declined.

Under the Abbasid Caliphate (750–1258 CE), Damascus was eclipsed and subordinated by Baghdad, which was closer to the Abbasids' key economic centers. Within the first six months of Abbasid rule, revolts began erupting in Damascus as its citizens tried to adjust to the decline in their status. However, the rioters were disorganized, and they proved to be little more than a nuisance to the Abbasids. Despite their lack of importance, the last of the prominent members of the Umayyad Caliphate were executed, ostracized, or dismissed. Finally, the city's walls were torn down, reducing Damascus to a provincial town of little importance. It then generally disappeared from written records for the next century, with the only significant improvement to the city being the Abbasid-built treasury dome in the Umayyad mosque in 789.

Damascus once again became the capital of an independent state in the late eleventh century CE with the arrival of the Seljuq Turks. It was ruled by Abu Sa'id Taj ad-Dawla Tutush I in 1079 and succeeded by Abu Nasr Duqaq in 1095. By the end of the eleventh century, Damascus was in serious danger as a result of the European Crusades. While the city did manage to escape direct occupation, it was forced to endure numerous attacks and sieges. It also lost a substantial portion of its hinterlands to the invading Crusaders. While the loss was a blow to the city, the Crusades forced the reconstruction of Damascus's walls as well as the construction of a citadel in the northwest corner of the city. The Crusades also affected the architecture of the city, as homogeneous and self-reliant residential quarters emerged in this period. By the twelfth century, the city was divided into segregated communities, each neighborhood equipped with its own amenities, including a mosque, bath, public oven, independent water supply, and small markets. The Great Mosque and central market became the last bastion of civic unity.

A new era opened when Nūr al-Dīn ibn Zangī, a powerful Turkish emir (military commander), captured the city in 1154 and made it once again the capital of a strong kingdom as well as the base for the Muslim military struggle against the Crusaders for the next 150 years. Under Zangī's rule, Damascus developed into a major religious and educational center, with emirs competing to build madrasahs (religious colleges) and *qubbahs* (funerary domes) and to bestow them with generous *waqfs* (land held in trust and dedicated to religious or educational purposes) to support their teachers and students. Having been revived once again, Damascus flourished under a group of Kurdish Muslim rulers known as the Ayyubids until 1260 when the Mongols invaded Syria. Following the Mongol defeat at Ain Jalut and their subsequent withdrawal from Syria in 1260, Damascus became a provincial capital of the Mamluk Empire, who ruled from Egypt. Damascus contracted the Black Death between 1348 and 1349, which led to the death of roughly half of its citizens.

In 1400, Damascus was besieged by Timur, a Turco-Mongol conqueror. The Mamluk sultan dispatched forces from Cairo to break the siege of their regional capital. While the Mamluk forces did break the siege of Damascus, after their withdrawal Timur sacked the city. During the sacking, the Umayyad Mosque was burnt and many of Damascus's citizens were taken into slavery. A large percentage of the population was slaughtered and had their heads piled up in a field outside the northeast corner of the walls. There is currently a city square that bears the name *burj al-ru'us*, originally "the tower of heads." Despite being sacked, Damascus was rebuilt and continued to serve as a Mamluk provincial capital until 1516.

In early 1516, the Ottoman Turks started a campaign of conquest against the Mamluk sultanate. On September 21, the Mamluk governor of Damascus fled the city, and on October 2, Damascus was pronounced part of the Ottoman territories—it would remain so until the end of World War I in 1918. Under the Ottomans, Damascus again lost its political prominence, though it did remain an important center of trade.

Before and during World War I, Arab nationalism flourished in Damascus, which had become a center of anti-Ottoman agitation. Faiṣal, son of the grand *sharīf* of Mecca, made secret visits there to enlist support for the Arab Revolt begun by his father in 1916. In a countermove, Cemal Paşa, the Ottoman commander in chief, hanged 21 Arab nationalists on May 6, 1916, a day that is still commemorated as Martyrs' Day. The Ottomans, however, were defeated by the double-pronged attack of the British and Arab forces and evacuated the city in September 1918. An independent Syrian state was declared in 1919, with Damascus as its capital; Faysal was proclaimed king early in 1920.

The independence of the Kingdom of Syria was short-lived as during World War I, European powers secretly held negotiations to divide among themselves the provinces of the Ottoman Empire. Syria was forcibly placed under French Mandate, and Damascus fell to the army of General Henri Gouraud on July 25, 1920. Damascus resisted the French takeover until early 1927. In an attempt to curb the resistance, a new urban plan was immediately put in place that resulted in a modern residential cordon around the Old City, effectively separating it from al-Ghūṭah, where rebels regularly took refuge. French rule lasted until April 1946, when French troops finally left the country. Once again, Damascus was the capital of an independent Syria.

While now independent, the fragile Syrian Republic was ill-equipped to withstand the major political upheavals racking the region, especially the partition of Palestine in 1948 and the first of the Arab-Israeli wars, which followed almost immediately. A series of coups from 1949 to 1970 brought a varied array of leadership to power and the rumble of tanks to the streets. During Syria's short-lived union with Egypt as the United Arab Republic (1958–61), Damascus lost its title of capital to Cairo. In 1963, the Ba'ath Party came to power through a coup and embarked on an experiment of socialist reform. In 1970, Ḥafiz al-Assad, then the minister of defense, led an internal coup and established himself at the helm of the country for 30 years, to be succeeded on his death in 2000 by his son Bashar. As of 2019, Damascus continued to function as the capital of Syria as well as the headquarters of the Assad regime.

Life in Damascus during the height of the civil war was described as "surreal" by some of its residents. As the center of Assad's regime, there was less fighting in the city than in many other parts of the country, but battles between insurgents and government forces were common. Throughout it all, however, the government took great steps toward maintaining life in the capital as normal as possible. It was not uncommon for there to be a battle in the morning, and then people going out to experience night life among the smoldering rubble. One thing is certain, this ancient city has endured much over thousands of years, and it is not likely to be beaten anytime soon.

Payton M. Kerr

Further Reading

van Dam, Nikolaos. *The Struggle for Power in Syria: Politics and Society under Asad and the Ba'ath Party*. I. B. Tauris, 2011.

van Dam, Nikolaos. *Destroying a Nation: The Civil War in Syria*. I. B. Tauris, 2017.

Daraa Offensive

In the Spring of 2018, the Syrian Arab Army (SAA) and its allied militias launched an offensive to wipe out rebel forces in southern Syria. Centered in the Daraa Governorate, a region in southwestern Syria bordering Jordan and a small portion of the demarcation line with the Israeli-controlled Golan Heights, the offensive was designed to strike a decisive blow against both Islamic State (IS) and other anti-government forces who had made significant territorial gains in 2017. The more than two months of intense fighting left many dead, wounded, and displaced, and dealt both a strategic and symbolic blow to anti-government forces as the Syrian Arab Army was able to regain the territory, which saw a significant Russian presence established along Daraa's border with the Golan Heights.

The Syrian government placed a high priority on retaking Daraa for both strategic and symbolic reasons. Strategically, border regions are always important for any sovereign state to control in order to secure access to and from their country with neighboring territories. Daraa is a particularly sensitive region for its border with Jordan—the main road between Amman (Jordan's capital) and Syria's capital, Damascus, runs through the territory—but perhaps more important is its border with the Israeli-controlled Golan Heights. Fighting in this area since the Syrian Civil War began in 2011 always brought with it the very real possibility that Israel could be drawn into the fighting, a situation that no one in the international community wanted to happen. The symbolic reasons for the government's strong desire to retake Daraa were, for Bashar al-Assad's regime at least, even more significant, however, as it was in Daraa that protests against his government began in the wake of the Arab Spring in 2011.

Daraa was the first major city in Syria to see mass, anti-government protests in 2011. As part of the pro-democracy Arab Spring sweeping across North Africa and into parts of the Levant, the Arab Spring marked a moment in which people attempted to call out their despotic leaders and institute representative governments with varying degrees of success. There had been small acts of defiance against Assad's regime earlier, especially in the Kurdish area of northeastern Syria, but Daraa is where the first large-scale anti-government protests took place. Resulting from popular outcry against the way government forces treated, or more accurately, mistreated at least 15 teenagers who had been caught writing anti-government graffiti, the protests paved the way for Daraa to become a kind of spiritual heartland for the anti-Assad movement; and rebel militias such as Jabhat al-Nusra and the Free Syrian Army, among others, quickly identified Daraa as a strategic necessity from which to base their operations in southern Syria.

The Syrian government's response to the 2011 protests in Daraa was swift, brutal, and according to most international observers, disproportionate. It did not take long for people across the country to learn of the government's brutal response, and Daraa became a symbolic center of resistance for various groups all over Syria. The very name of the city, Daraa, became a rallying cry for Syrian activists and rebels in much the same way that people in North Africa viewed the name of Mohammad Bouazizi, the man who lit himself on fire in an act of sacrifice at the despotism of Tunisia's then president Zine el-Abedine Ben Ali, as the martyr of the Arab Spring; or even how early Texans in the

United States recalled the valor of those who fought on despite overwhelming odds at the Alamo.

After daily protests in the late spring of 2011, and in spite of repeated government crackdowns, the government intensified its efforts to put down opposition groups in Daraa. One of the biggest challenges for the Assad regime in Daraa is its demographic makeup. Predominantly Sunni Muslim, Daraa Province as a whole has a strong tribal presence that has always been skeptical of Ba'athist rule in Damascus, but generally supportive of Bashar al-Assad as they had, for a long time, seen him as a more just ruler than his father had been. This, of course, changed when the government cracked down so hard on them in fear of the Arab Spring spreading wholesale into Syria. Culturally more similar to their neighbors to the south, the people of Daraa have formed tight-knit social networks that leave little room for outsiders to exert control or influence. In normal times, however, the government in Damascus had been content to maintain a light presence in the region so long as the people did not impede the workings of government or the economy, especially along the important trade route between Damascus and Amman. When the protests broke out in 2011, however, the mix of tribal loyalty, skepticism and mistrust of the government, and a deeply ingrained independent streak paved the way for what would escalate into a violent clash between State and local interests. In April 2011, the Syrian Arab Army launched an all-out offensive in Daraa resulting in violence and mass arrests. Fighting continued with rebel groups making significant territorial gains throughout the province by 2015—international observers agree that only Russian support for Syrian forces slowed them down.

In February 2017, anti-government militias launched a series of coordinated attacks against Syrian Arab Army positions in Daraa City. Led primarily by forces representing Jabhat al-Nusra and the Free Syrian Army, the rebels needed to act quickly and decisively in order to capitalize on the gains they made in fighting against their rivals, the Islamic State, throughout the first few months of 2016. Because of Daraa's strategic and symbolic value, the city was coveted by all sides in the conflict, and before any rebel force could make a decisive move against the government forces holding out in the city, the bitter rivalries among the rebel groups themselves had to be sorted out. The two best-funded anti-government militias in the conflict were, at that time, Jabhat al-Nusra (the Nusra Front) and the Islamic State. Both organizations had slightly different reasons for wanting to control the city. As a predominantly Syrian-focused organization, Jabhat al-Nusra and its allied Syrian militias saw Daraa as a necessary prize in order to claim legitimacy as an organization of and for a new Syria. IS, on the other hand, saw the city primarily in terms of its strategic importance in creating its new, pan-Islamic caliphate and had little regard for preserving Syria as a political entity. For this reason, Jabhat al-Nusra was able to cobble together a coalition of groups that, while disagreeing on many issues, found common ground in the idea that IS was a "foreign" organization that didn't have the best interests of the future of Syria in mind.

Initially, the rebel offensive against the Syrian Arab Army found great success, in part due to the rebels' use of unconventional fighting techniques such as improvised explosive devices and car bombs aimed at Syrian army targets. The fighting that ensued throughout February and March 2017 was brutal, with success being measured by how many individual buildings were gained and lost by each side every day. Some attribute the early success of the rebel forces to the fact that the Syrian army was undermanned in Daraa; and when reinforcements arrived in March, the tide turned, with government forces making significant gains. Throughout the month of March, the Syrian army seized many buildings, but the rebels had strategically retreated from most of them in order to fortify the most vital areas of the city, from which they regrouped and went back on the offensive in April. The most intense fighting took place in the Manshiyah District of Daraa, with almost the entire area shifting from government to rebel control in just a few days. With the Syrian Arab Army up against the ropes, a cease-fire was brokered by Russia, Iran, and Turkey with the consent of the United States in early May, and Daraa was designated as a "De-escalation Zone," meaning that all hostilities needed to come to a halt for a six-month cooling-off period. The cease-fire lasted for approximately three weeks, but a stalemate prevented either side from making significant territorial gains.

After a year of relative stalemate, the reinforced Syrian army redoubled its efforts and launched an offensive to decisively defeat the anti-government militias. Prior to the offensive, Russia negotiated with the Israeli government to guarantee that no Iranian forces would be used during the assault, as the presence of Iranian troops so close to the Golan Heights would have all but guaranteed involvement by the Israeli Defense Forces—something all sides wanted to avoid. Additionally, the United States under President Donald Trump took a neutral stance, informing the rebel forces not to expect American military support. In June 2018, the Syrian government's offensive began with a coordinated effort between special forces, the Syrian Air Force, and government-backed militias in a well-planned operation to systematically retake key strategic areas throughout the city. The monthlong offensive was intense, with both human casualties and loss to cultural heritage sites such as the centuries-old Roman theater. By the end of July, rebel forces surrendered and the Syrian Arab Army reestablished military control over the entire province, including the border with Jordan and the main road to Damascus.

Robert M. Kerr

Further Reading

Abouzeid, Rania. *No Turning Back: Life, Loss, and Hope in Wartime Syria.* W. W. Norton, 2018.

Druze

The Druze are a people who adhere to set of religious practices and beliefs derived from Ismaili Islam. The name "Druze" is a misnomer, probably derived from the eleventh-century figure Nashtakin al-Darazi, regarded as the first Druze, or heretic. The Druze call themselves *muwahhidun*, or believers in monotheism (*tawhid*), a central principle of Islam, meaning unicity, or strict monotheism. They are also known as Ahl al-Tawhid and Bana Maruf. Historically, some other Muslims treated the Druze as an extremist sect or disclaimed their beliefs and even considered them heretics. The Druze number about 1 million people and are most numerous in Syria (400,000–500,000) and Lebanon (300,000–400,000). Smaller communities exist in Israel (60,000), the Golan Heights (15,000), Jordan (10,000–20,000), and elsewhere in the world (90,000).

The Druze are Arabs and tribal in origin. They are divided between the Qays and Yaman, or northern and southern traditional family rivalries. Their esoteric teachings were not revealed to all Druze, meaning that the common folk (*juhhal*) were excluded from some of the secrets of the faith possessed by the *uqqal*, or wise elders, although commoners may seek initiation into the sect's esoteric teachings. The Druze are an endogamous group, marrying within the faith, and no longer accept converts. The earliest *muwahhidun* were followers of the Fatimid caliph al-Hakim (966–1021), who developed into a reform movement under Hamza ibn Ali and others. The group proselytized and established a community in the Levant among 12 Arab Tanukhi tribes.

An intra-Druze war in 1711 spelled defeat for one faction, some of whom moved to the Hawran and Suwaida districts of Syria. Maronite Christians moved from northern Lebanon into some formerly Druze areas in Lebanon at this time.

The Druze religion is an offshoot of Ismaili Islam that developed in the tenth century. The Druze adhere to five articles of faith and seven acts of worship that correspond to the so-called Five Pillars of Islam. However, the esoteric interpretation of the acts of worship differs, or goes beyond the exoteric (outward) practice in Sunni Islam. The articles of faith include (1) *tawhid*, or unicity of God, and the idea that He has no opponents (Satan is not a separate force); (2) veneration (*taqdis*) of seven who preached a Message (including Abraham, Muhammad, and Muhammad ibn Ismail) and their divine Helpers as well as five luminaries, or key principles; (3) metempsychosis (*taqamus*), the rebirth of souls in a new body; (4) the need for initiation (*ta'aqul*), as faith should be pursued through reason; and (5) erudition or esoteric knowledge, known as *ma'rifa*.

In addition, the required acts of worship must include key principles that correspond to pillars of the Druze: speaking truth to attain unicity; supporting fellow believers with pure hearts; abandonment of old (polytheistic) ways and of sin; self-purification, or fleeing from evil nature and oppression; declaring the unity of God (true declaration of the *shahada* following esoteric understanding); being content and patient (*ridha*) with God's will as the expression of jihad; and submission to God's will.

The Druze believe in *taqamus*, a doctrine meaning transmigration of the soul after death, and in tolerance of other faiths, or races. Their esoteric teachings sparked other sects' suspicion of their beliefs. These suspicions were politically promoted at times, for example in ibn Taymiyya's fatwa against them when the Mamluk forces aimed to reconquer local dynasties cooperating with the Mongols.

The Druze abstain from alcohol, tobacco, and pork. The five-pointed, multicolor star of the Druze represents the five Luminaries referred to above, or five seminal principles: reason and intelligence; the universal soul; the word; historical precedence; and immanence (*al-tali'*, or the following).

The Druze in Lebanon—mainly found in Mount Lebanon, the Wadi Taym area, and Beirut—became involved in the Lebanese Civil War (1975–1991). Under the leadership of Kamal Jumblat, their participation in the Lebanese National Movement pitted them against establishment Christian forces. The Druze fought effectively against the Christian Maronite Phalangist militia. Since the end of the war, certain Druze and Maronites have reconciled. In Lebanon, Israel, and Syria, the Druze are officially recognized by the respective governments and maintain their own religiously based court system.

In Israel, the Druze live mainly in the Galilee and Carmel regions. The Druze of the Golan Heights suffered from expulsion from their villages or actual separation of territory. In all, the Druze have had about 80 percent of their former lands confiscated by Israel. The Israeli government treated the Druze more favorably than other Arabs as part of a policy aimed at dividing Arabs and creating loyalty to the state. The Druze routinely serve in the Israel Defense Forces (IDF) but nevertheless experience discrimination as non-Jews. In 2013, Israel began reaching out to the Druze of the Golan Heights, hoping that they would increase the pressure on Assad's regime and act as a buffer during the ongoing Syrian Civil War.

Sometimes the Israeli, Syrian, and Lebanese Druze communities have tried to support one another. When the IDF attempted to establish Christian domination in Lebanon over the Shuf area, Palestinian Druze vocally opposed this policy, which may have partially prompted Israeli withdrawal from the area. Some Druze officers have, in recent years, risen to general officer rank in the IDF.

In Syria, the Druze were leaders in the nationalist resistance to the French. Later, some were involved in a coup attempt against the Hafez al-Assad government and were subsequently treated poorly by the central government. Their region remains underdeveloped and poorly funded to this day. Nonetheless, some key Druze politicians were supporters of the Ba'ath Party. Since the start of the Syrian Civil War in 2011, Syria's Druze population has been split in its loyalties. Initially, a number of Druze supported Bashar al-Assad's government, but by 2012, more and more Druze were joining anti-government and opposition forces, if not in arms, at least in sympathy and moral support. In July 2018, the majority-Druze, government-held city of Sweida in south-western Syria was attacked by ISIS, resulting in hundreds of casualties. The city had remained largely unscathed in the previous years, and it appears the attacks met their desired effect of turning the Druze against the Assad regime as many Druze took to the streets to protest the government's inability to keep them safe.

Paul G. Pierpaoli Jr., Sherifa Zuhur, and Robert M. Kerr

Further Reading

Abu Izzeddin, Nejla M. *The Druzes: A New Study of Their History, Faith, and Society*. Brill, 1984 and 1993.

Betts, Robert Brenton. *The Druze*. Yale University Press, 1990.

Dana, Nissim. *The Druze in the Middle East*. Sussex Academic, 2003.

Reuters. "Syrian Druze Bury Dead as Anger over Islamic State Grows," July 26, 2018. https://www.reuters.com/article/us-mideast -crisis-syria-druze/syrian-druze-bury-dead -as-anger-over-islamic-state-attacks-grows -idUSKBN1KG359.

Swayd, Samy S. *The Druzes: An Annotated Bibliography*. ISES Publications, 1998.

E

Erdogan, Recep Tayyip

Recep Tayyip Erdogan served as prime minister of Turkey from 2003 until 2014, when he was elected president. Due to a previous conviction on charges of Islamic sedition, or trying to stir up religious hatred, the leader of the ruling Justice and Development Party (Adalet Ve Kalkinma Partisi—AKP) had originally been barred from taking office when the AKP won legislative elections in November 2002. However, he was eventually elected to the National Assembly in by-elections held in early March 2003, thus paving the way for his premiership.

Recep Tayyip Erdogan was born in 1954, the son of a coast guard worker for the city of Rize, located on Turkey's Black Sea coast. He spent his early years in Rize, but in 1967, when Erdogan was 13, his father moved the family to Istanbul in search of a better life. As a teenager, Erdogan sold food on the streets of Istanbul to earn spending money and attended a local Islamic school. He became interested in politics at a relatively young age, joining the youth group of the Welfare Party, an Islamic fundamentalist political party, at the age of 15.

After graduating from Istanbul's Marmara University with a degree in business, Erdogan embarked on his first career, that of a professional soccer player. Although he enjoyed playing soccer, his involvement with the Welfare Party grew deeper, and after a few years as a professional athlete his political career began to take shape.

In 1980, while working for the Istanbul transport authority, Erdogan had his first brush with the law. The military was in charge of the government following a bloodless coup that same year, and Erdogan's boss, a retired colonel, ordered him to shave his mustache due to military laws against facial hair. Erdogan refused and as a result was forced to leave his job. However, his refusal gained him notice within the Welfare Party, and he quickly began to move up the ranks.

In 1994, Erdogan was elected mayor of Istanbul. Often thought of as one of Turkey's most charismatic politicians, he earned the praise of his followers as well as some of his opponents. Despite their dissatisfaction with his ban on alcohol in Istanbul's cafes, many of Erdogan's secular critics admitted that he did do a good job of cleaning up the city. He also scored points from many people who felt that, unlike many of Turkey's politicians, Erdogan was fair and honest and not corrupted by power.

As he became well known as a politician, Erdogan's pro-Islamist leanings made him popular with devout Muslims who felt slighted by Turkey's secular government, but also brought him controversy and legal trouble. In 1998, he was convicted for inciting religious hatred after he read an Islamic poem aloud at a public function. Containing the lines "The mosques are our barracks, the domes our helmets, the minarets our bayonets, and the faithful our soldiers," the poetry reading earned him a 10-month jail sentence; however, he was released after having served only four months. That same year, the government banned the Welfare Party because officials felt that the party was undermining the government's secular policies.

When Erdogan was released from jail, he joined the reformist wing of the Virtue Party, the pro-Islamic party that had been founded on the ashes of the Welfare Party. Working alongside his friend and fellow Virtue Party member, Abdullah Gul, Erdogan worked to disavow the hard-line religious views of his past. When the Virtue Party was banned in 2001, Erdogan and Gul formed the AKP.

With promises that the AKP would not follow the same lines as the Islamic movement's radical past, Erdogan's new party received much press attention and many followers. In November 2002 legislative elections, the AKP won a surprise landslide victory, placing Erdogan at the forefront of national politics. However, due to his previous conviction barring him from holding a government office and the Constitution (1982)—which states that the prime minister must be chosen from among parliamentary deputies—Erdogan was not allowed to take office as prime minister. Gul took office instead, promising to step down once the law was changed to allow the AKP leader to become premier. In February 2003, the Turkish national electoral board ruled that Erdogan was able to stand in by-elections. On March 9, it was announced that he had secured enough votes to become a member of the National Assembly, and two days later Gul tendered his resignation, paving the way for Erdogan to take office.

While there was concern about the AKP's Islamic-based policy, Erdogan has focused on economic reform and Turkey's entrance into the European Union. Throughout his tenure, Turkey's economy not only weathered the recession but has grown, contributing to the reelection of the AKP and Erdogan, in 2007 and 2011. In 2011, Erdogan became the country's first prime minister to win a third term. Despite protests in 2013 over the AKP's Islamist influence in the government, Erdogan was elected president by popular vote in August 2014.

Since becoming president, Erdogan has steadily increased his power. In May 2016, Binali Yildirim, a close ally of his, was installed as prime minister. Shortly thereafter, in July 2016, military forces attempted a coup d'etat to remove Erdogan from office and "restore constitutional order." Following the attempt, Erdogan declared a three-month state of emergency, which has since been extended. Ninety-nine top military officers were arrested, and about 100,000 state employees, including university and school employees, judges, and police, were fired or suspended from work. The government has also restricted Internet access and amended the constitution to give the president greater power. In late 2016, the European Parliament, alarmed by these developments, suspended Turkey's bid for European Union membership.

In April 2017, a public referendum gave Erdogan even more power. Eighty-five percent of the electorate voted in the referendum, with just more than half of those voting in support of increasing presidential powers. As a result of the referendum, the position of prime minister will be eliminated, leaving the president as head of government. The president will have the authority to select high public officials and intervene in the judiciary. International observers criticized the election as unfair, while Erdogan stated, "In the past it was the parliament who actually decided whether to make any constitutional changes but today, for the first time, the will of the people has shown through this referendum. . . . We would like other countries and institutions to show respect to the decision of the nation."

Erdogan has been outspoken in his dislike for the Assad regime. However, his relationship to the Syrian regime has been complicated by his deteriorating relationship with the United States, particularly after the failed coup against his government in 2016—a coup in which he suspects the Americans played a key role. Since the coup attempt, Erdogan has attempted to improve relations with Vladimir Putin, and because of Russia's support of the Assad regime, Turkey's stance on Syria has softened somewhat, particularly on the issue of working with the international community in removing Syrian refugees from Turkey. Erdogan is still not a supporter of Assad, but time will tell whether this relationship changes significantly if U.S.-Turkish relations do not improve.

Tamar Burris and Robert M. Kerr

Further Reading

Council on Foreign Relations. "What Erdogan's Victory Means for Turkey, the Kurds, and Syria," June 29, 2018. https://www.cfr.org/blog/what-erdogans-victory-means-turkey-kurds-and-syria.

Justice and Development Party. http://www.akparti.org.tr.

F

Free Syrian Army

The Free Syrian Army (FSA) is an armed opposition group formed in July 2011 by Syrian Army defectors based in Turkey and led by Colonel Riad al-Asad. The size and structure of the FSA evolved over time, as dozens of disparate groups claimed to fight on behalf of it. The group's original members were among the first fighters to engage regime forces in the Syrian Civil War. The Free Syrian Army became an umbrella organization for dozens of relatively moderate opposition groups fighting against the Assad regime and ISIS, but its influence steadily declined relative to other armed groups operating in Syria.

The FSA organized in response to the Syrian regime's brutal treatment of peaceful protestors beginning in March 2011. In a video clip released on July 29, 2011, the FSA issued a call to arms for Syrian Army soldiers to abandon their posts and join with the Syrian people to overthrow the Assad regime. In late September 2011, defectors from the Free Officer Movement joined the FSA, and several other militias began to fight under the FSA banner. Videos of soldiers in uniform declaring allegiance to the FSA in front of the three-starred "Istiqlal" flag were posted on YouTube throughout 2011. The FSA flag, used by Syria prior to Ba'athist control, remained a unifying artifact for moderate anti-regime forces.

The FSA's rapid growth and inability to manage the *katibas* (militias) that claimed to be a part of the FSA challenged its legitimacy. Rather than a coordinated effort directed against the Assad regime, the FSA was a loose confederation of localized militias. In some cases, *katibas* were local criminal gangs motivated by the financial benefits of a weakened Syrian state rather than the pursuit of liberty and justice; or local strongmen who seized the opportunity to strengthen personal power with little interest in effecting change across the country. In other instances, localized groups had the will but lacked the capacity to challenge the regime and grew frustrated with the FSA's inability to secure weapons and external funding. The need to coordinate activities among various FSA affiliates across the country led to the formation of regional councils in March 2012, under the name Higher Military Council.

The FSA had mixed success in 2011–2012. The rebel forces acquired more weapons in early 2012 through the capture of Syrian military bases. Its insurgent strategy focused on some rural areas of Syria, where the regime was less popular and had less control over military installations, with the belief that momentum could spark a wider uprising. This strategy required the regime to spread its forces across the country and left it vulnerable when the Free Syrian Army pivoted toward populated cities. Throughout 2012, the FSA claimed responsibility for several high-profile bombings that killed Syrian regime officials and members of Hezbollah. The various factions fighting under the FSA struggled to maintain a strategy as it conducted major operations around Damascus and Aleppo, where the regime had a base of support. FSA gains in 2012 were halted in July when some factions launched an uncoordinated attack in Aleppo that resulted in regime forces and rebels from the FSA, Kurdish YPD militia, and various Islamic militias vying for control of the city.

To better unite affiliated opposition groups, the FSA created a political affairs arm in November 2012 called the National Coalition for Syrian Revolutionary and Opposition Forces (SOC). The formation of SOC was followed by the organization of a 30-member council, the Supreme Military Command (SMC), to gain better command and control in military operations. Colonel Riad al-Asad remained the figurehead of FSA, but Selim Indriss, a former Syrian Army general, became chief of staff of the FSA-SMC. The FSA-SMC designated five geographic fronts with command structures to better coordinate resources and actions through General Indriss. The founding FSA-SMC meeting in Antalya, Turkey, also marked an increase in foreign intervention from Turkey, Jordan, Saudi Arabia, Qatar, as well as the United States, the United Kingdom, and France. The creation of the FSA-SMA triggered a splintering of some groups in early 2013. Prominent Islamist rebel groups such as Ahrar al-Sham, angered that they were not invited to participate in the FSA-SMA, convinced some of its members to align with a new Islamist umbrella organization, Islamic Front, in late 2013. This division and competition caused an overall decline in the Free Syrian Army as it struggled to recruit and retain members in 2013–2014.

The ineffectiveness of Syrian and ISIS opposition prompted a decentralization of the Free Syrian Army to localized groupings focused on anti-ISIS operations. Dozens of factions unified under four separate groups by mid-February 2014: Syrian Revolutionaries Front, Jaish al-Mujahideen, Harakat Hazm, and Southern Front. The centralized FSA-SMA, marred by infighting and changes in leadership, dissolved through this process. Between January and March 2014, groups claiming affiliation with the Free Syrian Army cooperated with a range of other rebel groups, including ISIS rival and al-Qaeda–linked group Jabhat al-Nusra, in an offensive that pushed ISIS from four provinces in Syria. The diffusion of the FSA in 2014–2016 and synchronization with jihadist groups complicated Western support. Periodic tensions with rebel groups and attacks from Iran and Russia challenged the splinter organizations of the FSA, but they remained formidable opponents of the regime and ISIS. Since 2016, a group known as the Turkish-backed Free Syrian Army has operated alongside the Turkish military to counter ISIS and the Kurdish People's Protection Units (YPG), which indicates a change in priorities for those fighting as the Free Syrian Army.

Melia Pfannenstiel

Further Reading

Gall, Carlotta, and Anne Barnard. "Syrian Rebels, Backed by Turkey, Seize Control of Afrin." *New York Times*, March 18, 2018. https://www.nytimes.com/2018/03/18/world/middleeast/afrin-turkey-syria.html.

Hokayem, Emile. *Syria's Uprising and the Fracturing of the Levant*. Routledge, 2013.

Lister, Charles R. "The Free Syrian Army: A Decentralized Insurgent Brand." Brookings Institution, Analysis Paper 26, November 2016: 1–44. https://www.brookings.edu/research/the-free-syrian-army-a-decentralized-insurgent-brand/.

Lister, Charles R. *The Syrian Jihad: Al Qaeda, the Islamic State and the Evolution of an Insurgency*. Oxford University Press, 2015.

Phillips, Christopher. *The Battle for Syria: International Rivalry in the New Middle East*. Yale University Press, 2016.

G

Golan Heights

The Golan Heights is an occupied territory of northern Israel captured from Syria during the 1967 Six-Day War. It is an area of great strategic importance for Israel, being within easy striking distance from Damascus, the Syrian capital. It also allows Israel greater control over Hezbollah activity in southern Lebanon. Syria insists on the return of the Golan Heights as a condition for normalizing relations with Israel, and bilateral peace talks on the highly volatile issue have thus far been unsuccessful. Lebanon claims a small portion of the Heights, known as the Shebaa Farms, as part of its territory, a claim that Syria acknowledges.

Following World War I, the Golan Heights was included in the French Mandate of Syria, although in 1924 a small portion of the Heights was designated as part of the British Mandate of Palestine. When Syria became independent in 1944, it gained control of the Golan, which was known within the country as the Syrian Heights. A plateau overlooking the Jordan River Valley and part of an ancient volcanic field, the Heights became a strategically important part of Syria due in part to its water resources, a valuable and often rare commodity in the Middle East.

During 1944–1967, Syria maintained control of the Heights. Following the Israeli War of Independence in 1948, Syria used the area as a launching ground for attacks against Israeli farming settlements. These actions, along with Israel's retaliation, were in violation of the Israel-Syrian Armistice Agreement that was established to end the war. Tensions between the two sides increased, and during the 1967 Six-Day War, Israel successfully captured the Golan on June 9–10. At this time, approximately 90 percent of the population (mostly Druze Syrians and Circassians) fled the area and have not been permitted to return. Israel immediately began building Jewish settlements in the Golan, with the first settlement town of Merom Golan being established in July.

Syria refused to make peace with Israel unless the Heights were returned, and Israel continued building settlements in the area, with 12 Jewish towns set up by 1970. Tensions culminated in 1973 with a surprise attack on Israel by Egypt and Syria that started a war. Despite having to fight a war on two fronts (the Sinai Peninsula and the Golan Heights) and being severely outnumbered (180 Israeli tanks faced 1,400 Syrian tanks), Israel was able to turn the tide of the war on October 8, putting the Syrians on the defensive and securing an Israeli victory. After Israeli forces pushed the Syrians back to the 1967 border, they continued to march into Syria proper, coming within 25 miles of Damascus before a combined force of Jordanians, Iraqis, and Syrians forced the Israelis to withdraw. At the end of the war, more than 1,000 United Nations (UN) peacekeeping troops were stationed in the Golan, and the armed conflict between the Syrian and Israeli armies came to an end.

The Golan Heights remained under Israeli military administration until 1981, when legislation was passed subjecting the area to

Israeli law and granting citizenship privileges to people living within the Heights. Although Israel did not use the word "annexation" within the legislation, much of the international community saw the move as such. The UN responded to the move with Security Resolution 497, which said that "the Israeli decision to impose its laws, jurisdiction and administration in the occupied Syrian Golan Heights is null and void and without international legal effect." However, the UN also avoided calling the move an annexation.

Possession of the Golan Heights remains central to the crisis in the Middle East, and Syria has repeatedly refused to normalize relations with the Jewish state until its return. Syria demands a withdrawal of Israel to the 1948 armistice line, which extends Syrian territory to the shores of the Sea of Galilee. Syria claims that its demands are in keeping with UN Security Council Resolution 242 and Resolution 338, which call for Israel to withdraw from the territories it occupied during the 1967 war. In 1999–2000 peace negotiations, Israel proposed returning most of the Golan to Syria; however, Syria refused on the grounds that this would not be a complete fulfillment of UN resolutions.

As of July 2014, about 19,000 Jewish settlers inhabited 32 settlements and nine other civilian use sites in the Golan. Due to the large-scale migration that occurred during the 1967 war, there are about as many Druze residents of the Golan as there are Jews. Israel has maintained that the Golan Heights is a strategically important buffer between Israel and Syria that is essential for security. Israel has refused to enter into direct peace negotiations with Syria (previous talks were brokered by the United States) unless the Arab state puts an end to Hezbollah attacks launched from Syria. Since the beginning of the Syrian Civil War in early 2011, Israel has viewed control of the Golan Heights as being more important than ever; indeed, it now sees the region as a bulwark against rebel activity and Islamic extremism occurring within Syria.

Jessica Britt

Further Reading

Asher, Jerry, and Eric Hammel. *Duel for the Golan: The 100-Hour Battle That Saved Israel*. Pacifica Press, 1987.

Dunstan, Simon. *The Yom Kippur War 1973: The Golan Heights*. Osprey Publishing, 2003.

Lerman, Hallie. *Crying for Imma: Battling for the Soul on the Golan Heights*. Night Vision Press, 1998.

Mo'az, Moshe. *Syria and Israel: From War to Peacemaking*. Oxford University Press, 1995.

Rabil, Robert G. *Embattled Neighbors: Syria, Israel, Lebanon*. Lynne Rienner Publishers, 2003.

H

Hezbollah

Hezbollah is a Lebanese Shia Islamist organization. Founded in Lebanon in 1984, it is a major political force in that country and, along with the Amal movement, a principal political party representing the Shia community there. There have been other, smaller parties by the name of Hezbollah in eastern Saudi Arabia and Iraq, and their activities have been mistakenly or deliberately associated with the Lebanese party. The Lebanese Hezbollah also operates a number of social service programs, schools, hospitals, clinics, and housing assistance programs to Lebanese Shiites. (Some Christians also attended Hezbollah's schools and ran on their electoral lists.)

One of the core founding groups of Hezbollah, meaning the "Party of God," actually fled from Iraq when Saddam Hussein cracked down on the Shia Islamic movement in Karbala and Najaf, the shrine cities. Lebanese as well as Iranians and Iraqis studied in Najaf and Karbala, and some 100 of these students returned to Beirut and became disciples of Sayyid Muhammad Husayn Fadlallah, a Lebanese cleric who was also educated in Najaf.

Meanwhile, in the midst of the ongoing civil war in Lebanon, a Shia resistance movement developed in response to Israel's invasion in 1982. Israel's first invasion of southern Lebanon had occurred in 1978, but the invasion of 1982 was more devastating to the region, with huge numbers of casualties and prisoners taken and peasants displaced.

The earliest political movement of Lebanese Shia was established under the cleric Musa al-Sadr and known as the Movement of the Dispossessed. The Shia were the largest but poorest sect in Lebanon and suffered from discrimination, underrepresentation, and a dearth of government programs or services that, despite some efforts by President Fuad Shihab, persist to this day. After al-Sadr's disappearance on a trip to Libya, his nonmilitaristic movement was subsumed by the Amal Party, which had a military wing and fought in the civil war. However, a wing of Amal, Islamic Amal led by Husayn al-Musawi, split off after it accused Amal of not resisting the Israeli invasion.

On the grounds of resistance to Israel (and its Lebanese proxies), Islamic Amal made contact with Iran's ambassador to Damascus, Akbar Muhtashimi, who had once found refuge as an Iranian dissident in the Palestinian camps in Lebanon. Iran sent between 1,000 and 1,200 Revolutionary Guards to the Bekáa Valley to aid an Islamic resistance to Israel. At a Lebanese Army barracks near Baalbek, the Revolutionary Guards began training Shia fighters identifying with the resistance, or Islamic Amal.

Fadlallah's followers now included displaced Beiruti Shia and displaced southerners, and some coordination between his group and the others began to emerge in 1984. The other strand of Hezbollah came from the Islamic Resistance in southern Lebanon led by Sheikh Raghib Harb, the imam of the village of Jibshit who was killed by the Israelis in 1984. In February 1985, Harb's supporters met and announced the formation of Hezbollah, led by Sheikh Subhi Tufayli.

Another militant Shia group was the Organization of the Islamic Jihad, led by Imad Mughniya. It was responsible for the 1983 bombings of the U.S. and French peacekeeping forces' barracks and the U.S. embassy and its annex in Beirut. This group received some support from the elements in Baalbek. Hezbollah, however, is to this day accused of bombings committed by Mughniya's group. While it had not yet officially formed, the degree of coordination or sympathy between the various militant groups operative in 1982 can only be ascertained on the level of individuals. Hezbollah stated officially that it did not commit the bombing of U.S. and French forces, but it also did not condemn those who did. Regardless, Hezbollah's continuing resistance in the south earned it great popularity with the Lebanese, whose army had split and had failed to defend the country against the Israelis.

With the Taif Agreement, the Lebanese Civil War should have ended, but in 1990 fighting broke out, and the next year Syria mounted a major campaign in Lebanon. The Taif Agreement did not end sectarianism or solve the problem of Muslim underrepresentation in government. Militias other than Hezbollah disbanded, but because the Lebanese government did not assent to the Israeli occupation of southern Lebanon, Hezbollah's militia remained in being.

The leadership of Hezbollah changed over time and adapted to Lebanon's realities. The multiplicity of sects in Lebanon meant that an Islamic republic there was impractical, and as a result Hezbollah ceased trying to impose the strictest Islamic rules and focused more on gaining the trust of the Lebanese community. The party's Shura Council was made up of seven clerics until 1989, from 1989 to 1991 it included three laypersons and

four clerics, and since 2001 it has been entirely composed of clerics. An advisory Politburo has from 11 to 14 members. Secretary-General Abbas Musawi took over from Tufayli in 1991. Soon after the Israelis assassinated Musawi, Hassan Nasrallah, who had studied in Najaf and briefly in Qum, took over as secretary-general.

In 1985, as a consequence of armed resistance in southern Lebanon, Israel withdrew into the so-called security zone. Just as resistance from Hezbollah provided Israel with the ready excuse to attack Lebanon, Israel's continued presence in the south fueled Lebanese resentment of Israel and support for Hezbollah's armed actions. In 1996, the Israelis mounted Operation Grapes of Wrath against Hezbollah in south Lebanon, pounding the entire region from the air for a two-week period.

Subhi Tufayli, the former Hezbollah secretary-general, opposed the party's decision to participate in the elections of 1992 and 1996. He launched the Revolt of the Hungry, demanding food and jobs for the impoverished people of the upper Bekáa, and was expelled from Hezbollah. He then began armed resistance, and the Lebanese Army was called in to defeat his faction.

In May 2000, after suffering repeated attacks and numerous casualties, Israel withdrew its forces from southern Lebanon, a move that was widely interpreted as a victory for Hezbollah and boosted its popularity hugely in Lebanon and throughout the Arab world. Hezbollah disarmed in some areas of the country but refused to do so in the border area because it contests the Jewish state's control of the Shaba Farms region.

Sheikh Fadlallah survived an assassination attempt in 1985 allegedly arranged by the United States. He illustrates Lebanonization of the Shia Islamist movement. He had moved away from Ayatollah Khomeini's doctrine of government by cleric (*wilaya al-faqih*), believing that it is not suitable in the Lebanese context, and called for dialogue with Christians. Fadlallah's stance is similar to that of Ayatollah Sistani in Iraq. He, like some of the Iraqi clerics, called for the restoration of Friday communal prayer for the Shia. He has also issued numerous reforming views, for example, decrying the abuse of women by men. Fadlallah is not, however, closely associated with Hezbollah's day-to-day policies.

Some Israeli and American sources charge that Iran directly conducts the affairs of Hezbollah and provides it with essential funding. While at one time Iranian support was crucial to Hezbollah, the Revolutionary Guards were withdrawn from Lebanon for some time. The party's social and charitable services claimed independence in the late 1990s. They are supported by a volunteer service, provided by medical personnel and other professionals, and by local and external donations. Iran has certainly provided weapons to Hezbollah. Some, apparently through the Iran-Contra deal, found their way to Lebanon, and Syria has also provided freedom of movement across its common border with Lebanon as well as supply routes for weapons.

Since 2000, Hezbollah has disputed Israeli control over the Shaba Farms area, which Israel claims belongs to Syria but Syria says belongs to Lebanon. Meanwhile, pressure began to build against Syrian influence in Lebanon with the constitutional amendment to allow Émile Lahoud (a Christian and pro-Syrian) an additional term. Assassinations of anti-Syrian, mainly Christian, figures had also periodically occurred. The turning point was the assassination of Prime Minister Rafik Hariri in February 2005. This led to significant international pressure on Syria to withdraw from Lebanon, although pro-Syrian elements remained throughout the country.

Hezbollah now found itself threatened by a new coalition of Christians and Hariri-supporting Sunnis who sought to deny its aim of greater power for the Shia in government. The two sides in this struggle were known as the March 14th Alliance, for the date of a large anti-Syrian rally, and the March 8th Alliance, for a prior and even larger rally consisting of Hezbollah and anti-Syrian Christian general Michel Aoun. These factions have been sparring since 2005 and in some ways since the civil war.

Demanding a response to the Israeli campaign against Gaza in the early summer of 2006, Hezbollah forces killed three Israeli soldiers and kidnapped two others, planning to hold them for a prisoner exchange as has occurred in the past. The Israel Defense Forces (IDF) responded with a massive campaign of air strikes throughout Lebanon, and not just on Hezbollah positions. Hezbollah responded by launching missiles into Israel, forcing much of that country's northern population into shelters. In this open warfare, the United States backed Israel. At the conflict's end, Sheikh Nasrallah's popularity surged in Lebanon and in the Arab world, and even members of the March 14th Alliance were furious over the destruction of the fragile peace in post–civil war Lebanon. Hezbollah offered cash assistance to the people of southern Lebanon displaced by the fighting and those in the southern districts of Beirut who had been struck there by the Israelis. They disbursed this aid immediately. The government offered assistance to other Lebanese, but this assistance was delayed.

In September 2006, Hezbollah and its ally Aoun began calling for a new national unity government. The existing government, dominated by the March 14th Alliance forces, refused to budge, however. Five Shia members and one Christian member of the Lebanese cabinet also resigned in response to disagreements over the proposed tribunal to investigate Syrian culpability in the Hariri assassination. At the same time, Hezbollah and Aoun argued for the ability of a sizable opposition group in the cabinet to veto government decisions. Hezbollah and Aoun called for public protests, which began as gigantic sit-ins and demonstrations in the downtown district of Beirut in December 2006. There was one violent clash in December and another in January 2007 between the supporters of the two March alliances. Meanwhile, the United Nations Interim Force in Lebanon (UNIFIL) has taken up position in southern Lebanon. Its mission, however, is not to disarm Hezbollah but only to prevent armed clashes between it and Israel. In 2008, when a unity government took hold in Lebanon, Hezbollah and its allies captured 11 of 30 cabinet seats, giving the coalition the power to veto.

Hezbollah and the Syrian Conflict

Beginning in 2012, amid the ongoing Syrian Civil War, Hezbollah decided to aid Bashar al-Assad's government in its fight against anti-government rebels. This support was, in part, a sign of the long-standing cooperation between Hezbollah and the Assad regime, with Hezbollah enjoying the protection of the Syrian government in terms of arms procurement and storage. Hezbollah is not necessarily single-minded in terms of its support of Assad exclusively, however, as it is in their best interest to retain access to Syria as a safe haven, weapons market and cache, and line of supply between itself and its Iranian sponsors. As a result of their involvement in Syria, however, they have suffered multiple Israeli air strikes against supply convoys; the convoys included antiaircraft

missiles. Hezbollah's involvement in the Syrian Civil War has raised concerns that the conflict might further destabilize Lebanon and the surrounding region.

Harry R. Hueston II and Sherifa Zuhur

Further Reading

Byman, Daniel. "Should Hezbollah Be Next?" *Foreign Affairs*, November–December 2003: 54–66. https://www.foreignaffairs.com/articles/lebanon/2003-11-01/should-hezbollah-be-next.

Council on Foreign Relations. "The Hezbollah Connection in Syria and Iran," February 15, 2013. https://www.cfr.org/interview/hezbollah-connection-syria-and-iran.

Macleod, Scott. "Hizballah's Herald." *Time*, February 2005.

Ranstorp, Magnus. *Hizb'allah in Lebanon: The Politics of the Western Hostage Crisis.* St. Martin's, 1997.

UPI. "Hezbollah for Arab Probe of Hariri Slaying," March 17, 2005. https://www.upi.com/Top_News/2005/03/17/Hezbollah-for-Arab-probe-of-Hariri-slaying/36181111057430/?ur3=1.

Homs

The ancient city of Homs, once the capital of a kingdom run by priest-kings called the Emesenes who worshipped the sun god Elagabalus and who pledged their allegiance to the Roman Empire, was reduced to little more than a collection of smoldering piles of rubble in the wake of the Syrian Civil War. Once dubbed "the Capital of the Revolution" by hopeful dissidents in the early stages of the conflict, Homs would see some of the Syrian Civil War's most intense fighting in the three years following the city's initial protests against the Assad regime in 2011. Even after the major fighting came to a conclusion in 2014, life in the city is hard and much of it lies in ruin. As of 2017 it is reported that there are almost 800,000 people in Homs, but many live in rudimentary conditions in buildings that are crumbling.

Homs occupies a geographically significant position in the Orontes River Valley, an important agricultural region that lies in the only natural gap in the mountains between Syria's interior and its Mediterranean coast, a geographic feature long known as the Homs Gap. The town is also about halfway between Damascus, modern Syria's capital, and Aleppo, its largest city. In Roman times the city was known as Emesa, and was intimately tied, economically, politically, and socially, to Palmyra. This is because the two cities were located on the ancient Silk Road, and Homs was the second-to-last stop along the southern branch of the trade route for goods traveling from the east on their way to the Mediterranean coast, where they then made their way through Southern Europe and North Africa on their way to Western Europe.

From the third through seventh centuries, Homs was a primarily Christian city, though still heavily influenced by the sun god cult that had existed in Emesa for so long. Many influential Christian figures in the early church came from Homs, including one of Christianity's early popes, Pope Anicetus, considered by the Vatican to be a martyr and a saint. Bishop of Rome from 155 to 166 CE, he was a converted Jew who grew up in Emesa and is perhaps best known for decreeing that Roman Catholic priests should not be allowed to have long hair; a decree that still stands in the church today by tradition, if not canon law. Islam came to Homs in 636, just 16 years after the death of the Prophet Muhammad in Mecca, and it played an important role in the young religion's history as tradition states that 500 of Islam's earliest converts moved here from the Arabian Peninsula in order to spread the faith in what was a predominantly Christian area (though there were significant Jewish communities throughout the region as well). Even in Roman times, Homs was a predominantly Arab City, and Arabs were in control of all of the city's civic and religious institutions. This remained the case until 1516 when the area fell under Ottoman rule and a ruling Turkish elite moved into the area. Though the bulk of the population remained Arab, Turkish became the language of governance, and old Arab institutions were replaced by ones that reflected Turkish norms and attitudes. Turkish elites remained entrenched in Homs, as well as much of the rest of Syria, until after the First World War in the twentieth century.

The Homs Governorate is the largest government administrative area in modern Syria. It is centered on a hill that rises to about 1,600 feet above sea level and provides a commanding view in all directions of the surrounding agricultural lands that have fed the city for centuries. Unlike the agricultural cities near the Mediterranean, which mainly produce fruit, the farmland around Homs produces wheat, corn, millet, cotton, and vegetables, and fruit, all staples of a diet that has made Homs self-reliant in terms of producing a balanced array of nutritious foods. Homs is the breadbasket of modern Syria, and even the country's once prosperous rail system put Homs at the center of a trade and transportation network that placed it in a position akin to Chicago's central role as a transportation center linking the East Coast of the United States to the Great Plains. Like Chicago, Homs's advantageous geography paved the way for economic development. It became Syria's most important industrial center and houses the country's largest oil refinery. It is for these historical and, more importantly, geographical and economic reasons that Bashar al-Assad could not tolerate the idea of losing Homs to rebellious forces trying to weaken his grip on power.

Within weeks of the famous anti-government protests in the southern city of Daraa, Homs began to see its own peaceful demonstrations. By the end of April 2011, thousands of people were regularly taking to the streets in Homs to call for democratic reforms to the government in Syria. This is in spite of the fact that government forces had already killed dozens of protestors in Homs; the more violent the government response, the more determined the protestors became to take to the streets. In May, the government sent infantry and even tanks into Homs, yet the protests continued to grow. By this time, however, protestors had started to take up arms—initially to defend themselves, but they were soon launching their own small-scale attacks against government positions. Newly formed, and very loosely organized militias began to form in neighborhoods throughout Homs, and the Syrian Arab Army became more nervous as the rebel attacks grew in frequency as well as sophistication. The strongest opposition was found in the most religiously conservative Sunni Muslim neighborhoods, and it is likely because this is where militants sponsored by international organizations, such as al-Qaeda, were training the nascent militia forces. Not wanting the opposition to get any more organized, the Syrian government forces began an offensive at the beginning of February 2012 that would last for more than two years.

Roughly half of Homs's residents are Sunni Muslim, and before the Syrian Civil War about 30 percent of the city was Christian. The remaining 20 percent of Homs's residents, however, were Alawites, the same ethnic group as Bashar al-Assad. The Christians and Alawites in Homs, as in the rest of Syria, were largely supportive of Assad primarily because they feared what their position in a Sunni-run government would be. While the city's Sunnis, Christians, and Alawites had lived together harmoniously for centuries (there simply is no basis for the often citied "centuries-old ethnic hatred" argument so common in some Western intellectual circles), the reality was that given a choice of a government that, while undeniably brutal and undemocratic, was favorable to your position in society versus the a Sunni-led government in which discrimination and retribution were very real possibilities, most of Syria's minority groups went with the former option.

Most of the Christians in Homs fled the city as the protests among the city's Sunni Muslims and the counterprotests of the Alawites grew into armed conflict among neighborhood militias. As the army got involved, many of the Alawites from Homs either left for Latakia or formed militias funded by the Syrian military. Fighting among the militias grew to a near-constant occurrence, and as the fighting intensified and it became clear that the Sunni militias were gaining an advantage, the Syrian military focused almost all of its attention on subduing the city (at the expense of allowing the resistance to grow in other areas, such as Idlib Province along the country's border with Turkey).

The rebel stronghold in Homs was centered in a neighborhood known as Baba Amr. The Free Syrian Army Forces that had gathered and organized had entrenched themselves in this conservative neighborhood, and it was on this neighborhood that the Syrian military focused its February 2012 offensive. It took about a month of intense bombardment, but Free Syrian Army forces finally collapsed and government troops moved into the district. Concerned by the reports coming out of Homs, the United

Nations pushed for a cease-fire, and by May 2012, the government controlled much of the city and there was a lull in violence. There were still rebel entrenchments throughout the city, however, and in spite of the cease-fire there were still skirmishes; the government slowly made progress in taking more of the city, and by December 2012, the rebels controlled only a few areas, including the Old City.

With the cease-fire slowly unraveling almost from the time it was brokered, the Syrian Army launched an operation to drive out the rebels completely from the city in March 2013. However, the cease-fire, while not complete, did allow the Free Syrian Army and allied militias to regroup and put up an effective resistance to the government forces. This stalemate lasted for a few months until the Syrian Army was reinforced by Iranian-backed Hezbollah troops from Lebanon. By July, rebel fighters had withdrawn and the Syrian government gained control of almost all of the city, though some rebel strongholds remained until May 2014 when government forces allowed remaining opposition fighters to flee to Idlib Province. A small pocket of resistance emerged in 2015, but it was short-lived and the government also allowed the rebels to move to Idlib Province in what most analysts believe was an attempt on the part of Assad to gather as many militants into the northwestern province as possible in order to justify a massive final, decisive blow to the opposition once and for all.

The Siege of Homs, especially the time from March 2012 through May 2014, was, in many ways, a watershed in the Syrian Conflict as far as the international community is concerned. Bolstered with the hope and expectations fueled by the success of the Arab Spring bringing about at least changes in policy, if not outright regime change, in countries throughout the Middle East, the international community responded with shock and revulsion with the resolution with which Bashar al-Assad met the opposition to his regime in Homs. It was in Homs that some of the most poignant images of the conflict emerged on the world's social media platforms, and it was the wholesale, intentional starvation of large areas of the city and the prevention of international aid that shocked the world.

Even five years after the end of the Siege of Homs, its legacy haunts the international community and, not least, the people of Homs. Many people still live in the city and are trying to rebuild, but it is under the watchful eye of a mistrustful regime that will not let what is arguably Syria's most important city in economic and strategic terms fall into the hands of the opposition again.

Robert M. Kerr

Further Reading

Butcher, Kevin. *Roman Syria and the Near East*. J. Paul Getty Museum, 2004.

Frankopan, Peter. *The Silk Roads: A New History of the World*. Vintage, 2017.

Grainger, John D. *Syrian Influences in the Roman Empire to AD 300*. Routledge, 2017.

Harrer, Gustavus Adolphus. *Studies in the History of the Roman Province of Syria*. University of California Libraries, 1915.

van Dam, Nikolaos. *Destroying a Nation: The Civil War in Syria*. I. B. Tauris, 2017.

I

Idlib

Idlib is the name of an administrative region, as well as a city in northwestern Syria. Bordering Turkey, the Idlib Governorate has been the site of some of the most intense fighting in the Syrian Conflict. Its border with Turkey is porous, and there is evidence that many militant groups, especially the Free Syrian Army, have been able to move freely between Syria and their safe havens in Turkey for the duration of the conflict. These safe havens are not necessarily the result of Turkey's support of the militias so much as the result of a very difficult geographical region to police.

Rebels started using Idlib as a safe haven early in the conflict, taking advantage of both its geography, which is good for hiding from government forces and its strategic location on the Turkish border. As a crossroads of civilizations for thousands of years, the people of Idlib are diverse and feel no particular loyalty to any outside political influences. They are fiercely independent, and neutral at best toward the Assad regime in Damascus. It is important to note that when the Syrian Arab Army was tasked with putting down protests in the rest of the country, thousands of soldiers from towns and villages throughout Idlib defected and returned home—many eventually joining the Free Syrian Army rebel militia.

Knowing that Idlib would be particularly hard, if not impossible, to take and hold, Bashar al-Assad began a policy of blockading the region as much as possible and trying to limit movement into and out of the Idlib governorate. In 2015, he actually started allowing rebels from other areas of Syria to take refuge in Idlib, and tens of thousands of anti-government militias have moved to the province with Assad's blessing. Analysts say there are two reasons why Assad has done this. The first is that he hopes by gathering all of the militias into one area, knowing they represent a variety of often conflicting goals and ambitions, they will eventually start fighting among themselves. The second, and most important reason, however, is that he seems to be gathering all his enemies in one place with the goal to mount a massive air campaign to kill them all. It is this second scenario that has the world's attention, and it poses the most significant unresolved question, as all indicators seem to be pointing to this possible next chapter in the Syrian Civil War.

Robert M. Kerr

Further Reading

Abouzeid, Rania. *No Turning Back: Life, Loss, and Hope in Wartime Syria*. W. W. Norton, 2018.

International Syria Support Group (ISSG)

The International Syria Support Group (ISSG) was founded in 2015 as a result of the "Vienna Talks" to bring about a diplomatic solution to the Syrian crisis. The Vienna talks, which took place from October 23 through November 14, 2015, involved the foreign ministers of 20 countries and organizations; and for the first time in the Syrian Conflict showed a real effort on the part of the international community to commit to concrete steps to help end the Syrian Civil War. Establishing the ISSG under the auspices of the United Nations (UN) was a significant accomplishment considering many earlier attempts to deal with the conflict at the diplomatic level had failed, most notably in 2012 when two members of the UN Security Council, Russia and China, refused to support a resolution condemning the Syrian government and with the creation of an official UN Contact Group on Syria after the al-Qubeir Massacre. The result of that significant setback was the establishment of the Friends of Syria Group, which is nothing more than an international discussion group that has served some purpose in creating a forum for back-channel talks and coordination primarily among nations supporting various anti-Assad forces. Unlike the Friends of Syria Group, the International Syria Support Group is an official United Nations initiative, and is cochaired by the United States and Russia. In addition to these two major players in the conflict, the ISSG includes the Arab League, Australia, Canada, China, Egypt, the European Union, France, Germany, Iran, Iraq, Italy, Japan, Jordan, Lebanon, the Netherlands, Oman, the Organization of Islamic Cooperation, Qatar, Saudi Arabia, Spain, Turkey, the United Arab Emirates, the United Kingdom, and the United Nations.

Unlike the Friends of Syria Group, which was set up as an open discussion forum without any clear agenda, the International Syria Support Group set out to not only encourage dialogue in an official international forum, but to develop a concrete plan to deal with the conflict's most significant issues in order to find an expedient end to the bloodshed.

The specific points outlined by the ISSG on November 14, 2015, in its peace plan were a stated commitment to ensure a Syrian-owned and -led political transition, calls for a nationwide cease-fire among all parties to begin as soon as Syrian governmental and opposition leaders take their initial steps toward dialogue, and to try to convene such dialogue no later than January 1, 2016. The communiqué of November 14, 2015, also stressed the need to defeat the two most significant terrorist groups operating in Syria, the Islamic State and the Nusra Front, with the full support of the UN Security Council. This effort was to be led by the Jordanians, who would use their intelligence assets to identify and track these threats within Syria while coordinating with the Syrians and other neighboring countries. The UN Security Council endorsed the agreement, listed as UN Security Council Resolution 2254, on December 18, 2015. Not surprisingly, the Assad regime did not consider any of these to be viable options.

One of the reasons for Syrian opposition to the ISSG, other than the obvious resistance of Bashar al-Assad in accepting any culpability in the conflict, was the fact that due to Russian involvement in the war, primarily through providing air strikes against opposition targets, the regime in Syria had gained the upper hand. Russian air strikes in Syria began in earnest in September 2015, which caused a major setback for U.S.- and European-backed insurgents. Knowing that Russia's involvement had tipped the military strategic balance, U.S. secretary of state John Kerry looked for ways to leverage the international community to use the diplomatic instrument of national power to convince Assad to end the conflict and agree to transition to a new government.

Tensions between the ISSG's cochairs, Russia and the United States, were evident throughout the Vienna Talks and reflected in the statements of the ISSG. While the United States claimed it did not wish to impose its will on the people of Syria, it also insisted that any real cessation of hostilities would have to involve a transition of government with Assad stepping aside. Russia, on the other hand, seized on the United States' repeated statements that its real enemy in Syria was the Islamic State (IS), and Russian foreign minister Lavrov insisted that the United States should only focus on defeating its declared enemy in the conflict and not interfere with Assad's sovereignty. As a result of this tension, the ISSG's final statement failed to address Assad's fate or what exactly his government's role should play in any post-conflict scenarios.

The International Syria Support Group was successful in bringing about UN-mandated peace talks in February 2016 in Geneva. Unfortunately, these talks broke down after just two days, largely because of Syria's concurrent military offensive against rebel groups north of Aleppo—complicated by Russia's involvement in providing air strikes during the offensive. Despite this setback, and many more like it in the ensuing years, the ISSG continues to work toward the goals laid out in its 2015 communiqué. While it has not been entirely successful, it has served as a means for the international community to hold the major players in the conflict, to include both Russia and the United States in addition to the Syrian government, somewhat accountable to the international community. Perhaps most importantly, it has made it difficult for the member states of the United Nations to ignore Syria and forced them to try to come up with creative solutions to the conflict.

Robert M. Kerr

Further Reading

European Union. "Final Declaration on the Results of the Syria Talks in Vienna as Agreed by Participants," October 30, 2015. https://eeas.europa.eu/headquarters/headquarters-homepage/5960_en.

International Syria Support Group. "Action Group for Syria: Final Communique," June 30, 2012. https://carnegie-mec.org/diwan/48975?lang=en.

Iran

Modern Iran is a country with an ancient and proud past. Strategically located at the geographic nexus of the Middle East, Europe, and Asia, it has long been an economic and cultural crossroads that has influenced global and regional geopolitics for centuries. Its ports on the Persian/Arabian Gulf have long served as Iran's links to the Western world, and its eastern hinterlands reach into Central Asia and the Far East. Its strategic importance has made it a perennial regional powerhouse, and its government, whether made up of ancient Persians or Babylonians, the sixteenth-century Safavids, the post–World War II Shah, or the Islamic revolutionary government put in place in 1979, has always tried to ensure that their land and people remain an important factor on the world stage. Since the 1800s, however, Iranian leaders have had to balance their desire for regional influence with their need to negotiate complex relationships with the world's great powers, primarily the United Kingdom, Russia, and the United States.

In the nineteenth century, Iran became part of a geopolitical struggle between the United Kingdom and Russia that was known as "the Great Game." The British saw Central Asia as an essential strategic location in their struggle to solidify their hold on their vast empire, but at the same time Tsarist Russia was trying to increase its geographical sphere of influence. Iran, known as Persia at that time, was on the frontlines of this great struggle, and in the early twentieth century, the country was divided into a Russian sphere of influence in the north and a British sphere in the south.

While the British did not get all the territory they desired, they did get a consolation prize that would forever change the destiny of not only Iran but the entire Middle East—the discovery of vast fields of oil in 1908. Britain quickly established the Anglo-Persian Oil Company (which today is known around the world as British Petroleum, or BP), a move that eventually paved the way for a growing sense of modern Iranian nationalism as the country's native population grew increasingly frustrated from an arrangement that really favored only the British. The most successful nationalist leader to emerge during this time was Mohammad Mosaddegh, who supported the nationalization of Iran's oil industry, removing it completely from the hands of the British and, since the end of World War II, the Americans. Mosaddegh's time as prime minister, from 1951 to 1953, was cut short by a coup orchestrated by the United States in order to install a government more favorable to U.S. and British interests. This coup, which remains largely unknown in American society, became a rallying point for the Islamic revolutionaries who seized power from a government they saw as a puppet of the United States in 1979.

The undisputed roots of the 1979 revolution lay in violence and public unrest that began in 1963. The leader of the antimonarchist movement that opposed the shah (Mohammad Reza Pahlavi, the pro-U.S. monarch) was Ayatollah Ruhollah Khomeini. The shah responded to the opposition with arrests and interrogations by the secret police, the SAVAK, and with military force. Khomeini was exiled to Iraq and protests were violently put down, resulting in thousands of dead. Khomeini continued to agitate against the shah from Iraq and later from France. From abroad he became the symbolic leader of the opposition to the shah's religious and economic policies.

In 1977, the United States put pressure on the shah to ease restrictions on human rights in Iran. As he loosened his grip on the country, a broad spectrum of Iranian society turned out to protest a variety of grievances. A core of the resistance to the shah were the religious student community and its clerical leadership. Resistance culminated in a general strike in October 1978. This convinced the shah of the need to change course. In January 1979, he left Iran and appointed as prime minister Shahpour Bakhtiar, who promised to launch a genuine social democracy.

The departure of the shah precipitated a power struggle in Iran that was quickly won by Khomeini and the advocates of a traditional Islamic-dominated government. The new government consolidated its power through ruthless intimidation and violence. The Ayatollah Khomeini was not only an ardent opponent of the shah, but also extremely anti-American. His youthful followers in Iran's universities reflected Khomeini's anti-Americanism. In November 1979, Iranian students stormed the U.S. Embassy in Tehran and took 90 occupants hostage. Over the next 14 months, the United States applied sanctions against Iran, froze Iranian assets, and attempted a military rescue of the hostages. All these efforts failed. In July 1980, the shah died of natural causes in Egypt, and this opened a diplomatic opportunity for negotiation. Algerian intermediaries helped negotiate a settlement in which the hostages were released on

January 21, 1981. Though the hostages were successfully released, the crisis destroyed Iranian relations with the United States.

Iran's neighbor, Syria, saw the 1979 revolution as an opportunity to forge relationships with a new regional ally. Syria's president, Hafez al-Assad, was an Alawite, a practitioner of a religious offshoot of Shia Islam. Assad saw the Shia-led revolutionary government of Ayatollah Khomeini as a natural friend in a region dominated by Sunni Muslims who were not necessarily comfortable with the emergence of a Shia-dominated theocracy in the region. Assad certainly had no interest in creating a theocracy, however, and the Ayatollah did not view him as a "true" Muslim. Assad was the first leader of an Arab nation to recognize the revolutionary government, however, and Khomeini did see the strategic and political advantages of allowing an Iranian-Syrian alliance.

The alliance between Iran and Syria was tested early in the revolutionary government's tenure as the war between Iran and Iraq erupted in 1980. Syria's place in the greater Middle East was solidified as Hafez al-Assad chose to support Iran rather than its fellow Arab neighbor, Iraq. This move created a tense relationship between Assad and Saddam Hussein, as well as with other Arab leaders throughout the region. In return for their support during the conflict, however, Iran has remained a steadfast, if somewhat overbearing, partner to Syria ever since. While there have been some minor disagreements over policy decisions between the two countries, none have been significant enough to threaten the alliance.

What do Iran and Syria get from their partnership? The benefits are quantifiably in favor of Iran: they get access to the Mediterranean Sea (in October 2019, under an agreement signed between the two countries, Iran has full operational control over Syria's most important port, Latakia); easy access to its proxy militia (which has become a functioning governing organization as well); and through this arrangement has access to the territory of its stated enemy, Israel, through both Syria and Lebanon. For its part, Syria gets funding and subsidies for just about everything ranging from its military to essential services and infrastructure (though these funds have largely dried up at various times due to U.S. sanctions against Iran). Throughout the Syrian Civil War, the Iranian government has provided support to the Assad regime by allowing its Revolutionary Guard and Hezbollah forces to participate in anti-rebel and anti–Islamic State operations, and has provided military supplies and advice to Syrian troops.

It is difficult to quantify exactly how much Iran has helped Syria in its civil war, but it is known that many Iranian troops, including some very high-ranking Iranian officers, have been killed in fighting. The strong relationship between the two countries ever since Syria's support for the revolutionary government in the Iran-Iraq War forged strong bonds between them, and it is reasonable to assume that Iranian support for the Assad regime runs even deeper than that as indicated by available evidence. Iran stands to lose much if the Ba'athist should fail in the fight—access to the Mediterranean, its proxies in Lebanon, its ability to wage a ground campaign against Israel, and regional significance would all be compromised if Assad falls to a Sunni-dominated opposition. This is a risk that is too great for Iran's leaders to contemplate.

Robert M. Kerr

Further Reading

Ansari, Ali M. *A History of Modern Iran since 1921: The Pahlavis and After.* Longman Publishing, 2003.

Karsh, Efraim. *The Iran-Iraq War, 1980–1988.* Osprey Publishing, 2002.

Kinzer, Stephen. *All the Shah's Men: An American Coup and the Roots of Middle East Terror.* John Wiley & Sons, 2003.

Iraq

The history of modern Iraq is believed to begin with the last phase of Turkish rule, when Sultan Ali Reza Pasha in 1831 ousted the last of the local Mesopotamian rulers and brought Iraq directly under Turkish administration. (The Turks had previously ruled through local sovereigns and thus failed to bring nomadic Arabs under Ottoman control.) Resentment of taxes introduced by the Turks stoked an intense Arab nationalism, while Great Britain and Germany vied for commercial development of the oil-rich area. After Turkey entered World War I on the side of Germany, British forces invaded southern Mesopotamia, pushed back the Turks, and occupied Baghdad. The British then offered Arab leaders independence if they joined a British offensive against the insurgent Turkish Army.

Iraqi military leader Faisal I thus led an uprising in 1916 under British tactical direction and defeated the Turks. The British-French Supreme Allied Council signed the Sykes-Picot Agreement with the assent of Russia in 1916. This agreement effectively divided the Middle East into British and French spheres of influence, and allowed Great Britain to remain in Iraq. Having been promised an independent Arab state in the earlier McMahon-Hussein Correspondence letters during WWI, Arabs were very upset when the details of the agreement were made public, and they launched a series of armed uprisings. In order to resolve the issue of Arab discontent, Great Britain held the Cairo Conference of 1921 and largely abandoned its mandate; retaining its territorial control of Palestine, but turning over control of the Transjordan to King Abdullah bin-Hussein, the Arab Peninsula to Abdul Aziz ibn Saud, and inviting Faisal to become ruler of the new kingdom of Iraq under the supervision of a British high commissioner. Faisal was popularly elected king in 1921 with 96 percent of the vote. However, Shiite Muslims of the Euphrates River area and Kurds from the north had separatist aspirations, which forced Great Britain to maintain troops in Iraq until a 20-year treaty of alliance was signed in 1922.

In 1925, King Faisal allowed foreign-owned companies to develop oil reserves in the Baghdad and al-Mawsil regions in return for hefty annual royalties. The same year, elections to Iraq's first legislature were held, and the king asked Great Britain to sponsor Iraq's membership in the League of Nations. Great Britain refused the request until 1932, when it sponsored Iraq as a fully independent state. Faisal was succeeded by his son Ghazi, who guided Iraq toward a treaty of nonaggression with its Arab neighbors. King Ghazi was killed in a car accident in 1939, which left his three-year-old son Faisal II titular king. The absence of direct leadership allowed ultranationalist elements to assume power and pursue a policy of noncooperation with Great Britain. A war ensued in May 1941 and ended in Iraq's defeat the same month. A moderate government was installed and was supplied with arms by Great Britain, the United States, and the Soviet Union. In 1943, Iraq became the first Arab country to declare war on the Axis powers, and in 1948, Iraq and Transjordan (Jordan) invaded the new state of Israel.

King Faisal II assumed the throne on his 18th birthday in 1953, and one year later,

Iraq secured U.S. military aid. Iraq signed a security pact with Turkey in 1955 that fostered the Middle East Treaty Organization, which included the United States, Great Britain, and other Arab states. In 1958, Iraq and Jordan formed the Arab Union to counterbalance the United Arab Republic (UAR), a recently formed federation between Egypt and Syria. The UAR was bitterly hostile to the pro-Western Arab Union and launched a propaganda campaign that urged the Iraqi people to overthrow their government. Iraqi general Abdul Karim Qassem led a successful coup in which the prime minister and King Faisal II were killed, and Qassem proclaimed Iraq a separate republic. Qassem himself was overthrown and killed in 1963 by a group of officers who belonged to the Arab Baath Socialist Party.

Iraq's governing Revolutionary Command Council declared war on Israel during the Six-Day War and severed all ties with the West in favor of relations with the Soviet Union. In 1970, a series of Kurdish revolts in the north led to the formation of a Kurdish Autonomous Region. Iraq's long friendship with Jordan ended in 1971 over Jordanian efforts to crush a Palestinian guerrilla movement in Iraq. Oil revenues soared in 1973, the same year Iraq armed Syria in the Yom Kippur War. Meanwhile, an Iranian-armed Kurdish independence movement gained force in the north under Mustafa al-Barzani. In July 1979, General Saddam Hussein, a Ba'ath Party member and Sunni Muslim, took power and changed the face of Iraqi history.

Tensions with the revolutionary regime in Iran erupted in the 1980–1988 Iran-Iraq War, which stifled Persian Gulf shipping and wrought heavy casualties on both sides. The United States resumed diplomatic relations with Iraq in 1984 and provided financial and technological support that in August

1990 helped Iraq invade and annex Kuwait, its former ally in the Iran-Iraq War. Iraq rejected ultimatums to withdraw, which sparked the Persian Gulf War, in which hundreds of thousands of Iraqis were killed. Shiite Muslims and Kurds took advantage of Iraq's perceived weakness after the war and staged rebellions in the north and south that were harshly put down by still-formidable government troops. Thousands of Kurdish refugees fled to Turkey and Iran, with some 600,000 sheltering in camps set up by American, British, and French troops to protect the Kurds from government reprisals. Since 1992, Iraq faced intense international pressure to destroy its remaining chemical and nuclear weapons, and the United Nations (UN) refused to lift devastating trade sanctions until it did so.

In June 1993, Washington launched a cruise missile attack on Iraq in retaliation for an assassination attempt on U.S. president George Bush. Despite claims that it had destroyed all its weapons of mass destruction, Iraq remained under UN sanctions because of its persecution of Kurdish and Shiite Muslim communities. Civil war caused by deteriorating economic and political conditions among rival Kurdish groups resulted in the deaths of some 900 people between May and August 1994. Hussein signed a decree that withdrew all territorial claims to Kuwait in November, which was one month after he provoked the deployment of American, British, and French troops to the Iraq-Kuwait border, where Iraq had secretly amassed troops. By 1995, with food and medicine shortages reportedly dire, the UN approved a plan under which Iraq could sell limited amounts of oil on a probationary basis to feed its people. The Iraqi legislature rejected the offer, but a deal was finally struck in May 1996. However, Iraq continued to face international sanctions for not cooperating with UN demands to destroy its weapons of mass destruction.

U.S. military forces remained in the region to enforce the trade embargo and the UN-sanctioned "no-fly zone" below the 32nd parallel in Iraq. With the ascension of George W. Bush as U.S. president in 2001, the United States adopted a hard-line approach toward Hussein and his regime. When the World Trade Center and Pentagon attacks on September 11, 2001, triggered Bush's war on terrorism, the Bush administration insisted that Hussein was still harboring weapons of mass destruction and was now allied with the terrorist organization al-Qaeda, although those charges have not been proven. Nevertheless, Bush's threats to attack Iraq began in earnest in the summer of 2002, and the UN reinserted weapons inspectors into Iraq in the fall of 2002. Although Bush and his ally, British prime minister Tony Blair, failed to secure UN approval for a war to oust Hussein, U.S.-led forces launched the Iraq War on March 20, 2003, which toppled Hussein's regime by mid-April.

Attempts at administration in Iraq were initially channeled through the U.S. Office of Reconstruction and Humanitarian Assistance and led by former U.S. general Jay Garner, which was superseded on May 7, 2003, by the U.S.-run Coalition Provisional Authority (CPA), headed by administrator L. Paul Bremer. Bremer appointed an Iraqi Governing Council (IGC) and government ministers in July 2003, and an interim constitution was signed by the IGC in March 2004. In preparation for the transfer of sovereignty from the CPA to the Iraqi people on June 30, 2004, an interim government was appointed by the IGC: Iyad Allawi, an exile Shiite, as prime minister; Ghazi al-Yawar, a Sunni tribal leader, as president; and two deputy presidents, Ibrahim Jaafari, a Shiite, and Nouri al-Shawis, a Sunni Kurd.

On January 30, 2005, Iraq held its first multiparty elections in half a century, selecting a 275-member transitional National Assembly. Despite the withdrawal of several Sunni parties from the poll and threats of Election Day violence from insurgents, turnout was high. After two months of deadlock, on April 6 the new legislature elected Kurdish leader Jalal Talabani as president and Ghazi al-Yawar and Adel Abdul Mahdi as vice presidents. The following day, Ibrahim al-Jaafari was selected to head the Iraqi government as prime minister.

In April 2006, Talabani was reelected and Nouri al-Maliki was selected to be prime minister after a nearly three-month deadlock in the Shia majority. The country continued to be racked by violence between Shiites and Sunnis that verged on wholesale civil war, and the government struggled to unite the disparate parties and warring factions. Hussein was found guilty of war crimes by an Iraqi court in November 2006 and executed on December 30, 2006. The execution sparked protests in Hussein's hometown of Tikrit.

In January 2007, President Bush presented his plan for "A New Way Forward" in Iraq. This was a new U.S. military strategy whose stated goal was to reduce the sectarian violence in Iraq and help the Iraqi people provide security and stability for themselves. Five additional U.S. Army brigades were deployed to Iraq between January and May 2007, totaling about 40,000 troops. Operations to secure Baghdad began immediately. The U.S. troop surge, as many commentators called the plan, continued into early 2009.

Interpretations of the results of the surge were mixed. Many U.S. media outlets, including CNN, reported that violence had dropped anywhere from 40 to 80 percent in Iraq following the surge. ABC ran many reports on its nightly news show that high-lighted the progress in Iraq. *New York Times* writer David Brooks argued that even Presi-dent Bush's harshest critics would have to concede that he finally got one right. Barack Obama, who was elected president of the United States in November 2008 and was once a harsh critic of the surge, later asserted that the new military strategy had led to an improved security situation in Iraq, although he was quick to point out that the war should not have been launched in the first place.

Between 2003 and 2007, tens of thousands of Iraqis fled to Syria. At the height of the sectarian violence in Iraq, Syria presented a good, stable environment for Iraqi refugees; they did not need a visa to enter the country, and the Syrian government provided them with essential services not available to them in Iraq. The refugee issue did pose a strain on Syrians, however, particularly in and around Damascus, where the unemployment rate skyrocketed and competition for resources put stress on the economy. Ironically, Iraq has become a shelter not only for Iraqis returning to their country, but for Syrians fleeing their own conflict in recent years.

On December 4, 2008, the U.S. and Iraqi governments concluded the Status of Forces Agreement, which stipulated that U.S. troops would depart from all Iraqi cities by June 30, 2009, and would leave Iraq entirely by December 31, 2011. U.S. forces were no lon-ger allowed to hold Iraqi citizens without charges for more than 24 hours. Also, immu-nity from prosecution in Iraqi courts was taken away from U.S. contractors. Maliki, however, was faced by detractors who called for the immediate removal of foreign troops from Iraq. They believed the agreement only prolonged an illegal occupation. Iraq's grand ayatollah, Sayyid Ali Husayn al-Sistani, led many of these protests and contended that

Maliki was ceding too much control to the Americans. In the end, Obama, who had pledged to remove all U.S. troops from Iraq before 2012, made good on his promise, and the last U.S. troops left the country on December 18, 2011. Prior to that, the last coalition nation to withdraw from Iraq was the United Kingdom (in May 2011).

During the occupation years, the Iraqi economy improved, largely due to an influx of money pouring in from abroad. Wages rose over 100 percent between 2003 and 2008, and taxes were cut by 15–45 percent, allowing many Iraqi citizens to increase their spending power. However, despite such suc-cesses, Iraq faced many economic problems as well. Unemployment remained high; the Iraq government estimated that unemploy-ment was between 60 and 70 percent in 2008. At the same time, the Iraqi foreign debt rose as high as $125 billion. Since the withdrawal of coalition troops in 2011, however, the Iraqi economy has failed to make any major gains, and in many sectors it has steadily deterio-rated. Much of this is the result of a growing insurgency and sectarian violence, com-bined with the ineffective Maliki govern-ment. Although unemployment had dropped to 30 percent by 2013, most Iraqis were employed in the public sector (60 percent), and Iraq's per capita gross domestic product (GDP) was only about $4,000 per year.

ISIS

In the years after Coalition Forces withdrew from Iraq, that nation witnessed an alarming reemergence of the anti-government insur-gency. This included sectarian violence and the rise to prominence of Islamic extremist groups, most notably the Islamic State of Iraq and Syria (ISIS). By early 2014, these groups had seized control of virtually all of Iraq's Anbar Province. Meanwhile, the

Iraqi government under Maliki, which was plagued by corruption and inefficiency, was unable to stem the rising tide of deadly violence. By late 2013, the situation had become so dire that the Obama administration agreed to ship Hellfire missiles to Iraq's government and pledged to provide it with increased intelligence support, military logistics, and specialized troop training. Meanwhile, the violence in Iraq continued to escalate, and May 2013 was the deadliest month in Iraq since the height of the Iraqi Civil War in 2006–2007. In May 2014, the U.S. government announced an arms deal with Iraq that promised at least $1 billion in new aircraft, armored vehicles, and surveillance technology. Meanwhile, the Iraqis also engaged in a major arms deal with the Russians, who agreed to sell them aircraft and bunker-busting rockets, among other items.

By the midsummer of 2014, the situation in Iraq was dire, and ISIS had advanced within 90 miles of Baghdad. Until then, the Iraqi army had performed abysmally in its fight against ISIS; indeed, many soldiers simply deserted or fled in the face of ISIS military operations. In August, Maliki was under great domestic and international pressure to step down. Even those in his own party believed he had to go. In the meantime, the United States began dispatching small deployments of military advisers to Iraq even as U.S. and allied aircraft began bombing raids against ISIS targets in northern and western Iraq. Maliki finally agreed to relinquish his office on September 8, 2014. He was succeeded by Haider al-Abadi, also of the Dawa Party. Abadi, a Shiite, vowed to reinvigorate Iraq's army and work closely with the new international coalition formed to stop and eventually eradicate ISIS. He also pledged more governmental transparency and efforts to bridge the gaping chasm between Iraq's Sunni and Shiite populations.

Throughout 2015, Iraqi forces battled ISIS, achieving modest success in winning back some territory claimed by the extremist group. Iran had also begun providing direct military support to the Iraqi government. The collapse of oil prices during the second half of 2015, however, had a chilling effect on Iraq's economy, which is highly dependent on oil exports. Indeed, by early 2016, the Abadi government announced that greatly reduced oil revenues were beginning to affect its ability to continue the fight against ISIS. Abadi, meanwhile, claimed that ISIS was siphoning Iraqi oil in areas under its control and shipping it into Turkey for sale; Turkey vehemently denied this, however. A January 2016 United Nations report stated that between January 2014 and November 2015, nearly 19,000 Iraqi civilians had died owing to violence in Iraq, while at least 40,000 others had been injured. An additional 3 million Iraqis had been displaced from their homes. On a more positive note, by early 2016, Abadi's efforts to reform Iraqi politics and rid the nation of corruption and cronyism had begun to bear fruit.

Gregory W. Morgan and Robert M. Kerr

Further Reading

Abdullah, Thabit. *A Short History of Iraq.* Pearson, 2003.

Brookings Institute. "Iraqi Refugees in the Syrian Arab Republic: A Field-Based Snapshot," June 11, 2007. https://www.brookings.edu/research/iraqi-refugees-in-the-syrian-arab-republic-a-field-based-snapshot.

Cockburn, Patrick. *The Occupation: War and Resistance in Iraq.* Verso, 2007.

Kagan, Kimberly. "The Iraq Report; From 'New Way Forward' to New Commander."

Weekly Standard, January 10, 2007–February 10, 2007, 7–10.

Marr, Phebe. *The Modern History of Iraq*. 2nd ed. Westview, 2003.

Tripp, Charles. *A History of Iraq*. Cambridge University Press, 2007.

Islamic Front

The Islamic Front is a conglomeration of Syrian Islamist rebel groups formed in November 2013 to unify efforts toward the establishment of an Islamic government in Syria. Unlike the goal of global jihad espoused by the Islamic State of Iraq and al-Sham (ISIS), the Islamic Front limited its focus to establishing a religious state in Syria.

Throughout 2011–2013, several Islamist groups operated independently but attempted mergers to share resources and seek external funding from Gulf states. The formation of the Islamic Front brought together an estimated 40,000–70,000 fighters from large Syrian Islamist rebel groups, Ahrar as-Sham, Liwa al-Tawheed, Jaish al-Islam, and Suqour al-Sham. The Islamic Front replaced the Islamist umbrella organization Syrian Islamic Front (formed in 2012 by Ahrar as-Sham) as it merged with members of the Syrian Islamic Liberation Front (formed in 2012 by Liwa al-Tawheed, Suqour al-Sham, and Kata'ib al Farouq), when many groups began to splinter from the more moderate Free Syrian Army-Supreme Military Council (FSA-SMC) coalition and began to sever ties with more extremist ISIS and Jabhat al-Nusra over ideological disagreements.

Despite its size, the Islamic Front was ineffective in uniting Sunni rebel groups to challenge both the Syrian regime and the Islamic State. The Islamic Front achieved mixed success in battles during 2013–2014.

The organization faced many challenges by early 2014 as factions disagreed over whether to foster a working relationship with ISIS, particularly after ISIS killed an Islamic Front commander in retaliation for criticizing ISIS leader Abu Bakr al-Baghdadi. Unable to compete with ISIS revenues and recruitment of fighters, remaining Islamic Front factions focused their attention on an information campaign to discredit ISIS ideology. Some factions fought alongside other anti-regime and anti-ISIS rebels in Aleppo and Idlib, while others defected to claim neutrality against ISIS.

Leaders from Jaish al-Islam and Ahrar al-Sham, the most prominent remaining groups of the Islamic Front, competed against one another for power. This rivalry eventually split the Islamic Front umbrella organization in late 2014, and many factions were absorbed into these two groups. Ahrar al-Sham became a key organizer of al-Jabhat al-Shamiyya, a coalition that fought in Aleppo but formally disbanded on April 19, 2015. The failure of Sunni Islamist rebel groups to coalesce under a single umbrella organization led rebel leaders supported by Turkey, Saudi Arabia, and other Western and Middle Eastern countries to create the Jaish al-Fatal coalition of seven armed groups that focused on the organization of a unified command to seize territory from the Assad regime. Jaish al-Fatal, which included Jaish al-Islam and Ahrar al-Sham, captured the Syrian provincial capital of Idlib on March 28, 2015, and continued fighting against the regime throughout summer 2015. While the Islamic Front umbrella organization dissolved by December 2014, many of its former members were absorbed by other groups or joined coalitions and continued to fight both the Assad regime and ISIS in Syria.

Melia Pfannenstiel

Further Reading

Hassan, Hassan. "Front to Back." *Foreign Policy*, March 4, 2014. https://foreignpolicy.com/2014/03/04/front-to-back.

Lister, Charles R. *The Syrian Jihad: Al Qaeda, the Islamic State and the Evolution of an Insurgency.* Oxford University Press, 2015.

Phillips, Christopher. *The Battle for Syria: International Rivalry in the New Middle East.* Yale University Press, 2016.

Islamic State of Iraq and al-Sham (ISIS)

Known also as the Islamic State of Iraq and Syria, the Islamic State of Iraq and the Levant (ISIL), or derogatively as Da'esh, the Islamic State is a Salafist takfiri organization currently active in Iraq and Syria. The group's name in Arabic is Dawlat al-Islamiyah f'al-Iraq wa al-Sham.

ISIS is a successor organization of al-Qaeda in Iraq (AQI), which was led by Abu Musa'b al-Zarqawi from 2003 to 2006. The relationship between al-Qaeda's leadership (Osama bin Laden and Ayman al-Zawahiri) and Zarqawi's AQI was always strained due to what bin Laden considered to be Zarqawi's excessive and unproductive hatred for Shia Muslims. After Zarqawi's death in 2006, AQI's successor organization, the Islamic State of Iraq (ISI), was never formally recognized by al-Qaeda. There were two leaders of ISI after Zarqawi's death, but the organization didn't really become powerful until Abu Bakr al-Baghdadi took over as its leader upon his release from U.S.-led Coalition Force detention at Camp Bucca, Iraq. Al-Baghdadi, whose birth name was Ibrahim Awwad Ibrahim al-Badri, was born in Samara, Iraq, in 1971. The name Abu Bakr is a *kunya*, a nickname that depicts either a relationship to one's child or a particular characteristic the child displays; in this case it is likely a reference to the historical figure Abu Bakr, the Prophet Muhammad's successor. "Al-Baghdadi" is simply a geographic reference to one who hails from Baghdad.

Origins of ISIS

As with al-Qaeda in Iraq, ISIS sought to 1) expel all foreign troops and personnel from Iraq, and 2) wage war against the Shia-dominated, secular government of Iraq. These organizations have not only battled coalition and Iraqi armed forces, but they have also engaged in myriad acts of terrorism and war crimes that have frequently involved civilians. ISIS, however, had ambitions beyond these activities. It sought to establish an Islamic regime within Iraq and Syria. It even hoped eventually to extend its reach into the Levant, which encompasses Lebanon, Palestine, and Jordan (which explains why some have referred to the group as ISIL).

By 2010, Baghdadi had emerged as a top leader of the Islamic State of Iraq. However, his vision of founding an Islamic emirate clashed with the more modest goals of that group, and so he began to assemble his own rebel group. Thereafter, he co-opted several other jihadist organizations, most notably the Mujahideen Shura Council (MSC), and began recruiting followers who shared his more expansive vision. Observers believed that Baghdadi enjoyed success in recruiting fighters (many are foreigners, and some even hailed from Western Europe and the United States) because he was a charismatic military strategist and battlefield commander rather than a theologian.

What Does ISIS Believe?

ISIS differs from al-Qaeda in significant ways. Whereas al-Qaeda was founded as a global movement intended largely to "awaken" potential followers to the possibility of rebuilding a modern version of the ancient Islamic empires (caliphates), it never really articulated anything other than a notional plan for doing so. ISIS, on the other hand, presents a well-defined and realistic plan for doing so in the immediate future in a particular location and with a well-structured civil and military organization. Another characteristic that makes ISIS very different from other militant Islamist organizations is its obsession with apocalyptic thought and doctrine. While they share many of the same beliefs as their Sunni counterparts, they are extreme in their approach to takfirism, the practice of declaring apostates within Islam—believing themselves to be the only true Muslims and entitled to kill lapsed Muslims, enslave pagans, and subjugate and tax Christians and Jews according to medieval literal interpretations of the Quran. They also consider all Shia Muslims to be apostate, and have been brutal in their approach to dealing with all of their conquered enemies.

ISIS is a territorial entity, which also differentiates it from al-Qaeda. Al-Qaeda is a global institution whose leadership has operated everywhere from Egypt to Sudan, Afghanistan, Pakistan, and perhaps even elsewhere. ISIS, on the other hand, sees control of Syria (al-Sham) and Iraq as essential to its existence, and uses its clearly defined territory as a visual symbol of the group's self-perceived legitimacy. Central to its territorial goals and apocalyptic vision is control of the city of Dabiq, in northern Syria. *Dabiq* is also the name of the organization's magazine, Again, perhaps the most significant difference between ISIS and virtually every other militant Islamist organization is its fixation on the end-times. End-time prophecies are extremely uncommon in

Sunni Islamic thought, yet ISIS defines itself by them. Dabiq is at the center of this apocalyptic vision because it is where the Prophet Muhammad said, in one of the *hadiths*, that Islam would ultimately defeat the "Armies of Rome" (i.e., Christendom). ISIS's leaders and propagandists focus a lot of time and attention on showing their followers how current events reflect such prophecies.

During its heyday, before large-scale offensives were launched against ISIS-held territory, many people from around the world were drawn to Syria with dreams of fighting for, and living in, the modern caliphate. The Internet was an essential recruitment tool as it allowed ISIS propagandists to reach even isolated individuals, many of whom felt disenfranchised in their life situations. Many recruits even came from Western countries drawn by the utopian visions and dreams of glory ISIS shared online. Many of these people have been killed in subsequent fighting, and some have tried to return to their home countries with varying degrees of success.

ISIS Control of Iraqi and Syrian Territory

By the spring of 2013, ISIS had become a potent force in both Iraq and Syria. In Syria, ISIS has taken full advantage of the bloody civil war that has been raging there since early 2011. ISIS rebels have been battling Syrian government forces under President Bashar al-Assad, as well as other rebel groups. Many Syrians have come to despise ISIS because of its violence toward civilians, attacks on other rebel groups, and uncompromising positions, which include the subjugation and enslavement of women. In early 2014, Western-backed rebels and even other Islamist groups launched a major campaign to expel ISIS from Syria. It met with only modest success, however, and after that time ISIS extended its reach within Syria, to include areas populated by the Kurds.

ISIS had an even greater impact in Iraq, however, and by the summer of 2014, it was threatening the very existence of the Iraqi government of then-prime minister Nuri al-Maliki. Throughout 2013, ISIS made major advances in northern and western Iraq. By late January 2014, ISIS and affiliated groups had managed to seize control of all of Anbar Province. In early June 2014, the group enjoyed even bigger gains, taking Mosul (Iraq's second-largest city) as well as Tikrit. ISIS forces reached to only some 60 miles north of Baghdad and were attempting to drive further south.

The fall of Mosul stunned the Iraqi government and much of the international community. By mid-June, the United States and other Western nations were involved in urgent negotiations to determine how they should aid Maliki's government and prevent all of Iraq from falling into the hands of ISIS. Unfortunately, the corrupt, ineffectual, and rabidly anti-Sunni Maliki regime proved virtually incapable of halting ISIS's advance, and many components of the Iraqi Army simply bolted and fled in the face of ISIS offensives.

Resistance to ISIS

During the summer of 2014, the Barack Obama administration began formulating a comprehensive strategy to reverse ISIS's advances. This would come to include cobbling together a multinational coalition, including a number of Arab states, to participate in air strikes against ISIS targets, arming moderate Syrian rebel groups combating ISIS fighters, sending more military hardware to the Iraqi government, dispatching some 3,000 military "advisers" to Iraq, and

commencing air strikes against ISIS. The air strikes began on August 8, 2014, and the U.S.-coalition air campaign against ISIS in Syria commenced on September 23.

Those operations, code-named Operation Inherent Resolve since October 15, 2014, have continued into 2017. Meanwhile, at the same time the Obama administration had announced its intent to defeat ISIS, it was lobbying for Maliki to be replaced as Iraqi prime minister. Under great internal and international pressure, he finally resigned on September 8, 2014, and was succeeded by Haider al-Abadi, who pledged to pursue conciliatory policies in Iraq and to work cooperatively with the United States and its coalition partners in order to subdue the ISIS insurgency.

By late December 2014, there were signs that the anti-ISIS effort was beginning to make progress. Although Syrian officials reported that ISIS had killed 1,878 people (the vast majority of them civilians) between June 2014 and January 2015, Kurdish fighters recaptured the Syrian border town of Kobani on January 26, 2015. They also pushed ISIS out of the Iraqi city of Sinjar, a development that was hailed as a turning point in the war against ISIS. In December 2015, the Iraqi Army regained control of the city of Ramadi, and six months later, in June 2016, the Iraqi forces recaptured the city of Fallujah. Because both cities' proximity to Baghdad is less than 70 miles, this marked a strategic victory in the country's fight against the Islamic State.

Continued Growth and Violence

The threat from ISIS was considerably larger than its military operations in Iraq and Syria might suggest. Indeed, the group routinely violated basic international law and human rights by kidnapping innocent foreign civilians, beheading them, and then releasing the videos of the executions on the Internet. In addition to targeting innocent civilians, ISIS also engaged in the severe repression of women in areas under its control, including the kidnapping, sexual exploitation, and enslavement of women and even young girls.

ISIS groups claimed responsibility for a number of terrorist attacks in recent years, including a suicide bombing at two Shiite mosques in Yemen that killed 137; a mass shooting at a Tunisian beach resort that killed 38, most of whom were British tourists; the bombing of a Russian airliner over the Sinai Peninsula that killed 224; two suicide bomb attacks in Beirut, Lebanon, that killed 43; coordinated bombings and shootings in Paris on the evening of November 13, 2015, that killed 129; and near-simultaneous attacks at the airport and metro in Brussels, Belgium, in April 2016 that killed 32. Many international observers speculated that the attacks signaled an expansion of the Islamic State's reach and potentially a change in tactics to suicide gunmen and bombers that would be more difficult to combat. Following the Paris attacks and the bombing of the Russian airliners, many world leaders, including French president François Hollande and Russian president Vladimir Putin, vowed to cooperate and intensify the fight against ISIS.

Additionally, a string of deadly attacks occurred during the summer of 2016 that have been linked to the Islamic State. These include multiple bombings at Istanbul's Ataturk Airport in Turkey that killed 44 on June 28. Just days later, ISIS militants killed 20 in an attack on a restaurant in Dhaka, Bangladesh, on July 1. Days later, on July 4, the group claimed responsibility for a bombing in Baghdad that killed 200. The group was also linked (although it did not claim responsibility for) three separate suicide bombings within a 24-hour period across Saudi Arabia that killed four. All of these attacks occurred during the final days of the Islamic holy month of Ramadan.

Losing Ground

A growing number of international forces have continued to put pressure on ISIS, which has caused the group to lose significant territory that it had once controlled. Since the summer of 2014, Iran has been launching air strikes against ISIS targets within Iraq. Iran has also sent special militia forces, known as the Quds Force, to Iraq to engage ISIS on the ground. On April 1, 2015, the Iraqi government declared a major victory over ISIS forces after having driven the group from Tikrit. Throughout the spring of 2015, Iraqi forces, aided by air support from the United States and other coalition governments, aggressively pursued ISIS. The United States and Iran, although fighting on the same side in this instance, have repeatedly declared that the two nations are not coordinating their military operations. Iranian militia units played a major role in the retaking of Tikrit.

The chaos caused by the ongoing civil war in Syria had allowed ISIS to gain control in several strategic areas of Aleppo Province, near Syria's largest city. Although ISIS still maintains a grip on some neighborhoods in the province, many places they once held were seized by U.S.-backed militias in 2016. ISIS forces were further pushed back in the fall of 2016 by blistering air strikes of Aleppo by Russian and Syrian government forces and the humanitarian crisis that was exacerbated in the wake of those air strikes. Turkish forces have also been successful in retaking control from ISIS in several cities in the northern part of Aleppo Province.

The Iraqi city of Mosul had been occupied by ISIS for more than two years when an international coalition, led by Iraqi, Kurdish, and U.S. forces, launched a major offensive in October 2016 to regain control from the terrorist group. The massive-scale operation to remove up to 5,000 ISIS fighters from the city was complicated by the 1.5 million civilians reported to still be inside the city. Thousands of refugees fled to Syria within the first week of the offensive, and thousands more were expected to join them on a constant basis until Mosul was back under Iraqi control. The United Nations warned that the flood of refugees could become a catastrophic humanitarian crisis because camps along the Syrian border were ill-equipped to handle such a massive influx of people. As people continued to flee, ISIS put up strong resistance and set fire to oil wells to reduce the tactical abilities of Coalition Forces. Al-Baghdadi was believed to be trapped within the city as the offensive was ongoing.

Mosul fell to Iraqi, Kurdish, and Coalition Forces in July 2017, marking a major defeat for ISIS. Three months later, in October 2017, the Syrian city of Raqqa, which had been controlled by ISIS for many months, was also retaken. The fall of Mosul and Raqqa were the two primary turning points in the war against ISIS. By late 2017, the group controlled only small pockets of Iraqi and Syrian territory, none of which included any major urban areas. In December 2018, U.S. president Donald Trump announced his intention to withdraw troops from Syria, declaring victory against ISIS.

ISIS had lost almost all of its territory in Iraq and Syria; however, a U.S. Department of Defense report estimated that the group retained around 30,000 active fighters in the two countries. Finally, in late March 2019, the Syrian Democratic Forces (SDF) coalition announced that it had reclaimed 100 percent of the territory formerly held by ISIS in Syria. This announcement followed the fall of the terrorist group's final stronghold in the eastern Syrian city of Baghouz. ISIS experienced another significant setback after U.S. forces killed Abu Bakr al-Baghdadi in Northern Syria in October of 2019.

Paul G. Pierpaoli Jr.

Further Reading

BBC News. "Syria Iraq: The Islamic State Militant Group." Accessed June 13, 2014. https://www.bbc.com/news/world-middle-east-24179084.

Brisard, Jean-Charles, and Damien Martinez. *Zarqawi: The New Face of al-Qaeda*. Other Press, 2005.

CNN. "ISIS Fast Facts." https://www.cnn.com/2014/08/08/world/isis-fast-facts/index.html. Accessed December 18, 2018.

Wood, Graeme. "What ISIS Really Wants." *The Atlantic*, March 15, 2015: 78–94.

Israel

Israel, the only Jewish country in the world, has had a problematic relationship with its Arab neighbors since its inception in 1948. Immediately upon declaring its independence at the end of the British Mandate period in Palestine after World War II, a coalition of Arab countries declared war against it, and with the exception of two of those countries, Jordan and Egypt, Israel's relationship with its Arab neighbors remains extremely volatile. Syria, on Israel's northeast border, has gone to war with the Jewish state on numerous occasions since then, and both countries have walked a fine line between war and tolerance throughout the Syrian Civil War starting in 2011.

After World War II, the United Nations (UN) developed a plan for partitioning the

British Mandate territory of Palestine into separate Arab and Jewish states, connected by an economic union. Jerusalem was to be internationalized under the UN. Although the Arab population in Palestine was then 1.2 million people and the Jews numbered just 600,000, the UN plan approved by the General Assembly on November 29, 1947, granted the proposed Jewish state some 55 percent of the land and the Arab state only 45 percent. The Arab states rejected the partition plan, while the Jewish Agency in Palestine accepted it. Immediately following the UN vote, militant Palestinian Arabs and foreign Arab fighters initiated attacks against Jewish communities in Palestine, beginning the Arab-Jewish Communal War (November 30, May 1947–1948). The United States, with the world's largest Jewish population, became the chief champion and most reliable ally of a Jewish state, a position that cost it dearly in its relations with the Arab world and greatly impacted subsequent geopolitics in the Middle East.

The British completed their pullout on May 14, 1948, and that same day David Ben-Gurion, executive chairman and defense minister of the Jewish Agency, declared the independent Jewish state of Israel. Ben-Gurion, who was from the Mapai (Worker's Party), became the new state's first prime minister, a post he held during 1948–1953 and 1955–1963.

Immediately following the Israeli declaration of independence, the Arab armies of Egypt, Lebanon, Jordan, Syria, and Iraq invaded, sparking the Israeli-Arab War (1948–1949), also known as the Israeli War for Independence. In the war, the Jewish forces defeated the Arab armies. A series of armistices in 1949 ended the war, with Israel left in control of an additional 26 percent of the land of Mandate Palestine west of the Jordan River. Jordan, however, controlled large portions of the West Bank. The establishment of Israel and subsequent war also produced 600,000–700,000 Palestinian Arab refugees.

The 1949 cease-fires that ended the 1948–1949 war were not followed by peace agreements. The Arab states not only refused to recognize the existence of Israel but also refused to concede defeat in the war. Throughout most of the 1950s, Israel suffered from repeated attacks and raids from neighboring Arab states, including Syria, as well as Palestinian Arab paramilitary and terrorist groups. Aggressive Israeli retaliation failed to stop them.

In 1956, Gamal Abdel Nasser, Egyptian president from 1954 to 1970, nationalized the Suez Canal. Israel joined France and Britain to develop a secret plan to topple Nasser and secure control of the canal. On October 29, 1956, Israeli forces invaded the Sinai and headed for the Suez Canal, providing the excuse for the British and the French to intervene. The U.S. government applied considerable pressure, and all three states agreed to withdraw. Israel was the one clear winner. It secured the right to free navigation through the Suez Canal and on the waterways through the Straits of Tiran and Gulf of Aqaba. The UN also deployed a peacekeeping force along the border between Egypt and Israel.

Throughout the spring of 1967, Israel faced increasing attacks along its borders from Syria and the Palestine Liberation Organization (PLO), a quasi-terrorist organization created in 1964 to represent the Palestinian Arabs and coordinate efforts with Arab states to liberate Palestine. The PLO mounted cross-border attacks from Jordan. By May, war seemed imminent. With the Arab states mobilizing, on May 23 Egypt closed the Straits of Tiran and blockaded the Gulf of Aqaba, thereby cutting off the Israeli port of Eilat. Fearing an imminent coordinated Arab attack, Israel launched a pre-emptive strike on June 5, 1967, crippling the air forces of Egypt, Syria, Jordan, and Iraq. Having achieved air supremacy, Israel then easily defeated the armies of Egypt, Jordan, and Syria as well as Iraqi units. Five days later, Israel occupied the Sinai and Gaza Strip from Egypt, the West Bank and eastern Jerusalem from Jordan, and the Golan Heights from Syria, doubling the size of the Jewish state and providing buffer zones in the new territories. In the wake of its military victory, Israel announced that it would not withdraw from these captured territories until negotiations with the Arab states took place leading to recognition of Israel's right to exist.

One of the most significant outcomes of the Six-Day War, as the 1967 conflict is now known, in terms of Israel's relationship to the Syrian Civil War, was its occupation of two-thirds of the Golan Heights region. The Golan Heights, a hilly elevated region, offers commanding views of the Jordan Valley, including the Sea of Galilee. It is strategically important to the Israelis because before the war in 1967 the area afforded Syria the ability to easily identify and hit Israeli targets. It is estimated that more than 100,000 Syrians were driven from their homes during the Six-Day War, and Israel's continued occupation of the territory is a sore spot for the Syrian government, which sees their presence as an afront to their sovereignty. Soon after the war, Jewish settlers began to move into the occupied territory, and the Syrians grew increasingly frustrated with the international community for allowing this to happen unchallenged. During the 1973 war with Israel, Syrian troops briefly held some of the occupied territory in the southern Golan, but they were eventually repelled by the Israeli Defense Forces. In 1981, Israel gave de facto recognition of the Golan as their territory by extending national law throughout the Heights, and it has remained part of Israel in its national consciousness ever since. There were some overtures of a willingness of both countries to negotiate the status of the Golan Heights in the mid-2000s, but this goodwill was short-lived and had fallen completely apart by the beginning of the Syrian Conflict in 2011.

Throughout the Syrian Civil War, all sides, especially the Syrian government itself, have been reluctant to take part in any action that might drag Israel into the conflict in any meaningful way. Some of the militant groups, however, have tried to provoke the Israelis in an attempt to destabilize the entire region. The al-Qaeda–backed Nusra Front, the Islamic State, and other rebel groups have tried to stir up trouble in the Syrian-held areas of the Golan Heights, and in areas directly adjacent to Israeli territory, in order to cause trouble, and in these operations the Syrian government forces have acted very carefully.

The Israelis have tried to maintain a position of neutrality throughout the conflict, though they have provided aid to relief organizations working directly with the civilian population. While they have not been directly involved in the civil war militarily, it is vitally important to understand that the mere existence of the State of Israel as a geopolitical actor in the region is always a factor when one considers the costs and consequences of destabilization in the region. The Israeli government is no friend to Assad's Ba'athist regime, but it is also fearful of a militant-backed government taking power in Damascus.

Stefan Brooks, Daniel E. Spector,
and Spencer C. Tucker

Further Reading

Dowty, Alan. *Israel/Palestine.* Polity, 2005.

Gilbert, Martin. *Israel: A History.* William Morrow, 1998.

Rabinovich, Itamar, and Jehuda Reinharz. *Israel in the Middle East: Documents and Readings on Society, Politics, and Foreign Relations, Pre-1948 to the Present.* Brandeis University Press, 2008.

Reich, Bernard. *A Brief History of Israel.* Checkmark Books, 2005.

Sachar, Howard M. *A History of Israel: From the Rise of Zionism to Our Time.* Knopf, 1976.

J

Jabal al-Zawiya

Jabal al-Zawiya is a highland region in the Idlib Governorate in northwest Syria that has been the site of much fighting throughout the Syrian Civil War; as of 2019 it remained the last true rebel stronghold in the Syrian Civil War. Consisting of a few dozen towns situated in mountain valleys, the region has a lot of remote areas, which made it an ideal location for anti-Assad militias to set up base camps. The primary militia members in the region referred to themselves as the Sham Falcons. Comprised almost exclusively of young men from throughout Jabal al-Zawiya, the Sham Falcons relied on tactics that took advantage of their vast knowledge of the local, mountainous terrain. They used this knowledge to launch guerrilla attacks against infantry units from the Syrian Arab Army. Their attacks were not enough to create mass casualties for the Syrian government's forces, but they were enough of a thorn in their side that by the end of 2011, the Assad regime determined that decisive action against the region's militias was needed. Many soldiers in the Syrian Arab Army who grew up in the region had defected in order to fight against their former army units; given a choice of defending their homes and families or deploying with the army to fight against relatives and childhood friends, most chose the former option.

Jabal al-Zawiya is, like other highland regions around the world, famous for the fierce independence of its people. People who live in rural, highland areas often identify, first and foremost, with the village, valley, or town they grew up in, and when given the choice to fight for Syria or defend their homes, many soldiers from Jabal al-Zawiya chose to desert their army units and return home. Some reports say that as many as 3,000 soldiers from Jabal al-Zawiya, and at least 10,000 soldiers overall, deserted the Syrian Army in the first year of the conflict alone. Many intended to flee into Turkey, across the border from Jabal al-Zawiya, in order to help form the Free Syrian Army. Because the Free Syrian Army was made up of a large number of well-trained former soldiers, it was one of the more effective rebel militias in the conflict, and they were eager to accept anyone who was well trained and motivated to overthrow Bashar al-Assad.

In December 2011, a sizable group of deserters from the Syrian Arab Army had made their way home and gathered to make their way into Turkey. Determined to make an example of the deserters to other potential defectors and to the people of Jabal al-Zawiya, the Syrian Army made it a priority to pursue them. On December 19 and 20, the Syrian Arab Army launched an offensive and killed at least 200 people in towns and villages throughout Jabal al-Zawiya, though that number could be higher. Most of those killed are believed to have been deserters from the army making their way to Turkey, and the event became known as the Jabal al-Zawiya Massacre.

Jabal al-Zawiya remained a hotbed of resistance throughout the conflict, and many of the region's towns and villages remain under rebel control, despite the Syrian Army's many attempts to take them. Throughout

2017, rebel groups launched many attacks against Syrian government assets throughout northwest Syria. Knowing that the previous six years of attempts to quell the resistance inside the region, the Syrian government turned to their Russian allies for support, and in September Russian and Syrian jets hit dozens of targets throughout Jabal al-Zawiya. These attacks, however, did not really help the Syrian government retake territory in the region. They did, however, serve as a reminder that the Syrian government still viewed the region as vital to its efforts to eliminate resistance to the Assad regime. In May 2019, Russian and Syrian jets launched extensive air strikes at rebel strongholds throughout Jabal al-Zawiya in an attempt to pave the way for Syrian ground forces to move into the highland region. The Syrian Army managed to take one town, but the region as a whole remained, as it had been since 2012, under rebel control.

Robert M. Kerr

Further Reading

BBC News. "Syria Unrest: Jabal al-Zawiya 'Massacres.'" January 19, 2012. https://www.bbc.com/news/world-middle-east-16287450.

Jihad

The term "jihad" is often translated as "holy war." It means "striving" or "to exert the utmost effort" and refers both to a religious duty to spread and defend Islam by waging war (lesser jihad) and an inward spiritual struggle to attain perfect faith (greater jihad). Although interpretations differ, the broad spectrum of modern Islam emphasizes the inner spiritual jihad.

Definitions of the term jihad have also been determined by historical circumstances. Indian reformer Sayyid Ahmad Khan (1817–1898) argued for a more limited interpretation of jihad whereby believers could perform charitable acts in place of armed struggle and it was only incumbent if Muslims could not practice their faith. The reform movement of Muhammad ibn abd al-Wahhab (1703–1792) in Arabia, by contrast, reasserted the incumbency of jihad as armed struggle for all believers. As the Quran contains verses that promote mercy and urge peacemaking but also those (referred to as the Sword Verses) that more ardently require jihad of believers, there is a scriptural basis for both sides of this argument.

Some scholars differentiate the fulfilling of jihad by the heart, the tongue, or the sword as a means of discouraging Muslims from seeing armed struggle as a commandment, but such teachings have by and large been contradicted by the revival of activist jihad, first in response to colonialism and then again in the twentieth century.

The broad spectrum of Islam considers foreign military intervention, foreign occupation, economic oppression, non-Islamic cultural realignment, colonialism, and the oppression of a domestic government, either secular or Islamic, of an Islamic people or country to be a sufficient reason, if not a Quranic mandate, to participate in a defensive jihad. The more militant and fundamental end of the Islamic spectrum asserts that a social, economic, and military defensive jihad is justifiable and necessary. However, a widespread discussion of jihad is ongoing in the Muslim world today in response to the rise of militancy, and there is a concerted effort to separate the concepts of jihad and martyrdom from each other when they are the rallying call of irrespon-sible extremists such as Osama bin Laden and his ilk.

Notable defensive jihads in the more recent history of Islam include the resistance of the Afghan (1979) and Chechnya (1940–1944, 1994–1996, and 1999–2009) mujahi-deen against their respective Soviet and Russian occupations and the Algerian War (1954–1962) against France.

Richard M. Edwards

Further Reading

Bostrom, Andrew G., ed. *The Legacy of Jihad: Islamic Holy War and the Fate of Non-Muslims*. Prometheus, 2005.

DeLong-Bas, Natana N. *Wahhabi Islam: From Revival and Reform to Global Jihad*. Oxford University Press, 2004.

Esposito, John L. *Unholy War: Terror in the Name of Islam*. Oxford University Press, 2002.

Kepel, Gilles. *Jihad: The Trail of Political Islam*. Belknap, 2003.

K

Kurdish Peoples Protection Units (YPG)

The Kurdish Peoples Protection Units (YPG) is a Kurdish autonomist group operating in Syria since 2011. Along with its female affiliate, Yekineyen Parasina Jin (YPJ), the YPG is the armed wing of the Kurdish political party Democratic Union Party (PYD). The YPG was also the dominant component of the Syrian Democratic Forces (SDF), an armed militia organized in 2015 to unite Arab and Kurdish rebel factions to better coordinate operations against the Islamic State. SDF fighters on the ground, in coordination with a U.S.-led air campaign, seized the Islamic State's remaining territory in early 2019, but credit for the success is largely assigned to the YPG. By mid-2019, the YPG and its partners gained control of major portions of territory and remain active in northeastern Syria, where they seek to maintain a self-governing region known as Rojava.

The Kurds in Syria, who make up approximately 10 percent of the population, have not traditionally been dedicated to a nationalist struggle for independence, unlike Kurdish minority populations in Turkey and Iraq. The Syrian Kurds were not among the first groups to join the 2011 uprising against President Bashar al-Assad, despite an increase in repressive policies implemented by the regime over the previous decade. Most ethnic Kurds are concentrated in Kobane and Afrin in the north and Jazeera in the east, but many assimilated into the culture across the country.

Opposition among Kurds and Arabs grew during 2011, and between May and October, 17 political parties met to discuss a strategy for seizing the opportunity for more political power in Syria. Much of the debate between parties centered on the extent of Kurdish autonomy, the role of religion, and the removal of the word "Arab" from the Syrian Arab Republic in a post-Assad Syria. Two coalitions emerged from the ongoing dialogue: the Syrian National Council (SNC) and the Kurdish National Council (KNC). The committees split largely along Arab nationalist/Islamist (SNC) and Kurdish/secular lines (KNC). Realizing its relative strength, the PYD ultimately decided not to align with either, exacerbating tensions among the factions. Both the SNC and KNC coalitions distrusted the PYD (and its armed wing, YPG), as they suspected the PYD/YPG was secretly negotiating with the Syrian regime. The PYD was the Syrian affiliate of the Turkish-based Kurdistan Workers' Party (PKK), and some YPG fighters had previously been PKK members or trained with the group. Moreover, the Syrian regime had allied with the PKK in the 1990s and renewed an association with the group in 2011 as Syrian-Turkish relations became strained.

In 2012, various coalitions of Arab rebels formed throughout the country, and the PYD/YPG focused attention on protecting the Kurdish areas from the fighting. The remaining KNC-PYD rivalry peaked in May-June when the armed factions of each Kurdish group clashed. Suspicions of regime-PYD/YPG coordination grew as Syrian security forces voluntarily withdrew from Kurdish areas soon after, allowing the YPG to take control of the most densely populated Kurdish cities in late July 2012. The PYD/YPG initially offered to work alongside the KNC to maintain security and govern the Kurdish cities. Iraqi Kurdish leader Massoud Barzani brokered the Erbil Agreement between the factions intended to establish the administrative structure, but the PYD refused to implement it in practice. The PYD/YPG announced plans to establish Rojava in November 2013, intended to be an autonomous region of Syria. The announcement marked its consolidation of power and further isolated the KNC, which relocated to northern Iraq.

The YPG demonstrated it was capable of defending Kurdish territory, beginning in the summer of 2013, when fighters clashed with Nusra along the border with Turkey. This marked the first of many battles with jihadist groups between 2013 and 2019. The earlier decision to undercut the KNC and Kurdish leaders in Iraq proved to be costly, however, as it left the YPG to defend hundreds of miles of border without consistent partners or a reliable logistics network.

As ISIS swept across Syria in 2014, the YPG coordinated with other anti-ISIS groups to defend northern Syria with limited success. Due to the YPG's relationship with the PKK, a group designated as a terrorist organization by Turkey and the United States, Turkey refused requests for logistics support as Islamic State fighters launched an offensive on the PYD stronghold of Kobane between September and October 2014. Kurdish Peshmerga forces from northern Iraq and the Free Syrian Army reinforced the YPG in November-December 2014 and pushed the Islamic State from Kobane in early 2015. The YPG, Free Syrian Army, and Kurdish Peshmerga, with coordinated air support from the United States, recaptured hundreds of villages and towns from ISIS throughout 2015.

U.S.-Turkish relations became increasingly strained after the United States assisted the YPG in the defense of Kobane. U.S. domestic and international audiences also questioned the long-term consequences of strengthening the PKK-affiliated group that was also suspected of coordination with the Syrian regime. Through direction from the United States, Arab and Kurdish militias united against the Islamic State were restructured in 2015 under the Syrian Democratic Forces (SDF). The SDF commander, identified as Mazlum Kobane, is known by the Turkish government to be a longtime member of the PKK, which added to Turkey's unease with Kurdish-controlled territory on its border.

Turkish forces and the Turkish-backed Free Syrian Army have continued to fight Kurdish militias along the border since 2018. In response, Kurdish militia leaders hoping to hold the territory opened ongoing discussions with the Syrian regime to negotiate protection from future attacks and an arrangement for regional autonomy.

Melia Pfannenstiel

Further Reading

Byman, Daniel. *Road Warriors: Foreign Fighters in the Armies of Jihad.* Oxford University Press, 2019.

The Economist. "Who Will Rule the North? The Kurds Are Creating a State of Their Own in Northern Syria," May 23, 2019. https://www.economist.com/middle-east -and-africa/2019/05/23/the-kurds-are-creat ing-a-state-of-their-own-in-northern-syria.

Lister, Charles R. *The Syrian Jihad: Al Qaeda, the Islamic State and the Evolution of an Insurgency.* Oxford University Press, 2015.

Phillips, Christopher. *The Battle for Syria: International Rivalry in the New Middle East.* Yale University Press, 2016.

Stein, Aaron. "Partner Operations in Syria." Atlantic Council Rafik Hariri Center for the Middle East, July 2017. https://www.atlantic council.org/images/publications/Partner _Operations_in_Syria_web_0710.pdf.

Kurdistan

Known by the ancient Sumerians as Karda and by the Babylonians as Qardu, the land of the Kurds stretches across the northern part of what was known historically as Mesopotamia. Today, the 74,000 square miles of mountainous and heavily forested terrain that "Kurdistan" covers encompasses southeastern Turkey, northwestern Iran, northern Iraq, and northeastern Syria. The Tigris and Euphrates rivers originate in the rugged mountains of Kurdistan. From before the time of Xenophon (427–355 BCE), this land was in the possession of the Kurds, who consider themselves the indigenous inhabitants of the region.

Kurds are an Indo-Aryan ethnic group distinct from the Turks, Persians, and Arabs, although the majority of Kurds share the Islamic faith of those populations. The vast majority of Kurds are Sunni Muslims, but there is a Shiite minority, known as the Feyli, who live in Iraq, primarily in northeast Baghdad. The Kurdish language, customs, traditions, and internal tribal structures are also distinct, though many Kurds are multilingual, adopting, at least in part, the languages and cultures of the countries in which they live. It is impossible to know the exact number of Kurds, but most estimate it to be around 45 million; the Kurds are the largest ethnic group in the world without a state, even though the unrecognized land of Kurdistan comprises an area the size of France. Instead, they have been incorporated as minority populations within larger surrounding states.

It is estimated that there are roughly 20 million Kurds in Turkey (which comprises almost 25 percent of that country's total population), about 10 million in Iran, a little more than 8 million in Iraq (which is actually about 27 percent of Iraq's total population), about 3.5 million in Syria, and about 3.5 million in the Kurdish diaspora throughout the world.

Wedged between the larger powers of Persians, Assyrians, and Babylonians, the Kurds were constantly pressed into service by the rulers of various empires up to and including that of the Greeks, which later gave way to their provincial incorporation into the Roman Empire. From the demise of Byzantium to rule by Arabs under the Caliph of Baghdad, the Kurds enjoyed brief periods of autonomy between foreign rulers, including the Mongols, until they were eventually incorporated into the Ottoman Empire. The collapse of the Ottomans after World War I offered the Kurds another chance at self-rule. Representatives of the crumbling Ottoman order signed the Treaty of Sèvres with the Allies in 1920 that dismembered the old empire into states under the supervision of Allied powers—one of which was reserved for the Kurds.

The Treaty of Sèvres, however, was rejected by the Turkish nationalist movement that had come to power under Mustafa Kemal Ataturk—the founder of a new secular Turkey. Before Kurdistan could be founded, Ataturk had consolidated power in Anatolia and pressed for a more favorable treaty. In 1923, the Turks signed the Treaty of Lausanne with the Allies, who were in no position to fight another war. The new treaty revoked the promise of an independent Kurdistan. Abandonment of promises made by Western powers in the Treaty of Sèvres was, from the perspective of the Kurds, a painful double-cross. The old Ottoman province of Mosul, rich with oil fields, was attached to the new state of Iraq along with the provinces of Basra and Baghdad. The Kurds who lived under Ottoman rule for so long were thereby partitioned between Turkish and Arab rulers. Kurds in Iran remained under the rule of the Iranians.

The post–World War I settlement remains the geographic fate of greater Kurdistan. Each of the areas of Kurdistan have suffered different degrees of repression from their foreign masters, perhaps mostly at the hands of the Turks and Arabs. Iraqi Kurdistan has over time come to enjoy the greatest level of autonomy amongst the larger Kurdish populations, but the journey to that level of autonomy has been a long and difficult one. The struggles within Iraq and Turkey began shortly after the war in 1918, and those struggles continue to the present day.

The Kurds in Syria have been placed in a precarious situation in terms of both their immediate safety and their geopolitical position relative to the Syrian government, the United States, Turkey, Iraq, and Iran. Making up the majority of the population in a sliver of land in northeastern Syria known by the Kurds as Rojava, as is the case in Iraq where the Kurds have been longtime allies of the United States, Kurds in Syria have been among the fiercest of opposition forces pitted against the Islamic State. In particular, the Kurdish People's Protection Units (YPG) have received arms and advice from the United States and have been key players in the fight against ISIS. The YPG, however, are the Syrian affiliate of the Kurdistan Workers Party (PKK), which has been engaged in an insurgency against the Turkish government since the 1980s, and this has significantly complicated U.S.-Turkish relations.

The relationship among the United States, Turkey, the Syrian Kurds, and the Syrian government was further complicated by President Donald Trump's announcement in late 2018 that U.S. troops would be unilaterally withdrawing from Syria; however, no immediate action followed this announcement, and as of early 2019, U.S. troops (primarily Special Forces) remained in place. The future of the Kurds in northeastern Syria remains in question; however, it is likely that the uneasy relationship among the Kurds in Syria and the Turkish government, the United States, the Syrian regime, and even their fellow Kurds in neighboring countries will remain complex and tense.

Michael J. Kelly and Robert M. Kerr

Further Reading

Chaliand, Gerard. *A People without a Country: The Kurds and Kurdistan.* Olive Branch Press, 1993.

Institute Kurde de Paris. "The Kurdish Population," 2018. https://www.institutkurde.org /en/info/the-kurdish-population-1232551 004.

Kelly, Michael J. *Ghosts of Halabja: Saddam Hussein and the Kurdish Genocide.* Praeger Security International, 2008.

L

Latakia

Latakia is one of Syria's most important cities. It is the country's principal port city, and the capital of the governorate that is Bashar al-Assad's ancestral homeland. Because of its strategically important location, Latakia has been an important port since the fourth century BCE, and it has been continuously inhabited since then. Like most port cities, it is a crossroad of cultures; it is a center of Alawite culture and politics with roughly half of Latakia's inhabitants being of Alawite descent. Just because it is the ancestral home of the Alawites, however, does not mean that there is complete loyalty to Bashar al-Assad in the region's rural hinterland. While the Syrian military has kept a foothold in the city throughout much of the conflict, as late as May 2019 the rebels maintained a stronghold on the mountains bordering the city.

Like many cities in the crossroad that is modern Syria, Latakia has been controlled by numerous groups from different civilizations throughout history. Various ancient societies controlled its port on the Mediterranean throughout history, In 638 CE, the city was conquered by Arabs who brought with them Islam, which was a very young religion at the time with the Prophet Muhammad having passed away only six years prior. Muslims controlled the port until the city was sacked by Christian Crusaders from Europe in 1103. Latakia was governed by Christians (though this does not mean all, or even most, of the people living in the city converted to Christianity). A few decades

later, in 1188, Saladin, the Kurdish founder of the Islamic Ayyubid Dynasty, which ruled over Egypt and the Levant for almost 90 years, took the city back from the Crusaders, but it changed hands again a few more times over the next few centuries. It was governed for a time by Christian merchants from Tripoli, Muslim merchants from Hama, the Ottomans, and finally the French before it became the most important port in the modern country of Syria.

Latakia is located on a good harbor with relatively deep water. Historically, one of the factors that made the port so important is that it is surrounded by very fertile agricultural lands. This gave Latakia's farmers direct access to European and North African markets and allowed them to compete economically with anyone throughout Syria and even Mediterranean Europe. Latakia is particularly famous for its unique tobacco, which is first sun cured and then smoke cured over embers of aromatic woods and herbs. It is an extremely potent tobacco, so it is usually blended with other tobaccos that are more subtle and then smoked primarily in pipes. Latakia tobacco became particularly popular in France and Great Britain. Today, most Latakia tobacco is grown in nearby Cyprus, however, and since the Syrian Conflict very few people in the region are cultivating it and the port's main exports are bitumen, asphalt, cereals, cotton, fruit, eggs, pottery, and vegetable oil. In fact, vegetable oil processing, along with sponge fishing, makes up a significant portion of Latakia city's economic base. Olive oil production in Latakia has actually continued to expand throughout the years of the civil war, but much of it has been wasted or unsold due to difficulties in getting the final product into the world market. Latakia's modern port facilities were established in 1950 with large loans provided by the United States and Saudi Arabia.

While Latakia's history is ancient, its twentieth-century history is the most relevant to understanding the current situation as it relates to the Syrian Civil War. When Latakia, like the rest of Syria, fell under the French Mandate, its Alawite population was quick to ally itself with the French administrators. The Alawites successfully lobbied the French for autonomous status in return for their loyalty to the European administrators, and they enjoyed that status and the freedom to practice their religion, which is a variation of Shia Islam, without the worry of persecution from the region's majority Sunni population; the "State of Latakia" was established in 1922. Some have argued that the French intended to grant autonomy to Syria's religious minorities in order to play them against the Arab majority and to quell any large-scale Syrian nationalist movements that might challenge French authority. The Alawites enjoyed autonomous status, with the exception of a three-year period from 1936 to 1939 when the territory was temporarily ceded to the Arab nationalists who were the semiautonomous administrators of Syria's Arab lands in an attempt by the French to buy their continued support. Alawite separatism was strong, however, and they were regranted their autonomous status from 1939 until 1942 when the French Mandate ended. The withdrawal of the French left the Alawites, as well as many of Syria's other minority groups who supported the French during the mandate period, in a tough situation, and relations between them and the larger Arab populations have never really recovered.

After Syrian independence in 1946, the Arab Sunni Muslim elite formed the basis of power in the government centered in Damascus, and they immediately set about erasing some of the privileges minority groups such as the Alawites enjoyed under their status as autonomous peoples. The new Sunni-dominated government painted the Alawites as religious outsiders, eliminated territorial autonomy of the Alawite state, and eliminated parliamentary seats reserved especially for them. Interestingly, however, the Sunni elites were reluctant to send their sons to the military, so Syria's minorities made up a significant proportion of the new state's military forces. Because the French were afraid of the possibility of a united Arab nationalist movement gaining military power, Syria's military forces during the French Mandate were disproportionately made up of minority groups, and the Arab Sunnis never really developed a culture of military service as a result. This is a condition that persisted into the new independent Syrian military, a fact that would come to have significant consequences down the road as the minority dominated Ba'ath party, and soon after that the Alawite father of Bashar al-Assad, would take over the country and set in motion a chain of events that would lead to the current civil war.

There were many Sunnis in the military, and they made up a significant number of the highest-ranking officers within the military. The Sunnis did not represent a single community of interest, however—a fact that remained apparent during the civil war when various Sunni interest groups spawned multiple, competing militias in the anti-Assad movement. The various competing interests of the Sunnis led to bitter infighting and factionalism in the highest officer ranks, and this opened the door for the lower-ranking Alawite officers, who did have unity of cause and unity of effort, to take advantage of the infighting among their superiors. The opportunity of the Alawites to exploit the fissures among the Sunni officers was exacerbated in the early 1950s after a series of failed Sunni-led military coups when the lower-ranking officers, who had earned respect by staying out of the Sunni politics, were elevated into higher positions of authority. Because the Alawites and other minorities represented single interests, they brought increasing stability to the military ranks and enjoyed the support of a very appreciative government. It is in this slow, methodical way that the once marginalized minority eventually came to rule the Syrian state; in a postcolonial environment where the numerically dominant group failed to reach a consensus on what the new state should look like, a more united minority seized opportunities where they found them and created a situation in which they gained the keys to the government. It was a rise to power that has always meant that the Alawites' grip on power was always dependent upon the Sunni Arabs remaining fractured into various interest groups, and no doubt Bashar al-Assad saw the unity that was emerging throughout Syria against his government in the wake of the Arab Spring as a threat he needed to try to put down as quickly as possible if he were to maintain not only his, but his Alawite kinsmen's privileged position. When people began to unite against him, he turned his attention to Latakia, the historical base of Alawite power and culture, in order to solidify his base.

Latakia has not been entirely supportive of the Assad regime; there were a lot of protests there in March 2011, early on in the conflict. After arresting a large number of people, however, the Syrian military made great efforts to secure the city, and even established an extensive series of roadblocks in order to control access to the city. This was done, in part, because Assad knew his strongest power base was in the relatively wealthy, and heavily Alawite, population of Latakia that was most satisfied with the status quo of his government. It was also crucial that Assad ensure that the port stay open in order to keep some semblance of economic life alive. Latakia's place as one of Assad's top priorities was solidified in 2015 when he allowed the Russian military to establish a base there, and the Russian Air Force has maintained a constant presence over the city, which has allowed life in Latakia to proceed fairly close to normal throughout much of the conflict. Latakia is also of great interest to Assad's longtime ally Iran. Iran and the Ba'ath party had an alliance that dates back to the early 1980s, and both countries have formed a mutually beneficial relationship. Iran has invested a lot of money into the relationship, and in April 2019 announced that it would be leasing port facilities in Latakia beginning on October 1 of that year. This complicates an already tense geopolitical situation in the eastern Mediterranean because it grants Iran not only economic but potentially naval access to this already volatile region. It remains to be seen what an Iranian military presence in a body of water that is already home to vessels from throughout Europe, Turkey, Egypt, Israel, and the United States, among others may bring.

Robert M. Kerr

Further Reading

Hourani, Albert. *A History of the Arab Peoples*. Belknap Press, 2010.

Podeh, Elie. *The Decline of Arab Unity: The Rise and Fall of the United Arab Republic*. Sussex Academic Press, 1999.

Reilly, James. *Fragile Nation, Shattered Land: The Modern History of Syria*. Lynne Rienner Publishers, 2018.

M

Maarrat al-Nu'man/Al-Ma'arra

Maarrat al-Nu'man, also known as al-Ma'arra, is a city in northwest Syria located about 20 miles south of Idlib and 35 miles north of Hama—two of the most hotly contested cities throughout the Syrian Civil War. In the conflict, the city was the site of two significant battles, in 2012 and again in 2016, between Syrian government and rebel forces, but the city's historical significance is much older than that and exists in a blur of fact and legend that shrouds it with a certain sense of infamy.

In ancient times, Maarrat al-Nu'man was an important trade center, but had declined in importance and was described by Muslim travelers through the region in the tenth century as laying largely in ruins. As the result of advances in agricultural techniques and irrigation technology, however, it had become an important agricultural market town by the eleventh century, and stone walls had been built around its perimeter to protect its commerce. Figs, olives, grapes, pistachios, and almonds quickly became the city's most important crops, and large numbers of people moved from the countryside into Maarrat al-Nu'man. However, the city's agricultural fortune became a liability in November 1098. This was the time of the First Crusade, a period in which European noblemen, under the sponsorship of Pope Urban II, set out to liberate Jerusalem from Muslim rule. One of the noblemen who answered the pope's call to arms was Raymond de Saint Gilles. Saint Gilles and his men had set out from France and had fought some of the most significant battles of the early Crusade, including the Siege of Nicaea, the Battle of Dorylaeum, and the Siege of Antioch in 1097. The Siege of Antioch proved extremely difficult, and after the victory his men were jubilant and invigorated, yet hungry. The European armies of the First Crusade were primarily private armies organized by wealthy nobles, and they did not have extensive experience or knowledge in fighting long wars far from home. As a result, supplying these armies on the road grew more and more complex, as the science of logistics and supply that is so essential to modern armies had not yet been developed. After Antioch, Saint Gilles and his men turned toward a city they knew could meet all their needs in terms of filling their hungry bellies—Maarrat al-Nu'man.

The siege and attack of Maarrat al-Nu'man is one of history's most gruesome and infamous events. Beginning on November 28, 1098, the siege lasted two weeks. It took constant and brutal fighting for the Christian Crusaders to breech the city walls, and when they finally did on December 11, they went on a rampage, killing at least 8,000 people. Not finding enough food to feed the entire army, a significant number of the hungry Crusaders turned to cannibalism, eating the flesh of dead Muslims. Historians argue about the exact number that were eaten, but this event is burned into the memory of not only Maarrat al-Nu'man's modern population, but of people throughout the Muslim world as well. Regardless of what Western historians say, the story of the cannibalism at Maarrat al-Nu'man is viewed as fact in the

Middle East, and it is important to understand this in terms of modern attitudes toward Westerners among some of the Syrian Conflict's militia groups.

Maarrat al-Nu'men's role in the Syrian Civil War dates to June 2011. One of the sites of the earliest and most vocal protests against the Assad regime, Maarrat also happened to be the home of a large number of Syrian Arab Army soldiers who defected after the government's initial brutal crackdowns in Daraa, the site of the conflict's earliest protests. The defectors, who had joined the rebel militia called the Free Syrian Army, attacked a government roadblock in October. After weeks of fighting the Syrian Arab Army and their allied pro-government militias, the Free Syrian Army took control of Maarrat in December and held it until June 2012. After it changed hands between the government and the rebels a few more times, the heavily battered city was under the control of the Syrian government until October 2012 after the first Battle of Maarrat al-Nu'man.

The 2012 Battle of Maarrat al-Nu'man pitted the Syrian Army and the rebel Free Syrian Army against each other for control of the strategically important town located on the heavily traveled M5 Highway. In early October, rebel forces knew that government forces needed the highway in order to reinforce their troops in and around Aleppo, and they decided that gaining control of Maarrat would hinder the Syrian Army significantly. The Syrian Air Force launched air strikes against rebel units, but the Free Syrian Army forces were strategically dispersed outside the town in small units, and the air strikes were not very effective in stopping their advance. On the second day of their offensive, rebel forces had seized eight out of nine of the government's checkpoints controlling access to the city, and they had set up their headquarters in one of the city's museums.

During the offensive, the rebels discovered that a detention facility the government forces had been using had been booby-trapped with an explosive device; 16 Free Syrian Army soldiers were killed when they triggered the trap. They also discovered that the detention facility contained the corpses of between 25 and 65 (sources conflict) dissidents and defectors from the military who had been arrested from Maarrat al-Nu'man. In just two days of fighting, it is estimated that around 60 people, most of them civilians, were killed. A day after losing their hold on the city, government forces launched a counteroffensive. There was intense fighting over the span of three days with the rebel forces coming out ahead—they held the town for about six months, which gave rebels fighting in Aleppo a distinct advantage due to the inability of Syrian troops to effectively bypass rebel-controlled Maarrat al-Nu'man.

The city remained a hotbed of fighting for the next three years, with skirmishes between government and opposition forces frequently breaking out between periods of fragile peace. On March 13, 2016, a coalition of forces from Jabhat al-Nusra and a group called Jund al-Aqsa launched an attack against a Syrian Army headquarters located in the city. This attack was significant because it is believed, though the Syrian Army denies it, that the rebel forces were able to seize two storage facilities' worth of American made anti-tank missiles. A fact that is not disputed, however, is that the anti-government militias acquired a large amount of ammunition and weapons. The success of the rebel forces in gaining weapons and equipment was significant, but what they did not expect was the very hostile reception they received from the citizens of Maarrat al-Mu'man after they tried to consolidate their gains after the Syrian Army division that had been holding the town fled. Civilian resistance to governance by Jabhat al-Nusra was intense unrest, and civil disobedience against the anti-government coalition became a significant thorn in the rebels' side for months. As of 2017, Maarrat al-Nu'man, like much of Idlib Province, was primarily under rebel control, even though the Syrian military has been able to regain control of a handful of neighborhoods throughout Maarrat and the city's population would largely welcome the return of Syrian government forces into the area.

Robert M. Kerr

Further Reading

Asbridge, Thomas. *The First Crusade: A New History.* Oxford University Press, 2005.

Phillips, Jonathan. *Holy Warriors: A Modern History of the Crusades.* Random House, 2010.

N

National Coordination Committee/Body for Democratic Change

The National Coordination Committee, also known as the National Coordination Body for Democratic Change, was a coalition of unarmed opposition parties and individuals based in Syria. It was created in the summer of 2011 to serve as a mouthpiece for people in Syria who opposed the Assad regime but did not want to take up arms because they believe true change can only be brought about peacefully. Its initial platform called for dialogue with the government in order to bring about the release of political prisoners, the withdrawal of the Syrian Arab Army from cities, the inclusion of opposition parties in national dialogue and elections, allowing foreign reporters to have unfettered access to all the places and people of Syria, and accountability for government officials who abuse their power. They also put forth a plan for a new government that addressed all of these issues and suggested changes to the constitution in order to safeguard certain rights in the future. The three principles of the organization were stated as: "No to foreign military intervention, no to religious and sectarian instigation, and no to violence and the militarization of the revolution."

The people who instigated the creation of the National Coordination Committee for Democratic Change were not newcomers to opposing the Assad regime. In fact, they had engaged in multiple attempts to try to introduce reforms into the Syrian system, and their efforts had varying degrees of success in garnering popular support. In 2005, for example, the group drafted a document called the Damascus Declaration that called for democratic reforms. This declaration was well received among the public, but the coalition was short-lived as internal rifts among the members stopped their momentum. The efforts of democratic reformers were mostly disorganized after the group's initial success in 2005, until the events of the Arab Spring and the Syrian government's violent crackdowns against peaceful protesters in the city of Daraa brought them back together. When the National Coordination Committee was formed in Damascus, 15 political parties representing various interests, along with several opposition figures both in and out of Syria, agreed to set their differences aside for the sake of unifying against the Ba'athist government of Bashar al-Assad.

In the fall of 2011, representatives of the various opposition groups met in Doha, Qatar, to discuss their plan. The idea was to develop a political platform; however, the best the group could accomplish at the Doha meeting was an agreement that the coalition's four main groups—the National Coordination Body, the signatories of the Damascus Declaration, the Muslim Brotherhood, and the independent Islamic Movement—needed to form a unified front. Even this small amount of momentum fell apart, however, after the Arab League announced its plan to bring about peace while allowing Assad to stay in power until 2015. Unwilling to compromise on its demand that Assad step down immediately, the Muslim Brotherhood, no doubt bolstered by the group's success in playing a key role in taking down Hosni Mubarak in Egypt, walked away from the coalition completely.

The National Coordination Committee was not the only political opposition working against the Assad regime. Its main competitor was the Syrian National Council, an opposition group made up of Syrian dissidents living in Turkey who successfully lobbied the Arab League to recognize them as the official representative of Syria on the regional stage. This was a huge coup for the Syrian National Council, and they assumed that if the Assad regime fell, they would be the rightful heirs to the keys to the government because of this recognition from the Arab League. Other international actors favored the militant route. Saudi Arabia and Qatar both favored arming the Free Syria Army with state-of-the-art weapons to aid in their fight.

One of the things that made the National Coordination Committee stand out was their initial desire to have direct talks with the Assad regime. As was illustrated earlier, some members of the coalition, such as the Muslim Brotherhood, opposed this approach, as did many of the National Coordination Committee's competitors. In general, the National Coordination Committee's relationship with other opposition groups is poor, and after their initial efforts, they lost momentum.

The National Coordination Committee, though moderate and not overly effective in the long run, is notable in that it showed that political opposition to the Ba'ath Party predated the Arab Spring in Syria by at least six years. When the peaceful protests against Bashar al-Assad first erupted in Daraa, and then spread rapidly across the country in the wake of the Arab Spring, they did so in the context of an anti-Ba'athist dialogue that had already been taking place, at least among the country's intelligentsia. It was, perhaps, because of this growing anti-regime dialogue outlined in the 2005 Damascus Declaration that Assad responded so violently to the initially peaceful protests. He knew that opposition to his government was widespread, and he felt the only way to retain his power was to do so forcefully.

Robert M. Kerr

Further Reading

Carnegie Middle East Center. "National Coordination Body for Democratic Change," January 25, 2012. https://carnegie-mec.org /diwan/48369?lang=en.

National Defence Force

The National Defence Force (NDF) is a pro-government militia fighting on behalf of the regime during the Syrian Civil War. Recruitment and organization of the NDF began in 2012 and was formally established in January 2013 to unify pro-regime local forces under provincial commands throughout Syria. Formation of the NDF amplified sectarian tensions due to its composition along ethnic lines, as most members were Alawite and Shia.

The group's origins may be traced to 2011, when several young Syrians suspected of taking direction from President Bashar al-Assad began inciting protestors and violently attacking civilians, specifically Sunni women. These individuals were collectively known as *shabiha*, either in reference to the Arabic word for "ghost" or the model of Mercedes they sometimes drove. As the Syrian Conflict escalated in 2011–2012, Assad increasingly relied on funding local militias to supplement the regime's security forces.

By April 2013, the NDF grew to an estimated 50,000 volunteers with the purported goal of reaching 100,000 trained fighters operating throughout the country. It became the largest pro-regime paramilitary force and was successful in countering anti-regime insurgents alongside the Syrian military. Local forces possessed different weapons and capabilities, but the NDF's most capable factions were allegedly funded and trained by Iran. Many fighters reportedly completed the same 15-day urban guerrilla warfare course used by the Iranian Revolutionary Guard Corps and Quds force to train Hezbollah.

Throughout 2014–2015, the NDF faced several challenges. NDF commander and Bashar al-Assad's cousin Hilal al-Assad was killed in Kessab (near the Turkish border) in March 2014, and the group endured heavy losses fighting the Islamic State and other rebels. The NDF also gained a reputation for corruption and brutality that hampered its legitimacy and recruitment efforts. Unable to enlist enough volunteer fighters, the Assad regime implemented an unpopular conscription policy throughout 2014, which led to protests. Reports of SDF activity waned throughout 2015, but trained, sectarian-based militias pose a long-term risk to stability in Syria.

Melia Pfannenstiel

Further Reading

Lister, Charles R. *The Syrian Jihad: Al Qaeda, the Islamic State and the Evolution of an Insurgency.* Oxford University Press, 2015.

Lund, Aron. "Syria in Crisis: Who Are the Pro-Assad Militias?" Carnegie Middle East Center, March 2, 2015. https://carnegie-mec.org/diwan/59215?lang=en.

Phillips, Christopher. *The Battle for Syria: International Rivalry in the New Middle East.* Yale University Press, 2016.

Obama, Barack

Barack Obama served as the 44th president of the United States from January 20, 2009, to January 20, 2017. Prior to becoming president, he represented Illinois in the U.S. Senate. A member of the Democratic Party whose star rose quickly, Obama was the first African American U.S. president. He served two terms, defeating Republican candidates John McCain in 2008 and Mitt Romney in 2012. The Syrian Conflict erupted in the wake of the Arab Spring in 2011 and became a constant thorn in the side of President Obama's administration as it gradually escalated, especially in his second term.

Early Life and Career

Barack Hussein Obama was born on August 4, 1961, in Honolulu, Hawaii, the son of a Kenyan economist and his American wife. Following his parents' divorce, Obama spent part of his childhood in Jakarta, Indonesia. Obama attended New York's Columbia University, graduating with a bachelor's degree in political science in 1983. He then moved to Chicago, where he worked as a community organizer. Obama moved to Massachusetts to study law at Harvard University in 1988, where he eventually became the first African American *Harvard Law Review* president. He received his law degree in 1991.

After graduating from law school, Obama returned to Chicago, where he worked as a lawyer and a law lecturer at the University of Chicago Law School. In 1993, Obama joined a public interest law firm. As a civil rights attorney at the firm, he dealt with such issues as fair housing, employment discrimination, and voting rights.

In 1996, Obama made a successful bid for the Illinois State Senate's 13th District, representing the South Side of Chicago. While in the Illinois Senate, Obama served on the Welfare Committee and the Health and Human Services Committee, eventually becoming chair. Controversy over the death penalty in Illinois led Obama to sponsor legislation to videotape interrogations in capital cases, a policy designed to eliminate coerced, false confessions; the legislation was passed. He also worked to curb racial profiling as well as to expand health-care coverage for the children of Illinois and to encourage the formation of charter schools.

U.S. Senate

In the election of 2004, Obama sought a seat in the U.S. Senate. During the campaign, he took a stand against the George W. Bush administration's march toward war in Iraq. While Obama believed that Saddam Hussein had weapons of mass destruction, he did not believe Hussein was an imminent threat. Obama's early opposition to the Iraq War would later be an important factor in his bid for the Democratic Party's 2008 presidential nomination. Obama's campaign received a boost after he delivered a well-received speech at the Democratic National Convention in Boston in July 2004. He went on to win 70 percent of the vote, carrying all but a handful of counties.

When he was sworn in on January 5, 2005, Obama became the only African American member of the Senate; he was only the fifth African American ever to have served in that body. In the Senate, Obama served on the Foreign Relations, Environment and Public Works, and Veterans' Affairs committees. He continued his criticism of the Bush administration's policies, including tax cuts for the wealthy, which he considered fiscally irresponsible. After just two years in the Senate, Obama announced he was seeking a higher office.

Rise to the Presidency

On February 10, 2007, at the town square where Abraham Lincoln gave his 1858 "House Divided" speech in Springfield, Illinois, Obama announced that he would seek the Democratic Party's nomination for president in the election of 2008. He got off to a strong start during primary season, winning the January 3, 2008, Iowa caucus and then placing second behind Sen. Hillary Clinton in the January 8 New Hampshire primary. Social media became a major campaign tool in the 2008 elections, and from the beginning of his presidential campaign, Obama had a substantial presence on such social media platforms as Facebook, MySpace, and Twitter. The campaign used social media to build grassroots support.

On March 18, Obama delivered a speech addressing racially charged comments made by his former pastor, the Rev. Jeremiah Wright. Though Obama had resisted making race a focus of his presidential campaign, public reaction to Wright's comments forced Obama to address the issue. In his speech, he denounced what Wright said but refused to disown Wright himself, instead discussing the pastor and his church in the larger context of race relations in the United States.

Obama officially became the first African American presidential nominee for a major party on August 27. His running mate was Democratic senator Joseph Biden, and they faced Senator John McCain of Arizona and Alaska governor Sarah Palin on the Republican ticket. For the general election, Obama turned down $85 million in federal funding for his campaign and instead raised $750 million. He was the first candidate to opt out of public financing since it had been established in 1976. Obama won the election on November 4.

As Obama's transition team prepared to take office, the United States faced an economic crisis; ongoing conflicts in Afghanistan and Iraq; and growing calls for affordable health care, energy independence, and education reform. Obama and his team underwent intense scrutiny as he assembled his cabinet and White House staff and began crafting policy and executive directives. As promised in his campaign, Obama took a bipartisan approach, keeping on Bush administration defense secretary Robert Gates and naming Republican Ray LaHood as secretary of transportation.

In his inaugural address on January 20, 2009, Obama spoke of the hardships facing the nation while optimistically assuring the country that such struggles could be overcome through unity and hard work: "Today I say to you that the challenges we face are real, they are serious and they are many. They will not be met easily or in a short span of time. But know this, America: They will be met."

Early Challenges

The first few months of Obama's presidency were dominated by the 2008 financial crisis. In February, Congress approved the American Recovery and Reinvestment

Act (ARRA) in a highly partisan, narrow vote. The $787 billion economic stimulus package included tax cuts, aid for state budgets, and funding for public works projects. Over the next several weeks, Obama announced that $15 billion in ARRA funds would be sent to states for immediate Medicaid relief and that $28 billion would be used to repair and build roads, highways, and bridges. Obama's fiscal year 2010 budget included a tax increase for those making more than $250,000 each year and emphasized energy initiatives and health-care reform. In addition, Obama set the goal of cutting the deficit in half by the end of his first term, which did not come to pass.

In early 2009, Obama announced that most U.S. troops would exit Iraq by the end of August 2010, with a small transitional force remaining until the end of 2011. The war was declared officially over by the U.S. military on December 15, 2011. Recognizing that the military effort in Afghanistan had suffered due to the U.S. commitment in Iraq, Obama refocused U.S. military efforts on Operation Enduring Freedom in Afghanistan by increasing U.S. combat troops and emphasizing nation-building and counterinsurgency in that country. In December 2009, Obama announced that the United States would begin handing over security responsibilities to the Afghan government by the middle of 2011 to allow the beginning of a drawdown in U.S. forces.

On multiple overseas trips to Europe, the Middle East, and Latin America, Obama often spoke of broader engagement within the international community and a readiness to listen and work with other nations. In recognition of this message, on October 9, 2009, he was awarded the Nobel Peace Prize for his "extraordinary efforts to strengthen international diplomacy and cooperation between peoples." The Nobel Prize Committee cited his work to promote multilateral diplomacy and rid the world of nuclear weapons. This recognition was later complicated, however, as international challenges such as the emergence of Violent Extremist Organizations (VEOs) (e.g., Boko Haram, Al-Shabaab, the Lord's Resistance Army, and the Islamic State of Iraq and Syria [ISIS], among others), as well as the capture and killing of Osama bin Laden in Abbottabad, Pakistan, forced Obama to use the military instrument of U.S. power on the international stage on multiple occasions. His extensive use of drones and remotely piloted aircraft (RPAs) was particularly controversial on the international stage.

2010 Midterms and Reelection

In the 2010 election, Republicans won control of the House of Representatives (Democrats maintained control of the Senate). The partisanship that had been building in Washington only increased in the second half of Obama's first term, as evidenced, for example, by the 2011 debt ceiling showdown. During the showdown between Republicans and Democrats, the United States came within days of defaulting on its debt obligations because the two parties in Congress and the president could not agree on a deal to raise the debt limit until the last possible minute. Gallup polls at the time showed both Obama and Congress with all-time low approval ratings: Congress's was below 20 percent, while Obama's dropped to 40 percent.

On April 4, 2011, Obama announced that he intended to run for reelection in 2012. His campaign used the slogan "Forward," citing job growth and the auto industry bailout among his domestic policy achievements and the end of the Iraq War. Among his most notable achievements in terms of national security was the capture and killing of Osama bin Laden under his direction in May 2011. Following a tight race against the Republican nominee, former Massachusetts governor Mitt Romney, Obama won reelection to a second term in office. He was the first president to win more than 51 percent of the vote in two elections since President Dwight D. Eisenhower had done so in the 1950s. Obama was officially sworn in to his second term on January 20, 2013. Because January 20 was a Sunday, inaugural ceremonies took place on January 21.

The Arab Spring and the Syrian Civil War

During his second term, Obama became increasingly concerned about the Arab Spring and the Syrian Civil War, both of which began, generally, in 2011. In the spring of 2011, a series of pro-democracy movements firmly took hold in Tunisia, Libya, Egypt, Yemen, Bahrain, and Syria. Triggered by an anti-government protest in Tunisia triggered by the self-immolation of Mohamed Bouazizi, a street vendor in the town of Sidi Bouzid, Tunisia, protesting corruption in the local, regional, and national government, the Arab Spring spread quickly throughout North Africa among people who had grown impatient with authoritarian regimes in their own countries.

The Arab Spring presented President Obama with complex diplomatic challenges; his goal was to support pro-democratic movements without throwing the international order into chaos. For this reason, he utilized the U.S. military sparingly, instead favoring an internationalist approach mediated through the United Nations. When necessary, he did authorize the use of military force, as in the case of Operations Odyssey Dawn and Unified Protector in Libya, but

generally shied away from overt uses of military force in other countries, especially Syria.

The Arab Spring in Syria began with peaceful protests in January 2011 but quickly escalated into an international conflict as Syria's president, Bashar al-Assad, forcefully resisted any ideas of reform in his country. The situation became particularly complicated for the Obama administration after Syrian military forces were accused of using chemical weapons against civilians. On August 31, 2013, Obama asked Congress to authorize the use of military force against Syria, but he withdrew that request a few weeks later due to significant congressional opposition. However, the rise of the radical organization known as the Islamic State of Iraq and Syria (ISIS), which had made significant territorial gains within those two countries, prompted the Obama administration to begin air strikes against ISIS targets in September 2014.

Obama's decision to not retaliate for Assad's use of chemical weapons, even after stating that Syria's employment of these weapons would constitute a "red line" and necessitate a military response (he made the now infamous "red line" statement in 2012), haunted him for the rest of his administration. Critics accused him of being too soft, and they eventually blamed him for this decision to not act on the rapid rise of ISIS within Syria, as well as opening the door for Russia's Vladimir Putin to send his own troops into Syria to support the Assad regime in direct opposition to American interests.

Election of 2016

During the presidential campaign of 2016, Obama endorsed former senator and secretary of state Hillary Clinton as his successor. He delivered a speech in support of Clinton's candidacy at the 2016 Democratic National Convention, and in the months leading up to the election he made appearances on the campaign trail on her behalf. Obama's support of Clinton was, undoubtedly, based largely on party loyalty. The fact that he saw Clinton as being likely to continue his foreign policy, especially in terms of Syria and the greater Middle East in the wake of the Arab Spring, cannot be underestimated. This was illustrated numerous times in the lead-up to the 2016 election in which the former secretary of state expressed her desire to continue Obama's foreign policy approach if she were elected president. However, Clinton was defeated on Election Day by Republican candidate Donald Trump, who made promises during his campaign to reverse many of Obama's key policies, including those on climate change, health care, and immigration.

During the final days of his presidency, Obama gave a farewell speech in which he expressed confidence in the future of the United States, but he also warned of threats to democracy resulting from economic inequality, political partisanship, and racism. He left office on January 20, 2017, with one of the highest approval ratings—57 percent, according to a Gallup poll—among outgoing U.S. presidents.

Nita Lang and Robert M. Kerr

Further Reading

Greenberg, David. "Syria Will Stain Obama's Legacy Forever." *Foreign Policy*, December 29, 2016. https://foreignpolicy.com/2016/12/29/obama-never-understood-how-history-works/.

Obama, Barack. *Dreams from My Father: A Story of Race and Inheritance*. Three Rivers Press, 1995.

Obama, Barack. *The Audacity of Hope: Thoughts on Reclaiming the American Dream*. Crown Publishing, 2006.

Operation Euphrates Shield

Operation Euphrates Shield was a Turkish military operation involving Turkish troops and their allied militias in northern Syria. It took place between August 2016 and March 2017, and resulted in Turkish occupation of parts of northern Syria. Turkey's interest in northern Syria was based on their concerns about two groups fighting in the Syrian Civil War: the Islamic State (IS) and the Kurdistan Workers' Party (PKK). The Turkish government, led by President Recep Tayyip Erdogan, feared that Islamic State influence would have a negative impact on Turkey's national security, and that any successes on the part of the Kurds in Syria would only embolden Turkey's large Kurdish population to act against his government.

Operation Euphrates Shield was not the first time Turkey had intervened militarily across its border with Syria; rather it was the culmination of a two-front campaign designed to contain the Islamic State and the PKK in order to limit their influence within Turkey that had begun over a year earlier. There had been a dramatic increase in violence and terrorist activity in Turkey in the spring of 2015, and Erdogan linked this activity to gains made by both the Islamic State and the Kurdistan Workers Party in the Syrian Conflict. Like all leaders of modern Turkey, Erdogan was most concerned not about IS, but that any successes achieved by the Kurds in Syria might embolden Turkey's own population of Kurds to rise against his government. His concern was not unfounded as he had to deal with this same issue in the wake of the Iraqi Kurds' military and economic successes in the years following the overthrow of Saddam Hussein. Unlike most of Iraq, which struggled after the 2003 ground invasion of Coalition Forces led by the United States, Iraqi Kurdistan quickly established itself as Iraq's most stable, secure, and prosperous region. This made the Turkish government nervous as Kurds in Turkey looked to Iraqi Kurdistan as a model of how an independent Kurdistan could flourish. Perhaps what made Erdogan most nervous was the effectiveness of the Kurdish militias that had perfected their training, tactics, and procedures in their fight against the Islamic State in Iraq. This put Turkish military intervention at the forefront of his mind as he considered options in determining how he was going to secure Turkey's border with Syria and prevent the spread of Kurdish nationalism.

The Kurds are considered to be a "stateless nation," that is, a nation of people without political representation on the international stage with their own country. What makes the members of a stateless nation different than other large groups of people is that they desire to have their own country, but for a variety of reasons that desire is not actualized. The Kurds make up one of the largest stateless nation groups in the world, with almost 30 million spread throughout a contiguous area within four different modern countries. In order for the Kurds to have a country—which they would call Kurdistan—Iran, Iraq, Syria, and Turkey would all have to be willing to give up large areas of their own countries in order to make this happen—this is not going to happen anytime soon. It does not help the Kurds' case that Kurdistan comprises some of the most resource rich—and in the case of Iraq, the most economically prosperous—parts of their respective countries. In Turkey, the Kurdish territory comprises almost a third of the entire territory of the state, and this land contains some of Turkey's most vital natural resources.

The Kurds are an old nation, and they have been fighting for an independent Kurdistan for hundreds of years. The first organized Kurdish insurgencies began more than 200 years ago as Kurdish militias rebelled against the Ottoman Empire. Modern Tukey's problematic relationship with the Kurds dates back to the country's war for independence in 1923. As Mustafa Kemal Ataturk was establishing a modern, secular, nationalist state, there was no room for competing national identities to challenge notions of what it meant to be a modern Turk, and he argued that all people within the territory of modern Turkey should abandon their old ethnic identities and customs and fully modernize according to his model. This approach worked in many areas, but the Kurds had their own distinct language, culture, and traditions, and they were not willing to abandon them in favor of accepting foreign cultural norms. The Kurds launched major rebellions against the Turkish government in 1925, 1930, and 1938, and maintained both armed and political resistance throughout the rest of the twentieth century. The Turkish government's problems with the Kurdistan Workers' Party, in particular, date back to the PKK's founding in the 1970s. The PKK's concern at the time of its founding was the fact that the Turkish government had banned the use of the Kurdish language and culture, and even the name "Kurd." In fact, the government had officially renamed the Kurds in Turkey "Mountain Turks" and had attempted to officially erase any trace of Kurdish existence within Turkey—this designation legally remained in place until 1991, though the Kurds themselves never accepted it. In 1984, following four years of particularly harsh treatment of the Kurds by the government, the PKK shifted its focus from advocating for Kurdish cultural rights toward an armed insurgency. The PKK declared an all-out insurgency against the government, and there have been intermittent periods of brutal fighting with acts of terrorism being committed by the PKK and responses on the part of the Turkish armed forces that have been classified as international human rights abuses.

The PKK is a paramilitary organization, and the Turkish military has been actively engaged in counterterrorism and counterinsurgency operations against them since the PKK launched a coordinated insurgency against the Turkish government in 1984. Since then, the PKK and the Turkish military have played a game of cat and mouse both within and outside of Turkish territory; it has not been uncommon for the Turkish military to operate outside their own borders in pursuit of the PKK with varying degrees of support and resistance from their neighbors.

The Syrian Conflict emerged in the midst of a particularly intense period in terms of Turkish relations with the PKK in 2011. Emboldened by military and economic success in Iraq, the PKK had seen an opportunity to renew its fight against the Turkish government, and Syria provided them with a strategic opportunity to broaden their own military forces and capabilities. Hoping to solidify their presence in Turkey and Syria using Iraqi Kurdistan as their base, the PKK focused their attention on supporting the reenergized, pro-Kurdish Peace and Democracy Party in the Turkish elections. Their efforts paid off, and for the first time a Kurdish political party had won more seats than the incumbent ruling party in Turkey's southeast. However, six of the Peace and Democracy Party's members were in Turkish jails as political prisoners, and calls for their immediate release were loud.

The year 2012 was a particularly violent one in the conflict between PKK militias and the Turkish government. More than 300 Kurdish militants and almost as many Turkish soldiers lost their lives that year, and the Turkish government quietly pursued secret talks with PKK leadership—Abdullah Ocalan, in particular—for a cease-fire. The negotiations did, in fact, result in relative peace between the two sides for almost two years until the Turkish military hit PKK targets during its bombing campaign against the Islamic State in 2015. It is rumored that the bombings were in response to suspected PKK terrorist attacks against Turkish police. With fighting resumed, violence quickly escalated, and the PKK turned its attention toward efforts to remove Turkish president Erdogan from power in Ankara. In 2016, the PKK played a crucial role in the formation of an anti-government coalition made up of a wide alliance of interest groups, to include the Kurds, political dissenters such as socialists and communists, and other leftist groups dedicated to the cause of removing Erdogan; the group is called the Peoples' United Revolutionary Movement.

Operation Euphrates Shield took place over the course of seven months, between August 2016 and March 2017. It was a cross-border operation planned and executed by Turkish forces and their Syrian militia allies to counter a coalition of Kurds and their allied militias under the guise of the Syrian Democratic Forces. Officially, the Turks identified Islamic State targets as their primary motivation for launching the cross-border military operation, but experts agree that their main objective was to weaken the PKK so that they could not entrench themselves in northern Syria in order to use it as a base from which to carry out their operations against the Turkish government. The Syrian region surrounding Aleppo was particularly problematic not only for the Syrian government but for the Turks as well. A hotbed of militia activity since the Syrian Civil War erupted in the wake of the Arab Spring, the region had become dominated by Kurdish militias and the Islamic State by 2015. This worried Erdogan for obvious reasons; no political leader wants that kind of instability directly on the other side of his country's border—especially a political leader in charge of a country with potential for that conflict to spill over into one's own country.

On August 24, 2016, Turkish artillery and air force jets attacked Islamic State and other targets of interest within Syrian territory. This was followed by Turkish ground troops moving into the region in order to establish a foothold in the territory to gain the strategic advantage over its enemies. One might wonder why the Syrian government would allow a foreign military to move into its territory without putting up a military resistance, but it is important to note that at this time the Syrian military had no control over the Aleppo Governorate region in northern Syria and really had no means of stopping the Turkish military. Fighting continued through the month of August, with Turkey taking land held by the Islamic State with relative ease. With this territory secured, Turkey turned its attention toward the areas held by the predominantly Kurdish Syrian Democratic Forces. There were casualties on all sides, but the Turkish military, aided by air strikes from their own air force and the expertise of their explosive ordinance divisions at diffusing mines and other explosive devices, had a distinct advantage.

At the end of August, the United States tried unsuccessfully to broker a cease-fire, and fighting continued on all sides, with a resurgence of Islamic State fighters, throughout the month of September 2016. The role of the United States in aiding the rebels during the offensive illustrated the very complex nature of the operation. As part of Operation Noble Lance, U.S. special operations forces provided training and assistance to Syrian rebels in northern Aleppo Province. However, the United States and Turkey had a common enemy in the Islamic State, and it was reported that American Special Operations forces accompanied Turkish military units in September 2016 and aided in defeating IS forces in the Syrian town of Jarabulus and other areas throughout the Aleppo region. Some speculated that the United States' interest in the operation was twofold: defeating Islamic State fighters and mitigating some of the conflict between the Turkish military and the Syrian Democratic Forces—the United States and the Kurds have been longtime allies.

Operation Euphrates Shield continued through the rest of 2016, with Turkey and their allies fighting back and forth throughout the Aleppo Governorate. At times, such as in October 2016, rebels made significant gains. The Syrian Arab Air Force got involved at times, as well, with a significant air strike launched against Turkish special operations forces in November. This incident led to a very tense international situation, and Syrian military claims that the attacks were carried out by the Islamic State. However, there is no indication that the Islamic State had any air assets at the time, so their claim is doubtful.

In February 2017, tensions between the United States and Turkey intensified as American Special Operations Forces deployed to the Syrian town of Manbij to support a Kurdish coalition of militias known as the Manbij Military Council—an organization actively opposed by Turkish forces. To complicate matters even more, the Manbij Military Council turned to Russia to help deal with the Turkish military presence in an effort to spare some villages near the town from Turkish military action by handing them over to the Syrian Army. This complex series of negotiations led to a high-level meeting between U.S. chairman of the Joint Chiefs of Staff General Dunford, Russian Chief of the General Staff General Gerasimov, and Turkish Chief of the General Staff General Akar in March 2017 in Turkey in which they all agreed that a diplomatic solution was the only viable option to solving the problems of northern Syria. This meeting officially ended Operation Euphrates Shield.

Operation Euphrates Shield represents the complexities of the modern battlefield in which the militaries of multiple countries and local, regional, and even international nonstate militias all compete simultaneously for a variety of desired outcomes. The objectives of battle are not clearly defined, and the classic struggle between two easily distinguishable armies with clearly understood objectives seems to be a thing of the past when one looks at armed conflict throughout the Syrian Civil War. The ever-present reality of international political intrigue complicates the Syrian Conflict even more, and Operation Euphrates Shield represents a new kind of conflict in which multiple parties use violence to influence their respective interests. While the operation began as part of Turkey's attempt to try to protect its own internal political stability, the conflict quickly escalated beyond a fight against the Islamic State and a group of predominantly Kurdish militias to one involving the Syrian, U.S., and Russian militaries. It should serve as a warning that future conflicts are likely to continue to be extremely complex, and that even the top military officers of three of the world's most powerful militaries all agreed at the end of the operation that such conflicts are best dealt with diplomatically.

Robert M. Kerr

Further Reading

Allsopp, Harriet. *The Kurds of Syria: Political Parties and Identities in the Middle East*. I. B. Tauris, 2015.

Cagaptay, Soner. *The New Sultan: Erdogan and the Crisis of Modern Turkey*. I. B. Tauris, 2017.

Garamone, Jim. "U.S., Turkish, Russian Defense Chiefs Meet to Discuss Syrian Battlespace." Department of Defense News, 2019. https://www.jcs.mil/Media/News/News-Display/Article/1111128/us-turkish-russian-defense-chiefs-meet-to-discuss-syrian-battlespace.

Global Security.Org. "Operation Euphrates Shield." https://www.globalsecurity.org/military/world/war/syria-euphrates-shield.htm.

Lawrence, Quil. *Invisible Nation: How the Kurds' Quest for Statehood Is Shaping the Middle East*. Walker, 2008.

Operation Shader

Operation Shader is the overall name of British military operations against the Islamic State of Iraq and Syria conducted under the auspices of the larger, U.S.-led mission called Inherent Resolve. Operation Shader began in September 2014 under the formal request of the government of Iraq, and it was formally expanded into operations in Syria in October 2014. Initially, British involvement in Syria was limited to intelligence gathering, surveillance, and reconnaissance missions conducted by the Royal Air Force (RAF), but in December 2015, the British mission had expanded to include air strikes against Islamic State targets throughout Syria. Since that time, the air mission of Operation Shader has evolved into the Royal Air Force's most intense involvement in a single theater of war since the Second World War.

The British House of Commons, under the leadership of Prime Minister David Cameron, voted to support Iraq's request for assistance against the Islamic State in September 2014. The parliament explicitly limited operations to within the border of Iraq, however, and initially had no intention of supporting an expansion of military operations into Syria. However, Islamic State militants who knew the limitations on British participation took full advantage of the fact that the Brits could not attack them in Syria. This on-the-ground reality posed an immediate problem for the British military, and the Royal Air Force successfully lobbied parliament to allow them to fly into Syrian airspace for surveillance missions. Over the course of late 2014 and almost all of 2015, British military leaders grew more and more frustrated with this arrangement as the Islamic State militias were fully aware that the Brits could watch them, but could not do anything to stop their actions or operations in Syrian territory. In fact, it is not coincidental that Islamic State operations hit their peak in Syria in 2015 as they knew that they were safe from Royal Air Force attacks. In the fall of 2015, the British House of Commons voted to allow the Royal Air Force to strike IS targets in Syrian territory by a margin of 397 votes for, and 223 votes against, expanding military action beyond Iraq's border.

Operation Shader is primarily, though not exclusively, an air operation. Headed by the Royal Air Force, the British have deployed a number of aircraft designed for controlling air superiority, surveillance, transport, refueling, and planes that can fire air-to-surface missiles with operations running out of a British air base in Cyprus. The Royal Navy has also deployed a destroyer to assist the U.S. Navy with air defense for its ships. The British Army also has advisors and

peacekeepers on the ground, primarily in Iraq, though none of the British ground forces deployed to the region in support of Operation Shader are serving in a combat role. It should be noted that the British government claims that there have been no civilian casualties resulting from air strikes under Operation Shader in either Iraq or Afghanistan.

While the air mission is the main effort of Operation Shader, ground troops are involved in training and advising both Kurdish and Iraqi troops in Iraq in their fight against the Islamic State. In the north, British efforts have centered on working with Kurdish Peshmerga forces. It is important to note that under Iraqi law, Iraqi military forces are forbidden from entering or operating in Iraqi Kurdistan, which is considered an autonomous region of Iraq. The Peshmerga are responsible for securing the region of Iraqi Kurdistan, and they have put up fierce resistance to IS militants. In addition to training, the British government has provided weapons, ammunition, and equipment to Peshmerga forces throughout their fight against the Islamic State in Iraqi Kurdistan. The British mission in Iraqi Kurdistan has focused primarily on training the Peshmerga on military tactics. Throughout the rest of Iraq, Operation Shader has focused on advising the Iraqi military on its counter–improvised explosive device (IED) training, tactics, and procedures. Improvised explosive devices are a cheap and effective means for insurgents to wreak havoc on any society, and finding and destroying them is a top priority for the Iraqi military as they attempt to provide a safe environment for the Iraqi people.

In 2016, the British military started training moderate Syrian opposition groups. The stipulation imposed by the British government was that these groups had to be vetted in order to make sure their primary goals were the defense of their cities, towns, and neighborhoods; the British people had no desire to aid large-scale militias with aims contrary to Western values. This training focused on basic military tactics, command and control, medical training, and explosive hazard awareness. In 2018, with Islamic State territory reduced to just 2 percent of its size when it was at its strongest, the British mission shifted to advising the Iraqi military on continuing to develop its long-term plan for training and educating its forces. Professional military education is a hallmark of every effective fighting force, and the Iraqi military had an extensive program to educate its troops, especially its officers, before the 2003 invasion by Coalition Forces. Iraqi military leaders had always wanted to rebuild the country's military education system, and with the defeat of IS within its borders, the Iraqis turned to the British to help them rebuild their education programs.

While British involvement in Iraq and Syria is not large in comparison to American military involvement, the fact that Operation Shader is the longest-sustained military operation in recent memory for the British military is significant, and speaks to the fact that the Brits view the fight against the Islamic State as one of its highest international priorities. In addition to a political desire to assist the United States, the British not only have a vested interest in the region in terms of geopolitical stability and the global economy, but they also have extensive knowledge of the region due to their long relationship, with at least the Iraqis going back to the days of the British Empire. This extensive knowledge has made them particularly effective trainers and advisers, and the British people have maintained their overall generally positive view toward Operation Shader as a result of the military's

effectiveness in carrying out its mission with positive outcomes. The British Ministry of Defence has even discussed maintaining a small military presence in the region with parliament, with largely favorable results. It is likely the British will try to maintain its long-standing role in the region as they have pointed out that while the Islamic State may have suffered a significant setback as a result of combined U.S. and UK operations, the threat is not completely defeated.

Operation Shader is highly significant in terms of how the British military views warfare in the twenty-first century. As the most intense air operation for the Royal Air Force since World War II, much of Operation Shader has taken place from bases outside the actual theater of war, and most of the British troops deployed in support of Operation Shader are airmen serving outside the actual theater of war. This has become normal for the United States Air Force which is used to conducting operations from bases far away from the actual fighting on the ground, but it has not historically been the case for the RAF. This has actually stirred much discussion and debate within British society regarding the nature of warfare, and has spurred a change in the law regarding who is and who is not eligible for military awards and decorations within the British military. Until Operation Shader, British soldiers, sailors, and airmen could only qualify for awards and decorations if they deployed to the theater where actual fighting took place. Under Operation Shader, the majority of service members are actually deployed to a Royal Air Force base in Cyprus, and some remotely piloted aircraft pilots are even stationed as far away from the fight as the Nevada desert in the United States. The Ministry of Defence and the British Parliament approved these troops to qualify for the Operation Shader Service Medal in a move that not only recognized the service of the volunteer soldiers, sailors, and airmen, but also acknowledged that the way British society views warfare in the twenty-first century needs to adjust to modern realities. For a society, and an organization, so steeped in tradition, this is no small event.

Robert M. Kerr

Further Reading

British House of Commons Defence Committee. "Oral Evidence: UK Military Operations in Mosul and Raqqa, HC 999," May 15, 2018. http://data.parliament.uk/writtenevi dence/committeeevidence.svc/evidenced ocument/defence-committee/uk-military -operations-in-mosul-and-raqqa/oral/82916 .pdf.

British House of Commons Library. "ISIS/ Daesh: The Military Response in Iraq and Syria," March 8, 2017. https://research briefings.parliament.uk/ResearchBriefing /Summary/SN06995.

British House of Commons Library. "ISIS/ Daesh: What Now for the Military Campaign in Iraq and Syria," July 10, 2018. https://researchbriefings.parliament.uk /ResearchBriefing/Summary/CBP-8248.

Operation Wrath of Euphrates

Operation Wrath of Euphrates is the official name of the military operation also known as the Raqqa Campaign. It took place for almost one year, starting in November 2016 and lasting until October 2017, and was led by the U.S.-backed Syrian Democratic Forces against the Islamic State (IS) in and around Raqqa, Syria. It met its main goal of isolating, and then defeating, Islamic State forces in Raqqa, as well as its secondary objectives of obtaining control of two crucial dams on the Euphrates River. The operation was a strategic success, and played a key role in diminishing the Islamic State's ability to wage war in the region, thereby marking a crucial step in achieving U.S. secretary of defense Ashton Carter's goal of a "lasting defeat" of IS in Iraq and Syria.

Syrian Democratic Forces (SDF) are a coalition of Kurdish, Arab, Turkmen, and Assyrian militias opposed to Syrian president Bashar al-Assad. While predominantly Sunni Muslim (though its Assyrian members are Christian), the SDF is secular in nature and does not advocate for a religious state government in Syria. Closely aligned with the Kurdish People's Protection Units (YPG), the SDF are well trained and have even employed all-female units in their fight against the Islamic State. Much of their training has been from American Special Operations Forces, and much of their equipment has been supplied by the United States.

U.S. secretary of defense Ashton Carter made the defeat of the Islamic State in Iraq and Syria his top priority in the region. Upon coming into office and discovering the ad hoc nature of the American fight against the Islamic State before 2015, he immediately set about coming up with a clear plan, and devoting necessary resources, to defeat the Islamic State. One of Secretary Carter's first actions was to appoint U.S. Army lieutenant general Sean MacFarland as the commander of the coalition fight against IS. This simple move allowed for resources and personnel to be dedicated specifically to that fight, and the benefits were felt almost immediately as the U.S. fight against the Islamic State yielded almost immediate results as the militants went on the defensive for the first time. Islamic State fighters made startlingly rapid gains throughout Iraq and Syria, and declared their intention to continue to expand into other parts of the Middle East in 2015. American allies, such as Turkey and Jordan, among others, immediately launched strikes against IS, but as effective as they were, there was no coordinating authority to maximize the informal coalition's efforts. Willing to allow the Americans to coordinate and deconflict their operations, the coalition became formalized and Islamic State fighters turned their attention from expanding their territory to digging in and entrenching themselves in the areas they already held. Raqqa was one of those cities, and they established it as one of their main bases of operation in Syria.

Raqqa was one of the first major Syrian cities to fall to the opposition. Taken by a coalition of opposition militias, including the Free Syrian Army and the Islamic State, in the summer of 2013, Raqqa met an uneasy peace teetering between varying degrees of Islamist ideologies. Unable to compete with the money and organization of the Islamic State, the other opposition forces either left Raqqa or acquiesced to IS ideology. By January 2014, Raqqa was an Islamic State city and run entirely by their draconian codes of public behavior. Akin to how the Taliban governed in parts of Afghanistan before the U.S. invasion in 2001, IS in Raqqa unleashed a reign of terror, murdering, beating, and raping anyone who did not adhere to their extremist views and code of conduct. This lasted from January 2013 until the city was liberated (though at huge costs in terms of destruction and loss of life) in October 2017.

The years in Raqqa under Islamic State control were brutal, but they did attempt to balance population control with the delivery of some essential services. It is important to remember that the ultimate goal of the Islamic State was to create a society in which Islamic law governed every aspect of life, but their view was that if such a society could be built, it would be one where people would actually want to live. Knowing that people (potential military recruits as well as

residents) around the world, especially the Islamic world, were watching, there was some effort made to make Raqqa look like a positive example of what life in the new caliphate might be like. Launching an extensive social media public relations campaign, Islamic State propagandists needed to show their audience all the benefits of moving to IS-controlled areas, and for that reason they did take some care to make sure that not too much of the city was destroyed; that people were seen as having food, shelter, and water; and that medical services were on par with those available in government-controlled areas. While this was little consolation to people living under the oppressive laws who had no desire to do so, it did create some constraints on what Islamic State would do in the city. An interesting RAND study pointed out that satellite imagery taken of Raqqa at night when the city was under IS control shows that efforts were made to ensure that hospitals, for example, retained access to electricity throughout the occupation.

As the Islamic State was digging in and treating Raqqa as one of its two main urban strongholds (along with Mosul in Iraq) and its de facto capital, U.S.-led coalition forces were planning their offensive to defeat them. It is important to understand that the desired end state of the coalition was not the liberation of Raqqa, but rather to deal a decisive blow against the Islamic State. This is important to know when assessing the aftermath of Operation Wrath of Euphrates. The 2016 Raqqa Campaign was not a surprise attack; and as it was launched, the international community, including Bashar al-Assad, watched with a mix of anticipation and trepidation. On November 5, 2016, commanders from the SDF announced the commencement of Operation Wrath of Euphrates. It was a well-calculated move on the part of the coalition to make sure that it was two female commanders from the Syrian Democratic Forces that announced the operation, given the Islamic State's attitude toward women. The Jordanians, too, had made sure to announce whenever one of their female fighter pilots flew a mission against Islamic State targets; it was also part of a calculated information operation aimed directly at IS. The announcement encouraged civilians to try to get away from Islamic State targets and to flee to areas outside their control. They were also up front about their plan: it would include 30,000 Kurdish, Arab, and Turkmen troops backed by American advisers and close air support from the U.S. Air Force. At the same time as the Raqqa Offensive, U.S. partners in Iraq also launched their offensive against the Islamic State in Mosul in an effort to divide the militants' attention between two isolated fronts.

One of the United States' biggest challenges in the Raqqa Offensive was managing their relationship with Turkey. The YPG, the main group comprising the Syrian Democratic Forces, is considered a terrorist organization by the Turkish government. The United States did manage to prevent Turkey from interrupting the mission, but U.S.-Turkish relations were damaged, and remained so after the mission. In 2019, the U.S. secretary of state was still working with the Turkish government to ensure they would not interfere with YPG/SDF operations in Syria and their American Special Forces advisers.

Phase One of Operation Wrath of Euphrates involved maneuvering troops into positions to isolate Raqqa from the north. On the first day of the operation, Syrian Democratic Forces liberated six towns from Islamic State control. SDF overcame light resistance in the next few days, and other than meeting fierce resistance in a village with a strong IS presence, Phase One was complete with 67 towns north of Raqqa under the control of the anti-IS coalition by November 19. Phase Two of the operation focused on setting up a blockade of anything trying to enter or leave Raqqa from the north, but this proved more difficult than Phase One, with one American casualty being taken on November 24. Part of the difficulty was that the Islamic State, somewhat unexpectedly, was diverted from resources from Iraq up to the north in order to defend Raqqa as opposed to Mosul. These troops forced a stalemate between the SDF and IS troops, but on December 10, the Syrian Democratic Forces set out to accomplish the key objectives of Phase Two, securing the northwestern and western countryside surrounding Raqqa and ultimately securing the Taqba Dam on the Euphrates River. As SDF troops spread throughout the countryside, surrounding Raqqa in an arc from the north to the west, the United States deployed 200 more troops in support of the operation. Overall, the SDF liberated almost 100 additional villages by December 19, but they fell short of securing the dam.

Phase Three of Operation Wrath of Euphrates began in February 2017 with an additional 3,000 SDF troops trained by U.S. forces joining the fight with the objective of securing the eastern hinterlands of Raqqa. Fighting between the U.S.-led coalition and the Islamic State was fierce, but SDF made advances throughout the countryside east of Raqqa. There were multiple incidents of civilian casualties that could have been the result of Islamic State fighters using them as human shields. In March, the SDF launched an operation to finally take control of the Taqba Dam and a military base that had been used by Islamic State forces. After fierce fighting, SDF took control of the area around the dam on March 26, though they wouldn't actually take the dam itself until after three more weeks of intense fighting. Phase Four of the Operation took place from April 13, after the SDF and U.S. Special Forces took the Taqba Dam, and lasted until June 2, 2017. Finally, the culminating battle, the fight to defeat IS in Raqqa, began on June 3.

Again, it must be understood the objective of the operation was to defeat the Islamic State, not liberate Raqqa. After launching a multipronged offensive from the north, east, and west, the SDF effectively blockaded the city, trapping thousands of militants, along with innocent civilians, in the city. Once the city was sealed off, SDF artillery and U.S. air strikes, followed by a ground invasion of the city, destroyed as much as half of the buildings in Raqqa. The Syrian Democratic Forces declared victory against the Islamic State on October 20, 2017.

The international community, as well as many of Raqqa's residents, have criticized Operation Wrath of Euphrates for being too heavy-handed in its attack on Raqqa. In its defense, it did indeed deal a significant blow to the Islamic State, a blow from which IS seems unlikely to recover anytime soon. The price was high, though; of that there can be no doubt. Some estimate that as much as 50 percent of the city was completely destroyed, and a huge number of international refugees and internally displaced persons are from Raqqa, and they will most likely never return to their homes. Finally, the people of Raqqa are left with little resolution as to their future in a Syria still ruled by Bashar al-Assad and the Ba'ath Party.

Robert M. Kerr

Further Reading

RAND. "What Life under ISIS Looked Like from Space," January 9, 2018. https://www .rand.org/blog/rand-review/2018/01/what -life-under-isis-looked-like-from-space .html.

Tax, Meredith. *A Road Unforeseen: Women Fight the Islamic State*. Bellevue Library Press, 2016.

Thomson, Mike, ed. *The Raqqa Diaries: Escape from the Islamic State*. Interlink Publication Group, 2017.

Williams, Brian Glyn. *Counter Jihad: America's Military Experience in Afghanistan, Iraq, and Syria*. University of Pennsylvania Press. 2017.

P

Palmyra

Palmyra is an ancient city in the Homs Governorate of modern Syria. Located in the central part of the country, Palmyra is built on an oasis surrounded by desert. Because of a *wadi* (a river whose banks are full only during the rainy season) and a nearby natural spring, Palmyra's soil is rich, but unable to sustain large-scale agriculture. In fact, the name Palmyra means "many palms," and it was bestowed on the city by the Romans to reflect the more than 20 different varieties of palm trees found in the area. What made Palmyra famous in the ancient world was not agriculture, or even its access to fresh water in the middle of the desert—it was its strategic location on the middle branch of the ancient Silk Road leading to Antioch on the Mediterranean Sea.

The Silk Road was not a single actual road. Rather, it was a network of trade routes connecting ancient China with the Mediterranean world. It was a two-way trade system, with horses, saddles, camels, textiles, animal furs and leather, honey, glassware, wool, gold and silver, slaves, and weapons and armor from the west being desired in places on the east side of the network, such as Mongolia and China. Places in the west, such as Rome and later Ottoman Turkey, and places throughout Western Europe coveted tea, spices, silk, dyes, precious stones, porcelain, bronze, perfumes, ivory, rice, paper, and gunpowder. The fact that many of the former items became indicators of wealth and status in the West illustrates how much time, effort, and money went into the cross-continental trade system. Goods traded over such a long distance became more and more expensive the farther they got from their point of origin. Middle men, warehousers, herdsmen, and even extortionists had to be paid, and the trade barons who oversaw the whole network became unbelievably wealthy. These trade barons established bases of operation on the route, and these bases grew into the some of the most influential cities in the ancient world. Anyone needing to find accommodations, shelter, supplies, provisions, protection, news, and literally anything else that can be found in a city that is a center of large-scale commerce went to one of these cities. On the western side of the trade network was Palmyra.

Palmyra was an Aramaic-speaking city where life revolved around agriculture, and later trade, and worship of the Mesopotamian celestial god Bel, the lunar god Aglibol, and the sun god Yarhibol. The city's Temple of Bel survived thousands of years unharmed and was in remarkable condition until the Islamic State destroyed a significant portion of it during the Syrian Civil War. When Palmyra came under the control of the Romans, it gradually shifted to a Christian city. Though it retained Aramaic as its main language, Latin and Greek became widely spoken as trade languages, and when the city came under the influence of Islam spread by Arabs in the seventh century, the dominant language of Palmyra gradually became Arabic. It is important to understand that while the international community knows the city as Palmyra, it is known colloquially in Syria, and throughout the Middle East, by its Arabic name, Tadmur. Although it was a regional administrative center under the Ottomans, Palmyra was governed primarily by Arabs from Lebanon, and it never really became a Turkish-influenced city.

In Roman times it took roughly three weeks to caravan between Antiochia (modern-day Antioch; it was the capital of Roman Syria) and Palmyra. For most caravans, the oasis town was perfectly placed as traders traveling from west to east were just about out of the supplies they packed in Antiochia, and those completing long journeys from the east restocked for the final push toward the Mediterranean. Palmyra was not a cheap city, as its merchants knew that traders had no choice but to fully stock their supplies because of the harsh desert conditions they faced regardless of what direction they were traveling. As a wealthy city, especially during Roman times, it was not spared from political turmoil and intrigue, and it acquired a reputation for being a fiercely independent city that, while not lawless, was certainly a place that had anything one was looking for—akin, perhaps, to Las Vegas or other towns in the American "Wild West" in its earliest days. Its role as a center of trade remained solid until the seventh century when two things, one political and one technological, changed the city forever.

The first change that occurred, the one that was political, was the taking of the city by one of Islam's first expansionist military leaders, Khalid ibn al-Walid. The new religion of Islam was, at that time, located primarily in an important trade center of the Arabian Peninsula called Mecca. Its prophet and founder, Muhammad, was a member of an elite trading family in Mecca, and many of his earliest converts were tradesmen whose families had traded in the peninsula

for centuries. The early Islamic expansionists wanted to keep the focus on the newly expanding empire on the Arabian Peninsula, and they emphasized trade centered on their existing networks, which were largely maritime based rather than the old east-west land routes of the Greeks and Romans. This is also related to the second reason for Palmyra's decline in importance as a trade city, and that is rapid improvements in seafaring technology. Maritime trade is far cheaper and more efficient than overland trade, and sailing ships became faster, more reliable, and larger, many of the once powerful cities along the Silk Road declined rapidly in importance.

Under the Ottomans, Palmyra served as a regional administrative center, but it was not, in any way, an important or powerful city. The Ottomans had a tense relationship with the Arabs in the region, however, and did garrison troops there in the nineteenth century to try to keep the area's residents, especially the nomadic Bedouin tribes, under control (with limited success), but the city's past glories were not reflected in its position under Turkish rule. The centuries-long Ottoman presence fizzled to an undramatic end in 1918 when the British Royal Air Force built an airstrip on the eastern edge of Palmyra and the remaining Turkish soldiers packed up their garrison and left. In 1920, Palmyra came under French administration, and it again became an important city (though never regaining its ancient prominence). The French saw Palmyra's strategic value in solidifying its power base in the desert. They were also interested in the city's archaeological treasures; and along with establishing the new city of Palmyra built alongside its ancient ruins, they brought the world's attention to the site that would eventually become a UNESCO World Heritage Site in 1980. For a brief period before

Syrian independence, the Nazis used Palmyra as a military base as it came under the control of the Nazi puppet Vichy regime, but the city was liberated by the British and the Free French forces in 1941.

In the modern state of Syria, Palmyra is widely known by its Arabic name, Tadmur, and it is the center of an administrative district of the same name. Its primary source of income is tourism, but there is also an important phosphate mining industry that emerged in the 1970s. Its population before the civil war was around 50,000, but this number actually grew during the conflict as many internally displaced persons (IDPs) moved to Palmyra from other parts of the country because they believed they would be safe there. It is also notable that anti-Assad forces also converged in Palmyra, and in 2013, the ancient Temple of Bel was damaged by mortar fire from the Syrian Arab Army trying to kill dissident militants who were using the city as a base of operations. In May 2015, the city came under the control of the Islamic State. In infamous videos and photos, the ancient Roman amphitheater is depicted as the scene of dozens of brutal executions of captured Syrian Army soldiers. Islamic State social media outlets also propagated videos of IS soldiers smashing ancient artifacts and cutting the heads off ancient statues. It did not take long, however, for Islamic State fighters to realize they were sitting on a black-market goldmine, and relics and artifacts from Palmyra started making their way into illegal art trading networks around the world. It is believed that the looting and selling of artifacts from dozens of sites from around the Middle East actually constituted the second-largest source of income for the Islamic State, after oil revenue from oil sold illegally. The Syrian Arab Army did liberate the city from the Islamic State in March 2016, but the riches to be had in Palmyra were too great for the militants to pass up, and they retook the city in December. Knowing their time there was limited based on their intelligence network's assessment of the Syrian military's planning, they set about heavily mining the city, especially the ancient ruins, while gathering as many artifacts as they could sell as possible. By early March 2017, Islamic State fighters had been completely driven out, but they left massive destruction of the ancient city in their wake.

The Islamic State destroyed much of the Temple of Bel, part of the Roman amphitheater, a triumphal arch, and other ancient structures. They looted countless artifacts, and left a permanent hole in the archaeological and anthropological heritage of the city, country, and even the world. As a city whose primary source of income is tourism, its residents have no choice but to try to rebuild what they can, but their task is monumental. International investors have already pledged billions of dollars to help restore the things that can be salvaged, but pledges do not always translate to actual donations, so it remains to be seen what the future holds for this ancient, once great city.

Robert M. Kerr

Further Reading

Anderson, Benjamin, and Robert G. Ousterhout. *Palmyra 1885: The Wolfe Expedition and the Photographs of John Henry Haynes.* Cornucopia Books, 2016.

ORBIS. "The Stanford Geospatial Network Model of the Roman World." http://orbis.stanford.edu.

Veyne, Paul. *Palmyra: An Irreplaceable Treasure.* University of Chicago Press, 2017.

White, Benjamin Thomas. *The Emergence of Minorities in the Middle East: The Politics of Community in French Mandate Syria.* Edinburgh University Press, 2012.

Peshmerga

The Peshmerga (meaning "those facing death") are armed Kurdish insurgents operating chiefly in Kurdistan (northern Iraq, Turkey, and Iran). They are Kurdish irregular (i.e., not part of a state-sponsored military) fighters whose origins predate the twentieth century. Although primarily Kurdish men, their demographic composition has come to include women and non-Kurds. In fact, the Peshmerga have become well known for their female soldiers, especially snipers, who have played a pivotal role in Kurdish resistance against ISIS. The role of women in the Peshmerga has inspired many women throughout the Middle East to fight not with guns but with words for more equal rights in their own countries as news of their fighting prowess has spread through social media and satellite news outlets. The fighters' chains of command were the successive leaders of the Kurdistan Democratic Party (KDP), namely Mullah Mustafa Barzani and, following his death, his successor and son Masoud Barzani, currently the president of the Kurdistan Regional Government (KRG), as well as the Patriotic Union of Kurdistan (PUK) led by Jalal Talabani. The Peshmerga in Turkey fall under the auspices of the Kurdistan Workers' Party (PKK).

In Iraq, the KDP and PUK comprise the current government of the KRG, by which the Peshmerga are largely governed. Historically, they have played a pivotal role in shaping Kurdish nationalist aspirations for independence since the early 1920s, particularly as a result of the dissolution of the Ottoman Empire after World War I and the quest for a Kurdish homeland.

The historical development of the Peshmerga was concurrent with the rise and fall of various Kurdish rebellions following the collapse of the Ottoman Empire. Failed promises by the Allied powers after World War I to grant Kurds local autonomy and possible independence as suggested in the Treaty of Sèvres (1920) helped solidify the Kurds' quest for independence thereafter. The 1920s witnessed various Kurdish uprisings led by Sheikh Mahmud Barzinji of Sulamaniyah, all of which were promptly quashed by the Iraqi government and the British Royal Air Force. In 1931, Sheikh Barzinji died in one such uprising. This critical juncture witnessed the rise of Mullah Mustafa Barzani as the leader of the Kurdish movement in Iraq and the first solidification of the Peshmerga as a united force.

Throughout the 1930s and 1940s, the Kurdish nationalist movement remained largely dormant, as Barzani was forced into exile first in the Soviet Union, then Iran, and finally Western Europe. However, the ouster of Reza Shah's dictatorship in Iran enabled Kurdish intellectuals along with various Barzani followers to declare an independent Kurdistan in the Mahabad region, in northwestern Iran. This saw the swift dissolution of the Imperial Iranian Army there, which was replaced by the National Army comprised of Peshmerga. However, Mahabad, or the Republic of Kurdistan, succumbed to an Iranian invasion in 1946 during which both external influences and internal divisions, primarily between Iranian and Iraqi Kurds, shifted the power of the Peshmerga. In exile, Mustafa Barzani, greatly influenced by Marxist-Leninist ideals, solidified the Kurdish movement by the creation of the KDP, whose political arm provided for the support of the Peshmerga. Instability in Iraq fueled by the decline of the Hashemite monarchy throughout the 1940s and 1950s created an opportunity for the KDP and the Peshmerga to affirm their position as a force to be reckoned with during the 1958 revolution in Iraq.

The 1958 coup witnessed the overthrow of the Iraqi monarchy by General Abd al-Karim Qasim. At the onset, Qasim favored the integration of Barzani and the KDP into the Iraqi political fabric; Qasim also legalized the KDP and the Peshmerga as political entities while recognizing Kurds as distinct but integral people of Iraq under Article 23 of the newly drafted constitution. This ephemeral success was short-lived, however, as Qasim's pan-Arabist ideology blunted any demands for Kurdish autonomy within Iraq.

Under the leadership of Barzani, the Peshmerga occupied the northern region of Zakho stretching to the Iranian border as a result of the Kurdish revolt of 1962. The revolt had brought an unrelenting bombardment of Kurdish villages and towns across the northeastern frontier. Soon thereafter, Qasim's regime was quickly overthrown by the Ba'athist rise to power in 1963. The Baathists would prove steadfastly intolerant of Kurdish demands and would quickly increase their military campaign against the Peshmerga and the KDP. The Peshmerga launched counterattacks, which sustained their position and demands for autonomy by controlling much of the northern frontier by 1968.

The growing strength of the KDP and Peshmerga led to the 1970 Manifesto on Kurdish Autonomy, a proposal drafted by the Ba'ath Party to dilute the rise of Kurdish power, particularly in the north. The ultimate futility of the manifesto led to the 1974 uprising headed by Barzani along with an estimated 50,000 trained Peshmerga. Geopolitical events forced Barzani to abandon the struggle and seek refuge in Iran along with thousands of trained fighters and civilians.

The 1988 Iraqi offensive against Kurds in northern Iraq saw the destruction of hundreds of Kurdish and non-Kurdish villages perceived as being in support of Peshmerga. Labeling the Peshmerga as traitors, the Saddam Hussein regime engineered the 1988 chemical weapons offensive against the town of Halabja, a PUK and Peshmerga stronghold. Kurdish leaders, along with thousands of Peshmerga and civilians, sought refuge in nearby countries. Estimates place the total number of militant and civilian deaths at 100,000.

After the 1991 Persian Gulf War, the Peshmerga became an even more vital military force. The creation of the northern no-fly zone by the United Nations (UN) in 1991 provided an opportunity for Kurdish parties to regroup and form the National Front of Kurdistan, which unified the Peshmerga as a force. In doing so, the Peshmerga, aided by Western powers, were able to secure key Iraqi government strongholds, namely Kirkuk, Arbil, and Sulamaniyah, during 1991–1992. Although friction between Kurds and the Iraqi Army continued, the creation of the no-fly zone enabled leaders of the KPD and the PUK to establish the Kurdish National Assembly, which sought to unite the two major factions of the Peshmerga.

Currently, the Peshmerga are part of the official military force of the KRG, established in 2006. Its mandate seeks the implementation of law and order in the KRG and throughout Iraq and has been instrumental in sustaining security both inside and outside Kurdish-controlled territories in coordination with the Iraqi, U.S., and coalition militaries. Since 2003, the two parties comprising the KRG signed the Kurdistan Regional Government Unification Agreement, which oversees the administration of various governmental departments, most specifically the Department of Peshmerga Affairs, all in an effort to bolster Kurdish self-rule. Because of Kurdish unity and the presence of the Peshmerga, northern Iraq has been relatively free of the fighting that has plagued the rest of Iraq since 2004 with the exception of the campaigns against Ansar al-Islam and the Turcomen and Arab conflicts with the Kurds. It should be noted, however, that in the past the Peshmerga have battled each other in tribal and intra-Kurdish conflicts. The classification of the Peshmerga as an irregular force is rather disingenuous, given its current position within the Iraqi Army. The Peshmerga also remain a tenacious force in the geopolitical compositions of northern Iraq as well as neighboring Turkey, Iran, and Syria.

The Peshmerga played a vital role in the U.S.-planned operation to defeat the Islamic State of Iraq and Syria known as Operation Wrath of Euphrates. U.S. secretary of defense Ashton Carter, in concert with Lieutenant General Sean MacFarland, oversaw the plan that would ultimately deal a decisive, if not fatal, blow to the Islamic State. As IS had developed strongholds in the Syrian city of Raqqa and the Iraqi city of Mosul, they also developed a steady supply line of materials, weapons, and fighters that moved freely across the Iraq-Syria border. While the Syrian Democratic Forces (SDF), made up of mostly Syrian Kurds, led the fight in Raqqa, the Iraqi Kurds in the Peshmerga sealed the border while they took Mosul. This coordinated effort among Kurds on both sides of the border proved critical to cutting off IS supply lines. It is also important to note that as the most organized Kurdish fighting force that has ever existed in terms of legitimacy, training, and equipment, the Peshmerga would likely be the basis upon which any military for an independent Kurdish state, should such a state ever come to exist, would be built.

The Rojava Peshmerga, the militia's arm in Syria, is made up of Kurds that are truly "stateless." Unlike Iraqi Kurds, who have been considered citizens of Iraq since the overthrow of Saddam Hussein, the Kurds in Rojava in northeastern Syria are not considered citizens of any country. There are multiple Kurdish militias in Syria, however, such as the Kurdish Peoples Protection Units (YPG), which currently control the Rojav region of Syria, but tend to be more left-leaning than the members of the Peshmerga. Syrian members of the Peshmerga, which contains some all-women units, identify more closely with the Kurdistan Democratic Party, which currently governs Iraqi Kurdistan.

Shamiran Mako and Robert M. Kerr

Further Reading

ABC News. "Women at War: Meet the Female Peshmerga Fighters Taking on ISIS." https://abcnews.go.com/International/women-war-meet-female-peshmerga-fighters-taking-isis/story?id=39142160.

Barkey, J. Henri, and Ellen Laipson. "Iraqi Kurds and Iraq's Future." *Middle East Policy* 12(4) (Winter 2005): 66–76.

Chaliand, Gerard, ed. *People without a Country*. Zed, 1980.

Frantzman, Seth J. "Rojava Peshmerga—The Group May Be the US's Ticket Out of Syria Crisis." *Jerusalem Post*, December 18, 2018. https://www.jpost.com/Middle-East/Rojava-Peshmerga-the-group-may-be-the-USs-ticket-out-of-Syria-crisis-574728.

Gunter, M. Michael. *The Kurds of Iraq*. St. Martin's, 1992.

Khezri, Haidar. "Kurdish Troops Fight for Freedom—and Women's Equality—on Battlegrounds across the Middle East." https://www.pri.org/stories/2018-03-19/kurdish-troops-fight-freedom-and-womens-equality-battlegrounds-across-middle-east.

Lawrence, Quil. *Invisible Nation: How the Kurds' Quest for Statehood Is Shaping Iraq and the Middle East*. Walker, 2008.

McDowall, David. *A Modern History of the Kurds*. I. B. Tauris, 2000.

O'Ballance, Edgar. *The Kurdish Struggle, 1920–94*. Macmillan, 1996.

O'Leary, Brendan, John McGarry, and Khaled Salih, eds. *The Future of Kurdistan in Iraq*. University of Pennsylvania Press, 2005.

Yildiz, Kerim, and Tom Blass. *The Kurds in Iraq: The Past, Present and Future*. Pluto, 2004.

Popular Front for the Liberation of Palestine–General Command (PFLP-GC)

The Popular Front for the Liberation of Palestine–General Command (PFLP-GC) is an insurgent group established in 1968 by Ahmad Jibril, a former Syrian army captain, who has led it since its founding. The PFLP-GC is sometimes referred to as the Ahmed Jibril Militia or the Jihad Jibril Brigades. The main goal of the group is the destruction of the state of Israel and the establishment of a Palestinian state, but the most pressing priority is the preservation of the Syrian Ba'athist regime. The group is estimated to have a few hundred members who have fought alongside other armed militias on behalf of the regime since 2012.

The PFLP-GC is a splinter group of the Palestinian Marxist group Popular Front for the Liberation of Palestine (PFLP). PFLP-GC members left the larger organization over opposition to its willingness to negotiate with Israel. Ahmad Jibril has remained an outspoken critic of the Palestinian Liberation Organization (PLO) and Palestinian National Authority (PNA), which has caused splinter factions and dwindling membership. PFLP-GC was most active in the 1970s and 1980s when it operated in Gaza, Israel, southern Lebanon, Syria, and Western Europe and carried out dozens of attacks in Europe and the Middle East. The group is well known for its unique methods, such as the use of hot air balloons and hang gliders to conduct cross-border attacks into Israel. Since the 1990s, the group has focused on supporting Hezbollah in attacks against Israel and smuggling weapons through Syria and Lebanon, although it does periodically claim responsibility for bombings and rocket attacks. The PFLP-GC has been designated a Foreign Terrorist Organization by the U.S. State Department since 1997.

PFLP-GC political leadership is currently headquartered in Damascus, Syria, and maintains bases in southern Lebanon and a presence at Palestinian refugee camps in Lebanon and Syria for recruitment of fighters. For decades the group has relied on the Syrian regime for safe haven and logistical support. Its primary funding source is derived from payments for training Palestinian paramilitary groups at its bases in southern Lebanon, but Iran and Hezbollah also provide financial and military support. In exchange for support, the PFLP-GC acts as an armed proxy and issues statements in support of Iran, Hezbollah, and Syria on social media.

Ahmed Jibril reportedly began assisting the Syrian regime in 2011 by collecting intelligence on dissenters in refugee camps in Damascus as protests spread across the country. Jibril's fighters were responsible for maintaining the Palestinian Yarmouk camp, a large suburb of Damascus where an estimated 150,000 refugees resided. Yarmouk inhabitants increasingly aligned with anti-regime rebels, and Jibril claimed Jabhat al-Nusra and the Free Syrian Army were infiltrating the camp to recruit fighters into their respective groups. The PFLP-GC began fighting alongside the Syrian Army, National Defence Force (NDF), and Shiite militias against anti-regime rebel groups in 2012, particularly in and around the Yarmouk camp. In November 2012, Jabhat al-Nusra and an anti-Assad Palestinian group known as Liwa al-Asifa launched an assault on the camp that lasted weeks. On December 15, 2012, the PFLP-GC and Syrian Army were overrun, and Ahmed Jibril fled to Tartous on the western coast of Syria. Little is known about the group's activities until 2015, when the PFLP-GC and other Palestinian groups attempted to retake control of Yarmouk after it was seized by the Islamic State. The regime-backed offensive lasted weeks before they were expelled and the Islamic State reestablished authority.

Members of the PFLP-GC are assumed to be active in Syria and Lebanon and working alongside pro-regime and Palestinian forces. Based on their losses in and around Yarmouk, the group is considered to possess minimal operational capabilities, but it remains a threat to civilians and security forces in Israel and Lebanon.

Melia Pfannenstiel

Further Reading

Hartley, Will, "Popular Front for the Liberation of Palestine- General Command." *Jane's World Insurgency and Terrorism*, 34 (2011): 817–822.

Lister, Charles R. *The Syrian Jihad: Al Qaeda, the Islamic State and the Evolution of an Insurgency.* Oxford University Press, 2015.

Lund, Aron. "Syria in Crisis: Who Are the Pro-Assad Militias?" Carnegie Middle East Center, March 2, 2015. https://carnegie-mec.org/diwan/59215?lang=en.

United States Department of State, Country Reports on Terrorism 2017—Foreign Terrorist Organizations: Popular Front for the Liberation of Palestine-General Command, September 19, 2018. https://www.state.gov/reports/country-reports-on-terrorism-2017.

Putin, Vladimir

Prime minister of the Russian Federation (1999–2000 and 2008–2012), acting president (December 1999–March 2000), and president of the Russian Federation (2000–2008, 2012–), Vladimir Vladimirovich Putin was born on October 7, 1952, in the city of Leningrad (present-day St. Petersburg). He graduated with a law degree from Leningrad State University in 1975 and then joined the foreign intelligence directorate of the Komitet Gosudarstvennoi Bezopasnosti (KGB), with which he served until 1990. For obvious reasons, little information has been made public regarding the details of Putin's KGB career other than that he spent some time during the Cold War in the German Democratic Republic (East Germany). However, since he became president, speculation about his intelligence career has flourished, with claims that he was involved in economic espionage in Western Europe; others allege that he was little more than a low-level domestic spy. Although international sources have raised concerns over Putin's background as an officer of one of history's most brutal internal police organizations, his KGB career has done little to detract from his growing popularity among Russians since his rise to power.

Returning to St. Petersburg after retiring from the KGB with the rank of colonel in 1990, Putin began his political career in the early 1990s under the tutelage of Anatoly Sobchak, who was then the mayor of St. Petersburg. Because Sobchak was known as a liberal democrat, Putin's role in his administration provides some of the few clues to his political orientation, which at the time of his later appointment to the federal government was not at all evident. Putin became deputy mayor of St. Petersburg in

1994 and proved himself a capable administrator. With just two years of political experience, he was brought to the Kremlin in 1996 to serve on President Boris Yeltsin's presidential staff. In 1998, Yeltsin appointed him to head the KGB's main successor organization, the Federal Security Service (FSB), where Putin managed all of Russia's intelligence agencies and ministries; on August 9, 1999, Yeltsin appointed Putin prime minister and indicated publicly that he favored him as his presidential successor.

As Yeltsin's fifth prime minister in less than two years, Putin quickly accomplished the improbable task of gaining the confidence of a wary Russian public that had grown tired and frustrated with government corruption and a flagging economy. He was swift and firm in his response to an Islamic insurgency in Dagestan that was threatening to erupt into war with Chechnya by the time of his confirmation as premier. This earned him a reputation among Russians as a pragmatist for his tough-minded conduct of a government invasion of Dagestan in the wake of a string of terrorist bombings that struck large apartment complexes in Moscow in September 1999.

Although Yeltsin's surprise resignation from the Russian presidency on New Year's Eve 1999 came as a shock to many, his appointment of Putin as acting president was not a surprise. Drawing speculation that a deal had been struck between the two, Putin, in his first official move as acting president, signed a decree granting Yeltsin, among other perks, full immunity from criminal prosecution as well as a lifetime pension.

While Putin did not win the March 2000 presidential elections by as large a margin as analysts had predicted, he nevertheless easily defeated his closest challenger, Communist Party leader Gennady Zyuganov, by some 20 percentage points. The vote demonstrated what experts and pollsters described as a profound shift in Russian public opinion, which for the first time in a decade rallied around one candidate—a newcomer to politics—who had amassed a significant support base from formerly split constituencies and disparate parties. Putin was inaugurated in May 2000 in the first democratic transfer of power in Russia's 1,100-year history.

Putin moved quickly to solidify his power base, and he acted aggressively to curb corruption in government and in Russia's large industries. His detractors claimed that he sometimes subverted democratic ideals in doing so. His administration also struggled to jump-start Russia's troubled economy, a task that was made considerably easier after 2001, when the soaring price of oil brought an economic windfall to the world's second-largest oil producer. Critics of Putin, however, claimed that the president merely substituted one type of corruption with another, which benefited him and his wealthy supporters. Some even accused him of running a "kleptocracy."

Putin's relations with Western leaders, particularly with President George W. Bush, began on a cordial and cooperative note. He voiced full support for the War on Terror after the September 11, 2001, terrorist attacks, and supported Operation Enduring Freedom in Afghanistan. Those relations suffered dramatically after the 2003 Iraq War, however, which Putin refused to endorse without a full United Nations (UN) authorization. He has also been angered over the expansion of the North Atlantic Treaty Organization (NATO) and is vehemently opposed to a U.S.-built missile defense system that would be deployed in Central and Eastern Europe. In December 2007, Putin pulled Russia out of the 1990 Treaty on Conventional Armed Forces in Europe (CFE), a move that was likely a show of Russian disdain for the missile defense plans. By now, many in the West began to talk about a renewed Cold War. Russia also refused to ratify crippling sanctions against Iran, although it has more recently sought to reach a multilateral deal with Iran over its suspected nuclear weapons program. Russia also began to move closer to the People's Republic of China in an attempt to check U.S. hegemony. Meanwhile, Putin's government was compelled to fight against a guerrilla insurgency in Chechnya from 2000 to 2004.

Putin came under fire by many in the West and in his own country for what were perceived as harsh crackdowns on the media and critics of his government. Nevertheless, he was reelected in March 2004 with over 70 percent of the vote. The result was never truly in doubt, as few sought to oppose him and those that did were unable to pierce the media blockade imposed on his critics. European and American election observers criticized both the media coverage and polling irregularities. In response, Putin said, "In many so-called developed democracies there are also many problems with their own democratic and voting procedures," a not so veiled reference to U.S. president George W. Bush's controversial victory over Vice President Al Gore in 2000. By the time he reluctantly gave up the presidency on May 7, 2008, the Russian economy was faring very well, and the Russian government was already making plans to augment its military capabilities. Putin's handpicked successor, Dmitry Medvedev, easily won the May 2008 election, although most believe that Putin, who was immediately made prime minister, continued to hold the majority of power in the Kremlin. He is also head of the powerful United Russia Party, which currently exercises sweeping power within the Russian political arena.

Following a change to Russia's constitution dictating presidential tenure, which Putin himself championed, he ran for a third, nonconsecutive term in 2012 and won; his term is not set to expire until 2018. Russia's economy has largely stagnated during Putin's third presidential term, a consequence mainly of falling oil prices and corruption and inefficiency within the Russian economy. Putin has increasingly promoted a cult of personality, which some Russians (and many foreigners) find odd and off-putting. He has spearheaded anti-LGBT legislation in Russia, and during the 2014 Winter Olympics in Sochi, several athletes boycotted the games because of this.

From a Western perspective, Putin's recent foreign policy initiatives have proven to be deeply troubling. In 2008, he was the main instigator of the five-day Russo-Georgian (South Ossetia) War, which witnessed Russian troops aiding South Ossetian separatists and seizing Georgian military and territorial assets. After the Syrian Civil War began in 2011, Medvedev and Putin were determined to aid the Syrian government under Bashar al-Assad, even though that government was waging war against its own people and was committing wholesale human rights violations. This placed Russia in direct opposition to all of the Western democracies, who decried al-Assad's actions. In late February 2014, Putin's government became involved with Crimean separatists and aided them in seizing the Crimean Peninsula from Ukraine. Within days, a plebiscite was held that approved of a separate Crimea with direct ties to Russia. The vote was taken while thousands of Russian troops were massed along the Russo-Crimean and Russo-Ukrainian border. Russia now controls Crimea, a move that proved highly unpopular in the West.

The United States and other nations put in place limited economic sanctions against Russia, but nothing short of military intervention, which is extremely unlikely, could force Russia out of Crimea. Putin's move caused a precipitous decline in Russia's relations with the West in what many observers say is the worst such crisis since the Cold War, which ended nearly 25 years earlier.

Russia's involvement in Syria has been a tremendous complicating factor for the West. Putin's true motives for supporting the Assad regime have been debated by Western scholars and political leaders, and in reality they are varied and complex. Perhaps his greatest motivation is, as stated in a study conducted by the Brookings Institution in 2013, his fear of state collapse. In the wake of the Arab Spring, in which Putin saw the downfall of long-standing governments in Tunisia, Libya, and Egypt, Putin became very concerned about the challenges to his own sovereignty posed by groups within Russia, particularly in the Caucasus and Chechnya. The Brookings report concluded that Putin saw in Syria the mirror image of the problems he faces from Dagestani and Chechen rebels, and feels a victory for Assad would be a victory for the status quo and his own sovereignty. It must also be considered that Putin stands to gain from complicating matters for the United States as they try to navigate the Syrian conflict.

Paul G. Pierpaoli Jr.

Further Reading

Brookings Institute. "The Real Reason Putin Supports Assad," 2013. https://www.brookings.edu/opinions/the-real-reason-putin-supports-assad.

Kampfner, John. *Inside Yeltsin's Russia: Corruption, Conflict, Capitalism.* Cassell, 1994.

Politkovskaya, Anna. *Putin's Russia: Life in a Failing Democracy.* Holt, 2007.

Sakwa, Richard. *Putin: Russia's Choice.* 2nd ed. Routledge, 2007.

R

Raqqa Campaign. *See* Operation Wrath of Euphrates

Refugee Crisis

It is no exaggeration to say that the refugee crisis caused by the Syrian Civil War has been one of the most significant international crises of the early twenty-first century. Initially an issue of internally displaced persons (IDPs) within Syria's boundaries, the sheer number of people fleeing violence or made homeless from the gradually increasing frequency and intensity of fighting grew exponentially from the initial protests in 2011 to the all-out warfare that ensued in the following months. By 2012, the crisis of refugees from the conflict grew into a regional issue with Syrians fleeing to neighboring countries such as Jordan, Iraq, Lebanon, and Turkey and then expanded to countries outside the region as the situation within Syria became more and more untenable for those with the ability to flee. Impacting the internal political situation in the European Union, the United States, Canada, and even Australia, among others, the Syrian refugee crisis became a hot-button issue as wealthy countries wrestled with balancing political realities at home with a responsibility to help those fleeing for their lives. It is an issue that has forever changed the lives of people both within and outside Syria for generations to come.

The problem of wartime refugees is not a new one. In his ancient history of the Peloponnesian War, Thucydides spoke of the problem of people who had been displaced by war, and it is a problem that has plagued people in every armed conflict since then. It is fair to say that the loss of one's home in war is a burden largely carried by the innocent noncombatants, and there are many times throughout history when an enemy's civilian population has been deliberately targeted by an army hoping to completely demoralize their enemy and to break their will to fight. The impact of people displaced from war can be short-term, with displaced people returning to their homes after the fighting stops, or it can be long-term, or even permanent in the case of displaced communities settling in new parts of the world, thereby creating something known as a diaspora community.

Diaspora communities are large groups of people who have been displaced, or have either moved due to some sort of push factor away from their homeland or been drawn by some sort of pull factor to another location. The most obvious push factor driving people from their homes is war, such as in the case of large numbers of Vietnamese people leaving their homeland during the decades-long conflict in that country and settling in France, the United States, and elsewhere around the world. The Vietnamese diaspora is global, and its members commonly intermarry, maintain their language and religious traditions, and increasingly strengthen ties back to Vietnam now that the Vietnamese government and economy have become more favorable toward them, despite their families' resistance to the Communists in the 1950s, 1960s, and 1970s. Another famous diaspora community displaced by the push factor of war are the Palestinians, who live in concentrated communities in Jordan and Lebanon, and dispersed throughout the rest of the world as the result of the Arab-Israeli War in 1948. The other, less violent push factor driving diasporas actually functions as a pull factor as well, and that is economics. The early twenty-first century has seen a dramatic increase in the number of people leaving their homes in Central America and Mexico due, in large part, to the lack of jobs in their own counties. Drawn by the significant pull factor of the U.S. economy, diaspora communities of Mexicans, Guatemalans, Salvadoreans, and others have settled in the United States; and like other diasporas throughout history, they each maintain their own customs, traditions, and ties with one another that form a strong sense of community for people within those groups. It is this tie to tradition, however, that makes diaspora communities unwelcome in many societies that are afraid of losing their own sense of identity in the wake of large numbers of foreigners moving to their countries.

Early in 2011, when the uprisings started in the Kurdish lands of Syria's northeast and in the southwestern city of Daraa, Syrian refugees were not yet a major concern. However, Syria had been the destination for a large number of Iraqi refugees fleeing the fighting in their own country after the 2003 U.S. invasion. The flow of Iraqi refugees started in 2003, but hit its peak in 2006 and 2007 as sectarian violence went rampant throughout Iraq and those with the means to escape did so; its proximity to Iraq and its porous border made Syria an obvious destination, and Syria largely accepted these refugees. It is estimated that by 2010 more than 150,000 Iraqis had fled to Syria, but that number could actually be higher due to lack of documentation. As the Syrian Conflict intensified, the country faced the problem of

having to deal not only with the large number of Iraqis living in the country, but also with a steadily increasing number of Syrians being driven from their homes as well. This double dilemma quickly escalated, and while ai first there was a problem of internally displaced persons—that is, people seeking to move within Syria—the situation quickly evolved into one of international concern.

In 2016, the United Nations estimated that there were roughly 6 million IDPs in Syria, and an additional 5 million Syrian refugees outside the country—there is no indication that this number is any smaller as of 2019, and it is likely bigger as no large-scale returns related to Syria have been recorded. Initially, the largest number of Syrians fleeing violence moved into Turkey from northeastern Syria by the summer of 2011. It is estimated that 10,000–15,000 Syrians fled into Turkey at that time, though roughly 5,000 moved back into Syria in order to live in newly established refugee camps later in the year. Additionally, thousands of Syrians sought refuge in Lebanon, Jordan, and even as far away as Libya. As Lebanon and Jordan already have large populations of Palestinian refugees that have been living in their countries since 1948 and Libya has severe political and economic challenges, it did not take long for these countries to appeal to the international community for support, and a worldwide dialogue on the responsibility to support and protect Syria's people was set in motion.

One year into the conflict it was reported that there were more than 200,000 IDPs in Syria, and another 70,000 Syrians who had officially registered as refugees. In 2012, after a failed attempt at brokering a peace deal, the United Nations declared the conflict in Syria a civil war, and the number of refugees driven from their homes after an intense period of fighting increased dramatically to around 1.5 million by the end of 2013. The issues in Syria were made worse by the spread of IS throughout Iraq in 2014 as thousands of Iraqis flooded into the northeast; the situation had truly reached crisis proportions, and it was then that the Syrian refugee issue spread into countries outside the Middle East.

The first Syrian refugees made their way to the European Union by boat toward the end of 2012. With their resources stretched to the limit, Syria's neighbors, such as Jordan, started to turn refugees away at the border, and Syrians with the means to do so were forced to look farther afield for safe havens. By 2015, debates surrounding the Syrian refugee crisis came to dominate the political scene in almost every European Union country, Yet, despite the debates, the numbers of Syrians seeking refuge grew, with greater numbers of people making desperate attempts to reach safety. In what became one of the defining images of the refugee crisis, a picture depicting a drowned Syrian toddler washed up on a Turkish beach went viral via social media, and people from around the world voiced the need to help the Syrians. However, as countries around the world struggled with the economic and political realities surrounding the issue of granting large numbers of asylum seekers refuge, a "not in my backyard" (NIMBY) attitude came to dominate in many Western countries. That is, people saw the need to help, but did not want to spend their resources to do it. As the years of the conflict went on, so did the refugee crisis. Images of desperate Syrians breaching borders en masse, overloaded boats, and hungry children existed parallel to debates surrounding national security, economics, and even religion, culture, and identity, and the crisis continued.

By 2017, leaving Syria had become much more difficult as its neighbors devoted more resources to controlling their borders. This has exacerbated the country's problem with internally displaced persons, and the living conditions in the IDP camps are said to be abysmal. This presents a serious security concern, as it is well established that violent extremist organizations recruit heavily from such camps where living conditions are so bad, yet the Syrian government has done little to nothing to improve conditions for these people. That being said, there is evidence that many IDPs have been able to return to their homes, or at least the places where their homes once stood; and if levels of violence remain low, as they have since the end of 2018, the number of those displaced within Syria may grow. The issue concerning refugees outside the country is more problematic, however, as international laws, economics, and the challenges of travel over long distances will complicate the matter, even if a lasting peace is achieved.

Syrian refugees have been settled in countries all around the world. In the Middle East, Jordan, Lebanon, Turkey, Egypt, and even Iraq house significant numbers of Syrians who have fled the conflict. The list of European Union countries that accepted Syrian refugees is extensive, though the bulk have settled in Germany, Sweden, and Austria. There are small numbers of Syrian refugees in South America, but the majority of the refugees from Syria in the Western Hemisphere are in Canada and the United States. Initially, President Barack Obama promised to take in 10,000 refugees, but the United States surpassed that number, eventually taking approximately 33,000. Canadian prime minister Justin Trudeau brought in roughly 55,000 refugees, but lamented that he could not bring in more.

The Syrian refugee crisis is a complex problem born from a complex conflict. No doubt, when peace is eventually restored to

Syria, many will return to their homes and rebuild the cities, towns, and villages that have been completely destroyed. Many, however, may never return, and those who do will never fully recreate the lives they once lived. For those who left, some will find success in their new homes and build lives there. Others will struggle to fit into societies that don't want them, and they will long to return to a land that really only exists in their memories. The countries that accepted them, willingly or grudgingly, will also be changed forever as the debate around the responsibility of the international community to take in refugees from conflicts in distant places remains completely unresolved.

Robert M. Kerr

Further Reading

Al-Rabeeah, Abu Bakr. *Homes: A Refugee Story*. Freehand Books, 2018.

Betts, Alexander. *Refugee: Rethinking Refugee Policy in a Changing World*. Oxford University Press, 2017.

Pace, Michelle, and Somdeep Sen, eds. *Syrian Refugee Children in the Middle East and Europe: Integrating the Young and the Exiled*. Routledge, 2018.

Russia

In the post–Cold War era, Russia has seen more than its share of violence. The violence has been spawned by two separate wars with Chechnya, a constitutional crisis in 1993, a brief conflict with the Republic of Georgia over the future of South Ossetia in 2008, and ongoing terrorism and suicide bombings perpetrated by militant Islamic rebels in the North Caucasus region, particularly from Chechnya and Dagestan.

In 1993, deteriorating relations between Russian president Boris Yeltsin and Russia's parliament led to a political stalemate by September. The crisis was sparked chiefly by Yeltsin's economic policies, which threatened to plunge the nation into a depression as it converted from a Soviet/communist system to a free-market system. A large parliamentary faction decried Yeltsin's policies and asserted that he did not have the power to institute such changes without legislative oversight. On September 21, 1993, Yeltsin unilaterally dissolved parliament, even though he was not constitutionally authorized to do so. The move precipitated a 10-day conflict that witnessed the worst street fighting in Moscow since the Russian Revolution of 1917. Yeltsin ordered troops in to staunch the fighting, and in the process the Russian White House, home to parliament, was badly damaged by artillery fire. When the crisis ended, more or less on Yeltsin's terms, 187 people lay dead (some sources claim the death toll was closer to 2,000), and another 437 were wounded.

A little more than a year later, in December 1994, the Russian government went to war with Chechen separatists who sought independence from Moscow. Beginning in early January 1995, Russian troops launched a brutal attack on the Chechen capital of Grozny. After surrounding the city, Russian artillery and fighter jets pounded the city, resulting in some 25,000 civilian deaths by the end of the month. In retaliation, Chechen rebels took several thousand Russians hostage, many of whom died. Russian forces also suffered high casualties in the fighting. After more fighting and many more civilian casualties, Moscow agreed to a truce in August 1996 and signed a tenuous peace treaty in May 1997. All told, 50,000–100,000 Chechen civilians died in the war. An additional 17,300 Chechen soldiers were killed, while Russia reported about 5,700 deaths among its soldiers.

A second Chechen conflict began in August 1999, a result of the Islamic International Peacekeeping Brigade's invasion of Dagestan. The brigade was an Islamic Chechen militia that sought to help Dagestan's separatists. Russia intervened in the crisis by dispatching troops to Chechnya. The conflict ended in May 2000, with 25,000–50,000 Chechen civilians dead or missing and as many as 11,000 Russian army casualties. Although the battle phase of the conflict was terminated in 2000, Chechen rebels and Islamic extremists fought a terroristic guerrilla war against Russia that did not substantially subside until 2009.

There were many atrocities and acts of terror perpetrated against the Russians between 2000 and 2009. In October 2002, militant Islamic Chechens seized a theater in Moscow and took 850 hostages. After police moved in, 130 hostages and 40 rebels lay dead; another 700 were wounded. In December 2003, the bombing of a train at Stavropol killed 46 civilians. Militants bombed a Moscow subway in February 2004, killing 40 people, and in August 2004, bombings of two Russian commercial airliners killed 89 people. In one of the worst acts of terrorism in modern Russia, Chechen and Dagestani militants stormed a school in Beslan, taking 777 children and some 320 adults hostage. The standoff endured for three days, until police and army troops moved against the school. When the crisis ended, 380 people (many of them children) lay dead, and nearly 700 were injured.

After 2005 or so, the militants began to change their tactics, increasingly employing suicide bombers to instill terror among the Russian public. In March 2010, two female suicide bombers attacked a Moscow subway during rush hour, killing 40 and injuring 75. In January 2011, a suicide bomber blew himself up at Moscow's Domodedovo Airport,

killing 36 and wounding an additional 180 people.

Russia also waged a short, five-day war against Georgia over the disputed region of South Ossetia in August 2008. The conflict ensued when Georgian forces launched a large military incursion into South Ossetia, claiming that its peacekeeping forces along the border had been fired upon. Moscow authorized an incursion into the disputed region, in the process killing 365 civilians, destroying the town of Tskhinvali, and badly damaging several Georgian towns. The Russians suffered 162 deaths in the fighting, while Georgia reported 224 civilians dead, 15 missing, and 542 wounded.

In more recent years, Russia's foreign and military policies have become even more belligerent and unpredictable. Some have attributed these developments to the expansion of the North Atlantic Treaty Organization (NATO) to the Russian border, while others have blamed U.S. unilateralist foreign policies and a temporary spike in world oil prices, the latter of which permitted Russian president Vladimir Putin to strengthen his military. Still others have pointed to Russia's traditional security imperatives and its desire to remain a great power as the reasons for Russia's renewed assertiveness.

In February 2014, Putin engineered the annexation of the Ukraine's Crimean Peninsula during a political crisis in Kiev that saw the deposition of pro-Russian president Viktor Yanukovych. Employing disguised Russian troops, Moscow helped secure Crimea and then sponsored a referendum that suggested the majority of Crimea's residents wished to become part of Russia. Many believed the vote to have been rigged, but Russia nevertheless formally annexed the region in March 2014. Putin asserted that it was not territorial annexation but rather "self-determination" for ethnic Russians living in Crimea. The Crimean annexation was a virtually bloodless affair, but much of the world condemned the move, and the West imposed economic sanctions on the Kremlin.

Meanwhile, in eastern and southern Ukraine, Russia is believed to be aiding a pro-Russian secession movement, although Moscow had steadfastly denied this despite overwhelming evidence to the contrary. Russia has reportedly provided Ukrainian rebels with ample weaponry and other aid, and some disguised Russian troops have been embedded among rebel army units. The result has been a "frozen," low-level conflict, which by early 2017 had killed some 10,000 people, including 2,000 civilians. In July 2014, a Malaysian jetliner was shot down over eastern Ukraine, killing all 298 aboard; it is believed that a Russian-made missile, fired by the rebels, was responsible for the tragedy. The conflict in eastern Ukraine continues, with numerous cease-fires having quickly unraveled. This conflict has resulted in more sanctions on Russia, which by 2015 had begun to adversely affect Russia's economy, as did the collapse of oil prices.

In late September 2015, Russia intervened in the ongoing Syrian Civil War, ostensibly to help in the fight against the Islamic State of Iraq and Syria (ISIS) and other Islamist extremist groups. However, it became quickly apparent that Russian air, artillery, and missile strikes were intended first and foremost to prop up the beleaguered government of Syrian president Bashar al-Assad, a long-standing Russian ally. The Russian intervention greatly complicated the civil war and brought with it substantial civilian casualties. The Americans and Russians tried repeatedly to broker cease-fires, but none held for more than a few days.

In late 2016, the United States withdrew from Syrian talks involving the Russians while Moscow aided Assad in a brutal and bloody campaign to capture Aleppo, which was finally achieved on December 22. The following month, another cease-fire went into effect, brokered by Russia and Turkey, although fighting continued among groups not bound by it. It is estimated that more than 31,000 people died in Aleppo alone between 2012 and 2017. On December 29, 2016, Putin announced a partial Russian withdrawal from the Syrian theater, but he had announced a similar withdrawal in March 2016 that never actually occurred.

The West's relations with Russia have been further harmed by Russian cyber warfare. By 2011, there was evidence that Russia had attempted to hack NATO computers. In April 2015, U.S. intelligence officials indicated that Moscow-directed hackers had breached "sensitive" parts of White House computers. During the 2016 U.S. presidential campaign, Russian hackers repeatedly broke into computer systems of both the Republican and Democratic parties, but leaked only information from the Democrats in a bid to discredit Hillary Clinton's campaign and boost that of Donald Trump. Trump went on to defeat Clinton, although he garnered almost 3 million fewer votes. In late December 2016, the White House levied more sanctions against Russia and expelled 35 Russian diplomatic and intelligence personnel from the United States. Trump has pledged to pursue better relations with Moscow.

Paul G. Pierpaoli Jr.

Further Reading

Politkovskaya, Anna. *Putin's Russia: Life in a Failed Democracy*. Holt, 2009.

Service, Robert. *A History of Modern Russia*. 3rd ed. Harvard University Press, 2009.

S

Salafism

"Salafism" is a term describing branches of reformist Islam as well as a widespread contemporary purist movement, an attempt to return to traditional Islamic roots and practices. Salafism (*salafiyya* in Arabic) is derived from the Arabic *salaf*, and means "(righteous) predecessors" or "(righteous) ancestors" in reference to the first three generations of Muslims. Some adherents seek a return to the spirit of that period.

Modernist reformers in the late nineteenth and early twentieth centuries have been considered Salafists. The name also applies to fervently observant or activist Sunni Muslims who follow the teachings of Muhammad abd al-Wahhab in the eighteenth century and other scholars. These latter are sometimes called the neo-Salafis.

A key concept undergirding Salafism is that the first several generations of Muslims were intent on following the Sunnah, or tradition of the Prophet, and sincere in their efforts to live according to Islamic teaching. One common thread in the different branches of Salafism is that Islam must be cleansed of illicit innovations, known as *bid'ah*. The modernist school argued that tradition had rendered various principles rigid and imitative and that a return to previous creative principles would be of benefit. This school implicitly supported some innovations.

Both the modernist and purist strands of Salafism have impacted such organizations as the Muslim Brotherhood. The purist trend of Salafism has informed the worldviews of

such organizations as al-Qaeda and its offshoots, Jemmah Islamiya, al-Shebaab, and Boko Haram. However, most Muslims who abide by the precepts of Salafism and who may be found in many countries are neither violent nor radical.

The term "Salafiyya" or "Salafism" dates back hundreds of years and was applied to movements like the Ikhwan al-Safa arising in previous centuries. The term "Salaf" appears in a number of early *hadith*, or sayings of the Prophet and his companions, as well as other writings, such as the *tafsirs* of al-Tabari and ibn Kathir.

The title was applied in the late nineteenth century to various Muslim thinkers, including Jamal al-Din al-Afghani and his disciple Muhammad Abduh, mainly in response to British colonialism in the Middle East.

Jamal ad-Din al-Afghani was born and raised in eastern Iran and was probably Shia by doctrinal association. Nevertheless, in his effort to see the revival of Islam as a counter to British colonial policy, he strove to hide his doctrinal sympathies, focusing instead on building a philosophical opposition movement to oppose British occupation of Muslim lands. He traveled extensively and typically portrayed himself in ways that were not consistent with his background and training. In each instance when his benefactors, whether in Great Britain, Egypt, or Istanbul, became suspicious of him and his motives, Afghani would depart to another area of the world to continue his self-appointed mission to throw off the British yoke. Wherever he went he continued to preach the revival of the Islamic community, or *ummah*, as based on the lives of the Prophet and his early companions.

In his desire to defeat British colonialism, Afghani was willing to engage in a wide range of political and insurgency-type activities, ranging from simple fund-raising to endorsing assassination attempts against those Middle Eastern rulers he considered to be British puppets. He spoke openly of killing the leader of Persia, Nasir ad-Din Shah, and one of his disciples eventually carried out the deed in 1896. Although supportive of the Ottoman Empire as the current seat of the Islamic Caliphate, Afghani spent his last years in Istanbul as a virtual political prisoner of the empire's sultan, and died of cancer in 1897.

Afghani's influence almost vanished after his death, but later his name would be resurrected as a folk hero to the revived Islamic movement in the Middle East. The principles of Salafism would be pushed eloquently by one of his main disciples, Muhammad Abduh. Abduh collaborated with Afghani on a number of publishing projects and helped to popularize Salafist ideas through what became known as "the Islamic League." He was savvy politically, and was able to secure the position as Grand Mufti of Egypt in 1899, a post he held until his death.

In some ways Abduh's influence was greater than Afghani's because Abduh was seen by many as more moderate and mainstream, even though his ideas were essentially no different than his mentor's. His writings were more readily accepted, and included a *tafsir* of the Quran along with other works defending the unity of Allah from Christian influences stemming from British colonial policy.

Abduh's ideas would have a tremendous impact on the thinking of Hassan al-Banna and the founding of the Muslim Brotherhood in Egypt in 1928. The focus of the brotherhood as well as other revivalist Muslim societies was initially based on personal piety and raising money through the imposition of *zakat*, or the charitable tax. Soon these activities turned to political activism, and the brotherhood surged to the forefront of political thought in the struggle against British colonial occupation of the country. Although Banna was assassinated in 1949, the ideas of the brotherhood spread throughout the Middle East and into the rest of the Islamic world, especially through the work of such apologists as Sayyid Qutb and Yusuf al-Qaradawi, and have in large measure become the foundation of the Islamic revival movement.

The principles of Salafism revolve around several key issues that involve the literal interpretation of the Quran and adopting certain aspects of the lifestyle of the Prophet and his companions. Shunning Western dress and grooming became important outward displays of this movement, although this was not always consistently done for political reasons. Coupled with this was a revival of interest in the writings of the Hanbalite jurist ibn Taymiyyah, who discussed the conflict inherent between the *salaf* and the *khalaf*, or the authentic believers of the Prophet with those who are merely substitutes of the real thing.

This led to sporadic conflict in the Muslim world between the members of the Salafist movement and the governments of the region. Efforts by Arabic governments to suppress Salafism culminated in the judicial execution of Sayyid Qutb by the Egyptian government of Gamal Abdel Nasser in 1966, and the 1982 destruction of the town of Hama, which had become the base of the movement in Syria, by the government of Hafez al-Assad in which close to 30,000 people died. These attempts to destroy the movement were only temporary, however.

Rebounding from these setbacks, the brotherhood continued its political activities throughout the Islamic world, spreading even into Europe and the United States.

Another important aspect of the Salafist movement is the rejection in general of the concept of *taqlid*, and the call to revive *ijtihad*. *Taqlid*, often incorrectly labeled as "blind following," stresses the need for a Muslim to simply follow the rulings of a particular *madhhab*, or school of law, without doing the necessary research themselves. This is a convenient approach for it does not require an inordinate amount of time and energy to be expended on learning the fundamentals of Islam, particularly those considered well established a few hundred years after the death of the Prophet Muhammad. Taking a ruling on faith, a Muslim can practice his religion on the basis of these early rulings by those much more learned than they.

The weakness of *taqlid*, however, is obvious, as for one to be a truly devoted follower it is best to learn the foundational material for oneself. This requires long hours of study and sometimes even formal training to become well versed in the early writings of Islam. This approach reopened the door to *ijtihad*, being the revival of personal interpretation of Quranic texts as well as other early writings. For many centuries, the learned within Islam had considered *ijtihad* closed because of the solidification and codification of Islamic practice through the *madhhabs*. Salafism called for the return of *ijtihad* to allow the typical believer to make up his mind for himself, and this led to a massive revival of interest in the classical and medieval works of Islam. Translations of the *hadith* and *sunnah* writings flourished, and the works of medieval scholars such as Qadi Iyad, ibn Taymiyyah, and ibn Qayyim were resurrected. Even the writings of some early Sufi scholars such as Imam Ghazzali

became popular, even though the Salafist movement by and large considers Sufism a heretical interpretation of Islam.

The return of *ijtihad* meant that many devout Muslims began to question some aspects of the juristic rulings from later scholars of the *madhhabs*, while still retaining interest in the rulings of the founders of those schools. This revival of personal interpretation had significant influence on bringing back the earliest teachings regarding *zakat*, the proper forms of prayer, and the need to engage in jihad. *Zakat* became the means for the Salafists to influence local politics through provision of welfare and family support, while jihad became more than an inward struggle, returning to the Prophet's own conception that jihad was a form of warfare to make Islam supreme. This revival not only spawned such groups as the Muslim Brotherhood but also led to a whole series of other, lesser groups generally striving for the same goals, being the imposition of Islamic sharia in the Muslim world, and a return to evangelistic operations to spread Islam throughout the non-Muslim world. The Salafist movement's teachings can be found in virtually every Islamic revival today, largely because those teachings were built upon the earliest ideas and writings of the Prophet and his companions.

One of the most important elements of Salafism is the door it opens to something in Islam known as *takfirism*, or the practice of discerning who or what is considered to be properly Islamic and who or what is not. Most Islamic scholars have warned against getting involved in *takfirism* as it can lead to a slippery slope of determining who is proper and who is improper, but those Salafists who have embraced violent jihad have almost all, invariably, incorporated *takfirism* into their practice in order to justify their violence. Islamic violent extremist organizations (VEOs) kill many more Muslims than non-Muslims, and they justify their actions by claiming their Muslim targets are either apostate or not proper Muslims. This is a practice that violent Salafists engage in constantly as they develop potential targets for their terrorist tactics.

In terms of the Syrian Civil War, Salafism is found among many of the Sunni Muslim resistance groups, primarily in the al-Qaeda-backed Nusra Front and those associated with the teachings of the Muslim Brotherhood. It is vitally important to note that Salafism and militancy do not have to go hand in hand, and there are militias in the Syrian Conflict that are Sunni Muslims, yet not Salafist; some are not overtly religious at all. Additionally, there are Islamic VEOs, such as the Islamic State, that are not necessarily Salafist in nature. Many assume IS is a Salafist group, but many of its views, especially those concerning the end-times, differentiate it from what most would consider to be mainstream Salafi teachings.

Russell G. Rodgers

Further Reading

'Abduh, Muhammad. *Risalat al-Tauhid*. [The Theology of Unit]. Translated by Ishaq Musa'ad and Kenneth Craig. Islamic Book Trust, 2004.

Al-Hashimi, Muhammad Ali. *The Ideal Muslim Society: As Defined in the Qur'an and Sunnah*. International Islamic Publishing House, 2007.

Al-Qaradawi, Yusuf. *The Eye of the Beholder: The Muslim Brotherhood over the Past 70 Years*. Al-Falah Foundation, 2003.

Keddie, Nikki. *An Islamic Response to Imperialism: Political and Religious Writings of Sayyid Jamal ad-Din "al-Afghani."* Translated by Nikki Keddie and Hamid Algar. University of California Press, 1968.

Philips, Abu Ameenah Bilal. *The Evolution of Fiqh: Islamic Law & the Madh-habs*. A. S. Noordeen, 2005.

Shabiha

Shabiha, which can mean either "ghost" or "thug" in the Syrian dialect of Arabic, is a term used to describe civilian thugs paid by the Syrian government to crack down on government dissent when official security forces cannot respond. They are a type of localized, government-sponsored attack-dog organization that is employed sporadically when the government needs them to enforce order.

The Shabiha are not particular to the Syrian Civil War; their origin dates back to 1980s Latakia when they acted as a government-sponsored smuggling/crime syndicate who helped fund the Alawite Assad regime. In the 1980s and 1990s the Shabiha were primarily involved in smuggling weapons, alcohol, luxury cars, and cigarettes through Lebanon's Bekaa Valley, and it is believed they provided an essential link between Iran and their proxy militia in Lebanon, Hezbollah. They became so powerful in the 1990s that the regime did not really have control over the most powerful leaders of the Shabiha, and they operated with almost total impunity, especially in the port city of Latakia. As a result of this challenge to government authority, Hafez al-Assad put his eldest son, and designated heir apparent, Basil, in charge of wiping them out—a task he worked toward until his untimely death in 1994.

In 2000, when Bashar al-Assad came into power, the Shabiha seemed to disband, and they remained so until Assad reorganized them into a state-sponsored militia to crack down on anti-government protestors in 2011. Throughout the conflict they have developed a reputation for cruelty and brutality, and they have been implicated in a number of state-sponsored atrocities. It is unclear what role, if any, they would play in a post–Syrian Civil War context.

Robert M. Kerr

Further Reading

Lesch, David W. *The New Lion of Damascus: Bashar Al-Asad and Modern Syria*. Yale University Press, 2005.

Seale, Patrick. *Asad of Syria: The Struggle for the Middle East*. University of California Press, 1989.

van Dam, Nikolaos. *The Struggle for Power in Syria: Politics and Society under Assad and the Ba'ath Party*. I. B. Tauris, 1996.

Shia Islam

Shia ("partisan") Muslims are followers of Islam who hold special reverence for Ali ibn Abi Talib, Muhammad's cousin and son-in-law. Ali was the closest male relative to Muhammad at his death, and the first male convert to Islam, and the Shiites believe that Ali was Muhammad's true successor as the leader of the Muslim people. An important contentious issue between the Sunnis and Shiites today concerns not merely the question of who was meant to succeed Muhammad, but also of what qualifications his successors must have and what roles they should play in the Muslim community. To the Shiites, Muhammad's successors must possess the deepest knowledge of Islamic law and esoteric knowledge of both the Quran and *hadith* (traditions and sayings of the Prophet Muhammad) and be a descendant of the Prophet Muhammad through the family line of Ali and the Prophet's daughter, Fatima. The Shiites believe that Muhammad did indeed choose Ali as his successor at Ghadir al-Khumm in modern-day Saudi Arabia in 630 CE and that Ali bore the divine light of Muhammad (*al-Nur al-Muhammadi*), thus being protected from making errors or committing sins.

Sunnis, on the other hand, are the descendants of those who believed that after Muhammad's death, his father-in-law and closest friend, Abu Bakr, was the rightful successor (caliph), and he was elected through consensus to lead the Muslims. Though Ali initially rejected Abu Bakr, he eventually came to work with him faithfully, later working with Abu Bakr's two successors, Umar and later Uthman, as well to promote Islam until he finally became caliph in 656 CE. Ali's time as caliph was contentious, however, and he was opposed militarily by the ruler of Damascus, who waged multiple campaigns against Ali's forces until the two announced a truce, or *hudna*; but the seeds of dissent continued to plague Ali until he was assassinated in Kufa, Iraq, in 661 CE. It was after Ali's death that the Shia and the Sunni started to see themselves as two distinct political communities. Early Shiites were persecuted by the Umayyad Empire, and most Shia eventually left the Arabian Peninsula (with the exception of a large Shia population on the western shore of the Gulf), bringing their interpretation of Islam north as they settled in modern-day Lebanon, Syria, Iraq, and Iran.

Perhaps the most distinctive feature of modern Shia Islam is its explicit focus on the commemoration of the martyrdom of Ali's son Hussein at the hands of the Umayyads at Karbala, Iraq, in 680 CE. This commemoration is a central facet of Islamic practice for the Shia, and is manifested in the annual mourning rituals of *Ashura*, which takes place on the 10th day of the month of Muharram on the Islamic calendar. Sunnis recognize *Ashura* not as the commemoration of Hussein's martyrdom, but as a day of remembrance of the day Moses parted the Red Sea to lead the Israelites out of Egypt.

There are two major schools of thought regarding the relationship between the government and religious leaders in Shia Islam, and there are three major sects that differ on slight religious matters. The traditional school of thought, which originated in the ancient Shia religious schools (*husseiniya*) of Najaf, Iraq, argues that the religious leadership should focus on spiritual matters, and stay out of government so long as the government is acting in accordance with Islamic law (*sharia*). This Najaf school of thought dominated the Shia world for centuries, but today another, much younger school of thought centered in the Iranian city of Qom is posing a major threat to the traditionalists.

Founded by the leader of the 1979 Islamic Revolution in Iran, Grand Ayatollah Ruhollah Khomeini, the Qom school of thought is centered on the concept of *velayat e faqih*, which argues that the religious leaders should also be in charge of all matters of the state. In other words, *velayat e faqih* calls for a theocracy. It is important to note that due to Iran's increasing geopolitical influence throughout the Shia Islamic world, the Qom school of thought is becoming increasingly influential, even in Iraq where the political insurgency being waged by Muqtada al-Sadr is squarely rooted in the concept of *velayat e faqih*. With Iran's long-standing influence in Syria, it is reasonable to believe that most Shia in the country, though small in number, are increasingly influenced by the Qom school of thought.

Beyond the two major schools of thought regarding political governance among the Shia, there are also three subsets, or sects, that differ slightly in terms of religious interpretations: the *Ithana Ashariyyah* (the "Twelvers"), the *Ismailis* (the "Seveners"), and the *Zaydiyyah*. Twelvers, dominant in Iran, Iraq, Azerbaijan, Bahrain, and Lebanon, believe that the twelfth leader of the Muslim people did not die, but rather went into a type of hiding (occultation). The Shia argue the rightful line of succession was Ali bin Abu Talib, al-Hasan, al-Huusayn,

Ali Zayn al-Abidin, Muhammad al-Baqir, Jafar al-Sadiq, Musa al-Kazim, Al-al-Rida, Muhammad al-Jawad, Ali al-Hadi, Hasan al-Askari, and Muhammad al-Muntazar (also known as the hidden Imam after disappearing in 874). The event of his hiding is known as "lesser occultation." They believe that Muhammad al-Muntazar (al-Mahdi) will come back one day to establish justice on earth. Before his return, the Shiite scholars (*mujtahids*) will spread justice and interpret the laws through intellectual effort (*ijtihad*) for the Muslims, but they are not infallible like the Twelve Imams. The Twelvers established a Safavid dynasty in 1499 in Persia and made the Isna ashariyyah the religion of the state.

Ismailis, or "Seveners," believe that Jafar Sadiq would have been succeeded by his son Ismail, rather than Musa al-Kasim, the seventh Imam, had Ismail not died before his father. Before his death, Jafar appointed Musa al-Kasim to succeed him, but the followers of Ismail rejected Musa as a legitimate heir, disregarding all future Imams. The Ismailis established the Fatimid Empire in Egypt in the tenth century and ruled Egypt and Syria until Salah al-Din al-Ayubi overthrew them in 1174. The Fatimid dynasty also established Al-Azhar University, the oldest and largest Islamic theological learning center in the Muslim world, in Cairo in the tenth century. Interestingly, Al-Azhar today is considered a Sunni center of learning, despite its Shia origins.

The Zaydiyyah, dominant in Yemen and moderate in their theological orientation, chose Zayd, the son of the fourth Imam, Zayn al-Abidin, as their leader. The Zaydiyyah share many doctrines with the Sunnis, in particular with regard to sharia law and its interpretations. They also do not condemn the Sunni caliphs and have their own school of law, the Zaydiyyah school.

Despite the differences between Shiites and Sunnis, there are common elements that unite them. Both strongly believe in one God and in the Quran as a book of guidance. Both believe in Muhammad as the Prophet and that the *hadith* (Muhammed's sayings and deeds) are explanations essential to a true understanding of the Quran and of Islam, though of course they express and hold different interpretations of both sources. Both believe that the law of God, sharia, should rule both religious and mundane aspects of life. Because of these shared beliefs, both Shiites and Sunnis also embrace the pillars of Islam, observing the five daily prayers, fasting at Ramadan, giving alms to the poor and performing a pilgrimage to Mecca at the same times. Ethically, both groups share the same Islamic values and morals and doctrinally seek to promote peace and justice. Both strive spiritually to win God's blessings and mercy in this world and the hereafter.

Robert M. Kerr and Yushau Sodiq

Further Reading

Hourani, Albert. *A History of the Arab Peoples*. Harvard University Press, 1991.

Nasr, Seyyed Hossein. *The Heart of Islam*. HarperCollins, 2002.

Nasr, Seyyed Hossein, Hamid Dabashi, and Seyyed Veli Reza Nasr, eds. *Shi'ism: Doctrines, Thought, and Spirituality*. State University of New York Press, 1998.

Tabataba'i, Allamah Sayyid Muhammad Husayn. *Shi'ite Islam*. State University of New York Press, 1975.

Sunni Islam

Sunni Muslims are followers of Islam who recognize the first four caliphs as the legitimate successors to the Prophet Muhammad. They represent over 85 percent of Muslims worldwide, and form the majority in all Muslim countries but Iran, Bahrain, Lebanon, and Iraq. The term *Sunni* is a short version of *ahl as-sunnah wal jamaat*, which means "the adherents of the Prophet's traditions and the majority," referring to a strong adherence to the *hadith* (recorded traditional sayings, deeds, and approvals of Muhammad). Disciples of Muhammad did not refer to themselves as Sunnis or Shiites during his lifetime. Rather, the classification is a late development that grew out of a political dispute about the leadership of Islam that occurred when a faction of Muslims (now known as Shiites) asserted that Ali ibn Abi Talib, Muhammad's cousin and son-in-law, should be the legitimate heir to Muhammad. By contrast, the majority, who came to be known as Sunnis, insisted that Muhammad did not appoint Ali as his successor, considering Abu Bakr, Umar I, and Uthman I instead to be Muhammad's legitimate successors.

Sunnis, who recognize the four caliphs to have been the legitimate leaders of the faith, espouse the teachings of the Quran and spreading Islam to the world. They reject the notion that Ali and his descendants were the exclusive executors and upholders of Muhammad's traditions, nor do they accept the idea that divine knowledge was transmitted to Ali or his descendants after Muhammad's death. Sunnis also do not share with the Shiites the concept of the *imamate,* which declares that 12 Imams, Ali and his descendants, were given exclusive right to the leadership of the Muslims of all ages. In Sunnism, Muslim leaders may be appointed or selected from members of the community, the only requirement being that they are qualified and knowledgeable about Islamic law and the traditions of the Prophet. Sunnis also reject the notion that the Imams are infallible.

The community of Sunni Muslims, like that of the Shiites, is divided into many groups and sects, some moderate in their interpretations of the Quran and *hadith* and some more extreme. Sunnis base their understanding of Islam on the Quran and *hadith* as understood by Muslim scholars known as *ulama* through their schools of thought, developed in the eighth and ninth centuries. Of the many schools of thought in Islam, Sunni Muslims recognize only four to be legitimate: the Hanafi, Maliki, Shafii, and Hanbali schools. These do not represent different sects of Islam per se, but instead simply espouse different elucidations of the Quran or take diverse approaches to the application of the laws themselves.

The Hanafi school was established in Kufa, Iraq, by a Persian merchant-scholar, Abu Hanifah, Numan bin Thabit (d. 768). The school accepts the Quran, Sunna, and *Ijma* (consensus) as the foundation for Islamic law. It also recognizes local customs (*Istihsan,* or what the community regards as good) and gives great attention to the role of the intellect in articulating and applying the laws of God. The Hanafi school has the largest number of followers in the Muslim world.

The Maliki school was founded in Medina by Malik bin Anas (d. 795), who also accepted the Quran, Sunna, and the practices of the people of Medina (*amal ahl al-Madinah*) as sources of Islamic law. Imam Anas's great contribution to Islam is his work *al-Muwatta*, or "the trodden path," considered one of the earliest books on Islamic law. The majority of North and West African Muslims follow the Maliki school.

The Shafii school was founded by Muhammad bin Idris al-Shafi'i (d. 820), a student of Imam Malik who disagreed with him on the legality of the practices of the people of Medina as a source of law. Considered to be the master architect of Islamic jurisprudence, Imam Shafi'i had many followers in Egypt and Southeast Asia and authored a number of books, including *al-Risalah,* "the treatise," and *al-Um,* "the foundation."

The Hanbali school was introduced in Baghdad, Iraq, by Ahmad bin Hanbal (d. 855), a student of Imam Shafii who relied heavily on the Quran and Sunna as the only sources of Islamic law and who interpreted them rather strictly. The Hanbali school is generally seen to be conservative and reactionary in comparison to the other three schools. It has many followers in Arabia, and in Saudi Arabia in particular. Wahabism, a puritanical revival movement of the eighteenth and nineteenth centuries made prominent in the dialogue about Islam and Saudi Arabia that followed the September 11, 2001, attacks, is an offshoot of Hanbali school.

All Sunnis revere these four schools of Islam, and conversion from one school to another is relatively common. However, the schools do differ on many issues of interpretation and application and thus are not interchangeable. Sunnis believe, however, that all the differences in legitimate religious practice emerge from the divergent practices of the Prophet Muhammad himself, and thus no one has the right to despise any Muslim for following any of them in place of another. In fact, Muslims generally regard such diversity as a boon from God that has the effect of fostering mutual respect and tolerance for the difference.

Despite the differences between Sunni Islam and Shia Islam, there are common elements that unite the two. Both Sunnis and Shiites strongly believe in one God and embrace the Quran as a book of guidance. Both believe in Muhammad as the Prophet and in his *hadith* as a scriptural context essential to any true understanding of the Quran and of Islam, though of course they do express and hold relatively different interpretations of these texts. Both groups believe in the law of God, or sharia, and the pillars of Islam as the governing rules for both their religious and daily lives. Hence, all Muslims observe the five daily prayers, all fast during Ramadan, all give alms to the poor, and all perform pilgrimage to Mecca at the same time. Beyond doctrinal discussion, they all share the same ethical foundation in Islamic values and morals, and all seek ultimately to foster peace and justice for humanity. Finally, both Sunnis and Shiites also strive spiritually to win God's blessings and mercy, both in this world and in the hereafter.

Yushau Sodiq

Further Reading

Hourani, Albert. *A History of the Arab Peoples.* Harvard University Press, 1991.

Nasr, Seyyed Hossein. *The Heart of Islam.* HarperCollins, 2002.

Nasr, Seyyed Hossein, Hamid Dabashi, and Sayyed Vali Reza Nasr, eds. *Shi'ism: Doctrines, Thought, and Spirituality.* State University of New York Press, 1998.

Tabataba'i, Allamah Sayyid Muhammad Husayn. *Shi'ite Islam.* State University of New York Press, 1975.

Sykes-Picot Agreement

This agreement was reached between the British, French, and Russian governments regarding claims of territory belonging to the Ottoman Empire toward the conclusion of World War I. In the spring of 1915, British High Commissioner in Egypt Sir Henry McMahon promised Hussein, Sharif of Mecca, that in return for Arab support in Britain's fight against the Turks, the British would fully support the establishment of an independent Arab state in the Ottoman-occupied lands of Arabia and the Levant. This promise, made throughout the course of a series of letters later known as the McMahon-Hussein Correspondence, had a profound effect on the motivation of the region's Arabs to align themselves with the British Army in defeating the Turks. The promise of an Arab state incensed the French government, however, as they had designs on parts of the Levant in the event of an Ottoman defeat. This caused McMahon to walk back some of his promises, but this did little to deter the Arabs, who were sure that the British would follow through with their end of the deal. After all, the Arabs had no love for their Turkish overlords, and they were more than ready to rid the area of Ottoman influence.

Aware of the British agreement with Hussein, the French pressed the British for recognition of its own claims in the Ottoman Empire. Englishman Sir Mark Sykes and Frenchman François Georges Picot were appointed by their respective governments to conduct the negotiations, which took place in the Russian city of Petrograd in the early spring of 1916. They secured Russian support of their deal on May 16, 1916; the deal became known as the Sykes-Picot Agreement.

The Sykes-Picot Agreement provided extensive territorial concessions to all three powers at the expense of the Ottoman Empire. Russia was to receive the provinces of Erzurum, Trebizond, Van, and Bitlis (known as Turkish Armenia) as well as northern Kurdistan from Mush, Sairt, ibn Omar, and Amadiya to the border with Persia (Iran). France would secure the coastal strip of Syria, the vilayet of Adana, and territory extending in the south from Aintab and Mardin to the future Russian border to a northern line drawn from Ala Dagh through Kaisariya Ak-Dagh, Jidiz-Dagh, and Zara to Egin-Kharput (the area known as Cilcia). Britain would secure southern Mesopotamia with Baghdad as well as the ports of Haifa and Acre in Palestine. The zone between the British and French territories would be formed into one or more Arab states, but this was to be divided into British and French spheres of influence. The French sphere would include the Syrian hinterland and the Mosul province of Mesopotamia, while the British would have influence over the territory from Palestine to the Persian border. The agreement also provided that Alexandetta would become a free port while Palestine would be internationalized.

The parties involved agreed to maintain strict secrecy regarding the agreement. Despite this, the Italian government learned of its existence by early 1917 and forced the French and British governments to agree in the Saint-Jean-de-Maurienne Agreement of April 17, 1917, that Italy would receive a large tract of purely Turkish land in southern Anatolia and a sphere of influence north of Smyrna. This was the final agreement among the Allies regarding the future partition of the Ottoman Empire. It was contingent on the approval of the Russian government, which was not forthcoming because of revolutionary upheaval there. Husayn did not learn of the Sykes-Picot Agreement until December 1917 when the information was published by the Bolshevik government of Russia and relayed to Hussein by the Turks, who vainly hoped thereby to reverse his pro-British stance.

The revelation of the Sykes-Picot Agreement certainly soured the general Arab view of the Brits, but not enough to deter them in their fight against the Turks; they still felt that a British-Arab victory would inevitably result in support for an independent Arab state, and such a state was actually declared from Damascus in 1920. The French,

completely unwilling to allow for this, went to war with the Arabs that same year, but the drive for an independent Arab state never subsided. Even after the post–World War II independence era, however, another thing that has never subsided is Arab resentment toward the British, the French, and the West in general for what they see as the act of betrayal illustrated in the Sykes-Picot Agreement.

Sykes-Picot was a direct predecessor for the Syrian Civil War. First, the betrayal prompted the Arab declaration of an independent state in the city where the Arab armies' most triumphant moment took place, Damascus—a city in the heart of the area promised to the French in the agreement. Second, this act of defiance, from the perspective of the French, led to a general attitude among the French that the Sunni Muslim Arab population of their new territory posed the greatest threat to their grip on power in Syria, so it forced them to privilege the region's minority groups at the expense of the Sunni majority. The biggest benefactor of this mistrust toward the Sunnis were the Alawites, a group given privileges disproportionate to their numbers in Syria; privileges that would pave the way for Hafez al-Assad to ascend all the way to the top of the Syrian power structure. This would never have happened had it not been for the events set into motion by this secret agreement in 1916.

Spencer C. Tucker and Robert M. Kerr

Further Reading

Andrew, Christopher M., and A. S. Kanya-Forstner. *The Climax of French Imperial Expansion, 1914–1924.* Stanford University Press, 1981.

Kedourie, Elie. *In the Anglo-Arab Labyrinth: The McMahon-Husayn Correspondence and Its Interpretations.* Cambridge University Press, 1976.

Kent, Marian, ed. *The Great Powers and the End of the Ottoman Empire*. 2nd ed. Cass, 1996.

MacMillan, Margaret. *Paris, 1919: Six Months That Changed the World*. Random House, 2002.

Tanenbaum, Jan Karl. *France and the Arab Middle East, 1914–1920*. American Philosophical Society, 1978.

Tauber, Eliezer. *The Arab Movements in World War I*. Cass, 1993.

Syria

Syria is a predominantly Arab country in the Levant region of the Middle East on the far eastern edge of the Mediterranean Sea. Covering 71,498 square miles (just slightly larger than the U.S. state of North Dakota), it borders Jordan and Israel to the south and southwest, respectively; Lebanon and the Mediterranean Sea to the west; Turkey to the north; and Iraq to the east. Due to its favorable strategic location between the Mediterranean Sea and the Euphrates River, the territory that makes up modern-day Syria has been coveted by great powers throughout history. Damascus and Aleppo, primarily, have been important world cities off and on for more than 3,500 years, and Syria's fertile soil has abundantly supported the needs of many empires. Because of these factors, Syria has attracted many diverse groups of people from both within and outside of the Middle East, and at various times these different groups have either coexisted peacefully or they have fought bitterly amongst themselves. In the second decade of the twenty-first century, the latter has been the case, and a brutal civil war has taken its toll on Syria and its people in ways that will have far-reaching effects for a long time to come.

Syria has six distinct geographical regions, each one fostering different historical culture groups and traditions. The agriculturally rich coastal plain along the Mediterranean Sea has long been Syria's doorway to the west, with all the costs and benefits that have come with it. East of the coast lay the mountains with their difficult terrain and historically isolated peoples. The center of the country is marked by the rocky folded terrain of the Palmyra Folds and its network of ancient cities along well-trodden trade routes. Northeast of this area and west of the Euphrates lie Syria's richest agricultural lands and the cities of Homs, Aleppo, and Hamah, and south of the Palmyra Folds lie extensive ancient lava flows and a volcanic landscape—the famous and controversial Golan Heights reflect this landscape. Finally, northeast Syria, the oil-rich, desert region known as al-Jazirah extends across the border into Iraq. Given Syria's geography, it is not hard to understand why it has been desired by so many throughout history, and the French were able to capitalize on the regional identities within Syria in order to divide and rule during the time of their UN Mandate.

The land of Syria, along with all of the land surrounding it and now making up Lebanon, Israel and Palestine, Jordan, and Iraq was part of the Ottoman Empire for almost 400 years. This period had profound effects on the cultures and societies that comprise modern-day Syria. Most significantly, Ottoman social policies, collectively known as the *millet* system, demanded political loyalty to the Turkish empire, but it did not require cultural or even religious uniformity among all its subjects. While the empire was dominated by Sunni Muslims, Christians, Jews, Shia Muslims, Zoroastrians, and practitioners of other variations of Islam, such as the Alawites and the Druze, among many others, all lived more or less peacefully with one another under the ultimate rule of the Turkish sultan. The empire's institutional multiculturalism was practical, not altruistic, and the legacy of its social policies was a patchwork of hundreds, if not thousands, of ethnic groups who had to figure out how to continue to coexist peacefully in the absence of the Ottoman rulers to maintain order. Because of Syria's history as a crossroads of cultures, it was an area of particular complexity in terms of the sometimes vast ethnic, linguistic, and religious differences of the people who lived there at the time of the empire's demise in 1918.

In their fight against the Ottomans in the Middle East during World War I, the British, or more specifically one Brit, T. E. Lawrence (aka "Lawrence of Arabia"), worked tirelessly to convince various Arab tribal leaders to rise up and aid the British military in defeating the Ottoman forces. In return, the British promised the Arabs that upon Ottoman defeat, they would be rewarded with their own independent state to encompass the former Ottoman lands in Arabia and the Levant. Eventually, Lawrence was successful, and in 1918 he and his Arab ally, Faisal bin Hussein Ali al-Hashemi, triumphantly rode into Damascus—today the capital of Syria and at that time the last bastion of Turkish military strength in the region. Unbeknownst to Faisal (and perhaps even Lawrence himself), however, the British and French governments had made a pact to divide the former Ottoman territories between themselves, and after a failed attempt to claim an independent state centered in Damascus in 1920, the French took administrative control of Syria and neighboring Lebanon under the auspices of a League of Nations mandate.

French rule after World War I resulted in repeated uprisings by Arab nationalists, members of the Muslim Brotherhood, and various ethnic minorities opposed to the French presence. After a tortuous series of negotiations and anti-French violence and brutal responses by the French and the government-sponsored militia in the late 1920s, Syria was granted considerable autonomy in 1936. World War II was felt in Syria when, in 1940, Syria came under the control of the French Vichy government, thus giving the Nazis easy access and basing rights within the country. This situation was obviously intolerable to the Allies, and in July 1941 Syria and Lebanon were retaken by British, Australian, and Free French forces along with their Arab partners.

In July 1943, under pressure from its allies, the Free French government-in-exile announced new elections. A nationalist government came to power that August, electing as president Syrian nationalist Shukri al-Quwatli. France granted Syria independence on January 1, 1944, but the country remained under Allied occupation for the rest of the war. In February 1945, Syria declared war on the Axis powers and became a member of the United Nations (UN) the next month.

In early May 1945, anti-French demonstrations erupted throughout Syria, whereupon French forces bombarded Damascus, killing 400 people before the British intervened. A UN resolution in February 1946 called on France to evacuate the country, and by mid-April all French and British forces were off Syrian soil. Evacuation Day, April 17, is still celebrated as a Syrian national holiday.

On March 22, 1945, Syria cofounded the Arab League, which advocated pan-Arab nationalism but without the consolidation of states and the resultant problems that such a movement would have witnessed. The Arab League was also aimed at blocking the creation of a Jewish state in Palestine, which the Syrians strongly opposed.

Syria played a relatively small role in the Israeli-Arab War of 1948–1949 that arose from the creation of the Jewish state in May 1948. At the beginning of the fighting, Syria had only some 4,500 troops to commit, almost all of whom were dispatched to the Syrian-Palestinian border. Just six days into the fighting, Syrian troops had been repelled, with heavy casualties. News of the Syrian defeat spread rapidly, and many Syrians blamed al-Quwatli for the setback. Al-Quwatli reacted by firing his defense minister and chief of staff. As time passed, however, Syrian troops enjoyed some success and managed to occupy a small strip of Palestinian territory along the border. They also occupied a small piece of land in northeastern Palestine. After these initial successes, the small Syrian military contingent remained rather inactive for the rest of 1948. For al-Quwatli, whose popularity was quickly eroding, the chief issue of the 1948–1949 war for Syria was whether the nation would fight alongside other Arab nations in a show of pan-Arabism or whether it would fight to retain its Syrian identity. In so doing, he diluted the Syrian effort against the Israelis and engendered opponents in other Arab states.

The Israeli victory in the war and disagreements over Syria's potential union with Iraq torpedoed al-Quwatli's government. There were three separate coups in 1949, the last one headed by Lieutenant Colonel Adib al-Shishakli, who governed with a heavy hand until 1954. In 1952, after a series of lengthy talks, al-Shishakli agreed in principle with an American offer that would have brought $400 million of U.S. aid to Syria in exchange for Syria's settling of as many as 500,000 displaced Palestinians. The plan was doomed from the start, however, as many Syrians—especially those on the political Left—decried the plan as an attempt to deny Palestinians their right to return to Palestine, which by now had UN backing.

Al-Shishakli was ousted in 1954, and late that year elections were held to determine the makeup of the new government, which would now be civilian. In the end, a three-party coalition (People's, National, and Ba'ath Parties) emerged with National Party chief Sabri al-Asali as its head. The coalition was a shaky one, and political instability plagued the new government. In the succeeding years, the Ba'athists, who combined Arab nationalism with socialist economic policies, became the most powerful political force in Syria, and Syria gradually entered into economic and military agreements with the Soviet Union.

In February 1958, Syria and Egypt joined to form the United Arab Republic (UAR), with Syrian political parties supposed to refrain from all political activity. Within a year, complete Egyptian domination of the UAR forced yet another coup against the Syrian government, in September 1961. The coup, carried out by military officers, promptly pulled Syria out of the UAR and established the Syrian Arab Republic. In December 1961, elections for a national assembly were held, and the body chose two conservative People's Party members to lead the new regime. However, another coup in late 1962 again toppled the government.

In 1963, a joint Ba'ath-military government came to power. The new government nationalized most industrial and large commercial concerns and engaged in land reforms that redistributed land to the peasants. Meanwhile, Syria continued to cultivate relations with the Soviet bloc. A schism in the Ba'ath Party resulted in more instability, and in 1966 the radical wing of the party staged a coup and installed Yusseff Zayen as prime minister. Nureddin al-Attassi became president. This new regime tightened Syria's ties with both the Soviets and Egyptians.

In the 1960s, tensions with Israel persisted and Syria fought Israel again in the June 1967 "Six-Day War," with disastrous consequences. This time, Syria's defeat included the loss of the Golan Heights to the Israelis. The outcome of the war eviscerated the ruling government, and when Syrian forces had to pull back after attempting to aid the Palestinians in Jordan during Black September (1970), the scene had been set for yet another change of government. On November 13, 1970, General Hafez al-Assad, the minister of defense, seized power in a bloodless coup. Assad referred to it as the "Corrective Resolution," which essentially ousted from power civilian Ba'athists in favor of the military Ba'athists. An ardent Ba'ath nationalist, Assad sought to strengthen ties to other Arab states, de-emphasize Syrian reliance on the Soviet Union, and defeat Israel.

In early 1971, Assad was elected president, and he immediately began to consolidate his power. He would rule the country until his death in 2000. Over the next several years, he modernized the Syrian Army and engaged in modest economic reforms as the Ba'ath Party gained even more strength. Befitting Assad's Ba'athist philosophy, the state played a central role in economic planning and implementation. Assad's tactics could be brutal, and there was little room for dissent or democracy in Syria.

Syria joined with Egypt in the October Yom Kippur (Ramadan) War with Israel of 1973. At the beginning of the fighting, Syria launched a massive ground attack that included 1,500 tanks (900 in the initial attack and 600 in reserve) and 144 batteries of artillery in an attempt to retake the Golan Heights. After some initial success and although their forces this time fought quite well, the Syrian attackers were finally driven back beyond their original positions. Syria did not take the Golan Heights but did regain control over a small portion of it as a result of U.S.-led negotiations after the war.

In the late 1970s and 1980s, Sunni Muslim fundamentalists began challenging the Baath Party's secular outlook. From 1976 to 1982, urban areas all across Syria became hotbeds of political unrest. Assad brutally crushed a February 1982 uprising by the Muslim Brotherhood in Hama, and troops killed several thousand people.

Assad also sent his army into Lebanon in 1976, ostensibly as a peacekeeping force during the civil war there. The troops stayed on, however, with Assad siding with the Muslims who were fighting Christian militias. By the mid-1980s, Syrian forces had become the preponderant political and military force in Lebanon. In 1990, the conflict was declared to have ended, although Syrian troops were not withdrawn from Lebanon until 2005. As a result of the long Syrian presence in Lebanon, nearly 1 million Syrians moved into Lebanon after 1990 to seek work. In 1994, the Lebanese government granted citizenship to 250,000 Syrians, a move that was, for obvious reasons, controversial among the Lebanese people.

At the same time, the 1980s saw the Assad regime taking harder-line Arab positions and moving closer to the Soviets. Assad's "get-tough" approach in regional politics included funding and encouragement of terrorism, both in the Middle East and internationally. Assad, who was always in the end a pragmatist, sought to ameliorate relations with the West as the Soviet Union began to implode in 1990. When Iraq invaded Kuwait in August 1990, Assad was the first Arab leader to denounce the attack. His government also provided 20,000 troops to the international coalition that defeated Iraqi forces in the 1991 Persian Gulf War. Assad's frontline position in the war reflected both his desire to strengthen relations with the West and his strong dislike of Iraqi dictator Saddam Hussein. Although Hussein was a Ba'athist, at least in name, he posed a direct threat to Assad, who saw himself as the pivotal leader in the region and retained some of the pan-Arab nationalism of his youth.

In 1991, Assad's government entered into peace negotiations with Israel, although the process broke down with no firm agreement in January 2000. Assad died unexpectedly in June 2000 after 30 years in power. He was succeeded by his third son, Bashar al-Assad. Bashar was an ophthalmologist who had attended medical school in Damascus, and after serving as a military doctor in Syria moved to London to further his medical studies. Bashar's older brother Basil had been expected to be their father's heir apparent, but he was unexpectedly killed in a car accident in 1994. Bashar was called back to Syria, forced to abandon his medical career, and groomed to become his father's heir by being sent to the military academy and commissioned as an officer, eventually achieving the rank of colonel in the Republican Guard. At the time of Hafez al-Assad's death, Syrian law required that the president be at least 40 years old; an emergency session of the legislature had to be held in order to change the constitution to lower the age to 34 years, Bashar's age at the time of his father's death in 2000. Allegedly a free-market proponent, the younger Assad attempted some economic reforms, but the process has been fraught with setbacks and obstacles. In 1998, 65 percent of all Syrian revenues came from petroleum products. The younger Assad also promised both political and democratic reform, but neither has come to fruition.

After the September 11, 2001, terrorist attacks against the United States, Syria pledged its cooperation in the so-called "War on Terror." But with the beginning of the U.S.-led 2003 Iraq War, which Assad refused to support, U.S.-Syrian relations sharply deteriorated. Syria's continued support of militant Palestinian groups and terrorist organizations such as Hezbollah have seriously strained relations with the United States and much of the West. To make matters worse, Syria's long and porous border with Iraq to the east has served as a conduit for Syrian weaponry and terrorist fighters involved in the insurgency in Iraq. President George W. Bush's administration repeatedly warned Damascus not to aid the Iraqi insurgents, but there is little evidence that the warnings were heeded.

Although Syrian troops were finally out of Lebanon by 2005, there is considerable evidence to suggest that the Syrians continue to involve themselves in the internal politics of that nation. Indeed, most observers agree that Syrian operatives were responsible for the assassination of former Lebanese prime minister Rafik Hariri in February 2005. By late 2006, some pundits and even a few foreign policy strategists feared that Syria, working in tandem with Iran, was attempting to undermine the shaky government in Lebanon in a bid to exert de facto control over that country.

Since the spring of 2011, Syria has been rocked by a bloody civil war as anti-government groups, including the Islamic State (IS), have attempted to destabilize and bring down Assad's government. Assad has responded to the violence and unrest by employing brute military force and strict repression over his adversaries. Government forces have even resorted to the use of chemical weapons, which elicited strong reactions from the international community. The civil war reached its zenith in the years between 2015 and 2018, and by 2019 more than

500,000 people had been killed, and more than 11 million Syrians had been displaced from their homes and had fled either to other parts of the country or to other countries altogether. It is far too soon to understand the full effect that the Syrian Civil War will have on the social, political, and geopolitical future of not just Syria, but the entire region as a whole.

Paul G. Pierpaoli Jr.

Further Reading

Held, Colbert, and John Thomas Cummings. *Middle East Patterns: People, Places, and Politics.* Westview Press, 2011.

Lesch, David W. *The New Lion of Damascus: Bashar Al-Assad and Modern Syria.* Yale University Press, 2005.

Maoz, Moshe, and Avner Yaniv, eds. *Syria under Assad: Domestic Constraints and Regional Risks.* Croom Helm, 1987.

Seale, Patrick. *Assad of Syria: The Struggle for the Middle East.* University of California Press, 1990.

Syrian Armed Forces

Syria has been inhabited continuously for thousands of years and has been the site of dozens of conquests by invading forces. Damascus, the capital, is one of the oldest surviving cities in the world. It became a Muslim city in 636 CE and was the heart of the Islamic world until the Abbasid Caliphate was established in Baghdad in the eighth century. By 1517, Syria had been incorporated into the Ottoman Empire, where it remained until World War I. After World War I when the Ottoman Empire was partitioned, Syria became a French protectorate. Syria did not achieve full independence until April 1946.

The modern Syrian Army was first formed as a mandate volunteer force in 1920. Designated the Troupes Speciales du Levant (Levantine Special Forces) in 1925, all of the unit's officers were originally French. During World War II, this force was under Vichy French control until the British occupied Syria. When the force passed to the control of the Free French, it was redesignated the Troupes du Levant (Levantine Forces). When the French finally departed in 1946, the Levantine Force became the Syrian Army, which by 1948 had grown to 12,000 troops.

In May 1948, the British Mandate for Palestine came to an end. The Jews there declared the independence of the State of Israel, and the forces of Egypt, Iraq, Lebanon, Syria, and Transjordan (later renamed Jordan) immediately invaded Israel.

Syrian involvement in the Israeli War of Independence (1948–1949) began with an advance of infantry and armored vehicles into the Galilee region. The newly established Israel Defense Forces (IDF) had few means to repel armored forces, which it faced on three fronts. The IDF also began the war with no combat aircraft. The Syrian Air Force in 1948 had 50 aircraft, although only 10 were of relatively modern World War II design. French influence on the Syrian military was still significant in 1948. Most Syrian tanks were French models, including the Renault R-35 and R-37. The Syrians also had a small number of French artillery pieces.

The first Syrian advances into Israel targeted the village of Zemach (Samakh), situated at the southern edge of the Sea of Galilee. Despite deploying tanks, armored cars, and artillery against a defensive force armed only with rifles, machine guns, and two small antitank guns, the Syrian Army took three days to capture the village. After the fall of Zemach, the Syrians pushed toward the Degania Kibbutzim. At Degania A, 70 Israelis armed with rifles and Molotov cocktails repelled a Syrian infantry company reinforced by tanks and artillery. After a similar defeat at Degania B, the Syrians withdrew, abandoning all their previous gains and providing a one-month respite to the exhausted Israeli defenders.

On June 10, 1948, Syrian forces successfully forded the Jordan River and attacked Mishmar Hayarden, a kibbutz north of the Sea of Galilee. The Israelis launched a series of fierce counterattacks but could not drive the Syrian Army back from Mishmar Hayarden. From that point on, however, the Syrians were content to consolidate their defensive positions and hold what Israeli territory they had.

The Syrian Army occasionally supported the Arab Liberation Army (ALA), a multinational force commanded by Syria's Fawzi al-Qawuqji. When the IDF launched an offensive to destroy the ALA in October 1948, however, Syria refused to support ALA units or to allow them to withdraw into Syrian territory. On July 20, 1949, Syria and Israel agreed to a cease-fire. Syria withdrew from the Mishmar Hayarden area, which became a demilitarized zone.

Dissatisfaction with the outcome of the Israeli War of Independence ran deep in the Syrian military. Although Syrian president Shukri al-Quwatli envisioned a greater Arab nation, encompassing both Syria and Palestine, he also believed in a republican form of government. He was removed from power during a series of military coups that erupted in 1949. In December, Colonel Adib al-Shishakli seized power. In 1951, he orchestrated his own election as president and dissolved the Syrian parliament. Another coup removed him from power in 1954, and he was replaced by an Arab nationalist coalition. In September 1961, another military coup occurred. Following more turmoil, Syrian Army officers created the National

Council of the Revolutionary Command (NCRC), dominated by the Ba'ath Party. The NCRC assumed power on March 8, 1963, and remained in place until 1970, although internal coups changed the face of the NCRC on a regular basis.

Meanwhile, two decades of sporadic raids across the Israeli-Syrian border exploded into an aerial battle over the Golan Heights on April 7, 1967. Israeli aircraft shot down six Syrian Mikoyan-Gurevich MiG-21 fighters, after which IDF warplanes flew over Damascus in a triumphant show of force.

Although the United Arab Republic had dissolved, Egypt and Syria continued to maintain close military ties. On May 30, 1967, Jordan joined the alliance. All three nations began mobilizing their military forces, deploying them to the Israeli border. In response to the overwhelming intelligence indicators, the IDF launched a preemptive strike against Egyptian airfields on June 5, 1967, triggering the Six-Day War. After destroying virtually the entire Egyptian Air Force on the ground, Israeli warplanes launched attacks against Jordanian, Syrian, and Iraqi airfields with much the same results.

With two-thirds of the Syrian Air Force destroyed and the remainder dispersed to distant airfields, Syrian military options against Israel were limited. After an abortive attack on the Tel Dan water plant, Syrian units began shelling Israeli towns from fortified positions atop the Golan Heights. The IDF retaliated with air strikes, attempting to silence Syrian artillery and disorganize or destroy the armored units.

On June 9, Israeli forces broke the Syrian defensive lines atop the Golan Heights plateau. The Syrian Army retreated in disarray, abandoning much of its heavy equipment. When the cease-fire took effect on June 11, IDF troops held the Golan Heights. During the Six-Day War, Israel lost only 141 soldiers on the Syrian front. The war cost Syria 2,500 killed as well as almost all of its equipment that had been deployed on the Golan Heights.

The Israeli occupation of the Golan Heights was a critical factor in the next outbreak of hostilities between the two nations. On October 6, 1973, Egyptian and Syrian forces launched a coordinated surprise attack against Israel. During the Yom Kippur War, Syria's primary objective was to retake the Golan Heights. Syria also sought to reclaim some measure of the respect it had lost in the humiliating 1967 defeat. During the first two days of fighting, Syrian forces made significant advances, regaining much of the lost territory.

For the IDF, the primary front of the war was the Golan Heights, the loss of which would represent the single most serious threat to the security of Israel. Combat against Egypt in the Sinai became the secondary theater, as the IDF rushed reserves to the northern front.

Early Syrian advances pushed the IDF back to the outskirts of Nafah. But as the Syrian units advanced, they left the protective umbrella of their antiaircraft defensive network, increasing their own vulnerability to Israeli air attack. By October 8, the initiative and momentum shifted to the Israelis, who began to push the Syrian forces from the Golan Heights and back into Syria. On October 14, Israeli forces began shelling the outskirts of Damascus. Israeli progress was halted by a surprise Iraqi and Jordanian attack into the IDF's flank, but even the combined Arab armies were insufficient to push the IDF out of Syria.

On October 22, the United Nations (UN) imposed a cease-fire on Egypt and Israel. Syria acceded to the cease-fire on October 23. U.S. secretary of state Henry Kissinger engaged in a series of diplomatic meetings

in Syria and Israel, eventually brokering a long-term armistice agreement signed on May 31, 1974. Israel agreed to withdraw its forces to the post–Six-Day War border, which left it in control of the Golan Heights. Both sides also agreed to the establishment of a demilitarized zone policed by UN troops.

In 1976, Syria sent 40,000 troops into neighboring Lebanon to intervene in the Lebanese Civil War. This led to a 30-year Syrian presence in Lebanon, as Syria sought to impose internal stability while also pursuing its own interests. In 1982, Israel invaded southern Lebanon in an attempt to preempt terrorist attacks across the border, primarily those launched by the Palestine Liberation Organization (PLO). During the first week of Operation Peace for Galilee, the Syrian Air Force lost 86 aircraft to the Israeli Air Force (IAF) in the skies over Lebanon. Although the Syrian-Israeli border remained relatively quiet thereafter, the two nations effectively fought a proxy war in Lebanon, as Syria funded and trained Lebanese and Palestinian fighters.

During the 1991 Persian Gulf War, Syria participated on the side of the UN coalition, led by the United States. This was an abrupt departure from previous Syrian policy, especially considering that Syria had been allied with Iraq in three wars against Israel. Following the Persian Gulf War, Syrian president Hafez al-Assad, in power since 1970, conducted discreet face-to-face negotiations with the Israeli government. The talks failed to produce a peace settlement, but the Israeli-Syrian border remained relatively peaceful and secure. When al-Assad died on June 10, 2000, he was succeeded by his son, Bashar al-Assad, who has attempted to continue his father's lower-profile policy toward Israel.

Prior to the 1991 Persian Gulf War, Syria imported most of its military technology from the Soviet Union. As a reward for its participation in that war, Syria received financial assistance from several Arab states in the Persian Gulf, including Kuwait and Saudi Arabia. Much of that funding was earmarked for military spending, in part to offset the costs of participation in the war. With the collapse of the Soviet Union, however, and the unwillingness of most Western governments to sell arms to Syria, that nation has experienced difficulty in procuring quality military hardware. Domestic manufacturing of conventional weapons in Syria remains limited primarily to small arms.

Syria currently fields one of the largest military forces in the world. The Syrian military is organized into the Syrian Arab Army, the Syrian Arab Navy, the Syrian Arab Air Force, the Syrian Arab Air Defense Forces, and the Police and Security Force. All Syrian men serve a compulsory two years in the Syrian military, beginning at age 18. The officer corps is highly politicized, with membership in the Ba'ath Party being a virtual prerequisite for advancement to flag rank. Annually, Syria spends approximately $1.5 billion on its military, representing almost 6 percent of its gross domestic product (GDP). Syria's military has been significantly compromised, however, since the beginning of the Syrian Civil War, which began in early 2011.

By late 2013, the Syrian Army had been cut in half, numbering 110,000 regular troops compared to some 200,000 regular troops prior to the civil war. They are organized into five armored and four mechanized divisions, a Special Forces division, and a Republican Guard division. Its 5,000 main battle tanks include 1,700 Soviet T-72s and 2,000 T-54/55s and T-62s. Many of the T54/55s are emplaced in hull-down static positions in the heavily fortified defensive zone between Damascus and the Golan Heights. Almost all of Syria's armored infantry fighting vehicles and armored personnel carriers are older Soviet BRDMs and BMP-1s. Syria also has significant numbers of field artillery pieces, including the 122-mm 2S-1 and 152-mm 2S-3.

The Syrian Air Force, established in 1948, has some 27,000 regular troops (compared to 100,000 regular troops and another 37,000 reservists before the civil war). Its 760-plus combat aircraft include Mikoyan-Gurevich MiG-21s, MiG-23s, MiG-25s, MiG-29s, and Sukhoi Su-24s. It also has some 70 attack helicopters, including Mil Mi-24s. The Air Defense Command, with about 26,000 personnel in late 2013 (compared to 65,000 pre–civil war) fields some 25 air defense brigades, each with six surface-to-air missile (SAM) batteries, as well as about 4,000 antiaircraft guns ranging from 23 mm to 100 mm. The air force inventory has undergone a marked reduction since 2011, with a number of aircraft lost or rendered inoperable due to insurgent attacks and accidents.

The Syrian Navy was established only in 1950. The relatively small force of 5,000 operates some 50–60 vessels, including two older Soviet diesel submarines and 21 missile attack craft. Syria had one of the most advanced unconventional weapons programs of all the Arab nations. Most intelligence assessments agree that Syria developed, stockpiled, and weaponized a significant amount of chemical agents, including the nerve agents GB (sarin) and VX and the blister agent HD (mustard). Syria's biological warfare agents include anthrax, cholera, and botulism. The country has a number of delivery options for its chemical weapons, including an arsenal of SAMs. In the autumn of 2013, however, the Syrian government agreed to disarm and destroy all of its chemical weapons, under international observation. This agreement, brokered by Russia and the United States, sought to avoid Western air strikes against Assad's regime in retaliation for its employment of chemical weapons during the civil war.

In its pursuit of missile technology, Syria has been aided by shipments of weapons and technological assistance from North Korea, which in the 1990s supplied variants of the Scud-C missile, with a range of 300 miles, and the Scud-D, with a range of 430 miles. Russia and Iran have also supplied Syria with military aid and technology, even after the civil war began in 2011.

Paul J. Springer and David T. Zabecki

Further Reading

Herzog, Chaim. *The Arab-Israeli Wars: War and Peace in the Middle East from the War of Independence through Lebanon.* Vintage Books, 1982.

Pollack, Kenneth M. *Arabs at War: Military Effectiveness, 1948–1991.* University of Nebraska Press, 2002.

Rabil, Robert G. *Embattled Neighbors: Syria, Israel, Lebanon.* Lynne Rienner Publishers, 2003.

Torr, James D. *Weapons of Mass Destruction: Opposing Viewpoints.* Greenhaven, 2005.

Syrian Democratic Council. See White Helmets

Syrian Democratic Forces

Syrian Democratic Forces (SDF) is an armed militia operating in Syria, following the merger of Kurdish and Arab groups seeking to challenge the Islamic State. Its political wing is the Syrian Democratic Council (SDC). Since its formation in 2015, the SDF has received support from and worked in close coordination with the United States to counter the spread of the Islamic State (IS) in Syria. The group was instrumental in capturing the remaining territory held by the Islamic State in March 2019. As of mid-2019, the SDF maintains territorial control across a major portion of northern Syria, encompassing approximately 25–30 percent of Syria.

The formation of the SDF was prompted by the seizure of large parts of Syria by IS in 2014. Although the Islamic State rapidly gained territory, IS militants were met with strong opposition from local Kurdish militias across Iraq and Syria. After IS surrounded the Kurdish town of Kobani along the Turkish border in northern Syria, the United States offered air support to an existing Syrian Kurdish militia, the People's Protection Units (YPG). Between October 2014 and February 2015, U.S. air strikes in coordination with Kurdish militias on the ground, as well as secular Arab rebels, successfully stopped the Islamic State's seizure of Kobani, although an estimated 11,000 Kurdish fighters were killed. The Kurdish YPG fighters and Arab fighters affiliated with the Free Syrian Army (FSA) united against IS extremists under the name Syrian Democratic Forces.

U.S. support for the Syrian Democratic Forces led to increased tensions between the United States and Turkey because many members and leaders of the YPG have longstanding ties to the Kurdistan Workers' Party (PKK), a Kurdish separatist group classified as a terrorist group by the United States and Turkey. The SDF commander, who goes by the name Mazlum Kobani, is a longtime member of the PKK, and the Turkish government views the presence of organized Kurdish fighters along its border as a serious security threat. U.S. support for the SDF is intended to defend against resurgent Islamic extremist groups, but the United States has wavered in its commitment to assist the group. In response to President Trump's announcement in December 2018 to withdraw U.S. troops from Syria, SDF leaders suggested the loss of U.S. support would hasten the release of nearly 700 fighters from over 40 countries captured and detained by the Syrian Democratic Forces. Considering the potential loss of external support, leaders opened talks with the Assad regime in 2018, seeking protection from Turkish attacks and an agreement to transform the group into an internal defense force with autonomy in northeastern Syria. The ability of the group to maintain de facto control of northern Syria is uncertain, due to reliance on U.S. support, the threat of attack from Turkey, and the Syrian government's desire to regain the territory held by the Syrian Democratic Forces.

Melia Pfannenstiel

Further Reading

Clarke, Colin P. *After the Caliphate*. Polity Press, 2019.

Hubbard, Ben, and Eric Schmitt. "U.S. Uncertainty in Syria Weighs on Kurdish Commander." *New York Times*, May 12, 2019: A7.

Stein, Aaron. "Partner Operations in Syria." Atlantic Council Rafik Hariri Center for the Middle East, July 2017. https://www.atlanticcouncil.org/images/publications/Partner_Operations_in_Syria_web_0710.pdf.

U.S. Library of Congress, Congressional Research Service. *Armed Conflict in Syria: Overview and U.S. Response*, by Carla E. Humud, Christopher M. Blanchard, and Mary Beth D. Nikitin, RL33487. March 25, 2019: 1–44.

Syrian Electronic Army (SEA)

The Syrian Electronic Army (SEA) was formed on March 15, 2011, by a group of hackers supporting Syrian president Bashar al-Assad.

Syria is the first Arab country with a public Internet army that has launched open cyberattacks on its enemies, through spamming, website defacement, malware, phishing, and distributed denial-of-service (DDoS) attacks. SEA has targeted government websites in the Middle East, Europe, and the United States. News organizations, Syrian opposition groups, and human rights groups have also been compromised. The attack style varies from serious political statements to pointed humor.

The foundation of SEA can be traced back to the Syrian Computer Society of the 1990s. Later, a Syrian malware team was discovered on January 1, 2011. The following month, Syria lifted a ban on Facebook and YouTube. Anti-regime protests soon emerged on Facebook. The Syrian Computer Society registered SEA's website on May 5, 2011, which signified the backing of the Syrian government. SEA initially claimed that it was not officially sanctioned but more like a group of patriotic hackers, but they removed all text that denied official sanction on May 27, 2011. By 2014, their activity showed links with Syrian, Iranian, Lebanese, and Hezbollah officials.

The SEA's activities concentrate on four styles of attack. Their primary goal comprised attacks against Syrian rebels, using surveillance to discover their identities and locations. This was later expanded to include foreign aid workers. Secondary intrusions were made against Western news websites that were hostile to the Syrian government. The group's third action consisted of spamming Facebook pages with pro-regime comments. The SEA's fourth concentration was on global cyber espionage, targeting technology and media companies, allied military procurement officers, U.S. defense contractors, and foreign attachés and embassies. The group's tools of attack included malware, phishing, and DDoS attacks. The SEA has used the Blackworm virus and spamming to achieve its goals.

Two members of the SEA were added to the FBI's "Cyber's Most Wanted" list on March 22, 2016: Ahmed al Agha and Firas Dardar ("The Shadow"). Both are believed to be in Syria, and there is a $100,000 reward for the capture of each. In 2018, both men were indicted *in absentia* in a U.S. Federal Court in Alexandria, Virginia, for actions taken in 2013 when they hacked into computers and threatened to damage, delete, or sell data unless paid a ransom. They compromised Twitter accounts of prominent U.S. media organizations and gained control of a U.S. Marine Corps recruiting website, urging Marines to refuse orders. The FBI reported that "While some of the activity sought to harm the economic and national security of the United States in the name of Syria, these detailed allegations reveal that the members also used extortion to try to line their pockets at the expense of law-abiding people all over the world." FBI agents and analysts continue to work with both domestic and international partners to curtail SEA operations.

The SEA was effectively countered to the point where many thought the organization dead by the end of 2016. However, toward the end of 2017, the SEA reemerged, though with more of a public relations type mission. Far from the clandestine nature of the SEA's early years, members today publicly acknowledge their affiliation, and act as a type of "cyber police" on various social media forums. Essentially, the SEA's new mission is to try to control the social media narrative within and about Syria. The events of the Arab Spring convinced the Assad regime of the importance of controlling the public narrative, but it remains to be seen how successful they will be in their quest to put a positive spin on the Syrian government.

Raymond D. Limbach and Robert M. Kerr

Further Reading

Abas, Anwar, and Abdulrahman al-Masri. "The New Face of the Syrian Electronic Army." OpenCanada.org, 2018. https://www.opencanada.org/features/new-face-syrian-electronic-army.

Kaplan, Fred. *Dark Territory: The Secret History of Cyber War* Simon & Schuster, 2016.

Libicki, Martin. *Cyberspace in Peace and War.* U.S. Naval Institute Press, 2016.

Weiner, Rachel. "Two Hackers Accused of Tricking Reporters Indicted." *Washington Post,* May 17, 2018. https://www.washingtonpost.com/local/public-safety/syrian-hackers-who-allegedly-tricked-reporters-indicted/2018/05/17/069ef328-59e7-11e8-858f-12becb4d6067_story.html?noredirect=on&utm_term=.6921056f1425.

T

Trump, Donald J.

Donald J. Trump is the 45th president of the United States. Born in New York City in 1943, he made a name for himself in American society as a businessman, real estate developer, and television personality before becoming president on the wave of a populist movement. With the campaign slogan "Make America Great Again," Trump appealed to American voters who were dissatisfied with the "politics as usual" mentality they felt had resulted in an entrenched political elite that was not looking out for their interests. A politically divisive figure, known to make daily use of the social media platform Twitter to bypass the media and communicate directly with his supporters, he developed a reputation for his no-holds-barred statements on everything from American popular culture to international relations. His supporters love him and his detractors vehemently dislike him, and because of his unorthodox approach to international relations, world leaders often do not know what to make of him.

While it may seem that President Trump's approach to politics is unprecedented in American history, the reality is that his is an approach deeply rooted in Jacksonian democracy. Named for President Andrew Jackson, Jacksonian democracy is based on the idea that the United States' government should represent the interests of "the common man." It decries elitism as being distinctly un-American, and it promotes self-sufficiency in terms of agricultural and industrial production. Jacksonian democracy had a dark side, however, in that in defining "the common man" it focused on the idea that the true American was white, Protestant, and owned land. Jackson is known for, among other things, the Indian Removal Act and enacting policies that rapidly expanded the plantation-based and slavery-dependent cotton industry in the South. Trump's political opponents have characterized many of his Jacksonian-like policies of being likewise discriminatory toward minority groups in the United States.

In terms of international relations, Trump's Jacksonian philosophy is reflected in his "America First" approach to interacting with the world. President Jackson was not overly concerned with the United States' foreign relations outside of trade. The most tension-filled moment of his presidency in the international arena came when he almost went to war with France over their decision to not pay a debt owed to the United States. Throughout Trump's election campaign he emphasized his desire to focus his foreign policy on making good, bilateral trade deals that would help the American economy and enact policies that were protectionist in nature (tariffs, import substitution, etc.), but expressed little taste for forging alliances or making any military commitments. This is perhaps why some of the critical international issues he inherited when he took office in 2016, such as Afghanistan, Iraq, and Syria, have been a thorn in his side throughout his presidency.

Trump is a defensive realist in terms of his approach to international involvement. Unlike President George W. Bush, who saw preemption and a policy to project American military power throughout the world in order to protect the homeland, Trump prefers a far more defensive posture, dealing with problems around the world only when, where, and if they happen and even then using only the amount of force necessary to deal with the issue directly. Syria, in particular, has presented Trump with a complex problem set for which he has taken a pragmatic approach—define specific problems that have direct implications for U.S. national security—the Islamic State and Syrian president Bashar al-Assad's stockpile of chemical weapons— and deal specifically with those issues. His official statements (see the Document section of this volume) focus very deliberately on how to defeat the Islamic State, and the prohibition on the use of chemical weapons. What they do not contain—which puts him in stark contrast to his predecessor President Barack Obama's statements on Syria—are ideological statements on the issues of democracy, free speech, and human rights.

Trump's approach to Syria is pragmatic but not hands-off. He continued and even expanded the U.S. mission in Syria that had begun under Obama, and allowed Secretary of Defense Ashton Carter to continue working with U.S. Army lieutenant general Sean MacFarland to prosecute the fight against the Islamic State, which ultimately led to dramatic defeats of the militants in Mosul, Iraq, and Raqqa, Syria, in 2017. Also, in April 2017, Trump authorized air strikes against a Syrian air base in response to al-Assad's chemical weapons attack in the town of Khan Shaykhun in Syria's northwestern Idlib Governorate. In 2018, President Trump announced that he would be withdrawing U.S. troops from Syria, but U.S. allies in the country, especially

the Kurds, have lobbied for an American presence to remain.

Robert M. Kerr

Further Reading

Brands, Hal. *American Grand Strategy in the Age of Trump.* Brookings Institution Press, 2018.

Johnston, David Cay. *The Making of Donald Trump.* Melville House, 2017.

Lim, Elvin T. *The Lovers' Quarrel: The Two Foundings and American Political Development.* Oxford University Press, 2014.

Turkey

Turkey is a Eurasian nation covering 300,948 square miles of territory. Strategically located both in Europe and Asia Minor, European Turkey borders Greece and Bulgaria to the east and north; in Asia Minor it shares common borders with Georgia to the northwest; Armenia and Iran to the east; and Syria and Iraq to the south. Turkey's 2016 population was estimated to be 79 million people.

The Turkish government is a representative parliamentary democracy with a president, elected by popular vote, as head of state. Executive power is invested in the prime minister, elected by parliament. In recent years, three political parties have vied for power. The largest of these by far is the Justice and Development Party, followed in order of magnitude by the Republican People's Party and the Nationalist Movement Party.

A secular republic with no official religion since the days of its great leader, Kemal Ataturk, Turkey is nonetheless 99 percent Muslim, with three-quarters of these Sunni. More than half of its Muslim population attends prayer services regularly. In recent years, the rise of religion, specifically Islam, in Turkish politics has been a matter of concern to many Turks as well as to the West. The Turkish Armed Forces number more than 1 million in five services branches. This makes it the second-largest military in the North Atlantic Treaty Organization (NATO) after only the U.S. Armed Forces. The country also has compulsory military service.

Turkey has been generally pro-Western in its foreign policy orientation and has enjoyed close ties with the United States since World War II. It has been a member of NATO since 1952; it joined the European Union (EU) in 2004.

Turkey was among the 34-member international coalition that helped to expel Iraqi forces from Kuwait in the 1991 Persian Gulf War, although it provided no ground troops to the effort. It dispatched two frigates to the Persian Gulf and was heavily involved in basing coalition forces on its military bases, including air assets.

The Turkish government also allowed overflights of its airspace when the air war began in January 1991. Despite its limited participation in the Gulf War, Turkey did benefit from the crisis. Having fought an insurgency against militant Kurds in southern Turkey that had killed thousands of Turks since the mid-1980s, the Turkish government was relieved by the outcome of the war in that Iraq continued as a unitary state and did not break into separate states to include an independent Kurdish nation laying claim to Turkish territory. At the same time, Turkey suffered economically, at least in the short term. By November 1990, rigid enforcement of the economic blockade against Iraq had cost Turkey an estimated $3 billion in revenues, chiefly from shutting down an oil pipeline through the country. This was later offset somewhat by U.S. loan and aid guarantees.

In the aftermath of the war, Turks came to resent the phobia expressed by many Americans and West Europeans toward its Muslim identity and what it perceived as a lack of support for Ankara's efforts to stamp out demands for autonomy by its Kurdish minority (20 percent of the country's overall population) in southern Turkey. This was evident in Operation Steel Curtain in March 1995, when Turkey sent 35,000 troops into the Kurdish zone of northern Iraq in an effort to trap several thousand guerrillas and halt cross-border raids by the Marxist Kurdistan Workers' Party (PKK). The PKK had been fighting for more than a decade in southeastern Turkey to establish a separate Kurdish state. More than 15,000 people had been killed since 1984, and Turkey mounted the military campaign in an effort to wipe out the movement.

In the immediate aftermath of the September 11, 2001, terrorist attacks on the United States, Turkey voiced support of the United States and the so-called War on Terror. It offered airspace and refueling rights as the U.S.-led coalition began operations against Afghanistan's Taliban regime in October 2001. Beginning in 2002, Turkey dispatched troops to the International Security Assistance Force (ISAF) in Afghanistan. The number of Turkish troops committed to Afghanistan rose steadily after that. In early 2009, Turkey took command of the ISAF for the second time. Many of the Turkish troops were responsible for security in and around Kabul (Turkey also leads the Kabul command). Turkish troops were also active in the Wardak Province, in east-central Afghanistan. Since Turkey increased its presence in Afghanistan, public opinion remained ambivalent about the nation's mission there. As of May 1, 2016, Turkey had 520 troops in Afghanistan, serving as part of Operation Resolute Support.

The United States had counted on active Turkish cooperation in the 2003 Iraq War that ousted Iraqi dictator Saddam Hussein from power, but the Turks balked at the last minute despite strong financial incentives, in part because public opinion was strongly opposed to the war and in part because of concerns of the possible breakup of Iraq and the creation of a Kurdish state. This decision by the Turkish government denied the United States a secure northern base of operations for the U.S. Army 4th Infantry Division and forced a recasting of the Anglo-American coalition's military plans, severely straining relations between the United States and Turkey.

In February 2008, Turkish military forces launched an incursion into northern Iraq, to again punish the PKK, which had been targeting Turks and Turkish forces in the southern part of the country. The brief punitive incursion, which lasted just eight days, had been preceded by Turkish air strikes against PKK targets beginning in December 2007. Both the Iraqi and U.S. governments voiced their displeasure with the incursion, terming it "counterproductive" to the stabilization of Iraq. The number of PKK fighters killed in the skirmish is subject to debate, but it is believed that as many as 550 died. Since February 2008, there have been numerous clashes between Turkish and Kurdish forces along the Iraqi-Turkish and Syrian-Turkish borders. Turkey continues to cast a watchful eye on Iraq and Syria and, because it is so strategically important geopolitically, much of the rest of the world continues to watch Turkey as well.

When the United States formed an international coalition to fight the Islamic State (IS) insurgency in Iraq and Syria in the summer of 2014, Turkey agreed to participate. However, its initial commitment was limited, and until the summer of 2015 it had refused to permit U.S. air assets to utilize its air bases in the south of Turkey. However, a rash of terror attacks in Turkey in June and July 2015 forced the Turks to substantially increase their efforts in the war against IS. At the same time, they also used the attacks as a pretense to hit Kurdish targets in nearby Syria, as the Turks blamed most of the terror attacks on "radical" Kurdish groups, including the PKK. This development, however, caused friction in Ankara's relations with Washington because the Americans had allied themselves with certain Kurdish organizations in the fight against IS. The Turkish government has remained extremely concerned that Kurds in Syria will demand their own autonomous region there, which might incite Kurds in Turkey to make a similar demand. Meanwhile, on November 24, 2015, a Turkish fighter jet shot down a Russian warplane, which Ankara claimed had violated its airspace during a bombing run into Syria. The incident caused Russian-Turkish relations to plummet and raised concerns that the internecine Syrian Civil War, and the complex coalition effort to bring it to an end, could result in a major confrontation between NATO and Russia.

On July 15, 2016, a small, disaffected faction of Turkish army officers (about 9,000) attempted to overthrow President Recep Tayyip Erdogan's government. The attempted coup failed within 24 hours of its start, however, after Erdogan rallied many Turks to his side. Within days, Erdogan launched a massive purge of the army and ordered the arrest of thousands of Turks suspected of having planned or supported the uprising. By the end of July, more than 130 media outlets throughout Turkey had also been closed down. Many observers feared Erdogan would use the attempted coup to strengthen his grip on power and to move his nation away from moderate secularism.

Some of Erdogan's critics even suggested that he had engineered the coup himself in order to purge his detractors and political enemies. Certainly the clumsily orchestrated coup attempt lent a certain amount of credence to these accusations. The abortive uprising precipitated a deterioration in U.S.-Turkish relations when Erdogan demanded that the American government extradite Turkish cleric and Erdogan detractor Fethullah Gulen to Turkey to stand trial for sedition. Erdogan's government claimed that the cleric had played a major role in fomenting the attempted putsch. Gulen had been living in the United States for many years after he fell out of favor with Erdogan. During and immediately after the attempted coup, the Turkish government closed the airspace around Incirlik Air Base, which was being used by U.S. air assets to conduct air strikes against insurgent targets in Syria and Iraq. The closure ended several days later.

Sedat Cem Karadeli, Keith A. Leitich,
Paul G. Pierpaoli Jr., and
Spencer C. Tucker

Further Reading

Carkoglu, Ali, and William Hale, eds. *The Politics of Modern Turkey*. Taylor and Francis, 2008.

Makovsky, Alan, and Sabri Sayari, eds. *Turkey's New World: Changing Dynamics in Turkish Foreign Policy*. Washington Institute for Near East Policy, 2000.

Robins, Philip. *Turkey and the Middle East*. Council on Foreign Relations Press, 1991.

Turkmani, Hassan al-

Syrian Army officer Hassan (Hasan) al-Turkmani, an ethnic Turkman, was born in Aleppo, Syria, in 1935. He joined the Syrian Army in 1954, and after graduating from the Syrian Military Academy at Homs, he served in the artillery. In the 1973 Yom Kippur War (Ramadan War) with Israel, al-Turkmani was the commander of a mechanized division. In 1978, he was promoted to major general, and in 1988 to lieutenant general.

On January 26, 2002, al-Turkmani became chief of staff of the Syrian Armed Forces. He set as the top national security goal the thorough modernization of the Syrian armed forces. Further, he believed that the Syrian military should be trained to remain at a high level of readiness to repel any Israeli attack.

In May 2004, al-Turkmani was appointed minister of defense. That October, a Ba'ath Party member, he became vice president of the Council of Ministers. Many saw his advancement as a move by President Bashar al-Assad to replace supporters of his late father, Hafez al-Assad, with younger loyalists.

On June 15, 2006, General al-Turkmani signed a defense agreement with Iran. It called for the elimination of weapons of mass destruction (WMD), a clear reference to WMDs held by the Israelis and American forces operating in the region. On June 17, 2006, al-Turkmani sealed an agreement with Iran to purchase Iranian missiles as a defense against both Israel and the United States. Al-Turkmani remained as defense minister until June 2009, at which time he was succeeded by General Ali Habib Mahmud.

Amid the ongoing Syrian Civil War, al-Assad named al-Turkmani assistant vice president on June 3, 2009, with the rank of minister. He was simultaneously appointed director of crisis operations, a post in which he played a key role in the suppression of Syrian rebels. In this post he was reportedly responsible for ordering the torture of detained rebels and their civilian supporters.

On July 18, 2012, al-Turkmani was killed in a bombing perpetrated by rebels in the northwestern section of Damascus. Also killed in the blast were the sitting Syrian defense minister and several other high-ranking government officials.

Andrew J. Waskey

Further Reading

Al-Turkmani, Imad Hasan. *Al-Sira' al-Ma'lumanti*. Al-Ula Li Al-Nashr Wa Al-tuzi, 2004.

Leverett, Flynt. *Inheriting Syria: Bashar's Trial by Fire*. Brookings Institution Press, 2005.

U

United States, Middle East Policy

Modern U.S. interest in the Middle East from a strategic perspective did not begin until the early 1940s, when the exigencies of World War II dictated that it pay increased attention to that region. Before that time, other than its involvement in the Barbary Wars in the late eighteenth and early nineteenth centuries, the U.S. government expressed little interest in the Middle East, maintaining only loose diplomatic and political relations with countries in the region. During this time, the United States largely deferred to the British and French, who controlled the area after World War I as per the Sykes-Picot Agreement of 1916. In the early twentieth century, U.S. petroleum companies had secured oil concessions in Iraq, Kuwait, Bahrain, and Saudi Arabia, but that was the extent of U.S. involvement until World War II. Worried about German and Italian efforts to seize oil fields and the strategic Suez Canal, Americans assisted and fought with the British in defeating German and Italian forces in North Africa during 1941–1942. From this point on, securing the Middle Eastern oil fields and maritime trade routes became a major foreign policy objective of the United States.

In early 1943, as the tide of the war began to turn in favor of the Allies and the Axis threat to the Middle East receded, the United States began to challenge European colonialism in the region. President Franklin D. Roosevelt and his successor, Harry S. Truman, supported in principle the independence of Arab states in the Middle East. In the United Kingdom, the government of Prime Minister Winston Churchill objected to the U.S. position, but by the end of war, bankrupt and war weary, the new Labour government of Clement Attlee was willing to release Britain's hold on much of the region—although it retained a considerable interest in Egypt and the Suez Canal. With the onset of the Cold War, the British government increasingly deferred to the United States on regional matters. For their part, the Americans sought to fill the power vacuum in the Middle East following the end of British and French rule and to challenge efforts by the Soviet Union (USSR) to project its power and influence in the region.

The U.S. government sought to deny Soviet efforts to gain control of the Persian Gulf's oil fields, acquire military bases and ports in the region, and sponsor or promote procommunist or Soviet-inclined regimes. The creation of the Jewish State of Israel in May 1948 greatly complicated the politics of the Middle East, and U.S. foreign policy, as it sparked the enduring Arab-Israeli conflict. It also put the United States in a delicate and arguably untenable position; Washington supported Israel but at the same time sought to maintain friendly relations with Arab states, whose support for the Palestinians conflicted with close U.S. ties with Israel.

Owing to the strategic location of Greece and Turkey relative to the Middle East and the Mediterranean Sea, both countries became a part of U.S. Middle East policy in 1947. Bankrupt and facing severe domestic troubles from the war, Britain announced that it was abandoning its military and financial support for Greece against communist insurgents and its efforts to protect Turkey against Soviet encroachments. This prompted the United States, in March 1947, to assume Britain's responsibilities in these nations. As a result, the U.S. Congress appropriated $400 million in aid and secured the pro-Western governments of both countries. Thus, the Truman Doctrine, which pledged U.S. assistance to any nation fighting communism, began in the Middle East.

After including Greece and Turkey in the North Atlantic Treaty Organization (NATO), the United States sought to create a similar collective security arrangement for the Middle East proper. Initially known as the Baghdad Pact and signed in 1955, after an Iraqi nationalist government seized power in July 1958, it was renamed the Central Treaty Organization (CENTO) and then included Iran, Turkey, and Pakistan. Because of the weak military positions of its members, however, both the Baghdad Pact and CENTO had serious limitations as deterrents to Soviet aggression. In addition, once Iraq withdrew from the Baghdad Pact in 1958, none of the remaining members were Arab states. Even Arab countries friendly to the United States, such as Saudi Arabia, refused to align with either organization, preferring to maintain their independence and avoid being seen as U.S. puppets and accused of serving American and, in the view of many Arabs, neocolonial and imperial interests.

Iran also figured prominently as an U.S. ally until the 1979 revolution there. In August 1953, U.S. and British intelligence agencies engineered a coup that deposed the nationalist prime minister of Iran, Mohammad Mosaddeq, after he nationalized the Anglo-American Oil Company. The bloodless coup restored to full power the pro-Western shah Mohammad Reza Pahlavi II. In the ensuing decades, the United States

equipped the shah's military with advanced weapons and trained his secret police, the Sazeman-e Ettelaat va Amniyat-e Keshvar (SAVAK, National Information and Security Organization), to consolidate and secure the shah's power and crush all political dissent. Indeed, by the early to mid-1970s, Iran was the bulwark of U.S. foreign policy in the Middle East. In 1979, an Islamic fundamentalist revolution deposed the shah and installed a theocratic government, which because of staunch U.S. support for the shah was rabidly anti-American. The United States and Iran remain bitter rivals to this day, and as recently as 2003 President George W. Bush labeled Iran a member of the so-called "Axis of Evil" along with North Korea and Saddam Hussein's Iraq. Preventing Iran from acquiring nuclear weapons became a high priority for both Bush and his Democratic successor, President Barack Obama, in part because these weapons might be used against Israel.

Successive U.S. administrations regarded Israel as an important ally against Soviet efforts to influence the region. This was particularly the case after 1953, when the Soviet Union under Nikita Khrushchev actively sought to challenge and undermine U.S. influence in the region by fostering closer ties and providing economic and military aid to Arab states such as Egypt, Syria, and Iraq.

The United States has enjoyed a close and strong relationship with Israel since 1948. Various reasons explain this special relationship, as it is sometimes called. Humanitarian factors—guilt over the Holocaust and the sympathy it created for both its victims and survivors—was a major reason behind U.S. support for the establishment of Israel. In addition, the fact that Americans regarded Jews arriving in Palestine as settlers or pioneers, much like the early English colonists to North America, almost certainly elicited a sense of communion. Culturally, despite obvious differences in faith—because many Jews were Westernized and thus viewed as less foreign or alien than Arabs—this fostered a sense of cultural affinity among many Americans. Also, the establishment of a democratic government in Israel created an instant political bond between both nations. Many Evangelical Christians supported the establishment of Israel and remain among its staunchest defenders. Finally, along with his Christian faith, electoral considerations certainly played a role in President Truman's decision to recognize Israel in 1948. Indeed, the powerful Jewish bloc of voters clearly contributed to his reelection that November. Since then, given their political success, pro-Israel interest groups—such as the American Israeli Public Affairs Committee (AIPAC) and the Christian Zionist Movement—continue to exert controversial but significant influence on both Congress and the White House. Due to Israel's strategic location and growing military might, Washington believed that the Jewish state would become the regional power and offer an effective way to check Soviet ambitions, not to mention being a rare example of pro-Western, democratic governance in the region. Over time, many Arab states either allied themselves, or at least fostered closer ties, with the Soviet Union to balance against U.S. support of Israel.

The United States' long-standing support for the state of Israel has not forged very close relations with many Arab countries. While U.S. ties to the region's non-Arab states such as Iran, and more recently Turkey, have been challenging, American ties to Saudi Arabia, though problematic, remain strong. The American relationship with Kuwait, Bahrain, and Qatar remains strong enough that the United States maintains semipermanent military bases in each of

these countries, and the United States provided massive amounts of military aid to Egypt throughout the late twentieth and early twenty-first centuries. Although the United States has provided economic assistance to Israel since its inception, until the late 1960s France was Israel's main patron and supplier of military aid. The United States remained decidedly neutral or aloof from the Arab-Israeli conflict until the late 1960s. After the June 1967 Six-Day War, however, U.S. president Lyndon B. Johnson fostered much closer ties with Israel, and the United States became its main supplier of military weapons, thereby establishing the precedent for subsequent U.S. military sales to the Jewish state, a policy that has continued to this day. Acting on the belief that by the late 1960s many Arab states, particularly Egypt and Syria, had decisively drifted into the Soviet orbit, Washington established much closer ties with Tel Aviv. The Soviets, meanwhile, severed diplomatic relations with Israel in 1967. In this context, Israel became a far more important ally to the Americans and was a key player in its foreign policy. During the October 1973 Yom Kippur War, the United States mounted a major airlift to resupply Israel's besieged military after it suffered heavy casualties in the opening days of the war following the surprise Egyptian-Syrian attack.

With respect to the Arab-Israeli conflict, the United States has generally been very supportive of Israel despite sometimes pressuring Israel to negotiate with its Arab neighbors or relinquish its control of occupied Arab lands. Such was the case during the 1956 Suez Crisis, when President Dwight D. Eisenhower ordered the Israelis to pull back from the Suez Canal. It was also evident in the late 1970s, when President Jimmy Carter sought to secure a peace treaty—the 1978 Camp David Accords—between Israel and

Egypt that brought Israel's withdrawal from the Sinai, which it had captured in 1967. Throughout the late twentieth century, U.S. aid to Israel was approximately $3 billion annually, and Washington continued its policy of equipping Israel with some of the most advanced weapons to assure its military superiority. It also implemented a free trade agreement in 1985 eliminating all tariffs between both countries.

At the same time, however, over Israeli objections, the United States has repeatedly sold military weapons to friendly Arab states, particularly Egypt and Saudi Arabia. Saudi Arabia figured prominently in U.S. foreign policy owing to its large oil reserves and generally pro-American leaders. As early as 1943, in fact, the United States provided military aid to the kingdom and constructed an air base at Dhahran. U.S. policymakers especially relished King Ibn Saud's anticommunism.

One area of noticeable friction between the United States and Israel, particularly during the late 1980s and 1990s, was the Israeli policy of constructing settlements in the occupied Arab territories of the Gaza Strip and the West Bank. In 1989, U.S. secretary of state James Baker went so far as to denounce Israel's expansionist policies, and President George H. W. Bush refused to grant loans to Israel if such funds were to be used to construct Israeli settlements in the occupied territories. This caused significant friction with Israeli prime minister Yitzhak Shamir.

Iraq's invasion of Kuwait on August 2, 1990, led the United States to organize a multinational coalition to compel Iraq's withdrawal and, following the failure of diplomacy, launch Operation Desert Storm, a sustained air and then ground offensive that routed and expelled the Iraqi military from Kuwait in late February 1991. The decision of the United States to repel Iraq's invasion of Kuwait was prompted by the fear that Iraq might invade Saudi Arabia and seize its northern oil fields located near the border with Kuwait. If Iraq were allowed to retain control of Kuwait's vast oil reserves, much less seize those of Saudi Arabia, Iraq would control a large share of the world's oil supply and thus potentially might engage in oil blackmail. Highly dependent upon Middle Eastern oil for its economy, the United States was unwilling to allow the free flow of oil to be threatened. Arab states were members of the coalition against Iraq, and for that reason the United States put heavy pressure on Israel not to attack Iraq in response to Iraqi Scud surface-to-surface missiles launched against Israel. Washington feared that if Israel entered the war, the Arab states would leave the coalition. The United States supplied Patriot missiles to Israel and was able, despite the missile attacks, to keep the Jewish state from intervening.

The September 11, 2001, terrorist attacks on the United States committed President Bush to waging the so-called War on Terror against the terrorist organization al-Qaeda and other terrorist groups and any country that harbors or supports them. The Americans launched an attack and invasion of Afghanistan in early October 2001 (Operation Enduring Freedom) to overthrow the Taliban government, which had offered sanctuary to the al-Qaeda terrorist network. By December, the Taliban had been routed, but the extent of al-Qaeda's losses remains unknown. A provisional government for Afghanistan was established that same month followed by democratic elections for president in 2004 and for the legislature in 2005. A recent escalation in Taliban attacks in Afghanistan has raised fears of a resurgent threat posed by the Taliban. In April 2014, there were over 30,000 U.S. troops in Afghanistan, along with 40,000 troops from

NATO member countries. These troops remained active in defending the country and government against Taliban and al-Qaeda forces.

In March 2003, the United States and Great Britain invaded Iraq—with a weak coalition of several other nations—and overthrew Saddam Hussein's government. President Bush justified the invasion by alleging Hussein's pursuit of weapons of mass destruction (WMDs) and ties to terrorism, including al-Qaeda. Following the end of the Persian Gulf War in 1991, per United Nations (UN) Resolution 687 (April 3, 1991), Hussein agreed to disable all of his WMDs. After Hussein's 12 years of defiance and violating 10 subsequent UN resolutions demanding Iraqi disarmament, Bush justified the invasion as the only way to enforce the will of the UN and assure that Iraq would never pose a threat to the region.

The U.S. government claimed that Iraq had failed to disarm and remained in possession of stockpiles of WMDs, including biological, chemical, and nuclear materials. In the aftermath of the war, however, no major stockpiles of WMDs were located. Nor have any direct links between Hussein and al-Qaeda ever been determined. This subsequently led critics of the Bush administration to suggest that the president at the very least deliberately exaggerated the threat posed by Iraq to convince Congress and the U.S. public to support the war. Defenders of the administration pointed out that before the war many of these same critics believed that Hussein had not disarmed and remained a threat. The Bush administration failed, however, to persuade the UN to authorize military action against Iraq and invaded Iraq on March 20, 2003. While most of the world denounced the invasion as illegal, the Bush administration defended its actions, claiming that UN Resolution 687 authorized any

state "to use all necessary means . . . to restore international peace and security in the area." What has become abundantly clear, however, is that U.S. intelligence gathering and the interpretation of that intelligence leading up to the war were deeply flawed.

As to the claim that Iraq had ties with al-Qaeda, in his 2003 State of the Union address Bush declared that "Saddam Hussein aids and protects terrorists, including members of Al Qaeda," and warned that he might even supply WMDs to al-Qaeda. Bush therefore sought to link the overthrow of Hussein with the War on Terror. No links between al-Qaeda and Hussein have yet been uncovered. In the absence of finding stockpiles of WMDs, Bush recast the reason for going to war from one of disarming Hussein to promoting democracy in Iraq. In a speech on September 11, 2006, he equated the War on Terror with the U.S. struggle against fascism during World War II.

Less than one month after the invasion of Iraq, Hussein's government fell. Although the war resulted in a seemingly quick and decisive victory with limited resistance from Iraq's military, the aftermath of the invasion proved far more problematic and bloody. U.S. forces faced much difficulty and were criticized for not aggressively restoring order in the wake of the collapse of Hussein's government. They were also blamed for allowing mass looting, including that of military depots, providing a significant source of ammunition and weapons for the subsequent insurgency. The disbanding of the Iraqi army immediately after the war was regarded as another critical mistake contributing to the disorder, if not anarchy, in the country.

By the summer of 2003, remnants of Hussein's military forces began attacking U.S. forces, leading to an insurgency characterized by guerrilla warfare and acts of terrorism including hundreds of car bombings. In response, a series of U.S. military operations was launched to suppress the insurgency, which also included radical Islamist militias in Iraq. Elections were held in January 2005 to select an assembly to draft a new constitution followed by elections in December of that year to seat a new parliament. Despite the establishment of a democratically elected government, and the withdrawal of the last U.S. forces in 2011—though 4,000 U.S. troops remained on two bases in Iraq—violence continued, often escalating into intersectarian conflict, mainly between Sunnis and Shias. From 2005 onward, relations between Iraq and Iran greatly improved; ironically, the U.S. military intervention ultimately dramatically enhanced Iranian influence over Iraq. Critics of the war in Iraq contended that it not only distracted the nation from the War on Terror but actually made the United States less safe because the war served as a rallying call for Islamic terrorism. Meanwhile, the United States also faced a challenge from Iran in a generally held belief that Iran is seeking to acquire nuclear weapons. Resolution to that crisis remains elusive.

The United States' relationship with Syria is long and complex. The U.S. government first sent a representative to Aleppo in the 1830s, and was quick to recognize Syrian independence by opening a consulate in Damascus in 1946 (two years before the creation of the state of Israel). Since 1946, however, U.S.-Syrian relations have been inconsistent, with the U.S. having orchestrated a failed coup attempt in 1957, diplomatic relations between the two countries being severed as a result of the Six-Day War in 1967, and the United States outright accusing Syria of state-sponsored terrorism in 1986. Interestingly, however, Syria lent its

support to the U.S.-led coalition in Operation Desert Storm, and Hafez al-Assad normalized relations between the two countries to participate in trilateral talks and agreements with the United States and Israel. By the early 2000s, there was even some speculation of a potential agreement between Israel and Syria under Bashar al-Assad regarding the controversial Golan Heights, but these hopes were never realized.

When Bashar al-Assad became president of Syria, he maintained his father's cautious engagement with the United States and Israel. Though the Syrian president had to walk a fine line between engagement with the West and maintaining good relations to its larger, more powerful patron, Iran. After the terrorist attacks on the United States in September 2001, Assad cooperated with the American administration in the Global War on Terror, even sharing intelligence on a limited basis. Assad was vehemently opposed to the U.S. invasion of Iraq in 2003, however, and relations between the two countries deteriorated rapidly since then and have never rebounded.

The events of the Arab Spring terrified Assad, and he saw it largely as an American plot to completely change the political makeup of the Middle East. It was this fear that led to his harsh reaction to any stirrings of revolution, even peaceful protest, in his own country. Syria quickly became one of the major holdouts to the sweeping change brought about by the Arab Spring, and Assad quickly styled himself as a champion of sovereignty and a great resister of imperial tyranny. It is this defiant attitude that led directly to the overall crisis in Syria, and that continues to fuel the escalation of the conflict into an increasingly global geopolitical crisis.

In August 2012, U.S. president Barack Obama, in response to an informal question posed by a reporter, said that if Bashar al-Assad were to use chemical or biological weapons against his own people, that would constitute a "red line" that might make him consider getting directly involved in the Syrian Civil War. He made this comment not long after imposing sanctions against the Assad regime for human rights violations committed in response to growing political protests throughout Syria. Soon thereafter, rumors about the Syrian military's use of chemical weapons began to circulate around the international community, and in August 2013 it was concluded that sarin nerve agent had definitely been used against civilians in Ghouta, a suburb of Damascus. In spite of President Obama's speculation about the "red line," however, the United States did not intervene directly in the conflict at that time. The U.S. military would be involved on the ground in Syria by 2014, but it would be the Islamic State and not chemical weapons that would be the catalyst.

When Secretary of Defense Ashton Carter took his position as head of the Pentagon in February 2015, he would find a Defense Department without a comprehensive plan on how to defeat the rapidly ascending Islamic State group. Given free rein to develop a plan under President Obama, Secretary Carter enlisted U.S. Army lieutenant general Sean MacFarland to head up the fight against IS. Together they developed a comprehensive plan to defeat IS in Iraq and Syria, and in 2014, as the Islamic State made significant military and territorial gains, President Obama authorized the use of American Special Operations Forces to begin training, assisting, and advising forces in Syria and Iraq to deal a decisive blow to IS. In both countries, the United States turned to its Kurdish allies (the Peshmerga in Iraqi Kurdistan) and the Kurdish-dominated Syrian Democratic Forces on the

Syrian side of the border. In a coordinated plan executed primarily by the Kurdish forces with U.S. assistance, the Islamic State's ability to wage war was significantly degraded, and the Americans' goal of dealing a devastating blow against IS was achieved. The United States did keep forces in Syria, however, in order to try to prevent the Islamic State from having a resurgence.

President Obama's successor, President Donald Trump, has also taken military action in Syria. He inherited the fight against IS from President Obama, and it was under President Trump that the most significant operation against IS fighters, Operation Wrath of Euphrates, took place in Raqqa, Syria, and Mosul, Iraq, simultaneously. President Trump did respond to Assad's continued use of chemical weapons as well. On April 4, 2017, Syrian troops launched a chemical attack against the town of Khan Shakhyun. Three days later, President Trump ordered a Tomahawk missile strike against the air base from which the Syrian Air Force launched the attack. This attack obviously did not dissuade Assad from launching more attacks, and on April 14, 2018, U.S. and British forces launched air and missile strikes against government sites in response to another chemical attack carried out by the regime, this time in the city of Douma.

The United States and the Middle East have had a long, complex relationship, and this is not likely to change anytime in the foreseeable future. Despite the conflicts in which the United States has been involved in the region, the reality is that the economic and political destinies of the United States and all countries in the Middle East are intimately related, and the relationship between the United States and almost all of the governments in the region remain strong. Bashar al-Assad has been a destabilizing force, however, and the United States will stay engaged in Syria at some level for however long it takes to bring about an acceptable level of security and stability.

Stefan Brooks

Further Reading

Abrams, Elliott. *Tested by Zion: The Bush Administration and the Israeli-Palestinian Conflict.* Cambridge University Press, 2013.

Bass, Warren. *Support Any Friend: Kennedy's Middle East and the Making of the U.S.-Israel Alliance.* Oxford University Press, 2003.

Buckley, Mary, et al. *The Bush Doctrine and the War on Terrorism: Global Reactions, Global Consequences.* Routledge, 2006.

Chamberlin, Paul Thomas. *The Global Offensive: The United States, the Palestine Liberation Organization, and the Making of the Post-Cold War Order.* Oxford University Press, 2012.

Citino, Matthew J. *From Arab Nationalism to OPEC: Eisenhower, King Saud, and the Making of U.S.-Saudi Relations.* 2nd ed. Indiana University Press, 2002.

Clark, Victoria. *Allies for Armageddon: The Rise of Christian Zionism.* Yale University Press, 2007.

Fisk, Robert. *The Great War for Civilization: The Conquest of the Middle East.* Knopf, 2005.

Freedman, Lawrence. *A Choice of Enemies: America Confronts the Middle East.* Public Affairs, 2008.

Gaddis, John Lewis. *Surprise, Security and the American Experience.* Harvard University Press, 2005.

Gardner, Lloyd C. *Three Kings: The Rise of an American Empire in the Middle East after World War II.* New Press, 2009.

Gerges, Fawaz A. *Obama and the Middle East: The End of America's Moment.* Palgrave Macmillan, 2012.

Hahn, Peter L. *Crisis and Crossfire: The United States and the Middle East since 1945.* Potomac Books, 2005.

Hurst, Steven. *The United States and Iraq since 1979: Hegemony, Oil, and War.* Edinburgh University Press, 2010.

Jacobs, Matthew F. *Imagining the Middle East: The Building of an American Foreign Policy, 1918–1967.* University of North Carolina Press, 2011.

Khalidi, Rashid. *Resurrecting Empire: Western Footprints and America's Perilous Path in the Middle East.* Beacon Press, 2004.

Khalidi, Rashid. *Sowing Crisis: The Cold War and American Dominance in the Middle East.* Beacon Press, 2009.

Kurtzer, Daniel C., Scott B. Lasensky, William B. Quandt, Steven L. Spiegel, and Shibley Z. Telhami. *The Peace Puzzle: America's Quest for Arab-Israeli Peace, 1989–2011.* Cornell University Press, 2013.

Lesch, David W., and Mark L. Haas, eds. *The Middle East and the United States: History, Politics, and Ideologies.* 5th ed. Westview, 2013.

Levey, Zach. *Israel and the Western Powers, 1952–1960.* University of North Carolina Press, 2011.

Little, Douglas. *American Orientalism: The United States and the Middle East.* 3rd ed. University of North Carolina Press, 2008.

Makdisi, Ussama. *Faith Misplaced: The Broken Promise of U.S.-Arab Relations: 1800–2001.* Public Affairs, 2010.

McAlister, Melani. *Epic Encounters: Culture, Media, and U.S. Interests in the Middle East since 1945.* University of California Press, 2001.

Palmer, Michael A. *Guardians of the Gulf: A History of America's Expanding Role in the Persian Gulf, 1883–1992.* Free Press, 1992.

Parsi, Trita. *Treacherous Alliance: The Secret Dealings of Israel, Iran, and the United States.* Yale University Press, 2007.

Quandt, William B. *Peace Process: American Diplomacy and the Arab-Israeli Peace Process since 1967.* 3rd ed. Brookings Institution Press and University of California Press, 2005.

Spector, Stephen. *Evangelicals and Israel: The Rise of American Christian Zionism.* Oxford University Press, 2008.

Spiegel, Stephen. *The Other Arab-Israeli Conflict: Making America's Middle East Policy, from Truman to Reagan.* University of Chicago Press, 1986.

Stein, Kenneth W. *Heroic Diplomacy: Kissinger, Sadat, Carter, Begin and the Quest for Arab- Israeli Peace.* Routledge, 1999.

Terry, Janice. *U.S. Foreign Policy in the Middle East: The Role of Lobbies and Special Interest Groups.* Pluto, 2005.

Tyler, Patrick. *A World of Trouble: The White House and the Middle East—From the Cold War to the War on Terror.* Farrar, Straus, and Giroux, 2008.

Yaqub, Salim. *Containing Arab Nationalism: The Eisenhower Doctrine and the Middle East.* University of North Carolina Press, 2006.

Weapons of Mass Destruction

Weapons of mass destruction (WMDs) are biological, chemical, and nuclear weapons capable of inflicting mass casualties. Use of these weapons is viewed as not only immoral but contrary to international law and the laws of war because WMDs have the ability to kill indiscriminately, meaning that their destructive nature is not limited to just combatants or military assets. During the Cold War, fears about nuclear weapons and their use was commonplace. Nevertheless, these weapons were under tight control, and neither side dared employ them for fear of the total destruction that a retaliatory strike would bring. With the end of the Cold War, however, nuclear proliferation has become a significant problem, and the likelihood of a rogue state or terrorist group attaining WMDs, including nuclear weapons, has increased substantially.

During the Iran-Iraq War (1980–1988), Iraq employed chemical weapons on Iranian troops, something that Iraqi dictator Saddam Hussein publicly admitted to in December 2006 during his trial for war crimes. It remains in dispute whether Iran employed them as well. The Iran-Iraq War was also the first conflict since World War I in which chemical weapons, apart from tear gas, had been employed. In 1988, as part of an operation to suppress a revolt by Iraqi Kurds, the Hussein government unleashed a chemical attack on the northern Iraqi town of Halabja, killing at least 5,000 people in the first recorded event of such weapons used against civilians. The terrorist bombings in Japan in

1994 and 1995, in which chemical weapons were released in a Tokyo neighborhood and subway, reminded the world of the destructive capability of WMDs.

Since the terror attacks of September 11, 2001, the fear of and danger posed by WMDs has increased significantly, owing to the desire of terrorist groups such as al-Qaeda and their affiliates to acquire and employ such weapons against the United States and other countries. The September 11 terrorist attacks on the United States and the 2004 Madrid bombings and 2005 London bombings clearly demonstrated the ability and willingness of al-Qaeda to engage in terrorism to inflict mass casualties, leaving no doubt about their willingness to use WMDs in future terrorist attacks. In March and April 2006 in Iraq, al-Qaeda is believed to have been responsible for a series of terrorist chemical attacks using chlorine gas that killed dozens and sickened hundreds.

Because of the instability and recurrence of war and conflict in the Middle East, the presence of WMDs has only heightened the arms race between Arab states and Israel and also among Arab states themselves. Egypt, Syria, Algeria, and Iran were believed to have significant stockpiles of biological and chemical weapons. In 2003, Libya, seeking to normalize relations with the United States and Europe and end its international isolation and reputation as a sponsor of terrorism, announced that it was abandoning its WMD programs. Some observers have suggested that President George W. Bush's decision to invade Iraq in 2003 and Libya's failure to end its isolation and convince the

United Nations (UN) to lift its sanctions prompted this change of behavior.

Egypt was the first country in the Middle East to develop chemical weapons, which may have been prompted, at least in part, by Israel's construction of a nuclear reactor in 1958. The size of Egypt's chemical weapons arsenal is thought to be perhaps as extensive as Iraq's prior to the 1991 Persian Gulf War, although the end of hostilities between Egypt and Israel since the 1978 Camp David Accords may have obviated the need for maintaining the same quantities of such weapons.

In 1993, as part of the Arab campaign against Israel's nuclear weapons program, Egypt and Syria (along with Iraq) refused to sign the Chemical Weapons Convention (CWC), which bans the acquisition, development, stockpiling, transfer, retention, and use of chemical weapons. These states also refused to sign the Biological Weapons Convention (BWC) of 1975, which prohibits the development, production, acquisition, transfer, retention, stockpiling, and use of biological and toxin weapons. Iraq later signed the BWC. The extent of Egypt's biological weapons program is unknown, but it clearly has the ability to develop such weapons if it already does not have weaponized stockpiles.

With respect to nuclear weapons, Israel is believed to possess as many as 100 nuclear warheads, although the Israeli government has never confirmed possessing such weapons. On December 12, 2006, Israeli prime minister Ehud Olmert admitted in an interview that Israel possessed nuclear weapons, only to be contradicted by a government spokesman the next day denying that Olmert had made such an admission. In the meantime, Israel has refused to sign the Nuclear Non-Proliferation Treaty (NPT) and has not allowed UN International Atomic Energy Agency (IAEA) inspectors to inspect its suspected nuclear sites.

Israel has repeatedly shown its willingness to use force to maintain its suspected nuclear monopoly and deny any Arab state the ability to acquire or develop nuclear weapons. In 1981, the Israeli Air Force destroyed an Iraqi nuclear reactor site under construction at Osirak, Iraq. Iran is currently enriching uranium for what it claims are peaceful purposes, but the United States and much of Western Europe have accused Iran of aspiring to build nuclear weapons. That state's refusal to cooperate with the IAEA led the UN in December 2006 and March 2007 to impose sanctions on Iran as punishment for its defiance. In late 2013, however, multilateral talks resulted in a preliminary framework within which Iran would work with the IAEA. Although the details of a final agreement had yet to be finalized by mid-2014, observers expect to see more Iranian transparency concerning its nuclear activities and regular inspections conducted by the IAEA. In return, the Iranians can expect to see the removal of economic sanctions.

In the fall of 2013, amid the ongoing Syrian Civil War, Syrian president Bashar al-Assad agreed to the complete destruction of his nation's chemical weapons arsenal. However, there is no evidence he actually took any steps toward eliminating his arsenal as he has launched multiple chemical weapons attacks against Syrians throughout his country's civil war (see entry for "Chemical Weapons and Warfare"). Syria has also long been suspected of trying to develop weaponized nuclear capabilities, with suspected nuclear sites being bombed by the Israeli Air Force in 2007. Subsequent inspections by the IAEA failed to reveal evidence of an organized program to develop nuclear weapons in Syria. The Syrian government is not the only concern regarding WMDs in that country's ongoing conflict. In 2016, the *New York Times* reported that ISIS had used chlorine agents and mustard gas at least 52 times in Syria and Iraq, but it is not known exactly where they obtained these weapons or if they produced them themselves.

Stefan Brooks

Further Reading

Hayes, Stephen F. *The Connection: How al Qaeda's Collaboration with Saddam Hussein Has Endangered America.* HarperCollins, 2004.

Hutchinson, Robert. *Weapons of Mass Destruction: The No-Nonsense Guide to Nuclear, Chemical and Biological Weapons Today.* George Weidenfeld & Nicholson, 2003.

"Iraq: Timeline of UNSCOM Related Events." http://www.mideastweb.org/iraqtimelineunscom.htm. Accessed October 27, 2006.

Langford, R. Everett. *Introduction to Weapons of Mass Destruction: Radiological, Chemical, and Biological.* Wiley-Interscience, 2004.

Meyer, Adrianne. *Greek Fire, Poison Arrows, and Scorpion Bombs: Biological and Chemical Warfare in the Ancient World.* Overlook-Duckworth, 2003.

Woodward, Bob. *Plan of Attack.* Simon & Schuster, 2004.

White Helmets

The White Helmets, pfficially known as the Syrian Civil Defense Force, is an organization made up of volunteers who operated in rebel-controlled areas of Syria during the civil war. It is one of the most controversial outgrowths of the Syrian Conflict, and its political motives and origin remain murky. Volunteers come from all walks of life and are primarily involved in medical triage and evacuation, urban search and rescue operations, evacuation of civilians from unsafe areas, and the delivery of essential services in the absence of governmental or nongovernmental organization involvement. White Helmet volunteers are officially unaligned in the conflict, and only operate in rebel-held areas. Putting themselves in harm's way, more than 200 volunteers have lost their lives; and they have been a thorn in the side of the Assad regime since their founding, since the regime feels the White Helmets secretly support anti-government forces, though there is no credible evidence to support this claim.

The White Helmets have a heavy Internet and social media presence, and they make a concerted effort to control the narrative regarding who they are and what they represent. Their website, syriacivildefense.org, is available in Arabic and English, and they use it to explain their history and their vision for the future, which is "We hope and pray for the cessation of bombing and fighting which target civilians and for peace and stability. We pledge that once fighting ends, we commit the Syria Civil Defence organisation to embark on the generational task of rebuilding Syria into a stable, prosperous and peace loving nation in which the social, economic and political aspirations of her people can be realized."

While the White Helmets claim to be completely neutral, it is clear from their webpage that they disagree with the Syrian government's tactics. Their official history begins with "When the peaceful revolution in Syria descended into a conflict, areas across the country became liberated from the control of the Syrian regime. The regime's response to this liberation was to attack these areas from the air, block aid and, in some instances, place them under siege." Statements such as this, and others, make it clear that the White Helmets' neutrality ends when it comes to Syrian armed forces and their supporters.

The White Helmets first organized in late 2012 in areas where rebels had taken over territory from the Syrian government. These areas faced an immediate crisis, losing government services as small groups of citizens banded together informally, initially in the areas of Idlib and Aleppo, to conduct search and rescue missions in their respective towns, villages, and neighborhoods after government forces' air and artillery strikes left them devastated. As the White Helmets gained visibility on the international stage, primarily through international media outlets such as CNN and al-Jazeera, they gained international support, primarily from non-governmental organizations in Turkey, the United Kingdom, and the Netherlands.

Perhaps most significant to the White Helmets' ability to organize throughout Syria and to grow from just a handful of volunteers in Idlib and Aleppo to more than 3,000 people country-wide by 2014, is a former British army officer named James Le Mesurier. Le Mesurier is a private military defense contractor often credited with founding the White Helmets, though the exact details of the organization's origins remain unclear. In a 2016 article, former United Nations weapons inspector Scott Ritter claimed that the origin of the White Helmets dated back to a March 2013 meeting between Le Mesurier and representatives of the Syrian National Council, a Syrian opposition coalition headquartered in Istanbul, Turkey, and members of the Qatari Red Crescent Society. Earlier that month the Syrian National Council had been awarded Syria's seat in the Arab League and was being treated as the de facto legitimate representative of Syria in the Arab intragovernmental organization based in Cairo, Egypt. At that meeting, the Arab

League voted to allow Arab nations to provide money, weapons, and support to the Syrian resistance and treated the Syrian National Council as the clearinghouse for this support. It is believed, according to Ritter, that Le Mesurier received as much as $300,000 to organize the White Helmets to provide services normally provided by the Syrian government in areas where the Syrian Arab Army had been defeated.

Regardless of the origins or claims of neutrality while actively condemning the Assad regime, the individuals who comprise the White Helmets are indeed average Syrians who repeatedly put themselves in harm's way throughout the conflict. In a May 2015 interview with CNN's Sanjay Gupta, Le Mesurier highlighted the main challenge that faced the people of Syria and the White Helmets' attempts to help them: barrel bombs and a tactic known as "double tapping." Barrel bombs are dropped by Syrian Arab Air Force helicopters equipped to carry two of these weapons, which are explosives filled with objects such as nails, jacks, spikes, and other pieces of shrapnel. They are designed to devastate large groups of people, and the wounds they inflict are horrific. Syrian government forces drop barrel bombs on targets and then hover until a group of people appears, in this case led primarily by White Helmets, to aid the injured survivors. Once the White Helmets arrive on the scene, along with large groups of their helpers, the pilots perform a "double tap" by dropping their second barrel bomb on the crowd. At the time of that 2015 CNN interview, 84 White Helmets had been killed and countless others injured as a result of this brutal tactic. It is difficult to know exactly how many additional White Helmets were killed after this time, but most estimates put the number at between 200 and 300, with most of them being the victims of a combination of barrel bombs and air strikes from the Russian Air Force. The year 2015 represented a watershed for the White Helmets in terms of international support as it is reported that at that time their operating budget was around $30 million.

While White Helmet volunteers conducted operations on the ground throughout Syria, their leadership worked tirelessly from their headquarters to lobby the international community to implement and enforce no-fly zones over the country to counter the Assad regime's use of barrel bombs. Their lobbying efforts, primarily through social media outlets, did have an impact on officials in President Obama's administration during his time in office and beyond—most notably, former U.S. ambassador to the United Nations Samantha Power. When Power was nominated for the position of UN ambassador, she was best known for a book she wrote as a professor at Harvard entitled *A Problem from Hell: America and the Age of Genocide* in which she argued that the United States has a responsibility to halt or prevent acts of mass violence around the world and to act as the guarantor of peace and stability for the world's peoples. This idea came to be known as "Responsibility to Protect," or more commonly by the shorthand tagline "R2P"; some even refer to it as the "Power Doctrine." As the White Helmets became better known through international news and social media, Ambassador Power became sympathetic to their mission and highlighted their actions as a rallying cry for the United States to support relief efforts based on the R2P approach—though her efforts had little direct impact on official U.S. policy in the form of direct action. It is notable that Power continued to be a strong supporter of the White Helmets even after her time at the UN as illustrated by a May 2018 tweet she made in response to the news that President

Trump's administration was officially freezing funding for the White Helmets, stating "This is beyond belief and must be fixed immediately. The White Helmets (@SyriaCivilDef) are volunteers who have heroically and selflessly saved tens of thousands of lives." In reality, however, the White House only cut direct funding to the White Helmets; it still allows for U.S. aid to go to the organization indirectly through other sources to include agencies contracted through USAID; and just one month after the freeze, President Trump released almost $7 million in aid to go directly to the organization. However, a July 2018 report by the Atlantic Council argued that the White Helmets were deeply impacted by the withdrawal of direct U.S. support, and that they were looking to other countries and organizations to make up for the shortfall in their operating budget. It should be noted that while the White Helmets are considered volunteers, the organization does make efforts to pay its workers a stipend of $150 per month to cover their costs.

The complex issue of the White Helmets is indicative of the overall complexity of the Syrian Conflict itself. It is a conflict in which local, national, and international interests intersect with ethnic, religious, and economic interests and present a multilayered and multifaceted scenario in which it is impossible to draw distinctions between two clear sides representing easily identifiable positions. The White Helmets, according to their own Internet and social media presence, is clearly against the regime of Bashar al-Assad, but aside from that, their position, origin, and strategic purpose becomes murky. It consists of an organizer who is a former British military officer who has been involved in various ventures as a private military contractor who has very close ties to the de facto Syrian opposition as represented by the Syrian National Council and has the ear of the Arab League. Its headquarters is in Istanbul, Turkey, and it has close ties to an international network of search and rescue organizations that provide training and equipment to the volunteer units throughout the country. It has garnered hundreds of millions of dollars in support from international non-governmental organizations as well as from governments of countries from around the world. It has, at various times, been considered by the U.S. government to represent both the best humanity has to offer and a shadow arm of international terrorist organizations such as al-Qaeda. It has captured the imaginations of people around the world through social media and even been the subject of an award-winning documentary produced in 2016 and viewed by millions. It is, for many, an enigma.

One thing is absolutely clear from social media and firsthand accounts, however, and that is that the White Helmets, the very individuals who don a piece of distinctive headgear and rush into harm's way without hesitating, are heroes to the people whose lives they have saved. Their narrative is, at the end of the day, the most important to the average Syrian, and whatever debates and intrigue surround the true nature of the organization's strategic purpose is irrelevant to those volunteers who are motivated to make their country safe and to try to protect their communities from harm.

Robert M. Kerr

Further Reading

ABC News. "Trump Administration Grants Release of $6.6 Million to Aid Syrian Group White Helmets," June 14, 2018. https://abcnews.go.com/Politics/trump-administration-grants-release-66-million-syrian-aid/story?id=55891552.

Hashemi, Nader. *The Syria Dilemma*. MIT Press, 2013.

Official Webpage of the White Helmets (Syrian Civil Defense Organization). https://syriacivildefense.org.

Ritter, Scott. "The 'White Helmets' and the Inherent Contradiction of America's Syria Policy," October 5, 2016. https://www.truthdig.com/articles/the-white-helmets-and-the-inherent-contradiction-of-americas-syria-policy.

Primary Documents

I. Executive Order 13582—Blocking Property of the Government of Syria and Prohibiting Certain Transactions with Respect to Syria (August 18, 2011)

U.S. president Barack Obama and his administration were very supportive of the Arab Spring protests throughout North Africa and the Middle East. He made many statements in support of the peaceful uprisings, and praised the bravery of those who were standing up for democracy and human rights during that historic moment. President Bashar al-Assad's violent reaction to peaceful protests, first in the southern Syrian city of Daraa and then throughout the rest of the country, stood in sharp contrast to the other countries where the Arab Spring had spread. President Obama reacted quickly to Assad's human rights violations, and enacted sanctions against his government. Executive Order 13582 provides a valuable glimpse at how governments enact their diplomatic and economic instruments of power to try to force other countries to change their policies and decisions.

By the authority vested in me as President by the Constitution and the laws of the United States of America, including the International Emergency Economic Powers Act (50 U.S.C. 1701 *et seq.*) (IEEPA), the National Emergencies Act (50 U.S.C. 1601 *et seq.*), and section 301 of title 3, United States Code,

I, BARACK OBAMA, President of the United States of America, in order to take additional steps with respect to the Government of Syria's continuing escalation of violence against the people of Syria and with respect to the national emergency declared in Executive Order 13338 of May 11, 2004, as modified in scope and relied upon for additional steps taken in Executive Order 13399 of April 25, 2006, Executive Order 13460 of February 13, 2008, Executive Order 13572 of April 29, 2011, and Executive Order 13573 of May 18, 2011, hereby order:

Section 1. (a) All property and interests in property that are in the United States, that hereafter come within the United States, or that are or hereafter come within the possession or control of any United States person, including any overseas branch, of the Government of Syria are blocked and may not be transferred, paid, exported, withdrawn, or otherwise dealt in.

(b) All property and interests in property that are in the United States, that hereafter come within the United States, or that are or hereafter come within the possession or control of any United States person, including any overseas branch, of the following persons are blocked and may not be transferred, paid, exported, withdrawn, or otherwise dealt in: any person determined by the Secretary of the Treasury, in consultation with the Secretary of State:

(i) to have materially assisted, sponsored, or provided financial, material, or technological support for, or goods or services in support of, any person whose property and interests in property are blocked pursuant to this order; or

(ii) to be owned or controlled by, or to have acted or purported to act for or on behalf of, directly or indirectly, any person whose property and interests in property are blocked pursuant to this order.

Sec. 2. The following are prohibited:
(a) new investment in Syria by a United States person, wherever located;

(b) the exportation, reexportation, sale, or supply, directly or indirectly, from the United States, or by a United States person, wherever located, of any services to Syria;

(c) the importation into the United States of petroleum or petroleum products of Syrian origin;

(d) any transaction or dealing by a United States person, wherever located, including purchasing, selling, transporting, swapping, brokering, approving, financing, facilitating, or guaranteeing, in or related to petroleum or petroleum products of Syrian origin; and

(e) any approval, financing, facilitation, or guarantee by a United States person, wherever located, of a transaction by a foreign person where the transaction by that foreign person would be prohibited by this section if

performed by a United States person or within the United States.

Sec. 3. I hereby determine that the making of donations of the type of articles specified in section 203(b)(2) of IEEPA (50 U.S.C. 1702(b)(2)) by, to, or for the benefit of any person whose property and interests in property are blocked pursuant to section 1 of this order would seriously impair my ability to deal with the national emergency declared in Executive Order 13338 and expanded in scope in Executive Order 13572, and I hereby prohibit such donations as provided by section 1 of this order.

Sec. 4. The prohibitions in section 1 of this order include but are not limited to:
(a) the making of any contribution or provision of funds, goods, or services by, to, or for the benefit of any person whose property and interests in property are blocked pursuant to this order; and

(b) the receipt of any contribution or provision of funds, goods, or services from any such person.

Sec. 5. The prohibitions in sections 1 and 2 of this order apply except to the extent provided by statutes, or in regulations, orders, directives, or licenses that may be issued pursuant to this order, and notwithstanding any contract entered into or any license or permit granted prior to the effective date of this order.

Sec. 6. (a) Any transaction by a United States person or within the United States that evades or avoids, has the purpose of evading or avoiding, causes a violation of, or attempts to violate any of the prohibitions set forth in this order is prohibited.

(b) Any conspiracy formed to violate any of the prohibitions set forth in this order is prohibited.

Sec. 7. Nothing in sections 1 or 2 of this order shall prohibit transactions for the conduct of the official business of the Federal Government by employees, grantees, or contractors thereof.

Sec. 8. For the purposes of this order:
(a) the term "person" means an individual or entity;

(b) the term "entity" means a partnership, association, trust, joint venture, corporation, group, subgroup, or other organization;

(c) the term "United States person" means any United States citizen, permanent resident alien, entity organized under the laws of the United States or any jurisdiction within the United States (including foreign branches), or any person in the United States; and

(d) the term "Government of Syria" means the Government of the Syrian Arab Republic, its agencies, instrumentalities, and controlled entities.

Sec. 9. For those persons whose property and interests in property are blocked pursuant to this order who might have a constitutional presence in the United States, I find that because of the ability to transfer funds or other assets instantaneously, prior notice to such persons of measures to be taken pursuant to this order would render those measures ineffectual. I therefore determine that for these measures to be effective in addressing the national emergency declared in Executive Order 13338 and expanded in scope in Executive Order 13572, there need be no prior notice of a listing or determination made pursuant to section 1 of this order.

Sec. 10. The Secretary of the Treasury, in consultation with the Secretary of State, is hereby authorized to take such actions, including the promulgation of rules and regulations, and to employ all powers granted to the President by IEEPA as may be necessary to carry out the purposes of this order. The Secretary of the Treasury may redelegate any of these functions to other officers and agencies of the United States Government consistent with applicable law. All agencies of the United States Government are hereby directed to take all appropriate measures within their authority to carry out the provisions of this order.

Sec. 11. This order is not intended to, and does not, create any right or benefit, substantive or procedural, enforceable at law or in equity by any party against the United States, its departments, agencies, or entities, its officers, employees, or agents, or any other person.

Sec. 12. This order is effective at 12:01 a.m. eastern daylight time on August 18, 2011.

Source: Blocking Property of the Government of Syria and Prohibiting Certain Transactions with Respect to Syria. August 17, 2011. 3 CFR 13582. https://www.govinfo.gov/content/pkg/DCPD -201100578/html/DCPD-201100578.htm

2. United Nations Security Council Resolution 2042 (April 14, 2012)

UNSC Resolution 2042 was unanimously adopted on April 14, 2012, and laid out a six-point proposal, the main goal of which was to persuade Bashar al-Assad to consider legitimate grievances with his government, cease all offensive military operations throughout Syria, ensure humanitarian assistance, release political prisoners, ensure freedom of movement for journalists, and allow peaceful protests. This resolution was obviously ignored by the Assad regime, but is significant in that it represents a moment when the entire UN Security

Council, including the often antagonistic permanent party members (the United States, Great Britain, France, Russia, and China), unanimously agreed on a plan to hold Assad accountable and allay the still young crisis. Within two years, the United States would actually be directly involved in the conflict, and Russia would follow suit in 2015. By 2018, the British and the French would also be involved in operations in and over Syria, leaving China the only permanent member of the UNSC without troops actively engaged in the Syrian Conflict.

Adopted by the Security Council at Its 6751st Meeting, on 14 April 2012

The Security Council,

Recalling its Presidential Statements of 3 August 2011, 21 March 2012 and 5 April 2012, and also *recalling* all relevant resolutions of the General Assembly,

Reaffirming its support to the Joint Special Envoy for the United Nations and the League of Arab States, Kofi Annan, and his work, following General Assembly resolution A/RES/66/253 of 16 February 2012 and relevant resolutions of the League of Arab States,

Reaffirming its strong commitment to the sovereignty, independence, unity and territorial integrity of Syria, and to the purposes and principles of the Charter,

Condemning the widespread violations of human rights by the Syrian authorities, as well as any human rights abuses by armed groups, *recalling* that those responsible shall be held accountable, and *expressing* its profound regret at the death of many thousands of people in Syria,

Noting the Syrian government's commitment on 25 March 2012 to implement the six-point proposal of the Joint Special Envoy of the United Nations and the League of

Arab States, and to implement urgently and visibly its commitments, as it agreed to do in its communication to the Envoy of 1 April 2012, to (a) cease troop movements towards population centres, (b) cease all use of heavy weapons in such centres, and (c) begin pullback of military concentrations in and around population centres, and to implement these in their entirety by no later than 10 April 2012, and *noting also* the Syrian opposition's expressed commitment to respect the cessation of violence, provided the government does so,

Noting the Envoy's assessment that, as of 12 April 2012, the parties appeared to be observing a cessation of fire and that the Syrian government had started to implement its commitments, and *supporting* the Envoy's call for an immediate and visible implementation by the Syrian government of all elements of the Envoy's six-point proposal in their entirety to achieve a sustained cessation of armed violence in all its forms by all parties,

1. *Reaffirms* its full support for and *calls for* the urgent, comprehensive, and immediate implementation of all elements of the Envoy's six-point proposal (annex) aimed at bringing an immediate end to all violence and human rights violations, securing humanitarian access and facilitating a Syrian-led political transition leading to a democratic, plural political system, in which citizens are equal regardless of their affiliations, ethnicities or beliefs, including through commencing a comprehensive political dialogue between the Syrian government and the whole spectrum of the Syrian opposition;

2. *Calls upon* the Syrian government to implement visibly its commitments in their entirety, as it agreed to do in its communication to the Envoy of 1 April 2012, to (a) cease troop movements towards population centres,

(b) cease all use of heavy weapons in such centres, and (c) begin pullback of military concentrations in and around population centres;

3. *Underlines* the importance attached by the Envoy to the withdrawal of all Syrian government troops and heavy weapons from population centres to their barracks to facilitate a sustained cessation of violence;

4. *Calls upon* all parties in Syria, including the opposition, immediately to cease all armed violence in all its forms;

5. *Expresses its intention*, subject to a sustained cessation of armed violence in all its forms by all parties, to establish immediately, after consultations between the Secretary-General and the Syrian government, a United Nations supervision mission in Syria to monitor a cessation of armed violence in all its forms by all parties and relevant aspects of the Envoy's six-point proposal, on the basis of a formal proposal from the Secretary-General, which the Security Council requests to receive not later than 18 April 2012;

6. *Calls upon* the Syrian government to ensure the effective operation of the mission, including its advance team, by: facilitating the expeditious and unhindered deployment of its personnel and capabilities as required to fulfil its mandate; ensuring its full, unimpeded, and immediate freedom of movement and access as necessary to fulfil its mandate; allowing its unobstructed communications; and allowing it to freely and privately communicate with individuals throughout Syria without retaliation against any person as a result of interaction with the mission;

7. *Decides* to authorize an advance team of up to 30 unarmed military observers to liaise with the parties and to begin to report on the implementation of a full cessation of armed violence in all its forms by all parties,

pending the deployment of the mission referred to in paragraph 5 and *calls upon* the Syrian government and all other parties to ensure that the advance team is able to carry out its functions according to the terms set forth in paragraph 6;

8. *Calls upon* the parties to guarantee the safety of the advance team without prejudice to its freedom of movement and access, and *stresses* that the primary responsibility in this regard lies with the Syrian authorities;

9. *Requests* the Secretary-General to report immediately to the Security Council any obstructions to the effective operation of the team by any party;

10. *Reiterates* its call for the Syrian authorities to allow immediate, full and unimpeded access of humanitarian personnel to all populations in need of assistance, in accordance with international law and guiding principles of humanitarian assistance and calls upon all parties in Syria, in particular the Syrian authorities, to cooperate fully with the United Nations and relevant humanitarian organizations to facilitate the provision of humanitarian assistance;

11. *Requests* the Secretary-General to report to the Council on the implementation of this resolution by 19 April 2012;

12. *Expresses its intention* to assess the implementation of this resolution and to consider further steps as appropriate;

13. *Decides* to remain seized of the matter.

Annex

Six-Point Proposal of the Joint Special Envoy of the United Nations and the League of Arab States

(1) commit to work with the Envoy in an inclusive Syrian-led political process to address the legitimate aspirations and concerns of the Syrian people, and, to this end,

commit to appoint an empowered interlocutor when invited to do so by the Envoy;

(2) commit to stop the fighting and achieve urgently an effective United Nations supervised cessation of armed violence in all its forms by all parties to protect civilians and stabilize the country;

To this end, the Syrian government should immediately cease troop movements towards, and end the use of heavy weapons in, population centres, and begin pullback of military concentrations in and around population centres;

As these actions are being taken on the ground, the Syrian government should work with the Envoy to bring about a sustained cessation of armed violence in all its forms by all parties with an effective United Nations supervision mechanism.

Similar commitments would be sought by the Envoy from the opposition and all relevant elements to stop the fighting and work with him to bring about a sustained cessation of armed violence in all its forms by all parties with an effective United Nations supervision mechanism;

(3) ensure timely provision of humanitarian assistance to all areas affected by the fighting, and to this end, as immediate steps, to accept and implement a daily two hour humanitarian pause and to coordinate exact time and modalities of the daily pause through an efficient mechanism, including at local level;

(4) intensify the pace and scale of release of arbitrarily detained persons, including especially vulnerable categories of persons, and persons involved in peaceful political activities, provide without delay through appropriate channels a list of all places in which such persons are being detained, immediately begin organizing access to such

locations and through appropriate channels respond promptly to all written requests for information, access or release regarding such persons;

(5) ensure freedom of movement throughout the country for journalists and a non-discriminatory visa policy for them;

(6) respect freedom of association and the right to demonstrate peacefully as legally guaranteed.

Source: United Nations. "The Situation in the Middle East." Security Council Resolution S/RES/2042, April 14, 2012. http://unscr.com/en/resolutions/2042

---

3. President Barack H. Obama: Remarks by the President in Address to the Nation on Syria (September 10, 2013)

As pro-democracy protests erupted in the wake of the Arab Spring in the Syrian City of Daraa in 2011, the United States imposed sanctions on the Assad regime in response to their heavy-handed response. These sanctions did not deter Assad, however, and tensions between the United States and Syria grew steadily through the summer of 2012 when the United States. pulled its diplomats from Damascus. Fearing this was a precursor to an American ground invasion, President Assad threatened to use chemical weapons if any foreign troops entered his territory. In early August 2012, President Obama famously answered a reporter's question about Assad's threat by stating that he would consider any use of chemical weapons a "red line" that if crossed, would likely spur the United States into military action. These words would haunt President Obama for the rest of his presidency as later that same month Assad's forces made good on his threat and used chemical weapons against innocent civilians in a rebel-held area just outside of Damascus. On September 10, just two and a half weeks after the attack, President Obama addressed the people of the United States in a speech from the White House.

THE PRESIDENT: My fellow Americans, tonight I want to talk to you about Syria— why it matters, and where we go from here.

Over the past two years, what began as a series of peaceful protests against the repressive regime of Bashar al-Assad has turned into a brutal civil war. Over 100,000 people have been killed. Millions have fled the country. In that time, America has worked with allies to provide humanitarian support, to help the moderate opposition, and to shape a political settlement. But I have resisted calls for military action, because we cannot resolve someone else's civil war through force, particularly after a decade of war in Iraq and Afghanistan.

The situation profoundly changed, though, on August 21st, when Assad's government gassed to death over a thousand people, including hundreds of children. The images from this massacre are sickening: Men, women, children lying in rows, killed by poison gas. Others foaming at the mouth, gasping for breath. A father clutching his dead children, imploring them to get up and walk. On that terrible night, the world saw in gruesome detail the terrible nature of chemical weapons, and why the overwhelming majority of humanity has declared them off-limits—a crime against humanity, and a violation of the laws of war.

This was not always the case. In World War I, American GIs were among the many thousands killed by deadly gas in the trenches of Europe. In World War II, the Nazis used gas to inflict the horror of the Holocaust. Because these weapons can kill on a mass scale, with no distinction between soldier and infant, the civilized world has spent a century working to ban them. And in 1997, the United States Senate overwhelmingly approved an international agreement prohibiting the use of chemical weapons, now joined by 189 governments that represent 98 percent of humanity.

On August 21st, these basic rules were violated, along with our sense of common humanity. No one disputes that chemical weapons were used in Syria. The world saw thousands of videos, cell phone pictures, and social media accounts from the attack, and humanitarian organizations told stories of hospitals packed with people who had symptoms of poison gas.

Moreover, we know the Assad regime was responsible. In the days leading up to August 21st, we know that Assad's chemical weapons personnel prepared for an attack near an area where they mix sarin gas. They distributed gasmasks to their troops. Then they fired rockets from a regime-controlled area into 11 neighborhoods that the regime has been trying to wipe clear of opposition forces. Shortly after those rockets landed, the gas spread, and hospitals filled with the dying and the wounded. We know senior figures in Assad's military machine reviewed the results of the attack, and the regime increased their shelling of the same neighborhoods in the days that followed. We've also studied samples of blood and hair from people at the site that tested positive for sarin.

When dictators commit atrocities, they depend upon the world to look the other way until those horrifying pictures fade from memory. But these things happened. The facts cannot be denied. The question now is what the United States of America, and the international community, is prepared to do about it. Because what happened to those people—to those children—is not only a violation of international law, it's also a danger to our security.

Let me explain why. If we fail to act, the Assad regime will see no reason to stop using chemical weapons. As the ban against these weapons erodes, other tyrants will have no reason to think twice about acquiring poison gas, and using them. Over time, our troops would again face the prospect of chemical warfare on the battlefield. And it could be easier for terrorist organizations to obtain these weapons, and to use them to attack civilians.

If fighting spills beyond Syria's borders, these weapons could threaten allies like Turkey, Jordan, and Israel. And a failure to stand against the use of chemical weapons would weaken prohibitions against other weapons of mass destruction, and embolden Assad's ally, Iran—which must decide whether to ignore international law by building a nuclear weapon, or to take a more peaceful path.

This is not a world we should accept. This is what's at stake. And that is why, after careful deliberation, I determined that it is in the national security interests of the United States to respond to the Assad regime's use of chemical weapons through a targeted military strike. The purpose of this strike would be to deter Assad from using chemical weapons, to degrade his regime's ability to use them, and to make clear to the world that we will not tolerate their use.

That's my judgment as Commander-in-Chief. But I'm also the President of the world's oldest constitutional democracy. So

even though I possess the authority to order military strikes, I believed it was right, in the absence of a direct or imminent threat to our security, to take this debate to Congress. I believe our democracy is stronger when the President acts with the support of Congress. And I believe that America acts more effectively abroad when we stand together.

This is especially true after a decade that put more and more war-making power in the hands of the President, and more and more burdens on the shoulders of our troops, while sidelining the people's representatives from the critical decisions about when we use force.

Now, I know that after the terrible toll of Iraq and Afghanistan, the idea of any military action, no matter how limited, is not going to be popular. After all, I've spent four and a half years working to end wars, not to start them. Our troops are out of Iraq. Our troops are coming home from Afghanistan. And I know Americans want all of us in Washington

—especially me—to concentrate on the task of building our nation here at home: putting people back to work, educating our kids, growing our middle class.

It's no wonder, then, that you're asking hard questions. So let me answer some of the most important questions that I've heard from members of Congress, and that I've read in letters that you've sent to me.

First, many of you have asked, won't this put us on a slippery slope to another war? One man wrote to me that we are "still recovering from our involvement in Iraq." A veteran put it more bluntly: "This nation is sick and tired of war."

My answer is simple: I will not put American boots on the ground in Syria. I will not pursue an open-ended action like Iraq or Afghanistan. I will not pursue a prolonged air campaign like Libya or Kosovo. This would be a targeted strike to achieve a clear objective: deterring the use of chemical weapons, and degrading Assad's capabilities.

Others have asked whether it's worth acting if we don't take out Assad. As some members of Congress have said, there's no point in simply doing a "pinprick" strike in Syria.

Let me make something clear: The United States military doesn't do pinpricks. Even a limited strike will send a message to Assad that no other nation can deliver. I don't think we should remove another dictator with force—we learned from Iraq that doing so makes us responsible for all that comes next. But a targeted strike can make Assad, or any other dictator, think twice before using chemical weapons.

Other questions involve the dangers of retaliation. We don't dismiss any threats, but the Assad regime does not have the ability to seriously threaten our military. Any other retaliation they might seek is in line with threats that we face every day. Neither Assad nor his allies have any interest in escalation that would lead to his demise. And our ally, Israel, can defend itself with overwhelming force, as well as the unshakeable support of the United States of America.

Many of you have asked a broader question: Why should we get involved at all in a place that's so complicated, and where—as one person wrote to me—"those who come after Assad may be enemies of human rights"?

It's true that some of Assad's opponents are extremists. But al Qaeda will only draw strength in a more chaotic Syria if people there see the world doing nothing to prevent innocent civilians from being gassed to death. The majority of the Syrian people—and the Syrian opposition we work with—just want

to live in peace, with dignity and freedom. And the day after any military action, we would redouble our efforts to achieve a political solution that strengthens those who reject the forces of tyranny and extremism.

Finally, many of you have asked: Why not leave this to other countries, or seek solutions short of force? As several people wrote to me, "We should not be the world's policeman."

I agree, and I have a deeply held preference for peaceful solutions. Over the last two years, my administration has tried diplomacy and sanctions, warning and negotiations—but chemical weapons were still used by the Assad regime.

However, over the last few days, we've seen some encouraging signs. In part because of the credible threat of U.S. military action, as well as constructive talks that I had with President Putin, the Russian government has indicated a willingness to join with the international community in pushing Assad to give up his chemical weapons. The Assad regime has now admitted that it has these weapons, and even said they'd join the Chemical Weapons Convention, which prohibits their use.

It's too early to tell whether this offer will succeed, and any agreement must verify that the Assad regime keeps its commitments. But this initiative has the potential to remove the threat of chemical weapons without the use of force, particularly because Russia is one of Assad's strongest allies.

I have, therefore, asked the leaders of Congress to postpone a vote to authorize the use of force while we pursue this diplomatic path. I'm sending Secretary of State John Kerry to meet his Russian counterpart on Thursday, and I will continue my own discussions with President Putin. I've spoken to the leaders of two of our closest allies, France and the United Kingdom, and we will work together in consultation with Russia and China to put forward a resolution at the U.N. Security Council requiring Assad to give up his chemical weapons, and to ultimately destroy them under international control. We'll also give U.N. inspectors the opportunity to report their findings about what happened on August 21st. And we will continue to rally support from allies from Europe to the Americas—from Asia to the Middle East—who agree on the need for action.

Meanwhile, I've ordered our military to maintain their current posture to keep the pressure on Assad, and to be in a position to respond if diplomacy fails. And tonight, I give thanks again to our military and their families for their incredible strength and sacrifices.

My fellow Americans, for nearly seven decades, the United States has been the anchor of global security. This has meant doing more than forging international agreements—it has meant enforcing them. The burdens of leadership are often heavy, but the world is a better place because we have borne them.

And so, to my friends on the right, I ask you to reconcile your commitment to America's military might with a failure to act when a cause is so plainly just. To my friends on the left, I ask you to reconcile your belief in freedom and dignity for all people with those images of children writhing in pain, and going still on a cold hospital floor. For sometimes resolutions and statements of condemnation are simply not enough.

Indeed, I'd ask every member of Congress, and those of you watching at home tonight, to view those videos of the attack, and then ask: What kind of world will we live in if the United States of America sees a dictator brazenly violate international law with poison gas, and we choose to look the other way?

Franklin Roosevelt once said, "Our national determination to keep free of foreign wars and foreign entanglements cannot prevent us from feeling deep concern when ideals and principles that we have cherished are challenged." Our ideals and principles, as well as our national security, are at stake in Syria, along with our leadership of a world where we seek to ensure that the worst weapons will never be used.

America is not the world's policeman. Terrible things happen across the globe, and it is beyond our means to right every wrong. But when, with modest effort and risk, we can stop children from being gassed to death, and thereby make our own children safer over the long run, I believe we should act. That's what makes America different. That's what makes us exceptional. With humility, but with resolve, let us never lose sight of that essential truth.

Thank you. God bless you. And God bless the United States of America.

Source: Obama, Barack. Remarks by the President in Address to the Nation on Syria. September 10, 2013. Compilation of Presidential Documents, Office of the Federal Register. https://www.govinfo.gov/content/pkg/DCPD-201300615/html/DCPD-201300615.htm

4. United Nations Security Council Resolution 2118 (September 27, 2013)

The first three UNSC resolutions on the Syrian Conflict (two in April 2012 and one in July) all dealt with the UN Observer force, commanded at its inception by Norwegian major general Robert Mood to monitor the actions of the Syrian Arab Army's actions regarding political protests around the country. Major General Mood suspended the observer mission in June 2012, stating that conditions in Syria had grown too dangerous for them. The observer mission actually continues in Syria, but it's extremely limited in scope. The violence in Syria escalated quickly throughout 2012 and 2013, and in August of that year Bashar al-Assad launched the now infamous chemical weapons attack in Ghouta, a suburb of Damascus. UNSC Resolution 2118 regarding Assad's use of chemical weapons was adopted about a month after the attack on Ghouta.

The Security Council,

Recalling the Statements of its President of 3 August 2011, 21 March 2012, 5 April 2012, and its resolutions 1540 (2004), 2042 (2012) and 2043 (2012),

Reaffirming its strong commitment to the sovereignty, independence and territorial integrity of the Syrian Arab Republic,

Reaffirming that the proliferation of chemical weapons, as well as their means of delivery, constitutes a threat to international peace and security,

Recalling that the Syrian Arab Republic on 22 November 1968 acceded to the Protocol for the Prohibition of the Use in War of Asphyxiating, Poisonous or Other Gases and of Bacteriological Methods of Warfare, signed at Geneva on 17 June 1925,

Noting that on 14 September 2013, the Syrian Arab Republic deposited with the Secretary-General its instrument of accession to the Convention on the Prohibition of

the Development, Production, Stockpiling and Use of Chemical Weapons and on their Destruction (Convention) and declared that it shall comply with its stipulations and observe them faithfully and sincerely, applying the Convention provisionally pending its entry into force for the Syrian Arab Republic,

Welcoming the establishment by the Secretary-General of the United Nations Mission to Investigate Allegations of the Use of Chemical Weapons in the Syrian Arab Republic (the Mission) pursuant to General Assembly resolution 42/37 C (1987) of 30 November 1987, and reaffirmed by resolution 620 (1988) of 26 August 1988, and *expressing* appreciation for the work of the Mission,

Acknowledging the report of 16 September 2013 (S/2013/553) by the Mission, *underscoring* the need for the Mission to fulfil its mandate, and *emphasizing* that future credible allegations of chemical weapons use in the Syrian Arab Republic should be investigated,

Deeply outraged by the use of chemical weapons on 21 August 2013 in Rif Damascus, as concluded in the Mission's report, *condemning* the killing of civilians that resulted from it, *affirming* that the use of chemical weapons constitutes a serious violation of international law, and *stressing* that those responsible for any use of chemical weapons must be held accountable,

Recalling the obligation under resolution 1540 (2004) that all States shall refrain from providing any form of support to non-State actors that attempt to develop, acquire, manufacture, possess, transport, transfer or use weapons of mass destruction, including chemical weapons, and their means of delivery,

Welcoming the Framework for Elimination of Syrian Chemical Weapons dated

14 September 2013, in Geneva, between the Russian Federation and the United States of America (S/2013/565), with a view to ensuring the destruction of the Syrian Arab Republic's chemical weapons program in the soonest and safest manner, and *expressing* its commitment to the immediate international control over chemical weapons and their components in the Syrian Arab Republic,

Welcoming the decision of the Executive Council of the Organization for the Prohibition of Chemical Weapons (OPCW) of 27 September 2013 establishing special procedures for the expeditious destruction of the Syrian Arab Republic's chemical weapons program and stringent verification thereof, and *expressing* its determination to ensure the destruction of the Syrian Arab Republic's chemical weapons program according to the timetable contained in the OPCW Executive Council decision of 27 September 2013,

Stressing that the only solution to the current crisis in the Syrian Arab Republic is through an inclusive and Syrian-led political process based on the Geneva Communiqué of 30 June 2012, and *emphasising* the need to convene the international conference on Syria as soon as possible,

Determining that the use of chemical weapons in the Syrian Arab Republic constitutes a threat to international peace and security,

Underscoring that Member States are obligated under Article 25 of the Charter of the United Nations to accept and carry out the Council's decisions,

1. *Determines* that the use of chemical weapons anywhere constitutes a threat to international peace and security;
2. *Condemns* in the strongest terms any use of chemical weapons in the Syrian Arab Republic, in particular the attack

on 21 August 2013, in violation of international law;

3. *Endorses* the decision of the OPCW Executive Council 27 September 2013, which contains special procedures for the expeditious destruction of the Syrian Arab Republic's chemical weapons program and stringent verification thereof and calls for its full implementation in the most expedient and safest manner;

4. *Decides* that the Syrian Arab Republic shall not use, develop, produce, otherwise acquire, stockpile or retain chemical weapons, or transfer, directly or indirectly, chemical weapons to other States or non-State actors;

5. *Underscores* that no party in Syria should use, develop, produce, acquire, stockpile, retain, or transfer chemical weapons;

6. *Decides* that the Syrian Arab Republic shall comply with all aspects of the decision of the OPCW Executive Council of 27 September 2013 (Annex I);

7. *Decides* that the Syrian Arab Republic shall cooperate fully with the OPCW and the United Nations, including by complying with their relevant recommendations, by accepting personnel designated by the OPCW or the United Nations, by providing for and ensuring the security of activities undertaken by these personnel, by providing these personnel with immediate and unfettered access to and the right to inspect, in discharging their functions, any and all sites, and by allowing immediate and unfettered access to individuals that the OPCW has grounds to believe to be of importance for the purpose of its mandate, and *decides* that all parties in Syria shall cooperate fully in this regard;

8. *Decides* to authorize an advance team of United Nations personnel to provide

early assistance to OPCW activities in Syria, *requests* the Director-General of the OPCW and the Secretary-General to closely cooperate in the implementation of the Executive Council decision of 27 September 2013 and this resolution, including through their operational activities on the ground, and *further requests* the Secretary-General, in consultation with the Director-General of the OPCW and, where appropriate, the Director-General of the World Health Organization, to submit to the Council within 10 days of the adoption of this resolution recommendations regarding the role of the United Nations in eliminating the Syrian Arab Republic's chemical weapons program;

9. *Notes* that the Syrian Arab Republic is a party to the Convention on the Privileges and Immunities of the United Nations, *decides* that OPCW-designated personnel undertaking activities provided for in this resolution or the decision of the OPCW Executive Council of 27 September 2013 shall enjoy the privileges and immunities contained in the Verification Annex, Part II(B) of the Chemical Weapons Convention, and *calls* on the Syrian Arab Republic to conclude modalities agreements with the United Nations and the OPCW;

10. *Encourages* Member States to provide support, including personnel, technical expertise, information, equipment, and financial and other resources and assistance, in coordination with the Director-General of the OPCW and the Secretary-General, to enable the OPCW and the United Nations to implement the elimination of the Syrian Arab Republic's chemical weapons program, and *decides* to authorize Member States to acquire, control, transport, transfer and

destroy chemical weapons identified by the Director-General of the OPCW, consistent with the objective of the Chemical Weapons Convention, to ensure the elimination of the Syrian Arab Republic's chemical weapons program in the soonest and safest manner;

11. *Urges* all Syrian parties and interested Member States with relevant capabilities to work closely together and with the OPCW and the United Nations to arrange for the security of the monitoring and destruction mission, recognizing the primary responsibility of the Syrian government in this regard;

12. *Decides* to review on a regular basis the implementation in the Syrian Arab Republic of the decision of the OPCW Executive Council of 27 September 2013 and this resolution, and *requests* the Director-General of the OPCW to report to the Security Council, through the Secretary-General, who shall include relevant information on United Nations activities related to the implementation of this resolution, within 30 days and every month thereafter, and *requests* further the Director-General of the OPCW and the Secretary-General to report in a coordinated manner, as needed, to the Security Council, non-compliance with this resolution or the OPCW Executive Council decision of 27 September 2013;

13. *Reaffirms* its readiness to consider promptly any reports of the OPCW under Article VIII of the Chemical Weapons Convention, which provides for the referral of cases of non-compliance to the United Nations Security Council;

14. *Decides* that Member States shall inform immediately the Security Council of any violation of resolution 1540 (2004), including acquisition by non-State actors

of chemical weapons, their means of delivery and related materials in order to take necessary measures therefore;

15. *Expresses* its strong conviction that those individuals responsible for the use of chemical weapons in the Syrian Arab Republic should be held accountable;

16. *Endorses* fully the Geneva Communiqué of 30 June 2012 (Annex II), which sets out a number of key steps beginning with the establishment of a transitional governing body exercising full executive powers, which could include members of the present Government and the opposition and other groups and shall be formed on the basis of mutual consent;

17. *Calls* for the convening, as soon as possible, of an international conference on Syria to implement the Geneva Communiqué, and *calls upon* all Syrian parties to engage seriously and constructively at the Geneva Conference on Syria, and *underscores* that they should be fully representative of the Syrian people and committed to the implementation of the Geneva Communiqué and to the achievement of stability and reconciliation;

18. *Reaffirms* that all Member States shall refrain from providing any form of support to non-State actors that attempt to develop, acquire, manufacture, possess, transport, transfer or use nuclear, chemical or biological weapons and their means of delivery, and *calls upon* all Member States, in particular Member States neighbouring the Syrian Arab Republic, to report any violations of this paragraph to the Security Council immediately;

19. *Demands* that non-State actors not develop, acquire, manufacture, possess, transport, transfer, or use nuclear, chemical or biological weapons and their means of delivery, and *calls upon*

all Member States, in particular Member States neighbouring the Syrian Arab Republic, to report any actions inconsistent with this paragraph to the Security Council immediately;

20. *Decides* that all Member States shall prohibit the procurement of chemical weapons, related equipment, goods and technology or assistance from the Syrian Arab Republic by their nationals, or using their flagged vessels or aircraft, whether or not originating in the territory of the Syrian Arab Republic;

21. *Decides*, in the event of non-compliance with this resolution, including unauthorized transfer of chemical weapons, or any use of chemical weapons by anyone in the Syrian Arab Republic, to impose measures under Chapter VII of the United Nations Charter;

22. *Decides* to remain actively seized of the matter.

Source: United Nations. "Middle East." Security Council Resolution S/RES/2118, September 27, 2013. http://unscr.com/en/resolutions/2118

---

5. Vladimir Putin's Address Following Adoption of a Joint Statement by Russia and the United States on Syria (February 22, 2016)

The Syrian Conflict has put the United States and Russia into a level of interaction and conflict not seen since the end of the Cold War in 1990. The already complex situation in Syria was made even more so after U.S. intervention in 2014, and then Russian involvement at the request of Bashar al-Assad in 2015. While the relationship between the United States and Russia has been tense, there have been periods of uneasy cooperation.

The two sides have made efforts to deconflict their airspace, for example, and both country's air forces have actively tried to avoid coming into contact with one another. In February 2016, the United States and Russia, under the auspices of the International Syria Support Group, made a joint statement on the cessation of hostilities in Syria. What follows is a relatively rare look at a response made by Vladimir Putin on that statement that was translated into English by the Kremlin.

President of Russia Vladimir Putin: Friends, I just had a telephone conversation with President of the United States of America Barack Obama. The phone call was initiated by the Russian side, but the interest was certainly mutual.

During our conversation, we approved joint statements of Russia and the US, as co-chairs of the ISSG, on the cessation of hostilities in Syria. Adoption of the statement was preceded by intensive work by Russian and American experts. We also made use of the positive experience we accumulated over the course of cooperation in eliminating chemical weapons in Syria.

Our negotiators held several rounds of closed consultations. As a result, we were able to reach an important, specific result. It was agreed that the cessation of hostilities in Syria commences at 00:00 (Damascus time) on February 27, 2016 on terms and conditions that are a part of the Russian-American statement.

The essence of these conditions is as follows: by 12:00 pm on February 26, 2016, all parties warring in Syria must indicate to the Russian Federation or our American partners their commitment to the cessation of hostilities. Russian and American troops will

jointly delineate the territories where these groups are active. No military action will be taken against them by the Armed Forces of the Syrian Arab Republic, Russian Armed Forces and the US-led coalition. In turn, the opposition will cease all military action against the Armed Forces of the Syrian Arab Republic and other groups supporting them.

ISIS, Jabhat Al-Nusra, and other terrorist organisations designated by the United Nations Security Council, are excluded from the cessation of hostilities. Strikes against them will continue.

It is fundamentally important that Russia and the US, as co-chairs of the ISSG, are prepared to launch effective mechanisms to promote and monitor compliance with the ceasefire by both the Syrian Government and the armed opposition groups.

To achieve this goal, we will establish a communication hotline and, if necessary, a working group to exchange relevant information. Russia will conduct the necessary work with Damascus and the legitimate Syrian leadership. We expect that the United States will do the same with regard to their allies and the groups they support.

I am sure that the joint actions agreed upon with the American side will be enough to radically reverse the crisis situation in Syria. We are finally seeing a real chance to bring an end to the long-standing bloodshed and violence. As a result, humanitarian access to all Syrian citizens in need should be made easier.

Most important is the creation of conditions for launching a long-term political process through a broad inter-Syrian dialogue in Geneva, under the auspices of the UN.

Unfortunately, recent history has many examples where one-sided actions not sanctioned by the UN, which favour short-term political or opportunistic interests, have led to dramatic results. These examples are on everyone's lips: Somalia, Iraq, Libya, Yemen.

Against this background, Russian-American agreements on the cessation of hostilities in Syria, and their joint implementation in coordination with all nations participating in the International Syria Support Group, can become an example of responsible actions the global community takes against the threat of terrorism, which are based on international law and UN principles.

I would like to hope that the Syrian leadership and all our partners in the region and beyond will support the set of actions chosen by representatives of Russia and the US.

Source: "Vladimir Putin's Address Following Adoption of a Joint Statement by Russia and US on Syria." February 22, 2016. http://en.kremlin.ru /events/president/news/51376

6. Presidential Memorandum on the Plan to Defeat the Islamic State of Iraq and Syria (January 28, 2017)

When Donald Trump became the 45th president of the United States, he took a very pragmatic approach to the Syrian Conflict. Rather than focusing on the broader issues of human rights violations committed by the Assad regime, he identified two main issues he felt had the most direct impact on U.S. national security—the Islamic State of Iraq and Syria (ISIS), and Assad's stockpile of chemical weapons. Choosing to retain Secretary of State Ashton Carter from the Obama administration in the initial phase of his administration, President Trump facilitated a plan initiated by Carter, and being

carried out by U.S. Army lieutenant general Sean MacFarland, to deal a decisive blow to the Islamic State by focusing on their strongholds in Mosul, Iraq, and Raqqa, Syria. This Presidential Memorandum illustrates Trump's effective endorsement of Secretary of Defense Carter's plan.

SUBJECT: Plan to Defeat the Islamic State of Iraq and Syria

The Islamic State of Iraq and Syria, or ISIS, is not the only threat from radical Islamic terrorism that the United States faces, but it is among the most vicious and aggressive. It is also attempting to create its own state, which ISIS claims as a "caliphate." But there can be no accommodation or negotiation with it. For those reasons I am directing my Administration to develop a comprehensive plan to defeat ISIS.

ISIS is responsible for the violent murder of American citizens in the Middle East, including the beheadings of James Foley, Steven Sotloff, and Peter Abdul-Rahman Kassig, as well as the death of Kayla Mueller. In addition, ISIS has inspired attacks in the United States, including the December 2015 attack in San Bernardino, California, and the June 2016 attack in Orlando, Florida. ISIS is complicit in a number of terrorist attacks on our allies in which Americans have been wounded or killed, such as the November 2015 attack in Paris, France, the March 2016 attack in Brussels, Belgium, the July 2016 attack in Nice, France, and the December 2016 attack in Berlin, Germany.

ISIS has engaged in a systematic campaign of persecution and extermination in those territories it enters or controls. If ISIS is left in power, the threat that it poses will only grow. We know it has attempted to develop chemical weapons capability. It continues to radicalize our own citizens, and its attacks against our allies and partners continue to mount. The United States must take decisive action to defeat ISIS.

Sec. 1. Policy. It is the policy of the United States that ISIS be defeated.

Sec. 2. Policy Coordination. Policy coordination, guidance, dispute resolution, and periodic in-progress reviews for the functions and programs described and assigned in this memorandum shall be provided through the interagency process established in National Security Presidential Memorandum—2 of January 28, 2017 (Organization of the National Security Council and the Homeland Security Council), or any successor.

(i) Development of a new plan to defeat ISIS (the Plan) shall commence immediately.

(ii) Within 30 days, a preliminary draft of the Plan to defeat ISIS shall be submitted to the President by the Secretary of Defense.

(iii) The Plan shall include:

(A) a comprehensive strategy and plans for the defeat of ISIS;

(B) recommended changes to any United States rules of engagement and other United States policy restrictions that exceed the requirements of international law regarding the use of force against ISIS;

(C) public diplomacy, information operations, and cyber strategies to isolate and delegitimize ISIS and its radical Islamist ideology;

(D) identification of new coalition partners in the fight against ISIS and policies to empower coalition partners to fight ISIS and its affiliates;

(E) mechanisms to cut off or seize ISIS's financial support, including financial transfers, money laundering, oil revenue, human trafficking, sales of looted art and historical artifacts, and other revenue sources; and

(F) a detailed strategy to robustly fund the Plan.

(b) Participants. The Secretary of Defense shall develop the Plan in collaboration with the Secretary of State, the Secretary of the Treasury, the Secretary of Homeland Security, the Director of National Intelligence, the Chairman of the Joint Chiefs of Staff, the Assistant to the President for National Security Affairs, and the Assistant to the President for Homeland Security and Counterterrorism.

(c) Development of the Plan. Consistent with applicable law, the Participants identified in subsection (b) of this section shall compile all information in the possession of the Federal Government relevant to the defeat of ISIS and its affiliates. All executive departments and agencies shall, to the extent permitted by law, promptly comply with any request of the Participants to provide information in their possession or control pertaining to ISIS. The Participants may seek further information relevant to the Plan from any appropriate source.

(d) The Secretary of Defense is hereby authorized and directed to publish this memorandum in the Federal Register

DONALD J. TRUMP

Source: Memorandum on the Plan to Defeat the Islamic State of Iraq and Syria, January 28, 2017. Compilation of Presidential Documents, Office of the Federal Register. https://www.govinfo.gov/content/pkg/DCPD-201700081/html/DCPD-2017 00081.htm

7. President Donald J. Trump, Statement on the Anniversary of the 2013 Syrian Chemical Weapons Attack (August 21, 2017)

When President Donald Trump became the forty fifth president of the United States, he took a very pragmatic approach to the Syrian Conflict. Rather than focusing in the broader issues of human rights violations committed by the Assad regime, he identified two main issues he felt had the most direct impact on U.S. national security—The Islamic State of Iraq and Syria (ISIS), and Assad's stockpile of chemical weapons. In fact, President Trump authorized U.S. missile Strikes on a Syrian Air Force airbase after a chemical weapon attack launched by Assad in Idlib Province in 2017, and he again authorized air and missile strikes in 2018. This statement made on the anniversary of Assad's first chemical weapons attack illustrates the strong stance the Trump administration has taken toward Syria's use of chemical weapons.

Today marks the 4th anniversary of the Syrian regime's deadly chemical weapons attack that killed more than 1,400 people in the Damascus suburb of Ghouta. This tragic event precipitated an international effort that led to the destruction of more than 1,000 metric tons of Syrian chemical weapons. Still, on April 4th of this year, Assad proved beyond a doubt that he still possesses these heinous weapons and is willing to use them against innocent civilians.

It is critical that the international community not forget these tragic events. We must speak with one voice and act with one purpose to ensure that the Syrian regime, and any other actor contemplating the use of chemical weapons, understands that doing so will result in serious consequences. As the President has made clear, the United States will do its part to prevent the use or spread of these weapons. Along with the many other nations that have signed the Chemical Weapons Convention, we commit to work together to create a world without chemical weapons.

Today is an appropriate reminder of the importance of that commitment. We reiterate our call for all countries to stand together and leave no doubt that the use of chemical weapons will not be tolerated.

Source: The White House. Statement on the Anniversary of the 2013 Syrian Chemical Weapons Attack. August 21, 2017. https://www.whitehouse.gov/briefings-statements/statement-anniversary-2013-syrian-chemical-weapons-attack

8. Statement by President Trump on Syria (April 13, 2018)

When Donald Trump became the 45th president of the United States, he took a very pragmatic approach to the Syrian Conflict. Rather than focusing o the broader issues of human rights violations committed by the Assad regime, he identified two main issues he felt had the most direct impact on U.S. national security—the Islamic State of Iraq and Syria (ISIS), and Assad's stockpile of chemical weapons. In fact, President Trump authorized U.S. missile strikes on a Syrian Air Force airbase after a chemical weapon attack launched by Assad in Idlib Province in 2017, and he again authorized air and missile strikes in 2018. What follows is a statement President Trump made from the White House to the American people when he authorized the 2018 American response to Assad's repeated use of chemical weapons.

THE PRESIDENT: My fellow Americans, a short time ago, I ordered the United States Armed Forces to launch precision strikes on targets associated with the chemical weapons capabilities of Syrian dictator Bashar al-Assad. A combined operation with the armed forces of France and the United Kingdom is now underway. We thank them both.

Tonight, I want to speak with you about why we have taken this action.

One year ago, Assad launched a savage chemical weapons attack against his own innocent people. The United States responded with 58 missile strikes that destroyed 20 percent of the Syrian Air Force.

Last Saturday, the Assad regime again deployed chemical weapons to slaughter innocent civilians—this time, in the town of Douma, near the Syrian capital of Damascus. This massacre was a significant escalation in a pattern of chemical weapons use by that very terrible regime.

The evil and the despicable attack left mothers and fathers, infants and children, thrashing in pain and gasping for air. These are not the actions of a man; they are crimes of a monster instead.

Following the horrors of World War I a century ago, civilized nations joined together to ban chemical warfare. Chemical weapons are uniquely dangerous not only because they inflict gruesome suffering, but because even small amounts can unleash widespread devastation.

The purpose of our actions tonight is to establish a strong deterrent against the production, spread, and use of chemical weapons. Establishing this deterrent is a vital national security interest of the United States. The combined American, British, and French response to these atrocities will integrate all instruments of our national power—military, economic, and diplomatic. We are prepared to sustain this response until the Syrian regime stops its use of prohibited chemical agents.

I also have a message tonight for the two governments most responsible for supporting, equipping, and financing the criminal Assad regime.

To Iran, and to Russia, I ask: What kind of a nation wants to be associated with the mass murder of innocent men, women, and children?

The nations of the world can be judged by the friends they keep. No nation can succeed in the long run by promoting rogue states, brutal tyrants, and murderous dictators.

In 2013, President Putin and his government promised the world that they would guarantee the elimination of Syria's chemical weapons. Assad's recent attack—and today's response—are the direct result of Russia's failure to keep that promise.

Russia must decide if it will continue down this dark path, or if it will join with civilized nations as a force for stability and peace. Hopefully, someday we'll get along with Russia, and maybe even Iran—but maybe not.

I will say this: The United States has a lot to offer, with the greatest and most powerful economy in the history of the world.

In Syria, the United States—with but a small force being used to eliminate what is left of ISIS—is doing what is necessary to protect the American people. Over the last year, nearly 100 percent of the territory once controlled by the so-called ISIS caliphate in Syria and Iraq has been liberated and eliminated.

The United States has also rebuilt our friend-ships across the Middle East. We have asked our partners to take greater responsibility for securing their home region, including con-tributing large amounts of money for the resources, equipment, and all of the anti-ISIS effort. Increased engagement from our friends, including Saudi Arabia, the United Arab Emirates, Qatar, Egypt, and others can ensure that Iran does not profit from the eradication of ISIS.

America does not seek an indefinite presence in Syria under no circumstances. As other nations step up their contributions, we look forward to the day when we can bring our warriors home. And great warriors they are.

Looking around our very troubled world, Americans have no illusions. We cannot purge the world of evil, or act everywhere there is tyranny.

No amount of American blood or treasure can produce lasting peace and security in the Middle East. It's a troubled place. We will try to make it better, but it is a troubled place. The United States will be a partner and a friend, but the fate of the region lies in the hands of its own people.

In the last century, we looked straight into the darkest places of the human soul. We saw the anguish that can be unleashed and the evil that can take hold. By the end of the World War I, more than one million people had been killed or injured by chemical weapons. We never want to see that ghastly specter return.

So today, the nations of Britain, France, and the United States of America have marshaled their righteous power against barbarism and brutality.

Tonight, I ask all Americans to say a prayer for our noble warriors and our allies as they carry out their missions.

We pray that God will bring comfort to those suffering in Syria. We pray that God will guide the whole region toward a future of dignity and of peace.

And we pray that God will continue to watch over and bless the United States of America.

Thank you, and goodnight. Thank you.

Source: The White House. "Statement by President Trump on Syria." April 13, 2018. https://www.whitehouse.gov/briefings-statements/statement-president-trump-syria/

9. United Nations General Assembly Summary Report on the High-Level Panel Discussion on Violations of the Human Rights of Children in the Syrian Arab Republic (May 15, 2018)

In September 2017, the United Nations Human Rights Council, affiliated with the Global Centre for the Responsibility to Pro-tect, resolved to convene an international, UN-sponsored committee to examine human rights violations in Syria as they pertain specifically to children. The United Nations Children's Fund (UNICEF) had long reported on the problems experienced spe-cifically by children in the conflict; and the fact that these children have known nothing but war for their entire lives will have pro-found effects not only on their lives, but in the wider community as they come into adulthood. This summary report highlights the myriad ways in which the war has severely impacted Syria's children.

Introduction

In its resolution 36/20, the Human Rights Council decided to convene, at its thirty-seventh session, a high-level panel discussion on violations of the human rights of children in the Syrian Arab Republic, in consultation with the Independent International Commission of Inquiry on the Syrian Arab Republic, with a specific focus on attacks against children, including attacks on schools and hospitals and denial of humanitarian access. The Council asked that the discussion feature witness testimony and Syrian voices, including children's views, through appropriate and safe means. The Council requested the Office of the United Nations High Commissioner for Human Rights (OHCHR) to prepare a summary report on the high-level panel discussion for submission at its thirty-eighth session . . .

Opening statements

The United Nations Deputy High Commissioner for Human Rights reminded participants that the conflict in the Syrian Arab Republic had started with the denigration of a child, referring to the detention and torture of 13-year-old Hamza Ali al-Khateeb, in 2011. The conflict was not only denying millions of children their fundamental rights, but it was also robbing them of their childhood. Nearly two thirds of the 8.35 million children in the Syrian Arab Republic required humanitarian assistance, with more than 1 million living in hard-to-reach areas and 170,000 in besieged areas. An entire generation of Syrians was making the journey from childhood to adulthood cowered by unending bombardment, under the shadow of constant violence, living in permanent fear, and deprived of basic goods and services. The Deputy High Commissioner referred to the deprivation of the right to education and health experienced by children in the Syrian Arab Republic . . .

Homes, ambulance bases, hospitals and schools had been ruthlessly targeted by all parties to the conflict, even though under international law they should be sanctuaries for children. The catastrophic humanitarian situation in the country underscored the failure of the international community to protect civilians, most notably children. The Deputy High Commissioner asked how many children would die in the current year and how much longer the international community would tolerate the intolerable suffering of children in the Syrian Arab Republic . . .

The Regional Humanitarian Coordinator for the Syrian crisis stressed that 40 per cent of the 13.1 million people in the Syrian Arab Republic requiring protection and assistance were children. Of the 5.6 million people in acute need, 663,000 were under 5 years old. The protection of civilians in the conduct of hostilities remained a critical concern. In that regard, the Regional Humanitarian Coordinator noted that Eastern Ghouta had been besieged for five years and that families had been sheltering in overcrowded basements, not knowing if they would survive another day. Children had been subjected to an unprecedented level of indiscriminate violence, causing long-lasting psychological trauma . . .

The monitoring and reporting mechanism had verified 108 attacks on hospitals and medical personnel in 2017. Those attacks, which severely undermined the delivery of health services, had a disproportionate impact on the lives of children. In any other country, an attack on a hospital would cause outrage and spark calls for action and accountability, while in the Syrian Arab Republic more than 100 such attacks had taken place in one year alone, with no end in sight.

The recruitment of children and their use in armed conflict by all parties continued to increase. In 2017, the recruitment of children as combatants under the age of 15—prohibited under international humanitarian law and constituting a war crime—represented 25 per cent of recruitment cases involving boys and girls. Out of every 10 recruited children, 9 served in a combat role in uniform, armed and with military training . . .

Contribution of the panelists

In her introductory remarks as moderator of the panel, Ms. von Hall shared stories from her travels to the Syrian Arab Republic as a journalist. She spoke about two children she had met: Hala, an 8-year-old girl, had sustained burns on 70 per cent of her body and had been completely disfigured when a bomb fell on her home in Aleppo; Hozaifa, a 17-year-old boy, was paralysed from the waist down, having been hit by a bomb on his way home from school, in Idlib. While those children had a long road to recovery, they were lucky because they had survived, which was not the case for many children in the Syrian Arab Republic. Ms. Von Hall had recently spoken to a man in Eastern Ghouta who was hiding in a basement with his six children. He had told her he had only one message to the world: "We do not primarily want food and medicine. We just want you to stop this war machine. Stop it now."

In his intervention, Mr. Zaza highlighted the gravity of the escalating situation in Eastern Ghouta, which had been besieged for several years by the Government of the Syrian Arab Republic and its allies. The population had been starved and deprived of basic goods due to the denial of humanitarian access, despite resolutions issued by the Security Council. Civilians, including 115,000 children, had been systematically and indiscriminately targeted in that area. Heavy and long-lasting bombing of civilians had previously been

carried out in other locations in the Syrian Arab Republic, notably in order to force the population to negotiate a forced displacement deal, which had led to the displacement of 3 million children. Mr. Zaza deplored the fact that the recent brutal attacks in Eastern Ghouta had halted efforts at maintaining education for children living there: five schools had been attacked in the first week of February 2018 alone . . .

Mr. Osman stressed that the gross violations of child rights in the Syrian Arab Republic, committed by all parties to the conflict, had resulted in countless deaths and injuries. According to the Syrian Network for Human Rights, some 27,000 children had been killed since the beginning of the conflict. His organization had documented human rights violations against children and conducted capacity-building activities on children's rights for civil society.

Weapons prohibited under international law had been used against civilians. With regard to the use of chemical weapons, he cited the report of the Commission of Inquiry (A/HRC/36/55), in which the Commission had indicated that 54 per cent of the 179 individuals killed by chemical weapons in April 2017 were children. The recruitment and use of children by armed groups was another serious type of violation against children. The military intervention of international forces in the conflict, and the weapons they used, was further exacerbating the risks faced by recruited children.

Mr. Alkasem described the conditions of detention of children and their treatment by Syrian authorities and armed groups. Arbitrary detention and enforced disappearance had been perpetrated by the Government of the Syrian Arab Republic for decades, and had increased in reaction to the 2011 uprising. Children had not been spared from arbitrary arrest and detention and faced torture, inhuman and degrading treatment similar to that endured by adults. Many children died in detention. The fear and trauma experienced by the children and their families were exacerbated by the impunity enjoyed by the perpetrators.

Mr. Alkasem outlined the conclusions of a report produced by his organization on enforced disappearance and detention of children. Children faced unbearable psychological and physical torture, including sexual violence. They were separated from their parents and detained with adults; used as witnesses against their own parents; forced to make false testimonies; accused of terrorism; and subjected to special courts. Most children in detention were between 13 and 18 years old. The conditions of detention were appalling, particularly in military detention facilities, and children were deprived of basic necessities, including food and access to health care.

When detained by armed groups, children would be accused of apostasy and spying on behalf of the Government or foreign intelligence agencies. Islamic State in Iraq and the Levant (ISIL) subjected children to sexual slavery, with girls being forcibly married to ISIL members, while boys were instilled with ISIL ideology and subjected to military training.

Fearing social stigmatization or reprisals, children would agree to report on human rights violations and abuses as witnesses, but not as victims, and such cases were consequently not documented. Ensuring accountability for human rights violations was a cornerstone for the rehabilitation of Syrian society. Mr. Alkasem called on the international community to assume its responsibility to ensure the protection of children in the Syrian Arab Republic. He recommended documenting cases of enforced disappearance, identifying burial sites and creating a DNA database for children separated from their families. He urged the Human Rights Council to remain seized of the matter of human rights violations of children in the Syrian Arab Republic. In conclusion, Mr. Alkasem emphasized the urgent need to protect children in order to spare them the terrible fate of those who had died in detention . . .

Comments and concluding remarks

The panelists emphasized that the failure of the international community was unacceptable and urged that it take prompt action to put an end to the atrocities.

One panelist recalled that the Government of the Syrian Arab Republic bore the primary responsibility for providing effective protection to its people. It was stressed that peace could not be achieved until there was accountability for the enforced disappearances, and that the Government should allow the Commission of Inquiry or the International Committee of the Red Cross to visit detention facilities.

The panelists reiterated their call for justice and accountability for crimes committed by all parties to the conflict, noting that the call was not rooted in revenge but aimed at seeking redress for violations of human rights.

The Regional Humanitarian Coordinator for the Syrian crisis stated there was no justification for attacks on children in the Syrian Arab Republic, and for people dying due to lack of medical care that was available just a few miles down the road. He stressed that the people of the Syrian Arab Republic needed peace and stability, and concluded that words were no longer sufficient; action should be the next move.

Closing the discussion, the moderator stated that after listening for two hours about the horrific violations of children's rights, there was a risk of becoming numb. She invited the participants to reflect on the following question: "What if these were your children, your son, or daughter raped, detained, starved to death, forcibly recruited to kill?" She observed that some victims might have been listening to the panel in Damascus, Idlib, Aleppo or Afrin. She hoped they had not just heard despair but had sensed some seeds of hope.

Source: United Nations Human Rights Council. "Summary Report on the High-Level Panel Discussion on Violations of the Human Rights of Children in the Syrian Arab Republic." A/HRC/38/29. May 15, 2018. https://documents-dds-ny.un.org/doc/UNDOC/GEN/G18/133/86/PDF/G1813386.pdf

10. Statement by H. E. Walid al-Moualem, Deputy Prime Minister of the Syrian Arab Republic, Made to the 73rd Session of the United Nations General Assembly (September 29, 2018)

Of all the voices speaking out on the Syrian Conflict, the one largely absent from the English-speaking world is the voice of the Syrian government itself. Regardless of what the world's opinion may be, it is important to read statements outlining the Syrian regime's position and the Syrian deputy's speech to the UN General Assembly, which provide a thorough overview of Bashar al-Assad's position regarding the civil war and the international community's response to it. It is clear the Syrian government feels the

international response has been an affront to its sovereignty, and that the United States, in particular, should be held accountable for initiating the problems in the first place. They cite U.S. support for groups that are destabilizing the region (e.g., the Kurds and the Israelis), and they point specifically to the destructive attack on Raqqa as an example of Kurdish and American aggression. They also speak of human rights violations and their desire to repatriate refugees and internally displaced persons. Readers may find it interesting to compare their statements with those of the United States and the United Nations also found in the Documents section of this volume.

Madam President of the 73rd session of the United Nations General Assembly,

I would like to congratulate you and your country Ecuador on your election as president of the current session of the General Assembly and I wish you all success. I would also like to thank your predecessor for presiding over the Assembly during the previous session.

Madam President, ladies and gentlemen,

Every year we arrive at this important international forum, hoping that every corner of this world has become more secure, stable, and prosperous. Today, our hope is stronger than ever, and so is our confidence that the will of the people shall eventually triumph. Our hope and confidence are the result of more than seven years of hardship, during which our people suffered from the scourge of terrorism. However, Syrians refused to compromise. They refused to succumb to terrorist and their external supporters. They stood their ground. They remained defiant, fully convinced that this was a battle for their existence, their history, and their future, and that they will ultimately emerge victorious.

To the disappointment of some, here we are today, more than seven years into this dirty war against my country, announcing to the world that the situation on the ground has become more secure and stable and that our war on terror is almost over, thanks to the heroism, resolve, and unity of the people and the army, and to the support of our allies and friends. However, we will not stop at these achievements. We remain committed to fighting this sacred battle until we purge all Syrian territories from terrorist groups, regardless of their names, and from any illegal foreign presence. We will pay no heed to any attacks, external pressure, lies or allegations that seek to discourage us. This is our duty and a non-negotiable right that we have exercised as we set out to eradicate terrorism from our land.

Madam President,

The governments of certain countries have denied us our right, under international law, and our national duty to combat terrorism and protect our people on our land and within our own borders. At the same time, these governments formed an illegitimate international coalition, led by the United States, on the pretext of combating terrorism in Syria. The so-called international coalition has done everything but fight terrorism. It has even become clear that the coalition's goals were in perfect alignment with those of terrorist groups; sowing chaos, death and destruction in their path. The coalition destroyed the Syrian city of Raqqa completely; it destroyed infrastructure and public services in the areas it targeted; it committed massacres against civilians, including children and women, which amount to war crimes under international law. The coalition

has also provided direct military support to terrorists, on multiple occasions, as they fought against the Syrian army. It should have been more aptly named 'The Coalition to Support Terrorists and War Crimes'.

The situation in Syria cannot be divorced from the battle raging between two camps on the world stage: one of the camps promotes peace, stability, and prosperity across the world, advocates dialogue and mutual understanding, respects international law, and upholds the principle of non-interference in the internal affairs of other states. The other camp tries to create chaos in international relations and employs colonization and hegemony as tools to further its narrow interests, even if that meant resorting to corrupt methods, such as supporting terrorism and imposing an economic blockade, to subjugate people and governments that reject external diktats and insist on making their own decisions.

What happened in Syria should have been a lesson to some countries but those countries refuse to learn. Instead, they choose to bury their head in the sand. This is why ladies and gentlemen we, the members of this organization, must make a clear and unequivocal choice: are we going to defend international law and the charter and be on the side of justice? Or are we going to submit to hegemonic tendencies and the law of the jungle that some are trying to impose on this organization and the world?

Ladies and gentlemen,

Today, the situation on the ground is more stable and secure thanks to progress made in combating terrorism. The government continues to rehabilitate the areas destroyed by terrorists to restore normalcy. All conditions are now present for the voluntary return of Syrian refugees to the country they had to leave because of terrorism and the unilateral economic measures that targeted their daily lives and their livelihoods. Thousands of Syrian refugees abroad have indeed started their journey back home.

The return of every Syrian refugee is a priority for the Syrian state. Doors are open for all Syrians abroad to return voluntarily and safely. And what applies to Syrians inside Syria also applies to Syrians abroad. No one is above the law. Thanks to the help of Russia, the Syrian government will spare no effort to facilitate the return of those refugees and meet their basic needs. A special committee was recently established to coordinate the return of refugees to their places of origin in Syria and to help them regain their lives.

We have called upon the international community and humanitarian organizations to facilitate these returns. However, some western countries and in line with their dishonest behavior since the start of the war on Syria continue to prevent the return of refugees. They are spreading irrational fears among refugees; they are politicizing what should be a purely humanitarian issue, using refugees as a bargaining chip to serve their political agenda, and linking the return of refugees to the political process.

Today, as we are about to close the last chapter in the crisis, Syrians are coming together to erase the traces of this terrorist war and to rebuild their country with their own hands, whether they stayed in Syria or were forced to leave. We welcome any assistance with reconstruction from those countries that were not part of the aggression on Syria and those that have come out clearly and explicitly against terrorism. However, the priority is for our friends that stood by us in our war on terror. As for the countries that offer only conditional assistance or continue

to support terrorism, they are neither invited nor welcome to help.

Madam President,

As we move ahead on counter-terrorism, reconstruction and the return of refugees, we remain committed to the political process without compromising on our national principles. These include preserving the sovereignty, independence, and territorial unity of the Syrian Arab Republic, protecting the exclusive right of Syrians to determine the future of their country without external interference, and eradicating terrorism from our country. We expressed time and again our readiness to respond to any initiative that would help Syrians end the crisis. We have engaged positively in the Geneva talks, the Astana process and the Syrian national dialogue in Sochi. However, it has always been the other parties that rejected dialogue and resorted to terrorism and foreign interference to achieve their goals.

Nevertheless, we continue to implement the outcomes of the Sochi Syrian national dialogue on the formation of a constitutional committee to review the current constitution. We presented a practical and comprehensive vision on the composition, prerogatives and working methods of the committee and submitted a list of representatives on behalf of the Syrian state. We stress that the mandate of the committee is limited to reviewing the of the current constitution, through a Syrian-led and Syrian-owned process that may be facilitated by the Special Envoy of the Secretary-General for Syria. No preconditions should be imposed on the committee, nor should its recommendations be prejudged. The committee must be independent since the constitution is a Syrian matter to be decided by Syrians themselves. Therefore, we will not accept any proposal that constitutes an interference in the internal affairs of Syria or leads to such interference. The Syrian people must have the final word regarding any constitutional or sovereign matter. We stand ready to work actively with our friends to convene the committee along the parameters I have just mentioned.

In addition to these international initiatives, local reconciliation is well underway. Reconciliation agreements allowed us to stem the bloodshed and prevent destruction in many areas around Syria. They restored stability and a normal life to these areas and allowed people to return to the homes they were forced to leave because of terrorism. Reconciliation, therefore, will remain our priority.

Ladies and gentlemen,

The battle we fought in Syria against terrorism was not only a military one. It was also an ideological battle, between the culture of destruction, extremism, and death, and the culture of construction, tolerance, and life. Therefore, I launch an appeal from this rostrum, calling for fighting the ideology of terrorism and violent extremism, drying up its support and financial resources, and implementing relevant Security Council resolutions, notably resolution 2253. The military battle against terrorism, albeit important, is not enough. Terrorism is like an epidemic. It will return, break out, and threaten everyone without exception.

Madam President, ladies and gentlemen,

We fully condemn and reject the use of chemical weapons under any circumstances, wherever, whenever, and regardless of the target. This is why Syria eliminated completely its chemical program and fulfilled all its commitments as a member of the Organization for the Prohibition of Chemical Weapons (OPCW), as confirmed by numerous OPCW reports. Although some western countries are constantly trying to politicize its work, we have always cooperated with the OPCW to the largest extent possible. Unfortunately, every time we express our readiness to receive objective and professional investigative teams to investigate the alleged use of chemical weapons, these countries would block such efforts because they know that the conclusions of the investigations would not satis5' the ill-intentions they harbor against Syria. These countries have ready-made accusations and scenarios to justify an aggression on Syria. This was the case when the United States, France, and the UK launched a wanton aggression on Syria last April, claiming that chemical weapons were used without any investigation or evidence and in a flagrant violation of Syria's sovereignty, international law and the UN charter.

Meanwhile, these same countries disregarded all reliable information we provided on chemical weapons in the possession of terrorist groups that used them on multiple occasions to blame the Syrian government and justify an attack against it. The terrorist organization known as 'the White Helmets' was the main tool used to mislead public opinion and fabricate accusations and come up with lies on the use of chemical weapons in Syria. The White Helmets was created by British intelligence under a humanitarian cover. It has been proven however that this organization is part of the Al-Qaeda-affiliated Nusra Front. Despite all allegations, we remain committed to liberating all our territory without concern for the black banners of terrorists or the theatrics of the White Helmets.

Ladies and gentlemen,

In another episode of the terrorist war on Syria since 2011, suicide bombings orchestrated by ISIL rocked the governorate of

Suwayda in southern Syria last July. It is worth noting that the terrorists behind that attack came from the Tanf area where US forces are present. The area has become a safe haven for ISIL remnants who are now hiding in the Rukban refugee camp on the border with Jordan, under the protection of US forces. The United States also sought to prolong the crisis in Syria by releasing terrorists from Guantanamo prison and sending them to Syria, where they became the effective leaders of the Nusra Front and other terrorist groups.

Meanwhile, the Turkish regime continues to support terrorists in Syria. Since day one of the war on Syria, the Turkish regime has trained and armed terrorists, turning Turkey into a hub and a corridor for terrorists on their way to Syria. When terrorists failed to serve its agenda, the Turkish regime resorted to direct military aggression, attacking cities and towns in northern Syria. However, all these actions that undermine Syria's sovereignty, unity, and territorial integrity and violate international law will not stop us from exercising our rights and fulfilling our duties to recover our land and purge it from terrorists, whether through military action or reconciliation agreements. We have always been open to any initiative that prevents further deaths and restores safety and security to areas affected by terrorism. That is why we welcomed the agreement on Idlib reached in Sochi on September 17th. The agreement was the result of intensive consultations and full coordination between Syria and Russia. The agreement is timebound, includes clear deadlines, and complements the agreements on the de-escalation zones reached in Astana. We hope that when the agreement is implemented, the Nusra Front and other terrorist groups will be eradicated, thus eliminating the last remnants of terrorism in Syria.

Any foreign presence on Syrian territory without the consent of the Syrian government is illegal and constitutes a flagrant violation of international law and the UN charter. It is an assault on our sovereignty, which undermines counter-terrorism efforts and threatens regional peace and security. We therefore consider any forces operating on Syrian territory without an explicit request from the Syrian government, including US, French, and Turkish forces, occupying forces and will be dealt with accordingly. They must withdraw immediately and without conditions.

Ladies and gentlemen,

Israel continues to occupy a dear part of our land in the Syrian Golan and our people there continue to suffer because of its oppressive and aggressive policies. Israel even supported terrorist groups that operated in southern Syria; protecting them through direct military intervention and launching repeated attacks on Syria. But just as we liberated southern Syria from terrorists, we are determined to liberate fully the occupied Syrian Golan to the lines of June 4th, 1967. Syria demands that the international community put an end to all these practices and compel Israel to implement relevant UN resolutions, notably resolution 497 on the occupied Syrian Golan. The international community must also help the Palestinian people establish its own independent state, with Jerusalem as its capital, and facilitate the return of Palestine refugees to their land, pursuant to international resolutions. Any actions that undermine these rights are null and void and threaten regional peace and security, especially the Israeli racist law known as "the nation-state law" and the decision of the US administration to move the US embassy to Jerusalem and stop funding UNRWA.

Madam President,

Syria strongly condemns the decision of the US administration to withdraw from the Iran nuclear agreement, which proves once again the United States' disregard for international treaties and conventions. We express once again our solidarity with the leaders and people of the Islamic Republic of Iran and trust that they will overcome the effects of this irresponsible decision. We also stand with the government and people of Venezuela in the face of US attempts to interfere in their internal affairs. We call once again for lifting the unilateral economic measures against the Syrian people and all other independent people around the world, especially the people of the DPRK, Cuba, and Belarus.

Madam President, ladies and gentlemen,

With the help of allies and friends, Syria will defeat terrorism. The world must never forget that and should treat us accordingly. It is time for all those detached from reality to wake up, let go of their fantasies, and come to their senses. They must realize that they will not achieve politically what they failed to achieve by force. We have never compromised on our national principles even when the war was at its peak. We will surely not do that today! At the same time, we want peace for the people of the world because we want peace for our people. We have never attacked others. We have never interfered in the affairs of others. We have never exported terrorists to other parts of the world. We have always maintained the best relations with other countries. Today, as we seek to defeat terrorism, we continue to advocate dialogue and mutual understanding to serve the interests of our people and to achieve security, stability, and prosperity for all.

Source: Statement by H. E. Walid Al-Moualem, Deputy Prime Minister, Minister of Foreign Affairs

and Expatriates, of the Syrian Arab Republic. September 29, 2018. https://gadebate.un.org/sites/default/files/gastatements/73/sy_en.pdf

II. Letter from the Representatives of the Islamic Republic of Iran, the Russian Federation, and Turkey to the United Nations (February 18, 2019)

On February 14, 2019, Iranian president Hassan Rouhani, Russian president Vladimir Putin, and Turkish president Recep Tayyip Erdogan met in Sochi, Russia, to discuss the future of Syria in light of American president Donald Trump's announcement that he was planning to withdraw his troops from the country. At the meeting, Putin expressed some doubts as to whether the United States would actually withdraw, however, and Rouhani called for the American president to reconsider his country's entire Middle East policy. Erdogan's main concern was making sure the United States did not aid the Kurdish Workers Party (YPG) in their attempts to assert Kurdish independence.

Joint statement of the President of the Islamic Republic of Iran, the President of the Russian Federation and the President of the Republic of Turkey Sochi, Russian Federation, 14 February 2019 . . .

The Presidents:

1. Discussed the current situation on the ground in Syria, took stock of the developments following their last meeting in Tehran on 7 September 2018 and underscored their determination to strengthen the trilateral coordination in light of their agreements.

2. Emphasized their strong and continued commitment to the sovereignty, independence,

unity and territorial integrity of the Syrian Arab Republic as well as to the purposes and principles of the UN Charter.

3. Highlighted that these principles should be universally respected and that no actions, no matter by whom they were undertaken, should undermine them.

4. Rejected all attempts to create new realities on the ground under the pretext of combating terrorism and expressed their determination to stand against separatist agendas aimed at undermining the sovereignty and territorial integrity of Syria as well as the national security of neighbouring countries.

5. Took note in this regard that the US decision on the withdrawal of its forces from Syria, if implemented, would be a step that would help strengthen stability and security in the country in compliance with the above-mentioned principles.

6. Examined in details the situation in the Idlib de-escalation area, denounced and expressed serious concern with the attempts of the terrorist organization "Hayat Tahrir al-Sham" to increase its control over the area, and agreed to effectively counter these attempts as well as to take concrete steps to reduce violations in the Idlib de-escalation area through full implementation of the agreements on Idlib, including the Memorandum on Stabilization of the Situation in the Idlib De-escalation Area of 17 September 2018. They also reaffirmed the determination to continue cooperation in order to ultimately eliminate DAESH/ISIL, Al-Nusra Front and all other individuals, groups, undertakings and entities associated with Al-Qaeda or DAESH/ISIL, and other terrorist groups, as designated by the UN Security Council.

7. Discussed the situation in the north-east of Syria and agreed to coordinate their activities to ensure security, safety and stability in this area including through existing agreements, while respecting sovereignty and territorial integrity of the country.

8. Reaffirmed their conviction that there could be no military solution to the Syrian conflict and that it could only be resolved through the Syrian-led and Syrian-owned, S/2019/155 19-02710 3/3 UN-facilitated political process in line with the UN Security Council Resolution 2254.

9. Reaffirmed their determination to facilitate the launch of the Constitutional Committee as soon as possible, including by agreeing on its composition and elaborating recommendations for its rules of procedure based on the work undertaken by the three guarantors. They emphasized in this regard the importance of continuing interaction and coordination with the Syrian parties and the United Nations Secretary-General's Special Envoy for Syria Geir O. Pedersen.

10. Welcomed the successful development of the second mutual release of detainees within the framework of efforts of the respective Working Group. The releases that took place on 24 November 2018 and 12 February 2019 constituted important contribution of the Astana format to building confidence between the Syrian parties and creating necessary conditions for advancing the political process.

11. Emphasized the need to continue all efforts to help all Syrians restore normal and peaceful life as well as alleviate their sufferings. In this regard, they called upon the international community, particularly the United Nations and its humanitarian agencies, to increase their assistance to Syria by providing additional humanitarian aid, restoring humanitarian infrastructure assets, including water and power supply facilities, schools and hospitals.

12. Highlighted the importance of creating conditions for the safe and voluntary return of refugees and internally displaced persons (IDPs) to their original places of residence in Syria. They assessed positively the interaction with all interested parties, including the Office of the United Nations High Commissioner for Refugees (UNHCR), and reaffirmed their readiness to continue this coordination.

13. Agreed to assign their representatives with the task of holding the next International Meeting on Syria in Astana in April 2019.

14. In addition to the Syrian issue, discussed recent developments in the world as well as their collaboration in different fields and decided to boost joint economic and commercial cooperation.

15. Condemned the recent terrorist attack in Iran (Sistan-Balouchestan Province). President of the Russian Federation H.E. Vladimir Putin and President of the Republic of Turkey H.E. Recep Tayyip Erdoğan expressed their condolences to the families of the victims of this attack and sympathy with the people and the government of the Islamic Republic of Iran.

16. Decided to hold the next Tripartite Summit in the Republic of Turkey upon the invitation of the President of the Republic of Turkey H.E. Recep Tayyip Erdoğan.

17. The Presidents of the Islamic Republic of Iran and the Republic of Turkey expressed their sincere gratitude to the President of the Russian Federation H.E. Vladimir Putin for hosting the Tripartite Summit in Sochi.

Source: Joint Statement by the President of the Islamic Republic of Iran, the President of the Russian Federation and the President of the Republic of Turkey. February 14, 2019. http://en.kremlin.ru /supplement/5388

12. Statement by UNHCR Special Envoy Angelina Jolie as Syria Crisis Enters Its Ninth Year (March 14, 2019)

The Syrian Crisis is not just a political and military crisis, it is a global humanitarian crisis as well. Millions of Syrians have been displaced and are now either living in poverty scattered throughout the country or they are part of a new diaspora of refugees spread around the world. In an effort to increase support and raise money to help refugees, the United Nations High Committee on Refugees often enlists the help of celebrities from around the world to help their cause reach a wide audience. In the spring of 2019, American actor Angelina Jolie traveled to the Middle East to see the humanitarian crisis firsthand and then wrote this statement.

My thoughts are with the Syrian people as we mark yet another year of devastating conflict. In particular, I think of the millions of Syrians struggling as refugees in the region and beyond, all the families displaced inside the country, and all those who have endured injury, trauma, hunger and the loss of family members.

Millions of Syrians have played no part in the war but live with its terrible consequences. It is impossible to describe the resilience and dignity of the Syrian families I have met. Every Syrian refugee I have spent time with over the last eight years, young and old, has spoken of longing for peace in Syria so that they can safely return home. Some have already started going back—internally displaced families and, to a lesser extent, refugees. It is critical that returns are driven by refugees themselves, based on informed decisions, and not by politics. Talking to refugees and placing their perspectives and concerns at the centre of future return planning is vital—it is a question of rights.

In the meantime, the gap between what Syrian refugees and IDPs need to survive, and the humanitarian assistance available to them, is growing by the day. There are Syrians inside the country who are trying to rebuild their lives around the rubble, without the necessary support. Millions of Syrian refugee families are living beneath the poverty line, and wake each day not knowing if they will find food or medicine for their children, and struggling with debt accumulated during eight years of exile.

Women and girls face additional burdens, including severely limited work opportunities and sexual and gender-based violence, such as forced and early marriage, sexual abuse and exploitation, and domestic violence. The host countries—Turkey, Lebanon, Jordan, Iraq and Egypt—have done so much to help refugees, but they are in severe need of financing to enable them to continue to support millions of refugees and assist their local populations in coping with the economic and social pressures.

While the conflict continues and until Syrians are able to return to their homes, the least we can do is to try to meet these urgent humanitarian needs: to minimize as much as we can the human suffering, and to try to mitigate some of the damage caused by these eight lost years of senseless conflict. This is the bare minimum that we can do for a people who deserve so much more: the right to live in peace and security and dignity in their country.

Source: United Nations High Commissioner for Refugees. "Statement by UNHCR Special Envoy Angelina Joie as Syria Crisis Enters Its Ninth Year." March 14, 2019. https://www.unhcr.org/en-us/news/press/2019/3/5c8aaed94/statement-unhcr-special-envoy-angelina-jolie-syria-crisis-enters-its-ninth.html

13. Statement of the Secretary-General on Syria (March 15, 2019)

As the Syrian Conflict entered its ninth year, the United Nations reflected on repeated failures to end the conflict through diplomatic means, the hundreds of thousands of lives lost, the human rights atrocities and millions of displaced persons, and the fact that no solution to the problem seemed to be in sight. As the conflict dragged on, the United Nations leadership grew increasingly frustrated with the United States, Russia, and Turkey—actors they saw as instigators in the conflict; and while official documents, such as this one, contain very broad and gentle wording when it came to the United States, in particular, the discussions behind the documents grew less guarded. Just days after this statement by Secretary General Antonio Guterres was released, for example, a meeting on the Syria issue devolved into a heated discussion of the large countries' role in exacerbating the problem, with each side accusing and defending their respective roles. Secretary-General Guterres's statement, though very diplomatic, belies the underlying frustration felt among the UN members that the situation was no closer to a resolution in 2019 than it was in 2011.

As the conflict enters its ninth year, Syrians continue to suffer from one of the worst conflicts of our time. Hundreds of thousands have been killed, many more maimed physically and psychologically, millions remain displaced, tens of thousands are detained and missing, hundreds of thousands have died and Syrians in the northeast and northwest remain under constant fear of yet another humanitarian catastrophe unfolding.

I issue four urgent appeals to all parties.

First, I urge all sides to maintain their commitments and uphold the ceasefire arrangement in Idlib. I am extremely concerned about reported increased military operations in the last few weeks. Counter-terrorism operations cannot override responsibilities to protect civilians. A ceasefire in Idlib is a necessary step to pave the way for a nation-wide ceasefire.

Second, where any form of military operation by any actor is contemplated, planned or executed, international humanitarian law needs to be fully respected and human rights protected. Innocent civilians, the majority of them women and children, have paid the highest price in this conflict because of the blatant disregard for International Humanitarian and Human Rights Law.

Third, sustained humanitarian access remains critical, with 11.7 million people in need of protection and assistance. I was encouraged with the international solidarity in the context of the Brussels III Conference on "Supporting the Future of Syria and the Region" and spoke forcefully of the need to address the needs of the Syrian people. I thank the generous support of international donors who have pledged a record $7 billion for 2019 for Syrians inside the country and outside.

Fourth, strengthened international support is urgently required if the parties to the conflict are to seriously move towards finding a political solution that meets the legitimate aspirations of all Syrians. I fully support my Special Envoy, Geir O. Pedersen, to facilitate a Syrian-led and Syrian-owned political process to implement Security Council resolution 2254 (2015) and the June 2012 Geneva Communiqué.

It is a moral obligation and a political imperative for the international community to support Syrians to unite around a vision for their common future that protects civilians, alleviates suffering, prevents further instability, addresses the root causes of the conflict and forges, at long last, a credible negotiated solution.

Source: United Nations. "Statement of the Secretary-General on Syria." March 15, 2019. https://www.un .org/sg/en/content/sg/statement/2019-03-15/state ment-of-the-secretary-general-syria

Chronology

1915–1916

The McMahon-Hussein Correspondence. Between July 1915 and March 1916, an exchange of 10 letters between the British High Commissioner to Egypt, Lieutenant Colonel Sir Henry McMahon, and Hussein Bin Ali, the Sharif of Mecca, resulted in a British promise to support Arab independence throughout the Arabian Peninsula and the Levant in exchange for their support in the British fight against the Ottomans. This promise was broken as it was superseded by the Sykes-Picot Agreement of 1916.

1916

The Sykes-Picot Agreement, a secret agreement made between the British and French to divide the Ottoman lands among themselves upon the fall of the Turkish forces, is signed with the assent of the Russians and Italians. This agreement comes to be seen as a betrayal of trust by the Arabs of the Middle East, and is still actively cited as evidence that the European powers (and other outside parties, including the United States) cannot be trusted to follow through on their diplomatic promises.

1918

October—Arab troops, under the leadership of Faisal ibn Hussein and aided by the British Army, take Damascus.

1919

The Syrian National Congress is established to represent the views of the Arab population of the areas that were to become Syria, Lebanon, Israel, Palestine, and Jordan (collectively these areas were known as Greater Syria at the time).

1920

On March 8, the Syrian National Congress declares the independent Arab Kingdom of Syria with Faisal ibn Hussein as its ruler. The French, who under the Sykes-Picot Agreement claimed much of the area encompassed by the new kingdom's borders, did not agree to this arrangement, and they sent troops to end what they saw as an insurgency against their claim. On July 17, Faisal's troops were defeated and the French sent him into exile (Faisal would later become the first King of Iraq, which was part of the British Mandate territory after World War I).

Under the auspices of a mandate from the League of Nations, and in accordance with the Sykes-Picot Agreement, France assumes full administrative control over the northern areas of the former Ottoman Territories of Syria, Lebanon, and parts of southeastern Turkey. In 1923, the mandate would be modified to the lands of Syria and Lebanon in recognition of Turkey's establishment as a republic in October of that year.

The French divide Syria and Lebanon into two separate administrative areas, and create separate regions within Syria, including autonomous states for the Alawites in northwestern Syria centered around the port city of Latakia, and for the Druze in southern Syria. Favoritism shown toward the Alawites in particular, a minority group that practices a variant of Shia Islam, would have direct consequences for the Syrian conflict which began in 2011.

1925–1927

The Great Syrian Revolt consisting of a series of uprisings against the French spreads throughout the French Mandate lands throughout Syria and Lebanon. Particularly insistent in their push against French rule, the Arab nationalists bore much of the brunt of the French military response against the uprisings. Lingering Arab nationalism, with its roots in promises made during World War I for an independent Arab state made by the British, continued throughout the mandate period, and the Arabs grew increasingly disgruntled with French policies they viewed as more favorable toward the Alawites than toward themselves. However, while the Alawites generally favored French rule out of fear of discrimination under Sunni Arab dominance, even they took part in many anti-French uprisings throughout this period, as did the Druze in the south.

1928

An assembly of anti-French groups comes together to draft a constitution for an independent Syrian state. An alliance of opposition groups, the National Front, is established under the leadership of Ibrahim Hannanu and Hashim Atassi, and a Constituent Assembly is created, with the cautious approval of the French in April. The French High Commissioner to Syria rejects the Constituent Committee's proposed constitution, and anti-French protests erupt as a result.

1930

Displeased with the work of the Constituent Committee, the French High Commissioner dissolves it and puts forth his own constitution for Syria on May 22. The new constitution does allow for a new representative council to be put in place, but he ensures that various minorities, such as the Alawites, will have the same weight in the government as the majority Sunni Arabs. This is done primarily as a measure to continue the French policy of trying to pit the ethnic groups against one another.

1933

France and the representatives of the Syrian assembly sign the Franco-Syrian Treaty, in which France promises to support the creation of an independent Syrian state by 1937.

1934–1936

Displeased with some parts of the Franco-Syrian Treaty, elements within Syria stage a series of uprisings against the French, and a period of violence between government troops and protestors ensues. Many of the government troops employed by the French are ethnic minorities, and their use as French proxies stirs much anti-minority (particularly Alawite) sentiment among the Arab population of Syria. This period represents the solidification of many fissures among Syria's ethnic groups that would become significant after the rise of the Alawite-dominated government under Hafez al-Assad in the 1960s.

1939

On July 10, the French High Commissioner to Syria suspends the Syrian Constitution in light of the events of World War II.

1940

One year later, on July 10, 1940, Syria officially comes under the control of Vichy France, and parts of the country are occupied by Nazi Germany.

1941

Syria is liberated by Free French and British troops on June 14, and the French appoint Taj al-Din al-Hasani as the president of the Republic of Syria. Though the emergence of an actually independent Syria would not be realized for a few more years, these events set the process in motion, and a series of moves by the French in the last years of the war would result in the Independent Syrian Republic's birth in 1946.

1946

Under the leadership of Syria's first elected president, Shukri al-Kuwaiti, the Independent Syrian Republic is born.

1947

The Syrian Ba'ath Party is founded. At the time of Syria's founding, there were a number of voices expressing what the role of religion should be in the new republic. The Islamism promulgated by the Muslim Brotherhood, founded by Hassan al-Banna in Egypt in 1928, was popular among many Arab nationalists throughout the Middle East, but there were just as many, if not more, secularists in the region. The Ba'ath Party was explicitly secularist in nature, and this appealed not only to less-religious Sunni Muslims, but to many minorities who feared discrimination under an explicitly religious government system. The Ba'ath party would come to rule Syria in 1961, and continue to do so until the present day.

1948

Syrian forces, along with those from other Arab states (including Iraq, Jordan, and Egypt), declare war against the newly declared Jewish state in Israel. The Syrians were defeated, as were all of the Arab armies, and the defeat resulted in political upheaval in Damascus.

1949

As a direct result of Syria's military defeat at the hands of the Israeli military, the first military coup d'état in the modern Middle East takes place in Syria in March. This coup was followed by two more that same year, and pointed toward the significant divisions that existed in the new Syrian military. These divisions would play a critical role in the rise of Alawite influence in the military throughout the 1950s and 1960s. The leader of the third coup, Colonel Adib Shishakli, would maintain military rule of Syria for the next five years until he himself was deposed in another coup and Shuri al-Kuwaiti regained his position as president.

1956

As a direct result of the Suez Crisis, Syria signs an agreement with the Soviet Union in which they allow Communist influence within Syria in exchange for military equipment. This was the first official step in the long-standing relationship between Syrians and Russians.

1958

As part of the wave of pan-Arabism sweeping through the region, Syria and Egypt form the United Arab Republic with Egyptian Gamal Abdel Nasser acting as president. He immediately disbands all Syrian political parties, and the Ba'ath Party, which supported the union, immediately regret their decision.

1961

Dissatisfied with Syria's position in the United Arab Republic relationship with

Egypt, a group of Syrian military officers reestablish Syrian independence and break out of the alliance.

1963

On March 8, the Syrian Ba'ath Party takes advantage of the political turmoil that ensued after the 1961 coup to reestablish Syria as an independent country after the United Arab Republic period.

1966

Dissatisfied with the leadership established in the 1963 coup, the Military Committee, the central power of the Syrian Ba'ath Party, carries out an overthrow of the party's leadership and establishes Nureddin al-Atassi as the president. While al-Atassi was the formal head of state, however, Salah Jadid was, in reality, the de facto leader of Syria until 1970.

1970

In a move that would lead directly to the events of the Syrian Conflict in 2011, an Alawite Ba'athist, Hafez al-Assad, leads a coup that ousts President Atassi and leaves Jadid imprisoned.

1973

Assad modifies the constitution to eliminate the law that the president must be a Muslim. This change reflects Assad's strict secularism, but is unpopular among many Syrians, who protest and start anti-government riots throughout the country. Assad suppresses the riots with the army and other supporting militias.

1982

Assad's rule is contested throughout the 1970s, especially among the country's Sunni Muslims, who are increasingly influenced by the Muslim Brotherhood. The Brotherhood stages an uprising against the government in Hama in February, and Assad responds with brutal military force, killing tens of thousands of civilians.

1994

President Assad's son and presumed successor, Basil, is killed in a car accident. Bashar al-Assad, an optometrist by training, starts the process to become the president upon his father's death.

2000

Hafez al-Assad dies, and his son Bashar becomes the president of Syria. In an act of consolation, Bashar releases 600 political prisoners, and there is some hope that his will be a more open government.

2001

The Muslim Brotherhood announces it will resume activity in Syria, and Syrian politicians become increasingly critical of the government's position. Bashar begins to jail many opposition leaders and hopes for a more gentle government are quickly dashed.

2002

Syria is singled out by the American president as a named member of the "Axis of Evil" in the wake of the attacks on New York City and Washington, D.C., on September 11, 2001.

2003

The United States invades Iraq, and over the course of the next five years more than 1 million Iraqis seek refuge in Syria. The Iraqi refugee crisis in Syria puts significant strain on the country's resources and services, and Syrians begin to put pressure on Bashar's government to maintain their services.

2004

The United States imposes economic sanctions against Syria for its support of terrorist organizations. These sanctions put further strain on a country already challenged by the Iraqi refugee crisis.

2007–2009

Syria's relationships with the United States and Europe (primarily France) improve, with diplomatic overtures being extended. Syria also establishes diplomatic relations with Lebanon for the first time as independent countries. There is a general sense of cautious optimism surrounding Syria's international relations.

2010

The United States renews economic sanctions against Syria in light of intelligence that shows it is still supporting organizations the United States considers terrorist groups. These sanctions hit the Syrian economy hard.

2011

Anti-government protests spring up in Syria in the wake of the Arab Spring movement, which is sweeping through North Africa and other parts of the Middle East. Fearful of losing his grip on power, Bashar emulates his father's handling of the Muslim Brotherhood uprisings in Hama in 1982 and responds to the protests with military force. The first city to experience his wrath is the southern city of Daraa in March.

July: Assad deposes the governor of Hama and sends troops to establish control over the area.

November: The Arab League votes to suspend Syria as a result of innumerable human rights violations it commits throughout the country in response to the protests.

2012

February: Government increases bombing and artillery campaigns in Homs and other major urban areas.

June: Al-Qubeir Massacre—government forces massacre all but five villagers under suspicion of supporting the Syrian Free Army.

July: The Free Syrian Army, an opposition group made up primarily of defectors from the Syrian Army, kill key military leaders in Damascus and seize a significant portion of Aleppo.

August: U.S. president Barack Obama, in an informal question-and-answer period, states that if Assad were to use chemical weapons against his own people, that would constitute a "red line" that would likely incur direct military intervention by the United States.

November: The National Coalition, a group of opposition forces that exclude Islamic militias (such as the Nusra Front, Al-Qaeda, and the Islamic State), is formed in Qatar.

December: The United States, Great Britain, France, Turkey, and the Arab Gulf states formally recognize the National Coalition as the legitimate representative of the Syrian people.

2013

August: Syrian forces launch a chemical weapons attack against rebels in the Damascus suburb of Ghouta.

2014

June: The Islamic State declares an independent caliphate in the territory of southern Syria and northern Iraq.

September: President Obama authorizes U.S. air strikes against Islamic State targets throughout Syria. The U.S. Air Force and five allied Arab nations conduct operations against IS in and around Aleppo and Raqqa.

2015

May: Islamic State fighters seize the ancient city of Palmyra. They destroy many priceless artifacts and architectural wonders at this UN World Heritage Site.

September: At the request of Bashar al-Assad, Russia intervenes and conducts its first air strikes against anti-government forces in Syria.

2016

August: Turkish troops enter Syria in an attempt to secure their border with Syria. It is widely believed their main motivation was fear of a Kurdish uprising in their own country.

December: Syrian troops, with help from Russian, Iranian, and allied militias, retake Aleppo from anti-government control. This represents a significant setback for anti-Assad forces as it was their last major urban stronghold.

2017

April: U.S. president Donald Trump orders air and missile strikes against an air base where it is believed the Syrian Air Force carried out chemical weapons attacks against civilians.

November: Islamic State forces are driven out of their last urban stronghold in Syria, Raqqa, by U.S.-backed Kurdish fighters.

2018

January: Turkey launches air strikes against Kurdish fighters in northern Syria. The Turks remain fearful of a Kurdish uprising within their territory.

April: News of a series of chemical weapons attacks by the Assad regime in cities around the country prompts a series of air strikes conducted by American and British air forces.

July: The Syrian Army recaptures almost all of southern Syria from rebel forces.

December: After a series of offensives, Kurdish forces effectively defeat Islamic State fighters and force them into a small territory along the Iraqi border.

2019

As of 2019, the Syrian military continues to solidify its hold throughout the country with opposition forces being limited primarily to the northwestern territory of the Idlib Governorate.

Bibliography

Abboud, Samer Nassif. *Syria*. Polity, 2015.

Abu Jaber, Kamel. *The Arab Ba'th Socialist Party: History, Ideology, and Organization*. Syracuse University Press, 1966.

Achcar, Gilbert. *The People Want: A Radical Exploration of the Arab Uprising*. Translated by G. M. Goshgarian. University of California Press, 2013.

Agha, Husayn. *Syria and Iran: Rivalry and Cooperation*. Royal Institute of International Affairs, 1995.

Amar, Paul, and Vijay Prashad, eds. *Dispatches from the Arab Spring: Understanding the New Middle East*. University of Minnesota Press, 2013.

Antoun, Richard T., and Donald Quataert. *Syria: Society, Culture, and Polity*. State University of New York, 1991.

Avon, Dominique, and Anais-Trissa Khatchadourian. *Hezbollah: A History of the "Party of God."* Harvard University Press, 2012.

Ball, Warwick. *Syria: A Historical and Architectural Guide*. Interlink Books, 2007.

Barkey, Henri. *Turkey's Kurdish Question*. Rowman and Littlefield, 1998.

Beck, Martin. *The Levant in Turmoil: Syria, Palestine, and the Transformation of Middle Eastern Politics*. Palgrave MacMillan, 2016.

Betts, Alexander. *Refuge: Rethinking Refugee Policy in a Changing World*. Oxford University Press, 2017.

Bey, Salma Mardam. *Syria's Quest for Independence*. Ithaca Press, 1994.

Bobrick, Benson. *The Caliph's Splendor: Islam and the West in the Golden Age of Baghdad*. Simon and Schuster, 2012.

Bodine-Baron, Elizabeth, Todd C. Helmus, Madeline Magnuson, and Zev Winkelman. *Examining ISIS Support and Opposition Networks on Twitter*. RAND Corporation, 2016.

Bradley, John R. *After the Arab Spring: How Islamists Hijacked the Middle East Revolts*. Palgrave Macmillan, 2012.

Burns, Ross. *Aleppo: A History*. Routledge, 2016.

Bryce, Trevor. *Ancient Syria: A Three Thousand Year History*. Oxford University Press, 2014.

Byman, Daniel. *Al-Qaeda, the Islamic State, and the Global Jihadist Movement: What Everyone Needs to Know*. Oxford University Press, 2015.

Cagaptay, Soner. *The New Sultan: Erdogan and the Crisis of Modern Turkey*. I. B. Tauris, 2017.

Chatty, Dawn. *Syria: The Making and Unmaking of a Refuge State*. Oxford University Press, 2018.

Cockburn, Patrick. *The Rise of the Islamic State: ISIS and the New Sunni Revolution*. Verso, 2015.

Cudi, Azad. *Long Shot: The Inside Story of the Snipers Who Broke ISIS*. Atlantic Monthly Press, 2019.

Culbertson, Shelly. *The Fires of Spring: A Post Arab Spring Journey through a Turbulent New Middle East*. St. Martin's Press, 2016.

Culbertson, Shelly, Olga Oliker, Ben Baruch, and Ilana Blum. *Rethinking Coordination of Services to Refugees in Urban Areas: Managing the Crisis in Jordan and Lebanon*. RAND Corporation, 2016.

Dabashi, Hamid. *The Arab Spring: The End of Postcolonialism*. Zed Books, 2012.

Danahar, Paul. *The New Middle East: The World after the Arab Spring*. Bloomsbury, 2013.

Diamond, Larry Jay, and Marc F. Plattner. *Democratization and Authoritarianism in the Arab World*. Johns Hopkins University Press, 2014.

Dodge, Toby, and Emile Hokayem. *Middle Eastern Security, the U.S. Pivot, and ISIS*. Routledge, 2014.

Erlich, Reese W. *Inside Syria: The Backstory of Their Civil War and What the World Can Expect*. Prometheus Books, 2014.

Faulkner, Neil. *Lawrence of Arabia's War: The Arabs, the British, and the Remaking of the Middle East in WWI*. Yale University Press, 2016.

Ferris, Elizabeth G. *The Consequences of Chaos: Syria's Humanitarian Crisis and the Failure to Protect*. Brookings Institution Press, 2016.

Fleming, Melissa. *A Hope More Powerful Than the Sea: One Refugee's Incredible Story of Love, Loss, and Survival*. Flatiron Books, 2017.

Gelvin, James L. *The New Middle East: What Everyone Needs to Know*. Oxford University Press, 2018.

Gerges, Fawaz. *ISIS: A History*. Princeton University Press, 2016.

Gunter, Michael M. *The Kurds Ascending: The Evolving Solution to the Kurdish Problem in Iraq and Turkey*. Palgrave MacMillan, 2011.

Hansen, Stig Jarle, Alte Mesoy, and Tuncay Kardas. *The Borders of Islam: Exploring Huntington's Faultlines, from Al-Andalus to the Virtual Ummah*. Columbia University Press, 2009.

Hashemi, Nader. *The Syria Dilemma*. MIT Press, 2013.

Held, Colbert C. *Middle East Patterns: Places, Peoples, and Politics*. Routledge, 2015.

Heydemann, Steven, and Reinoud Leenders. *Middle East Authoritarianisms: Governance, Contestations, and Regime Resilience in Syria and Iran*. Stanford University Press, 2013.

Hourani, Albert. *A History of the Arab Peoples*. Belknap Press, 2002.

Hudson, Leila. *Transforming Damascus: Space and Modernity in an Islamic City*. I. B. Tauris, 2008.

Ibrahim, Azeem. *The Resurgence of Al-Qaeda in Syria and Iraq*. Army War College Press, 2014.

Jenkins, Brian Michael. *The Dynamics of Syria's Civil War*. RAND Corporation, 2014.

Jones, Seth. *A Persistent Threat: The Evolution of Al-Qaeda and Other Salafi Jihadists*. RAND Corporation, 2014.

Jorum, Emma Lundgren. *Beyond Syria's Borders: A History of Territorial Disputes in the Middle East*. I. B. Tauris, 2014.

Kazimi, Nibras. *Syria through Jihadist Eyes: A Perfect Enemy*. Hoover Institution Press, 2010.

Khatib, Lina, and Ellen Lust. *Taking to the Streets: The Transformation of Arab Activism*. Johns Hopkins University Press, 2014.

Khoury, Philip S. *Syria and the French Mandate: The Politics of Arab Nationalism, 1920–1945*. Princeton University Press, 1987.

Kienle, Eberhard. *Ba'th vs. Ba'th: The Conflict between Syria and Iraq, 1968–1989*. I. B. Tauris, 1990.

King, Stephen J., Abdeslam Maghraoui, and Moulay Hicham, Prince of Morocco. *The Lure of Authoritarianism the Maghreb after the Arab Spring*. Indiana University Press, 2019.

Kinzer, Stephen. *All the Shah's Men: An American Coup and the Roots of Middle East Terror*. John Wiley and Sons, 2008.

Lapidus, Ira M. *A History of Islamic Societies*. Cambridge University Press, 2002.

Laremont, Ricardo Rene. *Revolution, Revolt, and Reform in North Africa: The Arab Spring and Beyond*. Routledge, 2014.

Lawrence, Quil. *Invisible Nation: How the Kurds' Quest for Statehood Is Shaping Iraq and the Middle East*. Walker, 2008.

Lefevre, Raphael. *Ashes of Hama: The Muslim Brotherhood in Syria*. Oxford University Press, 2013.

Lesch, David. *Syria*. Polity Press, 2019.

Lesch, David. *Syria: The Fall of the House of Assad*. Yale University Press, 2012.

Lesch, David. *The New Lion of Damascus: Basher Al-Asad and Modern Syria*. Yale University Press, 2005.

Leverett, Flynt Lawrence. *Inheriting Syria: Bashar's Trial by Fire*. Brookings Institution Press, 2005.

Levy, Avigdor. *Jews, Turks, and Ottomans: A Shared History, Fifteenth through the Twentieth Century*. Syracuse University Press, 2002.

Lewis, Bernard. *The Crisis of Islam: Holy War and Unholy Terror*. Oxford University Press, 2003.

Lewis, Bernard. *What Went Wrong? Western Impact and Middle Eastern Response*. Oxford University Press, 2002.

Lister, Charles R. *The Syrian Jihad: Al-Qaeda, the Islamic State, and the Evolution of an Insurgency*. Oxford University Press, 2015.

Longrigg, Stephen Hemsley. *Syria and Lebanon under French Mandate*. Oxford University Press, 1958.

Lynch, Marc. *The Arab Uprisings Explained: New Contentious Politics in the Middle East*. Columbia University Press, 2014.

Mansel, Philip. *Aleppo: The Rise and Fall of Syria's Great Merchant City*. I. B. Tauris, 2018.

McDowell, David. *A Modern History of the Kurds*. I. B. Tauris, 2006.

Migliorino, Nicola. *(Re)constructing Armenia in Lebanon and Syria: Ethno-cultural Diversity and the State in the Aftermath of a Refugee Crisis*. Berghahn Books, 2008.

Monsutti, Alessandro, and Silvia Naef. *The Other Shiites: From the Mediterranean to Central Asia*. Peter Lang, 2007.

Muasher, Marwan. *The Second Arab Awakening and the Battle for Pluralism*. Yale University Press, 2014.

Naylor, Sean. *Relentless Strike: The Secret History of Joint Special Operations Command*. St. Martin's Press, 2015.

Norton, Augustus R. *Hezbollah: A Short History*. Princeton University Press, 2018.

Noueihed, Lin, and Alex Warren. *The Battle for the Arab Spring: Revolution, Counter-Revolution and the Making of a New Era*. Yale University Press, 2012.

Olson, Robert W. *The Ba'th and Syria, 1947 to 1982: The Evolution of Ideology, Party, and State from the French Mandate to the Era of Hafiz al-Asad*. Princeton University Press, 1982.

Park, Bill. *Turkey-Kurdish Regional Government Relations after the U.S. Withdrawal from Iraq: Putting the Kurds on the Map?* Strategic Studies Institute, 2014.

Plater-Zyberk, Henry. *Russia's Contribution as a Partner in the War on Terror*. Strategic Studies Institute, 2014.

Provence, Michael. *The Last Ottoman Generation and the Making of the Modern Middle East*. Cambridge University Press, 2017.

Reilly, James A. *Fragile Nation, Shattered Land: The Modern History of Syria*. Lynne Rienner Publishers, 2019.

Roberts, David. *The Ba'th and the Creation of Modern Syria*. St. Martin's Press, 1987.

Rowe, Paul. *Routledge Handbook of Minorities in the Middle East*. Routledge, 2019.

Sahner, Christian C. *Among the Ruins: Syria Past and Present*. Oxford University Press, 2014.

Samer, Scott Coello, Mike Thomson, and Nader Ibrahim. *The Raqqa Diaries: Escape from "Islamic State."* Interlink Books, 2017.

Sluglett, Peter, and Stefan Weber, eds. *Syria and Bilad al-Sham under Ottoman Rule: Essays in Honour of Abdul Karim Rafeq*. Brill Academic Publications, 2010.

Smith, Lee. *The Consequences of Syria*. Hoover Institution Press, 2014.

Soufan, Ali H. *Anatomy of Terror: From the Death of bin Laden to the Rise of the Islamic State*. W. W. Norton, 2017.

Staffell, Simon, and Akir N. Awan. *Jihadism Transformed: Al-Qaeda and the Islamic State's Global Battle of Ideas.* Oxford University Press, 2016.

Starr, Stephen. *Revolt in Syria: Eye-Witness to the Uprising.* Columbia University Press, 2012.

Tax, Meredith. *A Road Unforeseen: Women Fight the Islamic State.* Bellevue Literary Press, 2016.

Taylor, William C. *Military Responses to the Arab Uprisings and the Future of Civil-Military Relations in the Middle East: Analysis from Egypt, Tunisia, Libya, and Syria.* Palgrave MacMillan, 2014.

Teixidor, Javier. *The Pagan God: Popular Religion in the Greco-Roman Near East.* Princeton University Press, 2015.

Terrill, W. Andrew. *Antiquities Destruction and Illicit Sales as Sources of ISIS Funding and Propaganda.* Strategic Studies Institute, 2017.

Tomass, Mark. *The Religious Roots of the Syrian Conflict: The Remaking of the Fertile Crescent.* Palgrave MacMillan, 2016.

UNESCO. *World Heritage: Archaeological Sites and Urban Centers.* Rizzoli International Publications through St. Martin's Press, 2002.

van Dam, Nikolaos. *The Struggle for Power in Syria: Politics and Society under Asad and the Ba'th Party.* I. B. Tauris, 1996.

van Dam, Nikolaos. *Destroying a Nation: The Civil War in Syria.* I. B. Tauris, 2017.

Von Welser, Maria, and Jamie McIntosh. *No Refuge for Women: The Tragic Fate of Syrian Refugees.* Greystone Books, 2017.

Warrick, Joby. *Black Flags: The Rise of ISIS.* Doubleday, 2015.

Weiss, Michael. *ISIS: Inside the Army of Terror.* Regan Arts, 2015.

Williams, Brian Glyn. *Counter Jihad: America's Military Experience in Afghanistan, Iraq, and Syria.* University of Pennsylvania Press, 2017.

Wood, Graeme. "What ISIS Really Wants." *The Atlantic*, March 2015.

Wright, Lawrence. *The Terror Years: From Al-Qaeda to the Islamic State.* Alfred A. Knopf, 2016.

Yassin-Kassab, Robin, and Laila al-Shami. *Burning Country: Syrians in Revolution and War.* Pluto Press, 2016.

Young, William, David Stebbins, Bryan A. Frederick, and Omar Al-Shahery. *Spillover from the Conflict in Syria: An Assessment of the Factors That Aid and Impede the Spread of Violence.* RAND Corporation, 2014.

Zabad, Ibrahim. *Middle Eastern Minorities: The Impact of the Arab Spring.* Routledge, 2017.

Ziadeh, Radwan. *The Kurds in Syria: Fueling Separatist Movements in the Region?* The United States Institute of Peace, 2009.

List of Contributors

EDITOR

Dr. Robert M. Kerr
Professor of Military and Security Studies
U.S. Air Force Air Command and Staff College, Maxwell AFB

CONTRIBUTORS

Amy Hackney Blackwell
Independent Scholar

Jessica Britt
Independent Scholar

Dr. Stefan Brooks
Assistant Professor of Political Science
Lindsey Wilson College

Tamar Burris
Independent Scholar

Dr. Richard M. Edwards
Senior Lecturer
University of Wisconsin Colleges

Dr. Harry R. Hueston II
Professor of Criminal Justice
West Texas A&M University

Dr. Sedat Cem Karadeli
Assistant Professor
Cankaya University

Michael J. Kelly
Professor, School of Law
Creighton University

Payton M. Kerr
University of Montevallo

Nita Lang
Independent Scholar

Keith A. Leitich
Independent Scholar

Raymond D. Limbach
Independent Historian

Dr. Shamiran Mako
Assistant Professor of International Relations
Boston University

Major Christopher G. Marquis
Instructor
U.S. Air Force Air Command and Staff College

Gregory W. Morgan

Independent Scholar

Dr. Melia Pfannenstiel

Assistant Professor

U.S. Air Force Air Command and Staff College

Dr. Paul G. Pierpaoli Jr.

Fellow

Military History, ABC-CLIO

Dr. Priscilla Roberts

Associate Professor of Business

Co-Director, Asia-Pacific Business Research Centre

City University of Macau

Taipa, Macao Special Administrative Region of China

Russell G. Rodgers

Staff Historian

U.S. Army

Dr. Yushau Sodiq

Associate Professor of Islamic and Religious Studies

Texas Christian University

Dr. Daniel E. Spector

Independent Scholar

Dr. Paul J. Springer

Professor of Comparative Military Studies

Chair of the Department of Research

Air Command and Staff College, Maxwell Air Force Base

Dr. Spencer C. Tucker

Senior Fellow

Military History, ABC-CLIO

Dr. Andrew J. Waskey

Professor of Social Science

Dalton State College

Dr. David T. Zabecki

Major General

Army of the United States, Retired

Dr. Sherifa Zuhur

Visiting Professor of National Security Affairs

Regional Strategy and Planning Department

Strategic Studies Institute

U.S. Army War College

Index

Page numbers in **bold** indicate main entries.

About the Editor

Robert M. Kerr, PhD, is professor of military and security studies in the Department of Joint Warfighting at the U.S. Air Force Air Command and Staff College. Dr. Kerr has spent more than two decades living in and researching the places and peoples of the Middle East, and he has worked directly on analyzing and advising on matters of U.S. national security.